THE BOOK OF
CITIES

PHILIP DODD AND BEN DONALD

MJF BOOKS
NEW YORK

London, UK, 0° 00'
Brighton, UK, 0° 08' W
Accra, Ghana, 0° 14' W
Valencia, Spain, 0° 21' W
Bordeaux, France, 0° 34' W
Oxford, UK, 1° 15' W
Ouagadougou,
      Burkina Faso, 1° 31' W
Nantes, France, 1° 33' W
Newcastle upon Tyne, UK, 1° 36' W
Manchester, UK, 2° 15' W
Bilbao, Spain, 2° 54' W,
Liverpool, UK, 2° 59' W
Timbuktu, Mali, 2° 59' W
Edinburgh, UK, 3° 11' W
Cardiff, UK, 3° 12' W
Granada, Spain, 3° 36' W
Madrid, Spain, 3° 40' W
Abidjan, Ivory Coast, 4° 02' W
Glasgow, UK, 4° 15' W
Cordoba, Spain, 4° 46' W
Fez, Morocco, 4° 57' W
Salamanca, Spain, 5° 39' W
Tangiers, Morocco, 5° 49' W
Belfast, UK, 5° 55' W
Seville, Spain, 5° 58' W
Dublin, Ireland, 6° 16' W
Casablanca, Morocco, 7° 34' W
Marrakesh, Morocco, 7° 58' W
Bamako, Mali, 7° 59' W
Cork, Ireland, 8° 28' W
Santiago de Compostela,
      Spain, 8° 32' W
Oporto, Portugal, 8° 36' W
Lisbon, Portugal, 9° 08' W
Santa Cruz de Tenerife,
      Canary Islands, 16° 15' W
St Louis, Senegal, 16° 29' W
Dakar, Senegal, 17° 28' W
Reykjavik, Iceland, 21° 55' W
Salvador, Brazil, 38° 25' W
Rio de Janeiro, Brazil, 43° 17' W
São Paulo, Brazil, 46° 43' W
Brasilia, Brazil, 47° 55' W

Nuuk, Greenland, 51° 45' W
Montevideo, Uruguay, 56° 13' W
Buenos Aires, Argentina, 58° 24' W
Port of Spain, Trinidad
      and Tobago, 61° 30' W
San Juan, Puerto Rico, 66° 04' W
Caracas, Venezuela, 66° 59' W
La Paz, Bolivia, 68° 10' W
Ushuaia, Argentina, 68° 19' W
Santiago, Chile, 70° 39' W
Boston, USA, 71° 06' W
Quebec City, Canada, 71° 15' W
Cuzco, Peru, 71° 59' W
Port Au Prince, Haiti, 72° 19' W
Montreal, Canada, 73° 39' W
Bogotá, Colombia, 74° 04' W
New York City, USA, 73° 59' W
Philadelphia, USA, 75° 10' W
Ottawa, Canada, 75° 40' W
Medellin, Colombia, 75° 35' W
Baltimore, USA, 76° 37' W
Kingston, Jamaica, 76° 47' W
Washington DC, USA, 77° 01' W
Lima, Peru, 77° 03' W
Quito, Ecuador, 78° 30' W
Panama City, Panama, 79° 36' W
Charleston, USA, 79° 58' W
Pittsburgh, USA, 79° 59' W
Miami, USA, 80° 18' W
Toronto, Canada, 80° 36' W
Cleveland, USA, 81° 41' W
Havana, Cuba, 82° 22' W
Tampa, USA, 82° 29' W
Detroit, USA, 83° 04' W
Atlanta, USA, 84° 22' W
Granada, Nicaragua, 85° 58' W
Nashville, USA, 86° 46' W
Chicago, USA, 87° 38' W
New Orleans, USA, 90° 03' W
Memphis, USA, 90° 04' W
St Louis, USA, 90° 14' W
Minneapolis, USA, 93° 18' W
Houston, USA, 95° 19' W
Dallas, USA, 96° 48' W

San Antonio, USA, 98° 27' W
Mexico City, Mexico, 99° 12' W
Acapulco, Mexico, 99° 52' W
Guadalajara, Mexico, 103° 24' W
Denver, USA, 105° 02' W
Santa Fe, USA, 105° 57' W
Salt Lake City, USA, 111° 54' W
Las Vegas, USA, 115° 09' W
Tijuana, Mexico, 117° 02' W
Los Angeles, USA, 118° 15' W
Seattle, USA, 122° 20' W
San Francisco, USA, 122° 25' W
Vancouver, Canada, 123° 08' W
Anchorage, USA, 149° 52'
Honolulu, USA, 157° 52' W
Auckland, New Zealand, 174° 46' E
Wellington, New Zealand, 174° 46' E
Brisbane, Australia, 153° 03' E
Sydney, Australia, 151° 11' E
Melbourne, Australia, 144° 59' E
Tokyo, Japan, 139° 48' E
Adelaide, Australia, 138° 40' E
Kyoto, Japan, 135° 46' E
Osaka, Japan, 135° 30' E
Vladivostock, Russia, 131° 56' E
Fukuoka, Japan, 130° 24' E
Nagasaki, Japan, 129° 52' E
Seoul, South Korea, 127° 00' E
Shanghai, China, 121° 30' E
Manila, Philippines, 120° 59' E
T'aipei, Taiwan, 121° 33' E
Nanjing, China, 118° 50' E
Beijing, China, 116° 27'
Perth, Australia, 115° 47' E
Hong Kong, China, 114° 11' E
Guangzhou, China, 113° 121' E
Ulan Bator, Mongolia, 106° 58' E
Jakarta, Indonesia, 106° 48' E
Ho Chi Minh City,
      Vietnam, 106° 42' E
Hanoi, Vietnam, 105° 51' E
Phnom Penh, Cambodia, 104° 57' E
Irkutsk, Russia, 104° 09' E
Singapore, Singapore, 103° 51' E

Vientiane, Laos, 102° 37′ E
Kuala Lumpur, Malaysia, 101° 42′ E
Bangkok, Thailand, 100° 33′ E
Yangon, Myanmar, 96° 08′ E
Lhasa, China, 91° 02′ E
Kolkata, India, 88° 21′ E
Kathmandu, Nepal, 85° 18′ E
Varanasi, India, 83° 04′ E
Chennai, India, 80° 16′ E
Colombo, Sri Lanka, 79° 50′ E
Delhi, India, 77° 17′ E
Almaty, Kazakhstan, 77° 01′ E
Kochi, India, 76° 14′ E
Kashgar, China, 76° 03′ E
Srinagar, India, 74° 51′ E
Lahore, Pakistan, 74° 23′ E
Mumbai, India, 72° 51′ E
Tashkent, Uzbekistan, 69° 15′ E
Kabul, Afghanistan, 69° 11′ E
Karachi, Pakistan, 67° 03′ E
Samarkand, Uzbekistan, 67° 01′ E
Bukhara, Uzbekistan, 64° 25′ E
Muscat, Oman, 58° 35′ E
Dubai, UAE, 55° 17′ E
Tehran, Iran, 51° 23′ E
Baku, Azerbaijan, 49° 50′ E
Tbilisi, Georgia, 44° 48′ E
Baghdad, Iraq, 44° 22′ E
San'a, Yemen, 44° 11′ E
Harar, Ethiopia, 42° 15′ E
Mombasa, Kenya, 39° 40′ E
Dar es Salaam, Tanzania, 39° 16′ E
Jeddah, Saudi Arabia, 39° 08′ E
Asmara, Eritrea, 38° 56′ E
Addis Ababa, Ethiopia, 38° 45′ E
Moscow, Russia, 37° 38′ E
Nairobi, Kenya, 36° 48′ E
Damascus, Syria, 36° 20′ E
Beirut, Lebanon, 35° 30′ E
Jerusalem,
        Israel/West Bank, 35° 13′ E
Tel Aviv, Israel, 34° 46′ E
Nicosia, Cyprus, 33° 22′ E
Aswan, Egypt, 32° 56′ E

Kampala, Uganda, 32° 34′ E
Maputo, Mozambique, 32° 34′ E
Khartoum, Sudan, 32° 32′ E
Cairo, Egypt, 31° 15′ E
Odessa, Ukraine, 30° 39′ E
Kiev, Ukraine, 30° 34′ E
St Petersburg, Russia, 30° 18′ E
Alexandria, Egypt, 29° 56′ E
Istanbul, Turkey, 28° 58′ E
Johannesburg,
        South Africa, 27° 59′ E
Bucharest, Romania, 26° 06′ E
Vilnius, Lithuania, 25° 16′ E
Helsinki, Finland, 24° 57′ E
Talinn, Estonia, 24° 45′ E
Riga, Latvia, 24° 07′ E
Athens, Greece, 23° 43′ E
Thessaloniki, Greece, 22° 57′ E
Warsaw, Poland, 21° 01′ E
Belgrade, Serbia, 20° 29′ E
Krakow, Poland, 19° 56′ E
Budapest, Hungary, 19° 04′ E
Gdansk, Poland, 18° 39′ E
Cape Town, South Africa, 18° 28′ E
Sarajevo,
        Bosnia-Herzegovina, 18° 25′ E
Dubrovnik, Croatia, 18° 06′ E
Stockholm, Sweden, 18° 04′ E
Bratislava, Slovakia, 17° 06′ E
Split, Croatia, 16° 27′ E
Vienna, Austria, 16° 23′ E
Zagreb, Croatia, 15° 58′ E
Brazzaville, Congo, 15° 11′ E
Ljubljana, Slovenia, 14° 30′ E
Prague, Czech Republic, 14° 26′ E
Naples, Italy, 14° 15′ E
Trieste, Italy, 13° 46′ E
Dresden, Germany, 13° 45′ E
Berlin, Germany, 13° 23′ E
Palermo, Italy, 13° 21′ E
Tripoli, Libya, 13° 08′ E
Salzburg, Austria, 13° 03′ E
Copenhagen, Denmark, 12° 34′ E
Rome, Italy, 12° 30′ E

Venice, Italy, 12° 20′ E
Gothenburg, Sweden, 11° 58′ E
Munich, Germany, 11° 35′ E
Bologna, Italy, 11° 22′ E
Siena, Italy, 11° 20′ E
Florence, Italy, 11° 16′ E
Oslo, Norway, 10° 46′ E
Tunis, Tunisia, 10° 16′ E
Aarhus, Denmark, 10° 12′ E
Hamburg, Germany, 9° 59′ E
Milan, Italy, 9° 11′ E
Genoa, Italy, 8° 56′ E
Frankfurt, Germany, 8° 41′ E
Zurich, Switzerland, 8° 32′ E
Strasbourg, France, 7° 44′ E
Turin, Italy, 7° 41′ E
Monte Carlo, Monaco, 7° 25′ E
Nice, France, 7° 17′ E
Cologne, Germany, 6° 57′ E
Düsseldorf, Germany, 6° 47′ E
Geneva, Switzerland, 6° 09′ E
Luxembourg, Luxembourg, 6° 08′ E
Grenoble, France, 5° 44′ E
Marseilles, France, 5° 23′ E
Amsterdam, Netherlands, 4° 54′ E
Lyons, France, 4° 52′ E
Rotterdam, Netherlands, 4° 30′ E
Antwerp, Belgium, 4° 26′ E
Brussels, Belgium, 4° 21′ E
Lagos, Nigeria, 3° 20′ E
Bruges, Belgium, 3° 15′ E
Algiers, Algeria, 3° 04′ E
Lille, France, 3° 04′ E
Palma, Spain, 2° 40′ E
Paris, France, 2° 21′ E
Barcelona, Spain, 2° 13′ E
Toulouse, France, 1° 26′ E
Cambridge, UK, 0° 07′ E

12:00	ZUR
12:05	PARIS
12:15	MILAN
12:25	AMSTERDAM
12:40	BERLIN-TEG
12:45	BRUSSELS
12:50	GENEVA
12:55	NICE

"Real cities have something else, some bony structure under the muck." Raymond Chandler

ANY REGULAR TRAVELLER has shared the same experience: a flight delayed by fog, winds or circumstances unknown, a few extra hours of your life evaporating in some anonymous airport lounge, while the departure and arrival screens click relentlessly through their litany of destinations, offering up the names of cities both exotic and familiar.

In his book *The Art of Travel*, Alain de Botton wrote eloquently about those screens, that their "workmanlike casing and pedestrian typefaces do nothing to disguise their emotional charge or imaginative allure. The screens bear all the poetic resonance of the last line of James Joyce's *Ulysses*; at once a record of where the novel was written and, no less importantly, a symbol of the cosmopolitan spirit behind its composition: 'Trieste, Zurich, Paris.'"

That spirit was the creative spark for this book. We found ourselves wanting to understand more about these many and varied cities. What does Caracas look like? What remains of Phnom Penh? Where on earth is Harar?

Cities are increasingly the focal points of human existence. For the first time in the history of the world, half the world's population lives either in or near major urban areas. People are coalescing around cities, which continue to evolve and change like living organisms. And while air travel has brought even the furthest-flung city within 36 hours of home, cheap-flight airlines offer the option of popping over to a new destination for the weekend.

The Book of Cities, then, is a gazetteer of 250 important and intriguing cities, a celebration of their diversity, energies and culture. Our first decision was to determine what constitutes a city. The dictionary defines the word at its simplest as "a large town". Other definitions are more specific, involving civic incorporation or the presence of a cathedral. We took the view that a city is more about a spirit, a state of mind, than any rules and regulations or the size of its population. In a small country, its principal city may be another nation's provincial town.

INTRODUCTION

When we set about selecting the 250 cities in this book, we found that perhaps a hundred cities were automatic inclusions, megacities whose global reputations and culture have permeated our imaginations through literature, art, music, TV and the movies – the likes of London, Paris, New York, Los Angeles, Cairo, Rome, Venice, Beijing or Sydney. A further hundred seemed generally incontrovertible. But the final fifty we fought over as fiercely as any number of invaders, colonizers or settlers. Second city or even capital city status was no guarantee of inclusion. We liked cities located at the far corners of continents – Nuuk or Ushuaia – and those that might have fallen on hard times in recent years, but whose names remain powerfully evocative: Baghdad, Algiers, Sarajevo.

We also decided to organize the book by longitude, the arcing imaginary lines that divide the globe from North to South Pole. And so our journey begins in London, on the Greenwich Meridian, at 0°, and heads west, jumping from Brighton down to Accra, Oxford to Ouagadougou, before swinging out across the Atlantic to the Americas and round the globe via Australasia, the Pacific Rim, Asia, the Middle East, Africa and Europe to arrive back in Cambridge, just east of London. It is a circumnavigation by way of every kind of urban environment.

The Book of Cities is not a guidebook. We have not recommended the most atmospheric or best budget hotels, nor hot new restaurants or hip clubs. For that information there are a host of guidebooks on the market, as varied as the establishments they grade. Instead we have tried to blend history, topography and architecture with sounds, aromas and vistas and the character of the citizens – whatever combines to make each city different and individual, especially in an age of global companies and brand names. Pollution and crime are virtual givens, which we have only mentioned when the level or absence of either merits comment. And we had a rule to try, if at all possible, to avoid saying that every African or Asian city had "a bustling market" – the stock standby of many guidebooks.

We selected a quote about each city from a wide range of observers. Of travel writers we wanted to include the old masters (Freya Stark on Kathmandu, Bruce Chatwin on Marseilles) as well as the younger stars (William Dalrymple on Delhi). But we also chose residents with attitude or transient visitors whose fame lay elsewhere: Che Guevara's take on Cuzco, Eminem on Detroit and Lenin on Vladivostok are piquant and heartfelt.

Each city is illustrated with an image or images chosen to capture something of its essence. For cities that are so widely photographed they have become over-familiar, we have often felt cheeky enough to use a slightly offbeat angle. For others it was important just to know what they looked like.

A concise paragraph of data gives the name (and where relevant the local name) and country of each city, plus the region, for those countries where states, provinces, *départements*, *Länder* or counties have an especial resonance. Next comes the longitude – which of course determines the city's position in the book – and its latitude. Astonishingly for something you might imagine as finite there is no central standard for these figures; every major atlas contains its own variation on the information. As our yardstick we settled on the *Times Atlas of the World*.

There are details on population, based on the latest available or authenticated figures, although populations flux daily, hourly, as inhabitants are born, die or migrate, just as a city's fame and fortune – commercial, cultural or political – ebb and flow, flitting in and out of the rest of the world's communal radar. The altitude, or elevation, above sea level gives an indication of its height; again, standard figures are virtually non-existent and figures are averages, so a hilly seaport will not be at sea level. We added information on "twin" – also known as "sister" – cities, those connections which either make perfect sense (Memphis, Tennessee and Memphis, Egypt is particularly sweet) or occasionally, one suspects, suggest that local councillors anticipated an expenses-paid holiday...

Finally we have listed a selection of famous natives and residents. The natives include favourite sons and daughters, and those who happened to be born in that city because it was their parents' temporary abode (Keanu Reeves in Beirut comes to mind). Residents are those who had a long connection with a city or whose stay, though relatively brief, had a major impact on the city or their own lives. The selection is by no means exhaustive – it can't be for a New York or a Berlin or a Budapest – but gives a sense of the people, celebrated, august or notorious, who seem to symbolize a city, or who prove somewhat of a surprise; suggestions for future editions are welcome.

We have generally not included presidents, prime ministers or monarchs who were technically resident in a capital city solely through their position in life, only if they were born there. Intriguingly, the more barbarous dictators seem to have been born in obscure peasant villages; professional tennis players mainly from major conurbations (as far as we know the twain have never met, although Mussolini apparently had a ferocious backhand!)

For the anthropologist Desmond Morris, the city, famously, was "not a concrete jungle, but a human zoo". Gabriel García Marquez wrote, "A writer needs a desert island in the morning and a big city at night". The author and journalist Cyril Connolly thought that "no city should be too large for a man to walk out of in a morning". Whatever our expectations, we all come away from a city with our own - and often completely opposite - impressions, a mental grab-bag of mementos, souvenirs and snapshots. *The Book of Cities* will, we hope, act as a spur to visit or revisit some of these metropolises and to replenish your own store of memories.

Philip Dodd and Ben Donald
(with sincere apologies to James Joyce) London, Istanbul, Los Angeles, Melbourne, Nice, Rome, San Francisco, Tokyo, Toronto

LONDON UNITED KINGDOM

AT ZERO DEGREES LONGITUDE, bestriding the Greenwich Meridian, London has always considered itself the very centre of the world. Like some jaded aristocrat, who wears frayed collars and shabby suede brogues at weekends, London knows its own position but disdains the need to show it.

London simply oozes history, especially that of the British Empire. The red post- and phoneboxes bear the stamp of kings and queens past. A polite BBC World Service voice announces the trains at Clapham Junction. Its royal parks and gardens still evoke the phlegmatic Victorian superiority and appetite for diversion that spawned a hundred world sports. And yet the city does not boast. Like its red double-decker buses and black taxis seemingly modelled on Rolls-Royces, the Tower of London,

St Paul's, Buckingham Palace and Big Ben are all comfortable in their grandeur and their global resonance.

London streets are not named after artists or revolutionaries. There is no Churchill Boulevard or Shakespeare Avenue. Such brashness would be in bad taste. London street names are understated and cryptic – Piccadilly, the Mall, Bakerloo – their origin lost in the annals of a long urban history. Instead of squares there are circuses.

Ever the individualist and satirist of puffed up ideology, London, despite Mayor Ken Livingstone's recent un-British draconian measures, has stubbornly defied Utopian planning, instead developing into a gloriously unruly patchwork of neighbourhoods. London is the genuine global village, a city of boroughs, each as distinct as the colours of the Monopoly board: leafy, affluent Chelsea, bohemian Notting Hill, tolerant, scruffy Camden Town, arty-socialist Islington, gentrified pie-and-mash East End and the looming gothic mansions of Clapham.

The odd cockney cab-driver aside there few original Londoners left. London has always been a clearing house for the world and a haven for refugees. Despite much introspection following the 7/7 attacks by terrorist elements from the Muslim community within, the city is resolved to uphold its tradition as Milton's "mansion house of liberty". Stretching for tens of miles "norf" and "sarf" of the winding flat banks of the murky Thames, here all the globe is represented: the Lebanese of Mayfair, the Indians of Brick Lane and Southall, the Jamaicans of Brixton, the French and Italians of Kensington, the Aussies of Earl's Court. London's Notting Hill Carnival – raw, cock-sure, ironic and aggressive – is a world party that epitomizes the modern cosmopolitan city.

Literary home of the Artful Dodger, Sherlock Holmes and James Bond, London stands at the core of global cultural consciousness. Its museums guard the vast booty of the Grand Tour, its West End theatres still attract Hollywood stars. London is a trend-setter – birthplace of the mini-skirt, punk and the original pin-stripe gentleman, epicentre of the recording industry and hothouse of experimentation across the arts.

Not conventionally beautiful and with a Victorian infrastructure beginning to creak under the demands of the 21st century, London stands resolute and majestic, a sceptered city, inexhaustible, and certain of the heritage at its irreducible core. London needs almost no introduction. It has been doing the big-city-thing longer than anyone else.

> "The man who is tired of London is tired of looking for a parking space."
>
> Paul Theroux

> LONDON, ENGLAND, UNITED KINGDOM > LONGITUDE: 0°00' > LATITUDE: 51°30' N > ALTITUDE: 50 feet/15 metres > POPULATION: 2,766,000 (metro: 7,651,600) > TWINNED WITH: New York
> NATIVES: Kingsley Amis, W.H. Auden, David Bailey, David Beckham, Dirk Bogarde, Michael Caine, Charlie Chaplin, John Gielgud, Alec Guinness, Alfred Hitchcock, William Hogarth, HM Queen Elizabeth II, Inigo Jones, Ben Jonson, Boris Karloff, Edward Lear, Christopher Lee, John Lydon, Roger Moore, Samuel Pepys, Henry Purcell, Oliver Reed, Elizabeth Taylor, Peter Ustinov, Virginia Woolf
> RESIDENTS: James Boswell, Samuel Taylor Coleridge, Charles Dickens, Benjamin Franklin, George Frederick Handel, Samuel Johnson, Karl Marx, Christopher Wren

BRIGHTON

IF BRIGHTON WAS A GIRL she'd be the pretty working-class lass who grew up with dreams of the big stage, but ended up acting out the desires of a different kind of audience in a no less red-cushioned boudoir.

On first impressions there's something alluringly slutty about Brighton – beautiful underneath but wearing too much make-up. Despite the flashing lights of the slot machines on the pier, and the overly-ornate façades of sea-front buildings it seems all that glisters is indeed not gold. Rust, brine, down-at-heel B&Bs, massive seagulls and shingle beach – on one level Brighton is the archetypal British seaside resort.

Ever since the Prince Regent began bringing his mistress here in the 1770s on the pretext of taking the healing waters, what was once a quiet fishing village turned into the original dirty weekend destination. Suddenly the city became host to deviants, dandies and dabblers from the city and guardian of a thousand illicit affairs following the royal trend. A love-nest conveniently close to the capital, London by the sea was born.

In many ways Brighton doesn't take itself too seriously, is not ashamed of its overt gaudiness and does not try to present its ritzy glamour as anything other than a veil. Brighton is happy to trade on its livin'it, lovin'it feel and reputation as a party town where anything goes. True to its permissive attitude and thespian artifice, Brighton is Britain's gay capital, focused around Kemptown – affectionately branded Camptown – which in turn feeds a vibrant arts scene. Summer 2002 saw DJ Fat Boy Slim host the Party on the Beach, the largest ever open-air party in the UK, where over 200,000 clubbers turned out to rave all day and night on the shingle.

But for all its skinny-dipping revellers, Brighton is not just skin-deep. Hippie shabbiness goes hand-in-hand with a fine architectural heritage and slick, retro urban fashion. Behind the sea front, the city is laid out in elegantly proportioned, regal Georgian crescents. The Holland- and Nash-designed Royal Pavilion is an extraordinary fusion of Empire-Hindu-Victorian styles. The Lanes of the old fishing village are a warren of small bohemian streets full of hip boutiques and cafés.

But the magnetic and most cosmopolitan centre of Brighton is the beachfront. In summer, while the old sit, teacup in hand, fixing the horizon in seaward windows, the beach is strewn with foreign language students of all nationalities in search of the textbook English experience. Unsuspecting, they become extras in another hen or stag weekend. And when the rest of the city has gone to sleep, house grooves still pump away in the clubs under the Arches until it's time to catch the morning train back to London, fish 'n' chips in hand and plastic bags swirling in the dawn. And as the train pulls out you think, "there goes the good time that was had by all".

> BRIGHTON, EAST SUSSEX, ENGLAND, UNITED KINGDOM > LONGITUDE: 0°08' W > LATITUDE: 50°49' N > ALTITUDE: 40 feet/12 metres
> POPULATION: 141,100 > TWINNED WITH: "No twinning" policy > NATIVES: Aubrey Beardsley, Frank Bridge, Norman Cook (aka Fat Boy Slim), Eric Gill, Nigel Kennedy, Steve Ovett, Roger Quilter, Gilbert Ryle, Martin Ryle, John Wisden > RESIDENTS: Emma Bunton, Julie Burchill, Steve Coogan, Chris Eubank, Anna Neagle, Annie Nightingale, Flora Robson

"Brighton is Dublin without priests.

Brighton is tolerance by the sea.

Dublin is intolerance by the sea." Brendan Behan

AS A POTENTIAL DESTINATION for city lovers, Accra has suffered from a pretty bad press over the years. When your least appealing slum area is known as Sodom and Gomorrah, that's hardly surprising. And when the military junta that ruled Ghana in the 1970s had been dubbed a kleptocracy, the overriding impression, certainly from the outside, was that Accra was best avoided unless you had a fetish for corruption, filth and disease. Needless to say, the truth is somewhat different. Few would claim that Accra is a visual feast (the description most often employed is "non-descript"), but it is simply a working oceanside city which,

after a period in the doldrums, is on the up. The light-hearted optimism of most Accrans is starting to win the day.

Nowhere is that more obvious than down on the beaches that lie to the east, further along the coast of the Gulf of Guinea. The city's kids go to party down at Labadi beach, also called La Pleasure Beach, some 15 miles (24km) away. Accra is, after all, the site of one of West Africa's first breweries. The original beer, Club – its taste barbed with quinine, visitors are always informed – along with Star (from the rival Ghanaian city of Kumasi, the old Asante capital) and *apatechi*, the local fire-water, provide the fuel for 24/7, full-on energy.

> ACCRA, GHANA > LONGITUDE: 0°14' W > LATITUDE: 5°35' N > ALTITUDE: 88 feet/27 metres > POPULATION: 1,661,400 > TWINNED WITH: Chicago > NATIVES: William Boyd, Marcel Desailly
> RESIDENTS: W.E.B. Dubois, Kwame Nkrumah

"No sophisticated architecture, no excess or pomp. **Accra is flat, single-storied, humble.**"

Ryszard Kapuściński, *The Shadow of the Sun*

Accra is a city that never stops. And because there is no clearly defined centre it can seem pretty out of control. The lack of a focus is due in part to its creation from three former and disputatious 17th-century trading posts, the Danish Christiansborg, the Dutch Usshertown and the British Fort James. The posts were there because of all the natural resources on tap. This used to be the Gold Coast, sitting side-by-side with the Ivory and Grain Coasts. When Ghana gained its independence from Britain in 1957 – the first African nation to free itself from colonial shackles – things looked bright. A quarter of the population was literate (high for the times), and the resources looked set to last; but then a series of juntas dissipated most of the riches.

Few Accrans have had even a sniff of that wealth. This is still a poor, low-rise city, where streets lined by trees provide an escape from the heat and humidity, and some small relief from the fumes of the buzzing bikes and crammed *tro-tro* buses. The flamboyant taxis displaying painted biblical slogans offer a different kind of deliverance. Accra is constantly in a state of criss-cross, in search of something, anything. But in this city without traffic-lights, even the chaos seems friendly.

"In Spanish terms it is neither north or south, but being in between, is blessed with a measure of modern, Catalan practicality and with a sun-filled meridional generosity." Adam Hopkins

TOUTED AS "THE NEW BARCELONA" and visibly undergoing a beachfront transformation similar to its upcoast Catalonian cousin, Valencia is a traditionally introvert city newly conscious of its image.

Often ignored in favour of Spain's heavyweight heritage haunts, the country's third largest city is beautifully virgin territory. There may be no gaudy (or Gaudi!) attractions, and less of the twirly baroque, but for urban freaks Valencia is a gritty, contemporary port city, known throughout the country for a boiling night-life and cutting-edge clubbing scene. It is said that the double-edged wave of Latin house and hallucinogens currently larging it in Ibiza was carried on the breeze from Valencia. What is now the Balearic beat started life as a groove called *bacalao* (yes, cod!), here on the Costa del Azahar, coast of the Orange Blossoms.

Known for its oranges, Valencia is a *Zeitgeist* city with a zest for life. One of Spain's richest, Valencia was bankrolled by the fruit of the blossom that cascades down to the sea in the surrounding citrus groves, and revered in the florid *azulejos* that tile the city's bars and restaurants, especially in Cabanyal and the pulsing Barrio del Carmen. The city is full of gardens, romantic 18th-century shrines to bloomers that brought it the folk appellation *"la tierra de las flores"*, the land of flowers – a paradox for a city that is also a vast, clunking port.

Oranges are not the only fruit. Valencians grew to their famed corpulent size on the food of the surrounding fertile plain, and one dish in particular with which a nation has become associated – *paella*. Food also built the city's handsome and lavish buildings, themselves a paella of styles, from the towering columns of the 15th-century silk exchange, the operatic cathedral and grandiose city gates to the brash Modernista Calle de la Paz.

With its bullring and hanging *jamons*, on the surface Valencia is a traditional Spanish city whose inhabitants are known by Spaniards as staid and narrow-minded. Why then, every spring, do they turn into pyromaniacs, setting fire to thousands of *fallas* – papier-mâché cartoon effigies – and millions of firecrackers? A year of proud home-made handiwork goes up in smoke in the name of the city's patron, San José. In the July festival the city is awash with flowers and the October Mocaora festival celebrates El Cid's victory over the Moors. Known for an explosive ability to party as if every festival were the last, one thing Valencianos are not is dull.

From razing their own city walls (to spite the conquering Moors) to diverting their own river when it flooded, Valencians have always been people of action. Like the bat of the city's heraldry, they are insatiably nocturnal, with a rebellious, devil-may-care attitude, and a dangerous capacity to spontaneously combust.

> VALENCIA, COMUNICAT VALENCIANA, SPAIN > LONGITUDE: 0°21' W > LATITUDE: 39°29' N > ALTITUDE: 26 feet/8 metres > POPULATION: 738,400
TWINNED WITH: Bologna, Moscow, Odessa > NATIVES: Santiago Calatrava, Antonio Gades, Vicente Blasco Ibáñez, Jean Luis Vives

APPROACHING BORDEAUX across the River Garonne via the Pont de Pierre, the vista revealed is of a beautifully preserved 18th-century façade of golden limestone buildings which curves proudly for half a mile (0.8km) along the crescent-shaped river-front. It would be far from unfair, and hopefully not too condescending to the locals, to say that Bordeaux is Parisian in aspect. The city certainly possesses all the presence and majesty of Paris, as befits the one-time capital of Aquitaine. The plain, undecorated architecture of the buildings forms a pleasing and homogeneous whole – which is equally reminiscent of Bath, say, or St Petersburg – but even better, there is a southern climate, and the lifestyle to match.

Bordeaux is definitely a place to explore on foot, to stroll about at leisure, a *flâneur's* delight. The great architectural glories – the showcase Grand Théâtre, the grand Place de la Bourse designed by Petit Trianon architect Jacques Gabriel, and the leafy Esplanade des Quinconces – are impressive, just as the city's *intendants* intended them to be, but the real heart of Bordeaux lies elsewhere, in the backstreets of the old town. Behind mundane pedestrian shopping streets there is a network of narrow roads which suddenly opens up into small squares, each, or so it seems, blessed with an antiques store, a quirky bookshop (Bordeaux is big on books) or a relaxed café. And further out, in contrast to the stately neoclassical buildings in the centre, are distinctively quirky stone bungalows, known as *échoppes*, which at the end of the 19th century sheltered the city's workers and which now house I.T. operatives.

Ultimately, though, everything in Bordeaux comes back to wine. When the feisty Eleanor of Aquitaine dumped and divorced her husband Louis VII in 1152 to marry Henry Plantagenet (soon to be Henry II of England), laying the foundations for the Hundred Years War, she also instigated centuries of serious trading in fine wines between Bordeaux's merchants and British oenophiles, who played a major role in boosting claret to its position as the most famous wine in the world. The 18th-century wine merchants' houses in the Chartrons area are testament to the revenues.

Bordeaux, not surprisingly, has an abundance of high-quality wine shops, but it's better to head out to the vineyards which start right at the edge of the city. To the east lie Sauternes, St-Emilion and Entre-Deux-Mers, but the holy grail is north-west of Bordeaux, in the Haut-Médoc peninsula set between the Garonne and the Atlantic. Puttering through its small towns and past its châteaux, a rich gazetteer of familiar names – Margaux, Lynch-Bages, Lafite-Rothschild – rolls past like a silver-tongued sommelier's sales pitch.

"This is a city which is
proud to be a city,
which doesn't yearn to be a conglomerate of suburbs."

Jonathan Meades

> BORDEAUX, GIRONDE, FRANCE > LONGITUDE: 0°34' W > LATITUDE: 44°51' N > ALTITUDE: 16 feet/5 metres > POPULATION: 218,900 (metro: 753,900) >
TWINNED WITH: Ashdod (Israel), Bristol, Boston, Casablanca, Fukuoka, Lima, Los Angeles, Madrid, Munich, Oporto, Quebec City >
NATIVES: Jean Anouilh, Yvonne Arnaud, Joseph Black, Rosa Bonheur, François Mauriac, Charles-Louis de Secondat, Baron de Montesquieu, Odilon Redon
> RESIDENTS: Jacques Chaban-Delmas, Jean Moulin

WHEN IT COMES TO SURVIVAL, Oxford should award itself a congratulatory first. Despite the onset of the 21st century, the charge of being out of touch with modern life and the threat of funding crises, the university – as it has done for centuries – has serenely adapted itself to the next brave new world. The Oxonian universe continues to revolve from year to year, from term to term, with the effortless ease of an undergraduate cycling slowly up the Woodstock Road.

The centre of Oxford is pure university. There is no campus, just the tight cluster of colleges, linked by their luminous yellow stone and the monastic-style Gothic look first established in the 13th century by Merton and University College (where Bill Clinton once studied). There are mavericks, like the Scandinavian modernity of St Catherine's, or the Victorian brick of Keble, but they are the exceptions that highlight the rule. Each of the 39 colleges possesses its own character: the public school veneer of Christ Church, the radicalism of Wadham, the fierce Welshness of Jesus.

Together they have formed the backdrop to the education of generations of Britain's ruling élite. Christ Church alone can claim 13 prime ministers. The high-walled streets have been walked by the great, the good and the eccentric, from Shelley and Oscar Wilde to Margaret Thatcher, J.R.R. Tolkien and William Archibald Spooner.

But, importantly, Oxford is not all academe. The tussle between the city and the university has been a running battle for centuries. During the Civil War the townsfolk sided with Cromwell; the university backed Charles I. The battlelines still exist: there is a world apart between the cosy, leafy roads of professorial residences north of the centre, and the outlying council estates of Blackbird Leys and Cowley, suffering from the decline in car production, an industry launched by William Morris, the Henry Ford of the UK (his Morris Oxford was England's Model-T). The pubs in Jericho that spawned bands like Radiohead and Supergrass are signs of a strong and healthy life outside the university. Nonetheless, the existence of Oxford without its dreaming spires is unthinkable. Town and gown coexist in a symbiotic relationship, and have done so for the best part of a millennium: kill off one and the other would founder.

Until that day, Magdalen's choristers will still ascend the college's medieval tower to sing greetings to the May Day dawn. There will be punting on the Cherwell and rowing regattas on the Thames (called the Isis where it flows through Oxford). And under the gaze of the gargoyles in the main university square, the Radcliffe Camera library will carry on purring – in Dorothy L. Sayers's phrase, "sleeping like a cat in the sunshine".

"London is **heaven,** and Oxford is **seventh heaven.**"

Isaiah Berlin

18 > OXFORD, OXFORDSHIRE, ENGLAND, UNITED KINGDOM > LONGITUDE: 1°15' W > LATITUDE: 51°45' N > ALTITUDE: 226 feet/69 metres > POPULATION: 119,400 > TWINNED WITH: Bonn, Grenoble, Leiden (Netherlands), Leon (Nicaragua), Perm (Russia) > NATIVES: Lennox Berkeley, Adam Clayton, Orlando Gibbons, Stephen Hawking, Jacqueline du Pré, Richard the Lionheart, Dorothy L. Sayers > RESIDENTS: Lewis Carroll, Joyce Cary, Colin Dexter, Kenneth Grahame, C.S. Lewis, Philip Pullman, William Archibald Spooner, J.R.R. Tolkien, Thom Yorke

"Ouagadougou is to the developing world what Cannes is to the developed world." Peter Biddlecombe

EVERY TWO YEARS the chic eyes of the cinema world turn their attentions on this unlikely African city for FESPACO, the festival of pan-African cinema that has put Burkina Faso's capital on the map.

In a part of the world where so many dusty city squares and streets herald the names of liberators (Avenue Nelson Mandela) and reaffirmed identity and independence from France (Place de la Nation), it is refreshing yet odd to find a square called Place des Cinéastes. During the festival the sight of tall and languid Burkinabes carrying stacks of film cans above their head is no less surprising.

And yet "Ouaga", as the place has become known to film fans and returning visitors, has become something of an African cultural capital, not only renowned for its biannual celebration of the *septième art* but for a rich creative seam that spans all art forms. A resident artist's colony produces a steady stream of striking, animist oil canvases, intricate hand-made musical instruments and hosts of tribal-abstract sculptures carved in the local granite stone, large examples of which are dotted like totems and sentinels around the city.

Burkina Faso means "the land of honest men" – a neat piece of 1980s rebranding by Thomas Sankara, perhaps the best of the megalomaniacs to rule a country that has seen more coups than a Swiss clock. Sankara was an eccentric and picaresque figure, whose chosen presidential car, presumably a gesture of generosity to the people, was a clapped-out Renault 4 and not the usually obligatory black Merc. A rare anti-Marxist figure in post-colonial African politics, legend has it that Sankara ordered the whole red-stone city to be painted its current white colour in a statement against the then prevailing wind of communism.

The city with the name like a sneeze (and which in the native Mossi language means "come and glorify me") is more of a large country town than a city, laid out in a spiral of Parisian *arrondissements* along wide, scorched red earth boulevards cast in the cool shade of tall green trees and thick "upside-down" baobabs. But it breathes with the 24-hour activity typical of African time. The bicycle is king, and Ouaga escapes the African curse of wheezing two-stroke ghost-cars, enjoying instead an alluring laid-back atmosphere, which in the absence of great monuments or grand buildings accounts for Ouaga's appeal.

Burkinabe are descendants of the Mossi settlers and unlike most of the Sahel peoples, they are animist, not Muslim; which means they enjoy a drink and a party. A virtual island of hedonism in this corner of Africa, Ouaga abounds with pulsating and welcoming bars and nightclubs which, as befits the Cannes of West Africa, stay open late into the night, packed with revellers, some of Africa's poorest but most gregarious people, gyrating to the rhythms of live Afro-latino grooves.

NANTES FRANCE

NANTES IS ONE OF THOSE CITIES that could easily slip under the radar of even the most assiduous Francophile. On the south-eastern cusp of the Brittany peninsular, Nantes sits well off to one side, away from the torrent of traffic that ploughs up and down the main autoroute from Paris to Bordeaux and beyond.

But Nantes is no backwater. In fact, in recent years it has been in the vanguard of a resurgence of France's provincial cities. Its football team has been riding high (League and Cup champions). A successful revival of its old tramway system in the late 1980s has sparked similar schemes in dozens of other towns. Most convincingly, while the recent census revealed that France's population had grown by two million, the population of Paris and its *banlieux* had fallen by 500,000, the main beneficiaries the likes of Nantes, Toulouse and Montpellier.

What may tempt the incomers is Nantes' setting on the north bank of that quintessential French river, the Loire, at its junction with the Erdre – the latter described as the most beautiful river in France by François I, no mean slouch when it came to an eye for the visual (he built the palace at Fontainebleau). In the last 50 years many of the river channels that gave Nantes that overused sobriquet "the Venice of the West" have been filled in, but there are still plenty of bridges and islands to maintain the illusion.

The natural world does well in Nantes. Its Floralies Internationales, held every five years, is one of Europe's finest flower shows, and the heavy, intoxicating aroma of magnolias hangs over the Jardin des Plantes. That scent, almost too lush, contains within it the exoticism and opulence that Nantes enjoyed when it boomed in the 18th century, becoming the largest port in France. Ships plied to and from the Indies, and corsairs mingled with slave traders: the slave past of Nantes still haunts the city, and is made tangible by the mansions of the Île Feydeau, which were built on the dubious proceeds.

However, Nantes was also the place where the Edict of Nantes was issued, granting Protestants religious freedom in 1598. Like Potsdam or Worms, Nantes is (vaguely) remembered by generations of history students as a moment, not a place. Yet the Nantes of today wears the past lightly. The Musée Jules Verne celebrates the vision of its favourite son, the galleried Passage Pomeraye, as frequented by Flaubert, is in demand as a movie location, and La Cigale, all mosaics and rococo decoration, is still a popular meeting-place.

More than anything, though, Nantes has left its mark on French culture in one completely iconic way. The city's Lefèvre-Utile Biscuiteries created the legendary Petit Beurre, that crisp, buttery biscuit that is unavoidable throughout France.

> NANTES, LOIRE ATLANTIQUE, FRANCE > LONGITUDE: 1°33' W > LATITUDE: 47°13' N > ALTITUDE: 16 feet/5 metres > POPULATION: 544,900 > TWINNED WITH: Cardiff, Jacksonville FL, Seattle
> NATIVES: Peter Abelard, Aristide Briand, Claude Cahun, Jean Metzinger, Anna Mouglalis, James Tissot, Jules Verne > RESIDENTS: Molière, Stendhal

"We would go to the Pommeraye Arcade to buy Chinese shades, Turkish sandals or Nile baskets…, the splendid, futile, colourful objects that make us dream of other worlds." Gustave Flaubert

"My idea of heaven is a place where the Tyne meets the Mississippi Delta." Mark Knopfler

BRIDGES HAVE DEFINED THE DEVELOPMENT of Newcastle upon Tyne. Its new Millennium Bridge, flickering open like the blink of an eye, is the latest in a long line. The Romans bridged the River Tyne at its lowest crossable point. George Stephenson's high level bridge of 1849 and the seminal half-moon Tyne Bridge of 1929 celebrated the great era of Newcastle, when it dominated not only the coal industry in the north-east but also produced a remarkable 25 per cent of the world's entire shipbuilding output. "Carrying coals to Newcastle" became a stock phrase for uselessness, or taking anything to where it was more abundant.

All these bridges span the Tyne, because this is Newcastle upon Tyne, just to make sure that we have not confused it with the other Newcastles around the world: Newcastle under Lyme or on Clun in the UK, or Newcastle, Wyoming, USA – so many others, there's a website dedicated to them all. The river is the aorta that feeds a catchment area of hardy, distinctive areas: Gateshead, Jarrow, Wallsend, Tynemouth and South Shields.

A new kind of span has taken the headlines recently: the vast reach (equivalent to the wings of a Boeing 767) of the *Angel Of The North*, Antony Gormley's soaring sculpture south of the city which motorway drivers or train passengers see before they ever reach the city. It's the symbol of a Newcastle that is regenerating itself with a vengeance. The Baltic, a former flour mill, is taking on the best of the country's art galleries. Norman Foster has created a huge music centre in Gateshead. Like the other great forcing-houses of Britain's industrial North, Newcastle upon Tyne has had to come to terms with the demands of a new non-industrial age – and Geordies are nothing if not resilient.

When the Great Depression kicked in during the 1930s, Geordies did not sit and moan. They marched from Jarrow to London to raise the consciousness of the nation. They are used to surviving the bad times, as any loyal Newcastle United fan who watched Kevin Keegan's Magpies blow the Premiership title in 1996 will know. Eric Burdon and the Animals created the city's very own blues, to be washed down with a can of Newcastle Brown Ale.

But Newcastle upon Tyne is not a grim city, far from it. Within easy reach are the airy, windswept uplands of the Northumbrian countryside and the parapets of Hadrian's Wall. And in 2002 the classical façade of Grey Street, curving gently through the centre of Newcastle, was voted the finest street in Britain. It was part of a Victorian makeover, of which the city's Theatre Royal is the prime and elegant example. J.B. Priestley once snidely remarked that Newcastle had been designed "by an enemy of the human race" – he should have taken a stroll along Grey Street first.

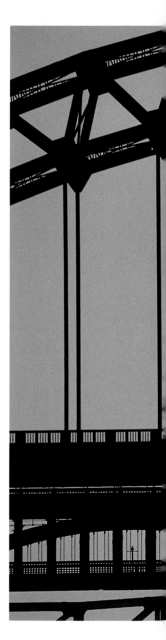

> NEWCASTLE UPON TYNE, TYNE AND WEAR, ENGLAND, UNITED KINGDOM > LONGITUDE: 1°36' W > LATITUDE: 54°59' N > ALTITUDE: 135 feet/41 metres > POPULATION: 254,800 (metro: 544,900)
> TWINNED WITH: Atlanta, Bergen (Norway), Gelsenkirchen (Germany,) Groningen (Netherlands), Haifa (Israel), Nancy (France), Newcastle (Australia), Taiyuan (China) > NATIVES: Ove Arup, Rowan Atkinson, Eric Burdon, Steve Cram, Bryan Ferry, Paul Gascoigne, Jack Higgins, Basil Hume, Jimmy Nail, Alan Shearer, Sting, Neil Tennant

196 W

"Manchester's got everything –
except a beach." Ian Brown of the Stone Roses

IT'S ODD THAT, although the city possesses no instantly recognizable iconic monument (no Big Ben, no Liver Birds), Manchester is nonetheless one of the best known of all British cities worldwide. Of course, that's principally down to the efforts, trophies and marketing nous of the lads over at Manchester United Football Club (even after David Beckham swopped his number 7 shirt for Real Madrid's number 23) and to a lesser extent the city's music scene, which have given Manchester a global corporate ID that any brand manager would die for.

The rest of the city has striven hard to match United's brand values. The new Urbis development, the Imperial War Museum and the Lowry Gallery in Salford are part of a campaign to trumpet Manchester's historical and artistic, rather than drug, culture. Confident new TV programmes set among its 20- and 30-somethings are erasing the opening sequence of Granada TV's decades-old soap *Coronation Street*, where mournful brass instruments play over images of cobbled streets, grim terraces and rain.

This was the Manchester of old, the Manchester that embraced the Industrial Revolution so brilliantly and so resolutely, using the arrival of the railways, canals and cutting-edge technology to propel itself to a position of prestige and power. Even the dreary rain came into its own, as it provided the perfect climate for spinning cotton. "Cottonopolis" was all-conquering: the Royal Exchange was the biggest room in the known universe, Manchester its wealthiest city. Some of the vast depositories of the period are still extant: the Britannia Hotel is the old Watts textile warehouse. On top of the Town Hall, the best relic of this wondrous age, there sits a golden cotton seed.

Not everyone thrived. The new wealth rarely filtered down outside the higher echelons, and Manchester gained a reputation for radical socialism: this was the birthplace of the still-campaigning *Guardian* newspaper. Once cheap imports had undercut the basis of Manchester's wealth in the 1950s, it took a while for the whole place to emerge from a post-industrial depression. Joy Division and Morrissey never did.

But led by the Stone Roses, the Happy Mondays and a revitalized New Order, Sadchester became Madchester. At the Hacienda, and down round Canal Street, it seemed everyone and everywhere rediscovered the old spring in the Mancunian step. As personified by Oasis's Man City fanatics, the Gallagher brothers, being bloody-minded (being "gobby") was revitalizing... and marketable, an attitude as spiky as the giant B Of The Bang sculpture, a sunburst of steel outside the City of Manchester Stadium. When the IRA planted the most powerful bomb to go off on the mainland since the Second World War, wiping out much of the less aesthetic parts of the centre, they did the city a strange favour, providing the stimulus for the whole place to come back stronger than ever.

> MANCHESTER, GREATER MANCHESTER, ENGLAND. UNITED KINGDOM > LONGITUDE: 2°15' W > LATITUDE: 53°29' N > ALTITUDE: 240 feet/73 metres > POPULATION: 438,200 (metro: 2,577,000) > TWINNED WITH: Bamako, Chemnitz (Germany), Córdoba, St Petersburg, Wuhan (China) > NATIVES: Caroline Aherne, John Alcock, Ian Brown, Anthony Burgess, Darren Campbell, Steve Coogan, Harold Evans, Norman Foster, Anna Friel, Liam & Noel Gallagher, Barry Gibb, Mick Hucknall, L.S. Lowry, Bernard Manning, Johnny Marr, Morrissey, Emmeline Pankhurst, Genesis P-Orridge, Joanne Whalley-Kilmer > RESIDENTS: Ben Kingsley, Alan Turing

2°54' W

NOW EVERYBODY WANTS A GUGGENHEIM. The impact on Bilbao of Frank Gehry's iridescent titanium gallery ("like a big fish at play", observed Dennis Hopper) was so instant and so resounding that, ever since, city fathers around the world have been desperately on the look out for cultural projects and ambitious architects to transform their own flagging metropolises. Situated on the route to Compostela, Bilbao has become a place of pilgrimage in its own right, a mecca of contemporary art and design.

Norman Foster's light, airy *fosterito* metro runs from the city centre down to the northern coast of Spain. Santiago Calatrava added a flowing footbridge over the river, and created a bird-like airport (La Paloma) up on the hillsides. Cesar Pelli (Canary Wharf) and Michael Wilford

gritty and drizzle-drenched.

Out along the river Nervión, the extraordinary Puente Colgante (an oscillating gondola bridge) remains as a tribute to the ingenuity and engineering of Bilbao's past; its vertiginous upper deck provides a panorama of the docks now undergoing a massive overhaul.

Bilbao also had plenty of culture, pre-Goog. Ernest Hemingway, Bertholt Brecht and Kurt Weill appreciated the city's robust character. Its university was renowned. The elegant 19th-century area of el Ensanche contains the Museo de Bellas Artes; many critics consider its collection of El Grecos, Goyas and Zurburáns to be one of Spain's finest. And Bilbao has always had great cuisine. Down around the exquisite Plaza Mayor in the

"On windy nights, the titanium skin seems to breathe." Frank Gehry

(Lowry Museum) are hot on their heels. Bilbao is a byword for urban regeneration.

Of course, Bilbao existed long before El Goog and Jeff Koons's iconic floral puppy took up residence in 1997. A focal point of fierce Basque nationalism, the city was a port somewhat down on its luck, with a seriously individualistic streak, like a Hamburg or a Liverpool. Built on the fat of a now beached whaling industry and littered with steel factories that had plundered the once ore-rich hillsides, Bilbao's slightly seedy reputation might not have had the chattering classes clamouring for weekend breaks; but it was its own city, grimy,

medieval quarter, the Casco Viejo, on the right bank of the river, spiky, spicy local tapas (*pintxos*, featuring mucho cod, just like the traditional *bacalao*) are bite-sized excuses for a *txikiteo*, or tapas crawl.

Resurgent, its distinctive Basque culture intact, perhaps the only thing that Bilbao is missing is Picasso's powerful painting of the horrific Spanish Civil War bombardment of Guernica, a town a dozen miles west. Curators at Madrid's Reina Sofia museum are stubbornly reluctant to part with this symbol of Basque pride. However, knowing Bilbao, Bilbao will doubtless get its way.

> BILBAO, VIZCAYA, SPAIN > LONGITUDE: 2°54' W > LATITUDE: 43°15' N > ALTITUDE: 702 feet/214 metres > POPULATION: 355,800 (metro; 880,300)
> TWINNED WITH: Dakhla (Western Sahara), Leixlip (Ireland), Pittsburgh > NATIVES: Kepa Junkera, Gaizka Mendieta, Miguel de Unamuno

29

LIVERPOOL UNITED KINGDOM

1960s LIVERPOOL PRODUCED FOUR PEOPLE responsible for changing the planet's *lingua franca* from French to English, according to beat poet Allen Ginsberg, putting the city momentarily at the "centre of the consciousness of the human universe." But although they are the city's most famous export, there was nothing intrinsically Liverpudlian about the vaudeville-soul music-hall songs of the Fab Four, or The Beatles as they are better known. Age-old sweet-nothings and the angst of adolescent unrequited love don't give much scope for the trademark acerbic wit of the city's native Scousers.

But from Merseybeat to Merseysound, music is still a major part of Liverpool's modern history. A mix of world-renowned DJs behind the wheels of steel at Cream nightclub have secured Liverpool's ongoing reputation as a kicking party city and launched the clubbing wave that has swept through the United Kingdom since the 1990s. The city has picked itself up from the "Hard Day's Night" of a depression that saw it fall from being England's most important seaport in the 18th century, the apex of the triangle of the slave trade between Africa and the Caribbean to a "Nowhere Man" disused dockland in the 1950s.

Half the country's exports were once handled on the Albert docks and at the end of the 19th century the Mersey estuary was the portal for European émigrés waiting to catch a boat for the American Dream. Many never made it, staying in Liverpool and making it one of the most cosmopolitan cities of the time. The centre sprouted the grand Victorian houses down Duke Street and Great Genge Street, built in the local purple granite, and the fine dockside warehouses and merchant buildings that define its modern skyline – which when approached from aboard the famous Mersey ferry recalls Manhattan approached from Staten Island.

The Depression formed the character of the Scouser (from the local sailors' old word for stew, *lobscouse*): resilience, obstinate energy, a healthy aggressiveness verging on an inferiority complex (though saying so can lose you your job as a politician) – especially when it comes to the fierce traditional rivalry with neighbouring Manchester – a dislike of emotional camouflage and intolerance of "bullshit". Such attributes have been sustained and exposed in good and bad through the recovery years, riddling the city with crime and exploding in the Toxteth riots, but best seen in the municipal solidarity after the Hillsborough disaster when over 80 Liverpool football fans were crushed in a Sheffield stadium.

Nothing is closer to a Scouser's heart than the red of Liverpool FC – unless you're a blue Evertonian – who in the 1980s held all before them at fortress Anfield, and were finally crowned European Champions again in 2005. There is no better forum for Scouse passion than in the famous Kop end, named after the hill in South Africa where many Liverpudlians lost their lives in the Boer war and where every Saturday afternoon they sing the city's anthem, "You'll Never Walk Alone".

> LIVERPOOL, MERSEYSIDE, ENGLAND > LONGITUDE: 2°59' W > LATITUDE: 53°25' N > ALTITUDE: 16 feet/5 metres > POPULATION: 460,933 (metro: 1,403,600) > TWINNED WITH: Cologne, Dublin, New Orleans, New York, Odessa, Shanghai > NATIVES: Beryl Bainbridge, Cilla Black, Cherie Blair, Alan Bleasdale, Kim Cattrall, Elvis Costello, Alex Cox, Ken Dodd, Robbie Fowler, Steven Gerrard, William Gladstone, George Harrison, John Lennon, Gerry Marsden, Paul McCartney, Roger McGough, George Melly, Simon Rattle, Patricia Routledge, Lily Savage, Alexei Sayle, Ringo Starr, Alison Steadman, George Stubbs, Ricky Tomlinson

"Liverpool is the pool of life." Carl Jung

TIMBUKTU MALI

THE MAIN THING ABOUT TIMBUKTU has always been the act of getting there. It is still a much sought-after destination, but for centuries those travellers with the necessary determination have invariably been disappointed, and seem to have spent their time in this fabled, desert-bound city either heading for the post office to get that all-important post-mark or simply plotting to leave.

Yet there are still riches to be found. The general feel of the town may be desolate, tired and impoverished, but there are fine limestone houses hiding behind heavy wooden doors. Haughty *tuareg* tribespeople in startling indigo-coloured robes patrol the streets. And three great mosques, structures of mud, plaster and limestone that would not look out of place among the adobe buildings of Santa Fe, are a direct link to Timbuktu's glory days.

The mystique of Timbuktu's name – synonymous with the back of beyond, or the very ends of the earth – came primarily from its inaccessibility, but also from its once mighty reputation. Located at the confluence of three great Saharan trading routes, it dominated the gold-salt commerce of the 14th century, at a time when salt was valued as much, if not more, than gold. Alongside this glamorous trade, Timbuktu was also a centre of Islamic scholarship, its Koranic university much admired for its status as an intellectual and spiritual centre.

But by 1600 Moroccan insurgents had captured the city, and the scholars were arrested, dispersed or worse. Simultaneously the trading boom declined as the focus of the world switched to what was happening on the other side of the Atlantic Ocean, and Timbuktu became a closed, mythical city.

In 1824 the Geographical Society of Paris offered a prize for anybody who could not only become the first European to reach Timbuktu in three centuries but also prove that they had actually been there. A fearless Scots explorer, Gordon Laing, completed the trip from Tripoli two years later, but was murdered shortly after setting out on the return leg. Then Frenchman René Caillié, after a year's torturous and dangerous travel, managed to make it there in disguise. However, he was so underimpressed that he left after a fortnight.

The city remains difficult to reach. There is a lazy riverboat journey up the Niger and a couple of flights a week from Bamako or Mopti, but even then the ever-encroaching Saharan sands always threaten to close the runway. This is a town in the middle of nowhere. The desert stretches north for the best part of a thousand miles towards the Atlas Mountains of Morocco. But, rumour has it, an Internet café has plugged Timbuktu into the 21st century; maybe notice has been given to go there before cyberspace, rather that the sand, overwhelms this legendary destination.

32

> TIMBUKTU, MALI > LOCAL NAME: Tombouctou > LONGITUDE: 2°59' W > LATITUDE: 16°46' N
> ALTITUDE: 860 feet/262 metres > POPULATION: 20,500 > TWINNED WITH: Tempe AZ

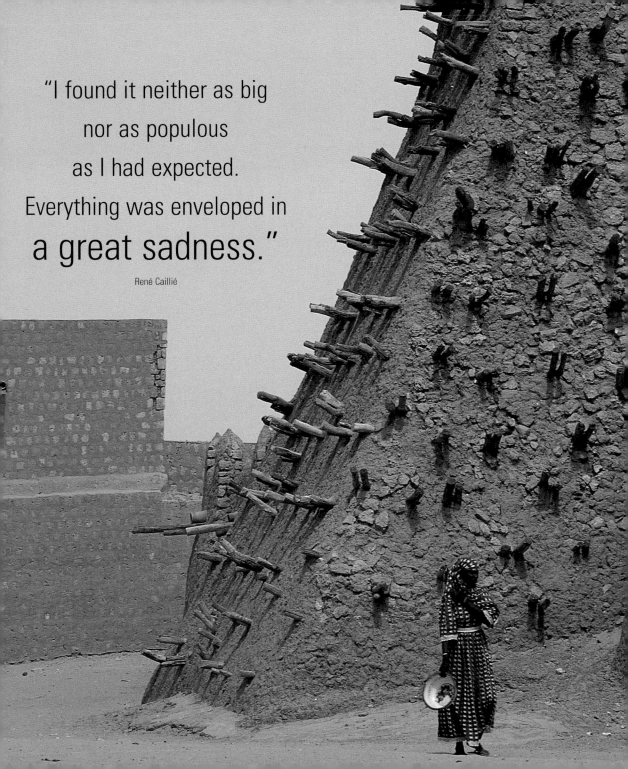

"I found it neither as big nor as populous as I had expected. Everything was enveloped in a great sadness."

René Caillié

THE THOROUGHFARE OF PRINCES STREET neatly sutures together the disparate halves of Edinburgh's character, like a hybrid beast created from the body parts snatched by Messrs Burke and Hare. The dichotomy is not hard to find. Verbally and topographically it makes itself unashamedly clear – Old Town and New Town are the self-proclaiming divisions. It's "Auld Reekie" versus the "Athens of the North".

Together they form a proud capital that soars up out of the Lothian landscape above the Firth of Forth. Edinburgh has sent out to the world the writings, wisdom and inventions of some of the greatest of Scots – Alexander Fleming, Alexander Graham Bell, Walter Scott. Every August, what feels like most of the rest of the world returns the compliment by arriving to revel in the Edinburgh Festival and its Fringe, one of the biggest arts extravaganzas on the planet.

to London in 1707, not to return for the best part of three centuries. Below is the New Town, a vision concocted in the 1760s by the 20-year-old James Craig, who won the competition to set about designing a physical manifestation of the Age of Enlightenment, with squares of symmetry and grace, towering Georgian houses, lashings of Grecian revivalism (hence the "Athens" tag) – the streets round Charlotte Square have lost none of their precision.

But while Glasgow, 60 miles (97km) west, revved itself up into the industrial revolution, Edinburgh fell into a van Winkle-style snooze. Edinburgh hung on to its past, and was sneered at by other Scots, seen as prim, haughty, high and mighty, very Miss Jean Brodie. Sex, so the joke ran, was what Edinburgh ladies kept their coal in. That was pretty much the perception until the 1990s, when Irvine Welsh,

"Edinburgh is a city the size of a town
that thinks like a village."

Ian Rankin

The Old Town is dark, brooding, earthy, Gothic – perched on the improbable though magnificent gorse-clad volcanic stack right in the heart of the city (and Midlothian), topped off by the Castle that is still a working military site, tattoo and all. Arthur's Seat is rich in Scottish heritage, a place of wending wynds and soot-covered buildings. Here lies the Edinburgh that was a celebrated European capital but which gradually saw much of its power whittled away, when James VI headed south to become James I, and again when the parliament descended

Ewan McGregor and the *Trainspotting* crew reminded everybody that Edinburgh was still there, still kicking.

Edinburgh grew up, and learned to enjoy its past and to relish its future (with the new Scottish parliament digging in at Holyrood and bistros nestling next to the old-style boozers). Now it is an all-year round city, topped and tailed by the boisterous Hogmanay celebrations, and the hybrid being is a civilized bohemian and party animal in equal measures.

> EDINBURGH, SCOTLAND, UNITED KINGDOM > LONGITUDE: 3°11' W > LATITUDE: 55°57' N > ALTITUDE: 105 feet/32 metres > POPULATION: 453,430 > TWINNED WITH: Dunedin (New Zealand), Florence, Kiev, Munich, Nice, San Diego CA, Vancouver, Xian (China) > NATIVES: Craigie Aitchison, Robert Ballantyne, Alexander Graham Bell, Tony Blair, Helen Brodie Bannerman, William Brodie, Ronnie Corbett, Arthur Conan Doyle, Sean Connery, Kenneth Grahame, Stephen Hendry, David Hume, Shirley Manson, Thea Musgrave, John Napier, Eduardo Paolozzi, Dougray Scott, Walter Scott, Graeme Souness, Muriel Spark, Robert Louis Stevenson > RESIDENTS: Burke & Hare, Thomas de Quincey, Joseph Lister, Alexander McCall Smith, Ian Rankin, J.K. Rowling

CARDIFF UNITED KINGDOM

AT THE TURN OF THE MILLENNIUM, Cardiff was on the move. John Malkovich took a stake in the Big Sleep, a hotel converted from a stark 1960s gas office tower block. Zaha Hadid was down to design a new opera house. The Chapter Arts Centre was a bohemian rhapsody in the Methodist stronghold of Canton. With the arrival in Cardiff of a new Welsh Assembly, style magazines like *Wallpaper** were already acclaiming the arrival of a new, Cool Cymru. It seemed that Cardiff was on the verge of (or perhaps in grave danger of) becoming very, very hip.

Cardiff is a comparatively young city – it only received its civic charter in 1905 and became the capital of Wales as late as 1955.

For much of the rest of the country, it was a bit of an upstart, and not particularly Welsh – far too English, if truth be told. In the early 19th century, Cardiff had not been much more than a docking bay for the great coal towns like Merthyr Tydfil, Swansea and Port Talbot, further along the South Wales coast, which had far more muscle.

As far as its Welsh credentials are concerned, the city has been making good progress; learning Welsh is now compulsory in schools and is seen as essential for career credibility. But Cardiff's strength is more than just Welshness. Its role as the port for the valleys created a population with a more cosmopolitan mix than the hinterland – among them Somalis, Chinese, Italians and the descendants of the

> "Cardiff has always been an **interesting place.** It's just that people are **taking** more notice of it now." Ioan Gruffydd

coloured *lascars* from the ships that stopped over: including, ladies and gennelmen, Miss Shirley Bassey... This was the Cardiff of Tiger Bay: rougher, readier, even notorious, and very much on the wrong side of the Great Western Railway tracks from the genteel Anglicized Cardiff of Victorian arcades, Glamorgan Cricket Club and manicured parks.

Both Cardiffs dwindled as the shipping trade disappeared, and a hefty regeneration programme for the docks tried to redress the balance. But when Hadid's vision of a national opera house got put on hold, and the city decided to construct the Millennium Stadium instead, the architectural critics felt that a great opportunity had been missed. However, the people of the city have quickly embraced the sports arena that replaced the historic Cardiff Arms Park. Rising in the heart of the city, the stadium has become a symbol of Cardiff's increasing pride. Pride in being a very liveable city, close to a string of great beaches, beautiful seascapes and the Brecon Beacons. And pride in being Welsh: a return to the tried and tested basics of rugby, laver bread, and *hwyl* (that uniquely Welsh intensity of emotional fervour) rather than a reliance on the faddishness of trendy design.

> CARDIFF, WALES, UNITED KINGDOM > LOCAL NAME: Caerdydd > LONGITUDE: 3°12' W > LATITUDE: 51°29' N > ALTITUDE: 53 feet/16 metres > POPULATION: 308,400 > TWINNED WITH: Baltimore, Lugansk (Ukraine), Nantes, Stuttgart (Germany), Xiamen (China) > NATIVES: Shirley Bassey, Charlotte Church, Gillian Clarke, Roald Dahl, Dave Edmunds, Ryan Giggs, Tanni Grey-Thompson, Ioan Gruffydd, John Humphrys, Rhys Ifans, Colin Jackson, Brian Josephson, Cerys Matthews, Ivor Novello, Griff Rhys Jones, Shakin' Stevens, J.P.R. Williams

JUST AS THE PEOPLE OF AGRA do not spend all their time in the Taj Mahal, so *granadinos* do not spend theirs inside the monument that so defines their city to the visiting world.

The hi-rise modern heart of a functioning city sprawling onto the plain will be disappointing foreplay to architecture lovers in search of a city more in tune with the Alhambra – the undisputed jewel of Moorish and royal Spanish architecture that sits on the hill, slightly detached both from reality and the city.

It's lucky the thing still exists. King Carlos V did a pretty good job of disrupting the original form of the Alcazaba castle and its Babylonian Generalife Gardens in order to build monuments to his own vanity. Napoleon used it as a depot and would have blown it up were it not for one of his own cultured soldiers who, despite crippling injuries, managed to cut the fuses. What remains of the Nasrid sultans' attempt to create "heaven on earth" is still one of the most awesome, sensual and romantic monuments in the world.

Ironic, then, that Granada is seen as a closed city, concealed by the Sierra Nevada mountains and that the *granadinos* are known among Castillians for their particular cantankerousness and bad humour. Lorca, who was born just outside Granada and shot there by partisans, was fond of saying, "When I go to Granada, only the air greets me". The city is as hard on the outside as the pomegranate from which it takes its name, supposedly inspired by Hercules' daughter, Granata.

Inside, however, like the same fruit, Granada courses with the scarlet juice of a wound. The city is haunted by the blood shed in Christianity's conflict with Islam. On the Alcahaba Hill lies the Albaicín, a Little Morocco of cobbled stone, a white-washed labyrinth of Morisco architecture that retains a strong Arabic feel and where you can once more hear the call to prayer. Architectural evidence of the crusade and the cleansing of Muslims is everywhere. Granada was the last bastion of Moorish Spain, falling in 1492 to signal the coming of a new world order. Columbus came to Granada to ask King Ferdinand for sponsorship for a certain voyage he was planning. The year that changed Granada's fate also changed that of the world.

Modern Granada is an exuberant university city full of plazas and *terrazas* to laze in. Young *granadinos* cruise the streets in *botellóns*, large groups with bottles of wine, especially around Plaza Alcon, and by the Darro River. This trend has attracted a glut of New Age travellers who also come to hang out with the troglodytes in their caves up on Sacromonte in an ironic continuation of the unwashed gypsy life. Meanwhile sensible showbiz gypsies stamp flamenco dances of fire and angst for the tourists downtown.

"Only sighs glide on the waters of Granada."

Federico García Lorca

MADRID SPAIN

IN THE 1980s *MADRILEÑOS* REDISCOVERED the fine art of enjoying themselves, following the end of the Franco regime, when fun had definitely not been part of the agenda. This fresh lease of life, known as *la movida*, was captured in the films of cheeky-boy director Pedro Almodóvar, harking back to an attitude that had once made Madrid one of Europe's top party towns in the 1600s.

Daytime in Madrid is essentially a time of preparation for the rigours of the night ahead. In the calm of the early afternoon, a little light exercise in the bars of the Plaza Santa Ana (a Hemingway haunt) is more than ample. All around, the city is in suspension; up above, the seemingly endless blue of the sky – dubbed *"velasqueño"* in tribute to the one-time court painter – is motionless. A siesta and a late dinner follows, then, as midnight approaches, Madrid gathers up its forces, gets dressed up, and heads off into the night. The timetable is unchanging. Madrid is notorious for never varying its routine. And after meeting in the

Plaza Mayor, there is plenty of nocturnal time to explore the myriad waterholes on offer; one rumour has it that the quarter of Antón Martín alone contains more bars than the whole of Norway.

After the heat of the day, the dry warmth of the night makes such an alfresco lifestyle easy. The climate is thanks to Madrid's location, slap bang in the middle of a vast plain in the heart of Spain. Some stroppy clerics and a wish to be close to his beloved palace of El Escorial gave Philip II the notion of moving the country's capital from Toledo to Madrid in 1561. The former market town embraced the panoply of court as well as its attendant airs and graces (social observer Taki once observed "If Castile is the country's soul, Madrid is Spain's ego"), a sense of majesty that lingers in the name of Real Madrid Club de Fútbol and the grandeur of the city's parks.

The parks, especially the Retiro, are where Madrid strolls in the evening or on Sunday mornings, resting with a glass of *horchata* – orgeat juice – to slake the thirst, above all never moving too fast. Madrid is not a city to run about in unless you're a Real or Atletico superstar, but rather a city to take time looking around – goggling at the baroque Palacio de Comunicaciones, which turns out to be the main post office; savouring the artistic riches of the Triangulo del Arte: the peerless Prado (Goya's *The 3rd of May*, Velázquez's *Las Meninas*), the new Reina Sofia (Picasso's *Guernica*) and the suave Thyssen-Bornemisza (van Eyck's *Annunciation*). And maybe some retail therapy – Madrid is a shopper's delight; after the Prado, a little Prada?

"Nobody goes to bed in Madrid
until they have killed the night."
Ernest Hemingway

> MADRID, SPAIN > LONGITUDE: 3°40' W > LATITUDE: 40°26' N > ALTITUDE: 1,932 feet/589 metres > POPULATION: 3,010, 500 (metro: 5,086,600) > TWINNED WITH: Bordeaux, New York
> NATIVES: Jacinto Benavente, Rafael Benitez, Teresa Berganza, Pedro Calderón de la Barca, Joaquin Cortes, Penelope Cruz, Placido Domingo, Farruquito, Francisco Goya, Juan Gris, Julio Iglesias, Carmen Maura, Tirso de Molina, Jean Muñoz, José Ortega y Gasset, Manuel Santana, George Santayana, Francisco Quevedo, Lope de Vega > RESIDENTS: Pedro Almodóvar, David and Victoria Beckham, Miguel de Cervantes

LOOMING OVER THE COCONUT PALMS and frangipani bushes which fringe the waterfront of the Ebrié lagoon, Abidjan's downtown skyscrapers have led to the city being frequently described as the New York of the tropics (although its lakeside setting suggests Chicago even more strongly). The city has never been quite in the Big Apple league, but its skyline remains an uncommon sight in West Africa, and reflects the decades of stability, peace and prosperity which Abidjan enjoyed in the years after the Ivory Coast, or Côte d'Ivoire, gained its independence from France in 1960. Stability, that was, until the death in 1993 of the country's founding father, Félix Houphouët-Boigny, led to a period of unexpected uncertainty: coups in 1999 and 2002 caught even old African hands by surprise.

Part of the problem was the amount of money that had been poured into the freshly-created and overblown city of Yamoussoukro in the interior of the country, and which became its new capital in the mid-1980s in a move designed to ease some of the problems that Abidjan was experiencing – too little space, a buckling infrastructure, and above all too many people. The appeal of Abidjan with its strong economy (the Côte d'Ivoire is still the world's biggest cocoa producer) has long attracted hordes of rural cousins and wide-eyed migrants from neighbouring African states. As a result Abidjan is throbbing with tensions.

The French influence – wide avenues named after Marseilles and General de Gaulle – and the modern cityscape have not eradicated the Africanness of Abidjan. Certainly the cathedral with its outstretched arms, designed by the aptly named Italian architect Aldo Spirito seems more relevant, more human than the vast equivalent in Yamoussoukro. Abidjan, though no longer the capital, remains the brain, the heart and the soul of the country. That soul resides partly down in the – albeit pretty odiferous – lagoon which first attracted the French colonists. Abundant and colourful fauna pushes up where it can into the nooks and crannies of the city, and the lagoon's fingers penetrate the half-dozen quarters of the city, from the exclusive ambassadorial elegance of Cocody to the gloriously sleazy vibrancy of Treichville.

Life here is down at street-level, particularly in the night-time, once the downtown quarter on the peninsula of the Plateau has closed down for business and after squadrons of fruit bats have left their daytime shelters in the city's mango trees in search of food – and to escape becoming food themselves. Now the emphasis shifts south, especially to rue 12 in Treichville, a place that comes into its own only after dark. The rhythms of the clubs, and the mingled chatter of creole, patois and *droula*, are the sounds of Abidjan and nowhere else.

"I don't believe in geography. Whether I am in America, Paris, or Abidjan, I am living in the big Israel." Alpha Blondy

SINCE 1990, when the city was handed the chalice of European City of Culture, the sages in the tourist offices have been marketing Glasgow as a city of art and culture. It's debatable whether any of the Glaswegians give a hoof.

They liked their city the way it was – and in many ways still is. Glasgow was built on the River Clyde and the Clyde with its shipbuilding industry made Glasgow, supplying the rich of the roaring twenties with the *Queen Mary* and *Queen Elizabeth I*, among the world's great luxury liners.

The city was built on the brawn of heavy industry, not butterflies of the brain, and no amount of packaging can disguise this. In its industrial heyday Glasgow was heralded as the second city of the British Empire. Only since the decline of the shipbuilding industry has it joined the ranks of post-industrial cities reinventing themselves through other aspects of their heritage. Enter Glasgow's favourite son-cum-export, Charles Rennie Mackintosh, whose radical designs

set a new trend in the decorative arts, now being rediscovered in retro Mockintosh imitations. Frommers recently voted the city the most culturally dynamic in the world.

Glasgow grew rich quick, in the space of a few decades, turning from a small estuary port town into a great Victorian merchant city with its own West End, a regal Argyle Street and stately George Square. But despite its importance to the Empire, it is perhaps the least British of cities on the sceptred isle. Glaswegians would be the first to assert this. The city's layout is a grid, more reminiscent of the American cities it sometimes doubles for in films. The M8 motorway runs virtually through it like an LA freeway. And the Glaswegians, reflecting their city's nouveau wealth, share something of the pragmatic American aversion to British obfuscation, understatement and reserve.

With its often grey and claustrophobic climate, one wonders how Glasgow got its Celtic name, Glas-cu, meaning "dear green place".

But it is the Glaswegians who define this place. They are an argumentative and hardened lot, with a devastating sense of humour, usually expressed in an unintelligible accent even other Scots need subtitles for. A night out in town is often sealed with a Glasgow kiss (a head-butt), even between friends who are bonded by lifelong friendships based on the fun of the brawl, where the camaraderie is unspoken. Glaswegians are passionate, especially along the old religious fault-line, traceable to the great Irish immigration, that occasionally threatens to erupt and which dividesthe city's population. In Glasgow you're either a Catholic or a Proddie, Celtic or Rangers, green or blue.

Deep down, while the cosmopolitan chic polishes the surface, real Glaswegians remain close to their socialist roots, neither showing nor suffering airs and graces – this is still the city of deep-fried Mars Bars before Chardonnay. They distrust the artsy snobbery of their Edinburgh cousins and resist attempts to gentrify a city they wouldn't have any other way.

"There is a lightness of touch about the town, without heavy industry. It's as if they discovered how to work the sunroof or something." Billy Connolly

> GLASGOW, SCOTLAND, UNITED KINGDOM > LONGITUDE: 4"15' W > LATITUDE: 55°52' N > ALTITUDE: 217 feet/66 metres > POPULATION: 607,200 (metro: 1,052,800) > TWINNED WITH: Havana, Nuremburg (Germany), Rostov-on-Don (Russia) > NATIVES: Stanley Baxter, Jimmy Boyle, Robert Carlyle, Robbie Coltrane, Billy Connolly, Kenny Dalgleish, Donald Dewar, Tommy Docherty, Lonnie Donegan, Donovan, Alex Ferguson, Bill Forsyth, Alisdair Gray, Alex Harvey, Jeremy Isaacs, Mark Knopfler, R.D. Laing, Lulu, Charles Rennie Mackintosh, John Martyn, Colin Montgomerie, Allan Pinkerton, Sharleen Spiteri, Midge Ure, Mortimer Wheeler

CORDOBA SPAIN

A VISIT TO CORDOBA CASTS Charlton Heston and the antics of El Cid in a new light. In its 10th-century golden age the Moorish culture of Cordoba represented the apex of human civilization. When the rest of Europe was still in the Dark Ages, without sewers, let alone illumination, Cordoba was a centre of scholarship, commerce, the arts and invention. The Moors were the new Romans, rescuing humanity from Visigoth barbarism and eventually begetting the Renaissance.

The Moors called it "El Andaluz" – "to become green after a drought". Exiled from the kingdom of the East, the Umayyad dynasty found the Iberian peninsula in a culturally and geologically desiccated state. They constructed Cordoba on its Roman roots at the highest point of the Guadalquivir River, whose evaporation to its current ochre trickle was to prove the city's downfall. A series of *noria*, vast wooden waterwheels, was constructed to elevate the water and irrigate the city from above. Only one of these, the Noria de la Albolafia, remains, but it has not revolved since Queen Isabella complained of its groaning noise while lodging at the *alcázar* (the royal palace) shortly after the conquistadors took over.

The breakaway Moors modelled Cordoba on their spiritual home in Damascus, but it was to be the capital of a rebellious Western caliphate. In defiance of the Koran, El Andaluz was a land of wine, women and song, a society that understood the richness and happiness of a life in which sense and intellect were equally cultivated. Beyond the city's spectacular red and white-striped Mezquita (the Great Mosque) this sensual Moorish lifestyle has bequeathed the city a rich legacy of atmospheric gardens and chequer-board patios of murmuring fountains and whitewash houses covered in the scented foliage of jasmines, geraniums and orange blossom. Lamp-lit and eerie at night, the tangled and time-locked streets and out-of-the-way plazas of the Juderia, the old Jewish quarter, are inspirationally beautiful and peaceful, perfect for serenades with a Spanish guitar.

The patios are still a feature of communal Cordovan life, and every year the Crosses of May festival sees the city festooned in the competitive blooms of a contest to find the most spectacular. But modern Cordoba is no longer a commercial hub, rather a quiet provincial city subsisting on the olive industry. Its food is still Moorish, in more ways than one, and the city has a lively young population that hangs out, sinking *montilla-moriles* fortified wine, in the cafés and bars of calle Romero.

Retrospectively, though, Cordoba seems a Utopian ideal of a city whose history challenges the crusades of the history books. Visitors may rush to Madrid, Barcelona and Granada; but this, as the locals would have it, is the mother of all cities.

> CORDOBA, ANDALUSIA, SPAIN > LOCAL NAME: Córdoba > LONGITUDE: 4°46' W > LATITUDE: 37°53' N
> ALTITUDE: 371 feet/113 metres > POPULATION: 314,000 > TWINNED WITH: Manchester
> NATIVES: Joaquín Cortés, Pepe Espaliú, Luis de Góngora, Martial, Moses Maimonides, Paco Peña, Lucius Anneus Seneca

"Nothing remains of it now but a white and calcined skeleton." Théophile Gautier

> "If you like
> your romance
> dark,
> Fez is probably
> the most
> romantic city
> on earth.
> It might have
> been dreamed
> up by Edgar
> Allen Poe —
> almost sinister
> in its
> secretiveness."
>
> John Gunther

AS THE MOST ANCIENT of Morocco's imperial cities and the country's spiritual, intellectual and cultural capital, it befits Fez to share its name with that famous Turkish red hat shaped like an inverted flowerpot, so evocative of the *Thousand and One Nights*.

The city's founder, Idriss I, was supposedly a descendant of the prophet Mohammed: the influence of its purist Koranic University is felt and respected throughout the Arab world, like a kind of Oxbridge. The *Koran* finds in Fez its most orthodox interpretation, practised within the walls of the city's magnificent, ancient Karawee Mosque.

Proud of a cultural and architectural heritage enriched by the subsequent influx of Andalusian Muslims, Jews, and *karaweens* from Tunis, the city's museums are home to Morocco's most significant collections of Arab-Andalusian art treasures.

And Fez's craftsmen are considered guardians of Morocco's traditional artistic skills. The steep, narrow and winding streets and alleyways of the Fes el-Bali medina are full with the sweet scent of cedar-wood shavings from carpenters' workshops, the mustiness and bright-diamond patterns of kilims and Barbary rugs and the earthy smell of raw leather strung up in rows of pelts like Spanish hams, waiting to be tanned and cut into cushion covers, belts and shoes. The traditional tanneries themselves, where leather is to this day dyed by hand, are set out on rooftops and in backyards, in rows of giant dipping vats like paint pots, each of a different hue, resembling the mixing trays of a child's paint set.

Fez's orthodoxy and self-appointed role as custodian of Moorish roots contrives to make the city a conservative place, compared to the exuberance of Marrakesh, modernity of Casablanca and Europeanness of Tangiers. Its tight enclosed layout and position inland, without access to the sea, reflects its hermetic introspection. The atmosphere of the medina with its Escher-like spiral stairways is apparently secretive and closed; where cloaked clerics waft like University dons up side passages, eyes retreat behind shadowed doors, and unkempt cats and dogs scuttle nonchalantly past.

Outside the old town is Fes el-Jedid, the half-ancient city of typical white, flat-roofed residences decorated in the paradox of washing and satellite dishes, and beyond that the wide, deserted roads of the modern administrative quarter. But the heart and soul of Fez is its medina, reputedly the largest, most perfectly preserved in existence, and generally regarded as the architectural pearl of the Arab world, and to the visitor probably the flagship of the "authentic" old-world Moroccan experience. Fez is beautiful, but like the beauty of a statue, cold, and for all its arts and crafts somewhat of a museum. So much for the hat. The fairytale labyrinth of the medina may evoke the magical world of Ali Baba, yet the city is not open, and, without the magic words, only with difficulty lets the visitor in.

SALAMANCA SPAIN

"As the afternoon sun hits the honeysuckle yellow stone of Salamanca,
a magical golden glow
suffuses the whole city with its warmth." Alistair Horne

SOME TRAVELLERS find Salamanca a sad city, fearing that its glorious past may have faded to the point of being threadbare; but they need not feel so downcast. The architectural splendours of its heyday have survived, and the city's venerable university is at the very least replenished annually by a new influx of students, whose energies keep the gracious old lady Señora Salamanca amused and youthful.

Stuck out on the western reaches of the great central plain of Spain, the comparative isolation of Salamanca has helped it retain its character over the centuries. Approaching across the flat reaches of the *Meseta* plain, the city rises unchallenged in the far distance. The predominant colour is the gold of the sandstone which is its signature building material. As the sun sets, the glow of the old town surrounding the cathedral hovers over the Roman bridge across the River Torme, providing a mesmerizing Hispanic variation of the dreaming spires.

The malleable sandstone proved to be a great canvas for two classic Spanish architectural styles – the Plateresque and the later Churrigueresque (created by the brothers Churriguera), both requiring detailed and ornate carving. The extravagant

> SALAMANCA, CASTILLA Y LEÓN, SPAIN > LONGITUDE: 5°39' W > LATITUDE: 40°58' N > ALTITUDE: 2,720 feet/829 metres > POPULATION: 152,600
> NATIVES: Tomas Breton, Francisco Vasquez de Coronado > RESIDENTS: Fray Luis de Léon, Miguel de Unamuno

ornamentation on the façade of the university building is a master-class in the carver's art.

At its peak, the university – Spain's oldest, founded in 1215 – was up there with the great European equivalents of Paris, Bologna, Oxford, its law and theology faculties undisputed leaders in the field. Here, Cervantes studied, Copernicus taught. But the Inquisition and anti-intellectual intolerance of Philip II, and four centuries later of Franco's regime, doused the intellectual fire, and now the university retains a social rather than cerebral prestige.

Salamancans have a reputation for being solemn, sombre, even austere (the antithesis of the Andalusian personality), but although they will admit to being reserved, they have a certain honest style. The academic and mystic Fray Luis de León, after years spent in the Inquisition's prison and torture rooms, reportedly returned to his lectern in 1576 with the Latin equivalent of "Before I was so rudely interrupted". This quirky individuality can still be seen in the stone frog that hides amidst the curlicues of the university façade and the celebrated Casa de las Conchas, with its beautiful carved scallop shells.

The current crop of students still gathers in the Plaza Mayor. Spain has many marvellous Plazas Mayor – Bilbao, Madrid – but Salamanca's is the most splendid, and the most gracious (Jan Morris described it as "the drawing-room of Salamanca") enhanced by yet more carving by Alberto, one of the Churriguera brothers. As the *tunas*, strolling bands of student minstrels in medieval costume, tour the bars, there is a sense that Salamanca's former glories are not so far away after all.

TANGIERS MOROCCO

JUST AS ISTANBUL MARKS THE JUNCTION between East and West at the Mediterranean's eastern inner sanctum, so Tangiers marks the divide between Europe and the Maghreb at the great sea's entrance. Set in a natural amphitheatre around a bay opening onto the Straits of Gibraltar the city sits between two worlds, a frontier zone, belonging fully to neither, a gateway to far-away places and itself a door open to all dreams.

Its special location lends Tangiers its unique mysterious aura, an aura in turn sustained by the city's colourful history. One of the oldest cites in north-west Africa, it was always coveted, disputed and besieged for its strategic position – first Phoenicians, then Romans, then Arabs, then the Portuguese. But Tangiers was never part of the Ottoman Empire and for this reason, despite a lively medina and typical modern Arab trappings, appears architecturally the

most western and is the most morally liberal of Moroccan cities. Designer labels are prevalent and young Tangerines walk around uncovered and in miniskirts.

In the decadent 1920s, when the rest of Morocco was a French protectorate, Tangiers was deemed an international port, a vacuum of political and military neutrality, a city without a nationality, arbitrarily governed by a handful of jaded, marginalized and bribable diplomats from a Graham Greene novel, who treated her as playground for their own ends and desires. Tangiers enjoyed total economic freedom and became an appealingly permissive place to live. Her geography had cast a spell, luring shady businessmen, adventurers, millionaires and artists to her mild and murky climate. The city became infamous for the sumptuous receptions held in the wooded affluence of the Montagne district, while she also served as a bolt-hole for the spleen and *idéal* of the Beat Generation who found here a heady escape from the perceived moral stultification of '50s America, perfect for their hallucinogenic wanderings.

America has always enjoyed a mercurial relationship with Tangiers. Morocco was the first country to recognize America's independence, and the American Legation remains the longest held American property on foreign soil. Yet 150 years later, during the Second World War, the legendary Barbary pirates of Tangiers were terrorizing the warships of the emerging superpower.

Tangiers may no longer be the cauldron of espionage and international intrigue it once was, now more of a holiday resort and transit town for those in search of a more old-world Morocco. But at its heart around the manic Grand Socco market-place of the new city, dominated by the multicoloured Sodo Abib mosque, or in its interior and the minty cafés in the picturesque Petit Socco of the old medina, the city stills oozes a tangy juice for those who peel back the skin of the Eastern fruit to which it gave its name.

> TANGIERS, MOROCCO > LOCAL NAME: Tanger/Tanjah > LONGITUDE: 5°49' W > LATITUDE: 35°47' N > ALTITUDE: 262 feet/80 metres
> POPULATION: 664,000 > TWINNED WITH: Chingdao (China) > NATIVES: Ibn Battuta, Eduardo Niebla > RESIDENTS: Paul Bowles, William Burroughs, Jean Genet, Paul Getty Jr, Jack Kerouac, Henri Matisse, Camille Saint-Saëns

"Tangiers is
a tired old hustler
of a city.
It's been living off
passing trade forever."

Jake Arnott, novelist

THERE WAS A TIME when a fanatical minority of its population could only look back and embroil Belfast's population in the blood-letting of a centuries-old sectarian feud. One apocryphal story tells of a British airline pilot who announced to his passengers that they were shortly to be arriving in Belfast and that they should set their watches back to local time – the year 1690.

Now Belfast is looking forward, and several years forward, instead of just as far as the next cease-fire. Even though the city narrowly missed being nominated European Capital of Culture for 2008 the lid of cloudy pessimism is off the Belfast sky. Today, although the reflex of suspicion is hard to shift and every promise is treated with the innate caution of a brow-beaten population, the aptly named Good Friday Agreement has brought the violence in the name of religion, euphemistically termed "the Troubles", if not to a complete end then to the tightrope-walk of a peace process.

Belfast is great if you're into wall-paintings. Now there's a bit of a distance one can begin to appreciate the great artistry that went into the sectarian murals that haunt parts of the city. They are even doing guided tours of them now. Like the Berlin Wall they will no doubt go, just as the painted lines on the street that used to divide people into green or orange, Falls Road or Shankhill, Catholic or Protestant, are being erased. The 30-foot wall that marks the Peace Line in West Belfast is still there, but the Berlin comparison is apt as the city is rebuilding itself and undergoing a similar cultural and night-life explosion.

Belfast used to be an after-hours ghost town, monitored by tanks and checkpoints. Now, as with Liverpool and Glasgow, two Victorian children of the Industrial Revolution with which it has closer ties than with the rest of Ireland, this small and compact city is reinventing itself. Engine room of the province of Ulster, built on the linen and shipbuilding industries, Belfast is rejuvenating its waterfront. On the banks of the Lagan River, the so-called Golden Mile of Great Victoria Street, bars, restaurants, juice joints and health emporiums are opening up as if daily. The streets are full of musicians, the wharf with its giant cranes where the *Titanic* was built has become a cultural focal point, the atmospheric cathedral quarter is a hive of warehouse gentrification and a clubbing Mecca (or clubbing Santiago if that is too many religions!), and the pub-filled streets of the Entries, old Belfast's famous narrow alleys, are filled with the Guinness-fuelled Irish spirit of a people that know how to have a good time. It is as if they are in catch-up mode.

Today this robust northern metropolis of stark, previously inflammatory red brickwork is a different kind of boom town and has rediscovered the liberalism and lust for life it was once known for.

"Had Belfast been an American city, it would have cashed in mightily on the *Titanic*. There would be a *Titanic* museum, a *Titanic* theme park and T-shirts bearing slogans like 'Do you get that sinking feeling?'"

Martin Fletcher, *Silver Linings*

> BELFAST, COUNTY ANTRIM, NORTHERN IRELAND, UNITED KINGDOM > LONGITUDE: 5°55' W > LATITUDE: 54°36' N > ALTITUDE: 26 feet/9 metres > POPULATION: 304,900
> TWINNED WITH: Nashville > NATIVES: Gerry Adams, Tony Banks, George Best, Danny Blanchflower, Kenneth Branagh, James Galway, Alex Higgins, Brian Hutton, C.S. Lewis, Louis MacNiece, Mary McAleese, Brian Moore, Van Morrison, Liam Neeson, Ian Paisley Jr, Stephen Rea > RESIDENTS: Seamus Heaney

55

"A city of traditional *alegría*, where gaiety was almost a civic duty, something which rich and poor bore with arrogant finesse simply because the rest of Spain expected it."

Laurie Lee

SEVILLE IS ONE OF THOSE CITIES where the sights and the buildings – fascinating though many of them are – seem almost incidental to the ambience. Seville is an experience, absolutely Andalusian, a crystallization of what most people imagine as "Spain". There is the full panoply of flamenco, castanets and bullfighting posters; the ladies wear mantillas, sherry is the lifeblood of the place. There are horse-drawn carriages and gypsies. After all, this is the city where Carmen cavorted – her tobacco factory is now part of the university buildings – where Figaro barbered and Don Juan seduced.

In a few weeks in early spring, Seville displays the full range of its deep Spanishness. First comes the mysterious Semana Santa. During this Holy Week, giant wooden figures representing the story of the Passion are borne aloft by local *Cofradia* fraternities, preceded and followed by penitents whose Klu Klux Klan-style hooded garb adds an extra layer of mystery and darkness to the sombre devotional parade, cloaked in incense and prayers. But once Seville has paid its religious dues, the city erupts in unbridled exuberance. The Feria de Abril is a week-long celebration of drinking, eating, equestrianism and dancing (especially the exotic, sexy *sevillana* dance).

Both events are theatrical, and the people of Seville are great performers. They are used to having the world in their thrall. Originally founded by Hercules, according to lore, Seville's fertile site on the Guadalquivir River and its sunny clime attracted a procession of invaders, Phoenicians, Carthaginians, Romans, Visigoths, Arabs, Vikings and the French. The Moors were in residence for the best part of 800 years, and their mark is easy to see in the minaret of la Giralda, one of Seville's landmarks.

While everybody else was queuing to get in, Seville was also a base for leaving to the Americas – the historical records for the continent are kept in the Archive of the Indies, including the diaries of Christopher Columbus, who set out across the Atlantic from nearby. Initially all the trade from the Americas came through Seville, and it is said that when that monopoly ended the city shut itself off, in something of a sulk, only re-emerging when local boy Felipe González became Spain's prime minister in the 1980s. The one-time Jewish quarter of Santa Cruz is full of hidden interiors, orange blossom and window grilles, but the hermetically sealed patios are exactly what gives the old city its charm. Not all Seville is quite so inward-looking, though: Triana, on the other side of the Guadalquivir, is a funky working-class district with a piquancy all of its own, and out along the river is a massive industrial zone that comes as a rude shock after all the lace mantillas and the jasmine.

> SEVILLE, ANDALUCÍA, SPAIN > LOCAL NAME: Sevilla > LONGITUDE: 5°58' W > LATITUDE: 37°24' N > ALTITUDE: 26 feet/9 metres > POPULATION: 684,600 (metro: 1,100,000)
> TWINNED WITH: Columbus OH, Cuzco, Kansas City MO > NATIVES: Joaquín Cortés, Farruquito, Felipe González, Antonio Machado, Bartolomé Murillo, Joaquín Turina, Diego Velázquez

DUBLIN

ANYONE WHO'S SPENT even the briefest time in Dublin knows that the *craic* is never more than a few paces away. But the stag and hen parties who fly in for a weekend's intensive celebrations in the taverns of Temple Bar will doubtless miss out on Dublin's other attractions, which lie equally close at hand. For Dublin is a tiny city. Not only is everything pretty much within gentle walking distance, but everybody, or so it seems, has known everyone else all their lives, which only reinforces the city's warm, close-knit, fiercely loyal character.

However far you wander from the River Liffey as it slouches through the middle of this small-town capital, there are reminders for Dubliners of the culture and hardships that forged them. The General Post Office on O'Connell Street was the launch-pad of the doomed martyrdom of the Easter Rising of 1916. The surprisingly elegant, even theatrical Dublin Castle was for seven centuries the symbol of British occupation. The magnificent illuminations of the *Book of Kells* glow in the calm of Trinity College. And everywhere there are statues: of Yeats and Joyce of course, or that cockle and mussel-vending Molly Malone, or the vast monument to nationalist hero Wolfe Tone in St Stephen's Green, an edifice known locally as "Tonehenge".

The hangover of British influence can still be found, in the imposing Custom House and the Four Courts, or the Georgian doors of the houses lining St Stephen's Green. But it's probably more valuable to celebrate local talent, especially in the written word which has always flourished here, whether the cultured wit of Jonathan Swift, the epigrams of Oscar Wilde or the belligerence of Brendan Behan.

Music also lies deep within the soul of the city, from traditional fiddles and *bodhrán* drums playing in the corner of a pub to the anthems of U2, whose Clarence Hotel is just along from the Ha'penny Bridge. Bono and the boys – along with *Riverdance*, the Commitments and Mary Robinson – were integral to Dublin's great resurgence. The Celtic Tiger roared loudly throughout the 1990s and added an extra sheen to Dublin's shabby chic (though tell that to the residents of the downtrodden estates on the north side).

Walking along Dublin's quays and canals, beside water as slow-moving as the black pool, or "Dubh Linn", that gave the city its name, helps clear the mind after a pint or three of Guinness and a shot of Jameson's. And to appreciate the true Irishness of Dublin, the horse fair in Smithfield Market, on the first Sunday of each month, could be set in County Clare, with kids riding bareback on mares trotting across cobbled streets. At its very heart, Dublin is still pure, undiluted Irish.

"When I die I want to **decompose in a barrel of porter** and have it served in all the pubs of Dublin." J.P. Donleavy

58 > DUBLIN, COUNTY DUBLIN, IRELAND > LOCAL NAME: Baile Átha Cliath > LONGITUDE: 6°16' W > LATITUDE: 53°20' N > ALTITUDE: 29 feet/9 metres > POPULATION: 1,108,500 > TWINNED WITH: Liverpool, San Jose CA > NATIVES: Francis Bacon, Thomas Barnardo, Samuel Beckett, Brendan Behan, Bono, Gabriel Byrne, Roddy Doyle, John Field, Michael Gambon, Bob Geldof, James Joyce, Phil Lynott, Larry Mullen, Sean O'Casey, Sinead O'Connor, Graham Norton, Stephen Roche, George Bernard Shaw, Bram Stoker, Jonathan Swift, Arthur Wellesley (Duke of Wellington), Oscar Wilde, Theobald Wolfe Tone, W.B. Yeats > RESIDENTS: Oliver Goldsmith, Arthur Guinness, Constance Markiewicz, Mary Robinson, Eamon de Valera

7°34' W

VISITORS EXPECTING A CITY that lives up to a name that was, for a time, the last word in celluloid cool and romance, will be disappointed. Time really has gone by, and nowadays it is hard to conjure up visions of the moody golden age of espionage painted on the silver screen – an atmosphere that was anyway arguably more true of Tangiers than Casablanca. Casa, as the city is known, is an industrial port, the economic capital of the country and the very symbol of modern Morocco. It may have no tourist vocation or old-world charm to exude, but instead a forward-looking, open, dynamic mentality whose expression is less obvious to the eye in search only for stereotypes.

that lends Casablanca its charm. His legacy is the grand Parisian boulevards of Hassan II, El Meskini and Mohammed V with their sequences of grand façades combining classical columns and pediments with cedar wood balconies, stucco artwork and wrought iron features.

These main arteries converge on the Place des Nations Unies, a would-be Étoile, now dominated by the huge ship-like construction of the Hassan II Mosque, the second largest in the world after Mecca.

Protected by the old Moulay Youssef pier, the port is the focus of Casa life by day, a rusty, oily theatre of foreign containers and tankers named in Arabic script. By night, along the Corniche,

"I had no idea that the city of Casablanca belonged exclusively to Warner Brothers."

Groucho Marx, on a legal threat to the Marx Brothers' *A Night in Casablanca*

Truth is, Casablanca is no longer the old colonial town that was built for the studio set. A devastating earthquake in 1755 saw to that, destroying the original Portuguese town of Casa Branca. The city was promptly rebuilt by Sidi ben Abdallah in Arab-Muslim style, but it is the legacy of French occupation that most characterizes the city.

During his tenure as head of the French Protectorate in the 1920s, the charismatic General Lyautey – perhaps the basis for the film's Capitaine Renault – was the man responsible for encouraging and overseeing the city's expansion and for choosing it, against Paris's advice, as the capital. An aesthete, he merged neo-Moorish respect with European art deco influences, creating a combination of Moroccan traditions and modernity

where old canons still point out to sea, in the old fishing port of Sqala the city comes alive with the liveliest DJ and clubbing scene in Morocco – St Germain meets Manu Chao to the mellow taste of *tagines*, pistachio pastries and minty *caipirinhas*.

Up in the hills, the residential Anfa quarter, Casa's answer to Beverly Hills and now another chic clubbing district, was where Churchill and Roosevelt met to plan the Allied Landings. Legend has it the Nazis got wind of the meeting, where it was to be held, and tried to tune in. But as with so many people's preconceptions about this city, they got the wrong place. Thinking "Casa Blanca" meant "White House" they tuned into Washington. But on Capitol Hill they found the president not at home.

> CASABLANCA, MOROCCO > LOCAL NAME: Dar el Beida > LONGITUDE: 7°34' W > LATITUDE: 33°35' N > ALTITUDE: 56 feet/17 metres
> POPULATION: 3,535,000 > TWINNED WITH: Bordeaux, Chicago, Dubai, Jakarta
> NATIVES: Hicham Arazi, Alber Elbaz, Nawal El Moutawakel, Guy Forget, Kitty Morse

61

MARRAKESH MOROCCO

CAN THERE BE ANY MARKETPLACE in the world so evocative of everything a market should be as Marrakesh's Djemma el-Fna Square? Empty of people it would be nothing special. No towering monument, no distinctive buildings. It's not even square. Under French rule it was a car park, and under the founding dynasties originally a place of public execution – from which it takes its name, "dead man's place". Yet now it represents something fundamental about life and the human need for social interaction in all its weird and wonderful forms.

the sweet incense of sandalwood sap and cedar shavings, the earthy smell of leather and that pervasive body odour of Morocco herself – mint. With spices piled high in pyramids of saffron and coriander, and a roof hung with myriad drapes, lamps and teapots, Marrakesh's souk is a veritable Aladdin's Cave.

But there is more to the city than its market. An earthy red fortress set at the feet of the Atlas Mountains, the city's ramparts, the great gates of Bab Debbagh and Bab Aghmat and the harmonious Koutoubia Mosque, symbol of the city, are still intact, despite the attentions of numerous suitors and pillagers. Within its walls is not only the frenetic activity of trade, but an oasis of gardens and pavilions, such as the Majorelle, thick with hibiscus and bougainvillaea, and shaded in palm groves and plantain trees. Now a parfumier's muse, these were once the retreats of scholars who placed their city at the centre of Morocco's civilization, an alternative pole to Fez's conservatism.

Rooted in such tradition Marrakesh is not just commerce and molecules on the breeze. Like a dance of the veils she weaves a spell and hides a mystery whose undressing is a veritable feast for the senses.

"You can't live in Marrakesh without liking scents. Here perfume is very mystical. It is part and parcel of life." Serge Lutens, perfumier

By day the square is framed by lines of carts piled high with oranges fresh for the squeezing. Inside this perimeter are lain out all manner of goods, from teapots to rugs, woodwork to leatherware, and more stalls selling sweet pastries, spicy *tagines*, ratatouilles and *shashliks*. Music from all corners collides, mixes and confuses in a delirious eddy in the middle. By night the place transforms into a Fellinian circus of acts: from jesters and flame-throwers, to impromptu boxing contests, snake-charmers and more smoke and spice of the grill. From somewhere comes the insistent tribal beat of a *tam-tam*, as if the whole thing were some elaborate daily ritual.

Inside the souk is an equal assault on the senses, the heady mix of aromas giving you a natural high – although there's plenty of the other stuff on sale should you need assistance. Passing each stall, through the pillars of dusty sunlight that seep through the slatted ceiling, the nose is invaded by the musky scent of cinammon, mingled with

> MARRAKESH, MOROCCO > LOCAL NAME: Marrakech > LONGITUDE: 7°58' W > LATITUDE: 31°39' N > ALTITUDE: 1,480 feet/451 metres > POPULATION: 755,200
> NATIVES: Just Fontaine, Hassan Hakmoun, Mordechai Vanunu > RESIDENTS: Alain Delon, Serge Lutens, Yves Saint-Laurent

BAMAKO MALI

BAMAKO IS A CITY of *gri-gri* and *griots*. The exotic shopping list that the black magician, or marabout, requires to practise his secretive arts (the *gri-gri*) includes unrecognizable sections of various unnamed animals, and a portion or two of crocodile from the city's markets. An equally long tradition is the musical thread that weaves its way back through generations of *griots*, the tribal troubadours who have been passing down ancient legends and tales since the Malian Empire of the 13th century.

In recent years, this musical heritage has been attracting a high-profile bunch of pilgrims, heading into Bamako to absorb the vibes of the hypnotic rhythms and harmonies of bambara music. Damon Albarn, the former frontman for Britpop band Blur, has been a regular visitor. Bonnie Raitt and Jackson Browne have made the journey to Bamako to seek out the Malian blues. Musicians like the Bamako-born Toumani Diabaté – the master of the harp-like *kora* – and incomers from elsewhere in Mali, including Ali Farka Touré and Salif Keita (who pitched up in the city at the age of 18 to play with the Rail Band at the Buffet de la Gare), have been at the forefront of putting Bamako on the world music map. The 2002 Cup of African Nations did much the same amongst cable soccer freaks.

Unusually for African cities, the bands and musicians of Bamako not only play in the bars and clubs but everywhere throughout the city, tucked away in courtyards, out-of-the-way halls or in the Institut National des Arts. Their music emerges as evening falls, and the dust and traffic of the day subside: the traffic is both physical (a scramble of bikes, *bashée* pick-up trucks, bright green *dou dourenis*, mobylettes and lovingly preserved old cars) and commercial (all the *bambara* music cassettes and *Tuareg* weapons you could wish for).

> "One of my favourite memories is Les Escrocs playing a party at Tourani Diabaté's house. Bass and drums doing **dead funky Malian reggae.**"

Damon Albarn

Thirty-five years ago, the city's night-life was also booming, as Bamako's jeunesse donned miniskirts and bell-bottoms, and grooved in clubs to hits like Boubacar Traoré's "Mali Twist", celebrating a new lease of life following independence from France in 1960.

The French had arrived in force in 1883, recognizing Bamako's strategic value on the navigable section of the wide, shallow River Niger. They left plenty of traces, not least the terracotta-tiled, red sandstone elegance of the main station. However, although a couple of hi-rises have popped up alongside the old colonial buildings – including an extraordinary mud-effect bank HQ that could easily double for one of the great mosques of Timbuktu – Bamako has remained resolutely African. And the music plays on, wending its way through the present and the past like the broad reaches of the Niger River, whose timeless flow ultimately provides Bamako's most eternal rhythm and pulse.

> BAMAKO, MALI > LONGITUDE: 7°59' W > LATITUDE: 12°38' N > ALTITUDE: 1,148 feet/350 metres > POPULATION: 935,400 > TWINNED WITH: Achkabad (Turkmenistan), Angers (France), Bobo-Dioulasso (Burkina Faso), Dakar, Manchester, Niamey (Nigeria), Rochester NY > NATIVES: Kouyate Lamine Badian, Amadou Bagayoko, Souleymane Cisse, Toumani Diabaté, Mariam Doumbia, Saydou Keita, Seydou Keita
> RESIDENTS: Salif Keita

65

CORK IRELAND

SECOND CITY STATUS CAN BE TRYING, especially in a small
country like Ireland where there aren't many other cities to vie with.
When the capital is so dominant – as far as the rest of the world is
concerned – jealousy and rancour could be forgiven. Luckily for Cork,
its inhabitants are individualistic and independent by nature, and
possess a bubbling undertow of humour that can amply temper
any angst they might feel about playing second fiddle – or second
bodhrán – to Dublin. They simply call Cork "the real capital".

Cork has always stood its own ground, although that ground
was for a long time a boggy, marshy area around the River Lee.
Once the land had been reclaimed, a strong and distinctive city
evolved in the valley and on the hills around, with an ability to
rile and rankle the governing classes of the day with a niggly
aggression that local boy-done-good Roy Keane, Manchester
United and Celtic's midfield warrior, would be proud of.

This is a self-confident merchant city which sided with the
pretender Perkin Warbeck in 1492, was besieged by William III in
1690, and whose Fenian tradition – Michael Collins was from just
up the road – meant that the city suffered badly at the hand of the
notorious Black and Tan bully boys who enthusiastically overstepped
their orders during the Anglo-Irish Wars.

The city's harbour, Cobh, has also suffered its share of tragedy.
Here is where the *Titanic* made its final call, from where the
Lusitania left for a watery grave, and whence millions of Irish
immigrants fled in an attempt to replace grinding poverty and
hunger with the hope and a dream of a better life elsewhere.

But despite these memories of grief, the laid-backness of Cork
seems to transcend the pain. The peal of bells from St Anne's
Church in Shandon – as essential a sound for Corkonians as the
Bow Bells once were for London's Cockneys – is a gentle melody,
not a call to arms. County Cork itself, "Sweet Cork",
is soothing: plentiful, prosperous, where good food is a must.
Myrtle Allen's Ballymaloe is nearby, Kinsale, the gourmet centre
of Southern Ireland, only 15 miles (24km) west, and the English
Market in the heart of Cork is crammed with organic delights
and rings of rich black pudding.

Among the grey stone wharves and warehouses and the
bridges across the Lee, Cork is having a ball. The local brews –
Murphy's and Beamish – slip down a treat, and the talk can keep
you up all night (nothing to do with the presence on the outskirts
of the city of the world's biggest Viagra factory). After all, just
north of Cork is Blarney Castle, where a kiss of the stone is
meant to guarantee you the sweetest of tongues...

> CORK, COUNTY CORK, IRELAND > LOCAL NAME: Corcaigh > LONGITUDE: 8°28' W
> LATITUDE: 51°54' N > ALTITUDE: 187 feet/57 metres > POPULATION: 193,400
> TWINNED WITH: Cologne, Coventry (UK), Rennes (France), San Francisco, Swansea (UK)
> NATIVES: James Barry, Thomas Crofton Croker, Edward Dowden, Roy Keane, James Sheridan
Knowles, Jack Lynch, Michael Mac Liammóir, Daniel Maclise, Frank O'Connor, Séan Ó Faoláin

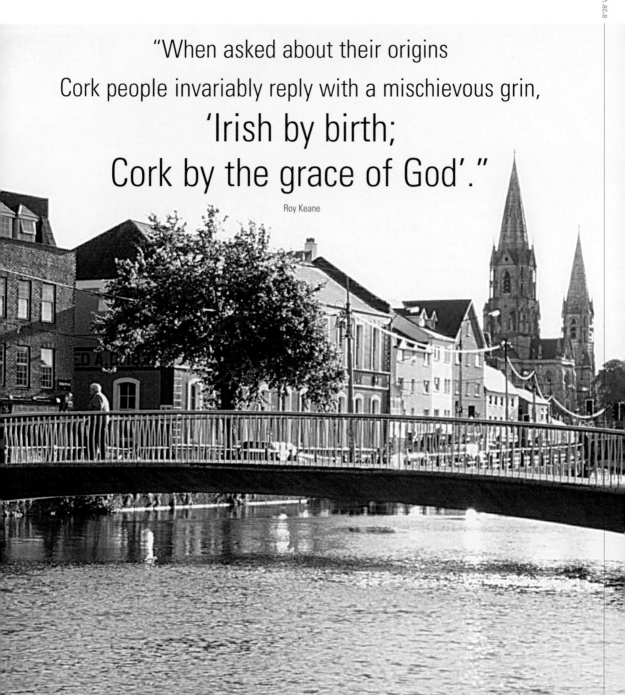

"When asked about their origins
Cork people invariably reply with a mischievous grin,
'Irish by birth;
Cork by the grace of God'."

Roy Keane

"There are, however, times and places when those who have lived before seem almost to touch us on the shoulder, and **midnight is the time and Santiago one of those places."** H.V. Morton

NESTLED IN THE NORTH-WEST corner of Spain, Santiago is located at the end of the Way of St James, the saint from whom the city takes its name. But, if for so many Santiago is a place of pilgrimage (one and a quarter million people tread el Camino each year), then what do the people do who already live there?

Modern Santiago is not a city-in-waiting, but a dynamic place with a vibrant university and thriving non-pilgrim industry, such as its own breast-shaped *tetilla* cheese, and where almost every one of its medieval granite streets has a cyber café. There is no longer any need for wandering apostles when the Internet brings the world into our homes. The credulity of the Middle Ages has long since been replaced, and devoted surfers now genuflect before the oracle of the electronic ether.

Nowadays people can fly to Santiago, stay in the posh Parador opposite the cathedral and get the scallop shell without having travelled hopefully. Most of those who act out the walk, a holiday from city life or a personal challenge in the name of charity, do so shod in AirMax comfort. So you can forgive the slightly jaded countenance of the locals at the mass of people, credulous to the god of tourism, who descend on their city year round. Among Spaniards the residents of Santiago are known for their drizzly personalities, just as the city, surrounded by the lush green bowl of the Sar Valley, is known for its prodigious rainfall.

Many Galicians would not think of themselves as Spanish. They are a race of Celts, bagpipes and all, whose *galego* dialect is closer to Portuguese. Galicia has an autonomous government within the Spanish kingdom, and as rabid separatist graffiti around the station shows, some would see Galicia as a nation – a poignant, modern antithesis to the unifying message of St James.

Not that the saint's legacy is all sweetness and piety. Far from it. Brought back from Palestine where he was murdered (having returned there from an unreceptive Spanish audience!) St James' relics were discovered in the 9th century by a hermit who was led to them by a *compostela*, a shining star. Thereafter he was used by the conquistadors as a military icon against the Moors, conveniently posted on the front line of Christianity's war with Islam. Until they were vanquished he was Santiago Matamoros, St James the Moorbasher. Whatever the rights and wrongs of that, his relics became a shrine, Catholicism's holiest site outside the Vatican. The cult in turn spawned a whole city. Europe's original tourist destination was born.

Faith brought great beauty, not only in the arcaded, cobble streets, but in the vast Plaza do Obrodorio main square, to which they all magnetically lead and where stands the city's 18th-century neo-Romanesque cathedral, shrine and core. It is still a dramatic sight to stir the most profound cynic – no matter how you have arrived.

OPORTO PORTUGAL

DOWN IN THE BOTTOM OF THE VALLEY of the River Douro, where mists swirl of an early morning, where the rain falls and mosses-up the stonework, a string of traditional boats proclaim their allegiance, on each sail a famous logo. The essence of Oporto's very name is port, and the companies which flourished here as far back as the 18th century and supplied post-prandial bottles to be passed at the high tables of the civilized world provide a rich catalogue of warming familiarity: Taylors, Cockburns, Sandeman, Graham's, Dow's.

Commerce and enterprise have always been the backbone of this city. Passing crusaders, on the way to the Holy Land, refuelled here. The expeditions that expanded the Portuguese Empire were victualled by the locals. After supplying one such flotilla with all their available fresh meat, the citizens of Oporto had to resort to the left-overs – and to this day their nickname is "*tripeiros*" or "tripe-eaters". A proverb distinguishes the characteristics of Portugal's main cities: "Coimbra studies, Braga prays, Lisbon shows off and Porto works". The catty comment about Lisbon might suggest this is an Oporto proverb – there's no great love lost between the two cities.

Both have wonderful settings. Oporto's old town tumbles higgledy-piggledy down a sheer hillside to where the Douro has sliced its way through granite rock to create nothing less than a gorge. To prove the point, the Ponte Dom Luis I, one of the city's half-dozen bridges and its iconic monument, is a two-tiered bridge, one span linking the upper towns of each bank, the lower one the riverside. It was designed by Téophile Seyrig, a disciple of Gustav Eiffel; the great man himself built another ironwork bridge just upstream. The streets are vertiginous, flat spaces at a premium. To explore the city on foot requires good stamina and a powerful set of quads.

However, climbing up to the city's Cathedral, the Sé, is worth the effort for the view alone; the 225 steps of the nearby dos Clérigos tower offer a little extra workout. Downhill, the Sao Francisco church illustrates the riches Oporto acquired from its trading prowess: in the 18th century gold leaf was applied lavishly, on altars, columns, cherubs, animals and the bizarre Tree of Jesse. Along the riverfront, where the painted houses of the Ribeira look across the Douro to the well-to-do port lodges in Vila Nova de Gaia, life is less precious: watching FC Porto (steered to Champions League victory in 2004 by the shy and retiring José Mourinho) on the bar room TV or listening to the melodic melancholy of a *fado* singer. Oporto may work – and it is still more a thriving industrial centre than a tourist destination – but it is perfectly happy to play, sauntering round the gardens of the Fundaçao de Serralves, the city's airy modern art museum, or concert-going at Rem Koolhaas's brand-new, strikingly polyhedral Casa da Música.

"There's a secret here that nobody can explain, as deep a mystery as the shady streets with their earth-coloured houses, as fascinating in their way as the lights which begin to emerge in the dusk…"

José Saramago

> OPORTO, PORTUGAL > LOCAL NAME: Porto > LONGITUDE: 8°36' W > LATITUDE: 41°11' N > ALTITUDE: 0 feet/0 metres > POPULATION: 293,400 > TWINNED WITH: Beira (Mozambique), Bordeaux, Bristol (UK), Nagasaki > NATIVES: Uriel d'Acosta, Sophia de Mello Breyner Andresen, João Batista de Almeida Garrett, Henry the Navigator, Ferdinand Magellan, Misia, Manoel de Oliveira, Guihermina Suggia > RESIDENTS: Albilio Guerra Junqueira, Alvaro Siza

IN ITS 15TH-CENTURY HEYDAY, following Vasco de Gama's pioneering of the trade route to India, Lisbon was one of the most important ports in the world, the trading hub of a nation that ruled the seas. The spices that furnished an entire empire and allowed its rulers to construct flamboyant palaces to their vanity are now only to be found in its food. Lisbon is a humble and unassuming capital, a quiet party in the European merry-go-round, its ornate colonial and regal buildings slowly crumbling into disrepair.

Yet its faded, mortal glory is the city's charm and attraction. In testament to their quixotism, Lisbon's patrons found their architectural follies all but devastated by the huge earthquake of 1755. However, in the lively Bairro Alto and the more secretive Moorish quarter of Alfama, up on the two hills that flank the

the vast Oceanarium and revamped subway of utopian stations culminating in the giant concrete and aluminium locust of Santiago Calatrava's mainline station.

Across the River Tejo, Revolution Bridge joins northern Lisbon to its poorer south bank district, Cacilhas, redolent with the smell of fried sardines and home to rust and tangled fishing-nets. The sad metronomic clanking of one of Europe's major shipping centres rings out like a bell-toll as from dawn till dusk ships and ferries lazily go by, and at sunset ruddy fishermen with rough hands strike up the slow beat of a *fado*, the Portuguese blues. They sit and sing dreams of love and loss, flowers of the fate in whose belief lives a whole nation, knowing, as its quixotic Dons discovered, that any flight of mortal fancy is subject to ruin by nature.

"It was beautiful, that capital, with its quiet heart, its unruly hills, its houses with pastel-coloured icing, its huge water ships."

Simone de Beauvoir

modern commercial district, many old buildings still survive. A stroll through the winding narrow streets of these quarters reveals a succession of florid arches and balconies, spiral staircases, courtyards, columns and brightly coloured façades, playfully decorated with the brightly-coloured *azulejos* which are the country's signature.

As if the truth of things lay in their dilapidation, the beauty of these streets lies in their oblivion. Time has eaten away at the stone and plaster, the salty air dulled and blotched the tiles. In the silent hours of the midday sun it feels like Pompeii.

Rickety trams out of a little boy's model train set grind and wobble around sharp and hair-raising bends and inclines. More reminiscent of the Wild West than modern urban transport they look completely out of control, like the caboose of a runaway train. By night their screeching echoes around the walls and their lights cast the glow of a ghost train.

Against this time-locked backdrop stand modern and equally extravagant statements of a new vanity, vestiges of Expo '98:

> LISBON, PORTUGAL > LOCAL NAME: Lisboa > LONGITUDE: 9°08' W > LATITUDE: 38°44' N > ALTITUDE: 52 feet/16 metres > POPULATION: 556,800 (metro: 1,971,000)
> NATIVES: Luis Boa Morte, Luis de Camões, Luis Figo, Frederico de Freitas, Fernando Pessoa, Paula Rego, Amália Rodriguez, Manuel Rui Costa, Juliao Sarmento, Maria-Elena Vieira da Silva > RESIDENTS: Mariza, Gil Vicente

73

SANTA CRUZ DE TENERIFE SPAIN

> SANTA CRUZ DE TENERIFE, CANARY ISLANDS, SPAIN > LONGITUDE: 16º15' W > LATITUDE: 28º27' N > ALTITUDE: 299 feet/91 metres > POPULATION: 208,800
> TWINNED WITH: San Antonio, Santa Cruz CA > NATIVES: Angel Guimera, Rodrigo Moynihan

EVERY WINTER TENERIFE is the chosen destination of migrating plane-loads of pasty sunseekers. But in general they head straight down to the custom-built resorts of Playa de las Americas or Los Cristianos in the deep south of the island, where the sun is at its most reliable. They tend to bypass the north, where Tenerife's capital, Santa Cruz, does not offer them the right mix of pubs, chips and child-friendly waterworlds.

That is a blessing, as it has allowed Santa Cruz to remain a pleasant slice of colonial Spain, benefiting from the climate of the Canaries: it lies on the same latitude as Florida, and a hundred miles or so off the coast of Morocco. Walking along the broad avenues that head up into the city away from the hazy waters of its port area, or sitting on cool tiled benches beside restful fountains in shaded squares, there is a sense of having stumbled across some forgotten outpost of Spain's Latin American adventure – a feeling enhanced by the presence of the volcanic hills and mountains which act as a backdrop.

In fact, ships on the way to the New World frequently dropped in to take advantage of Santa Cruz's exceptionally deep harbour for refitting, refuelling, rest and recreation. The port still bustles with container ships, while cruise liners, moored up in the natural amphitheatre, offload their passengers so they can explore the streets of the city, which offers up its charm in a discreet, unforceful way.

However, Santa Cruz was distinctly forceful when it became the only city to have defeated the all-conquering Horatio Nelson. In 1797 Nelson, lured to the island by reports of gold-laden galleons in the harbour, launched a daring raid. But stiff resistance, high surf and the stinging rains of northern Tenerife – one reason why tourists head south – turned his audacity into chaos. Worse, grapeshot shattered Nelson's right elbow (he had already lost one eye off Calvi in Corsica). With Nelsonian grit he insisted on immediate amputation, with but a slug of grog as an anaesthetic, and within hours was practising a left-handed signature to drop a civilized note to the governor of Santa Cruz, congratulating him on a splendid battle.

The cannon that supposedly did the damage to Nelson is still on display in the town, as is a piece of the original Holy Cross (the Santa Cruz) planted here in 1493 by the Spanish conquistador Alfonso

> "Whatever the hour of the day or the angle of the sun, one can always find a seat in the shade..."
>
> Henry Myhill

Fernandez de Lugo as he celebrated mass. Santa Cruz still celebrates – enjoying a three-week carnival in February that fiestaphiles consider to be more than a shadow of Rio's in terms of all-out flamboyance and energy, and honouring the art of the aria at Santiago Calatrava's new and curvaceous white opera house.

ST LOUIS SENEGAL

ST LOUIS IS A SPLENDID time capsule, a lost city that was trapped in the 19th century once the power centre of Senegal moved to Dakar. The ancient capital of Senegal-Mauritania has an abandoned air that can appear either beautiful or tatty, but this most French of African cities is rediscovering an energy that for many decades was woefully missing. Now its jazz festival can summon up the likes of Gilberto Gil, Archie Shepp or Weather Report founder Joe Zawinul to help boost the overall funkiness.

A glance at a street map of St Louis suggests a kind of West African Manhattan – there are no Abidjan-style skyscrapers, but the city is laid out in a grid pattern on an island slap bang in the middle of the Senegal River, as though pinioned between the Hudson and the East River. This is where the old French influence lingers most, an imprint left by the

The residence of the governors who preceded and succeeded Faidherbe is still in fine fettle, but many of the other colonial buildings are boarded up, burnt out, with paint that is flaking and shutters long closed to the outside world. The decrepitude, however, does not mean the inhabitants are listless – they have a reputation of being amongst the pushiest hustlers of the region, as well as the most upfront whores, with bar fights a-plenty. St Louis's spiciness is like the hot sauce on its staple diet of fish.

Although the Senegal River finally reaches the ocean 25 miles further south, St Louis is but a short hop from the sea, because it is only separated from the Atlantic by a long sandbar – la Langue de Barbarie, which is the site of fishing villages and surf huts, as well as a Parc National that is a major target for ornithologists (further north, the Oiseaux du

> "Quite suddenly, we appear to have time-travelled to provincial France. Cyclists everywhere, clipped hedges, shady balconies ..." Michael Palin

zealous General Louis Faidherbe, who arrived in 1854 and set about bringing his own vision of order and discipline to the city. His memory lives on in the railway line to Dakar and an arched iron bridge which links the island to the mainland, a bridge designed by Gustave Eiffel that was originally destined to cross the Danube in Prague, but which mysteriously turned up in St Louis – no one seems to know how or why.

Djoudj is one of the top reserves in the world). An aroma of fishiness pervades this area, adding to the sense of decay, but there are more graceful old houses along the Avenue Dodds, as well as the remains of a seaplane base for the intrepid airmail pilots of the 1930s who flew their flimsy craft across the waters to South America. Contemporary St Louis still retains something of the air of an Antoine de Saint-Exupéry novel.

> ST LOUIS, SENEGAL > LONGITUDE: 16°29' W > LATITUDE: 16°00' N > ALTITUDE: 3 feet/1 metre > POPULATION: 132,400
> TWINNED WITH: Bologna, Lille, St Louis MO > NATIVES: Alfred Dodds, Louis Phal (Battling Siki) > RESIDENTS: Louis Faidherbe, Jean Mermoz

> "A challenge
> for those
> who go.
> A **dream** for
> those who stay
> behind."
>
> Thierry Sabine,
> founder of the Paris-Dakar rally

THIERRY SABINE WAS THE MAN who got lost in the Libyan desert and came up with the idea of getting people to race cars across the Sahara. And so it was that since 1978 Dakar has been the city at the end of the world's most famous rally, a far-off, mystical city and undeniable presence in the French post-colonial consciousness. His credo sums up what Africa is to many people.

In the plundered landscape of what became the scramble for Africa, the continent's most westerly *finisterre* was at the centre of the Anglo-French game. Today still Dakar lures *émigrés* from France, attracted by thoughts of a neocolonial lifestyle and the striking setting. The city lies on a two-pronged promontory jutting out into the Atlantic, a natural fortress with sheltered bays that the Portuguese christened Cape Verde for its perennial lush cloak of tropical vegetation. Dakar was the first of the West African cities and its comparative sophistication and maturity bear witness to this. With terracotta rooftops, old French apartment blocks and battered Renaults, downtown Dakar feels more like Marseilles. Old mixes startlingly with new as the past is punctuated by shiny skyscrapers.

Unlike elsewhere in Africa, Dakar lives at the challenging, frenetic pace of a Western metropolis. It is all the more intoxicating for the modern mix of the local colours, scents and music. The city has a well-established fashion industry that has incorporated Senegal's exuberant

> DAKAR, SENEGAL > LONGITUDE: 17°28' W > LATITUDE: 14°43' N > ALTITUDE: 0 feet/0 metres > POPULATION: 2,476,400 > TWINNED WITH: Bamako, Washington DC
> NATIVES: Youssou N'Dour, Patrick Viera > RESIDENTS: Paul Bowles, Allen Ginsberg

red, gold and green natural colours and extravagant designs of Senegal's national costume into the grammar of international *haute couture*. No less rich is the city's spicy food whose smell wafts through the streets paradoxically reminiscent of the Caribbean to which it was once forcefully transported. And finally the *mbalax* rhythm and myriad unique instruments of Senegalese music, latterly discovered by the West in a Buena Vista Social Club Dakar styl-ee. Every two years the city hosts Dak'art, an international festival of contemporary African art in which all these art forms are proudly showcased to the world.

To escape the urban clamour, Dakarois head for the white-sand beaches of the *corniche*: the sheltered manicure of Tahiti and Voile d'Or beaches to the east or the wilder fringes of the plage de l'Institut Pasteur facing the Atlantic wrath. From a beach towel sun-worshippers can see the spectre of Île Gorée whose past haunts the city. Here, for over a century, thousands of "pieces of ebony" from all over black Africa were amassed ready for transportation to the plantations of the New World. Today it is a gaunt pilgrimage for black Americans returning to their roots.

Occasionally the boot is on the other foot, as when the Lions famously defeated World Champions France, their former masters, in the opener of the 2002 Football World Cup – a local derby in as much as many of the opposition were originally their compatriots.

GONE ARE THE DAYS when the only people in Reykjavik's bars were hikers drinking hot chocolate before an expedition into Iceland's rugged interior. Rucksacks and binoculars have been as good as banned in favour of the shiniest in trainers, surf-tops and combat trousers. This is the alternative night-life Mecca of Europe – an ironic winter Ibiza for seasonally affected clubbers. In winter here there is no end to the night and therefore no end to the party.

The odd chess match aside, it was the 1986 Reagan–Gorbachev peace summit that put Reykjavik on the map. Until then all we knew about Iceland were occasional volcanic eruptions on the Discovery Channel and that their natives were particularly belligerent about fish.

Even the city's founders didn't seem particularly confident the city would take off. Legend has it that the first settler, Viking Ingolfur

gloom beneath the dark slopes of Mount Esja patched with snow like local killer whale, Keiko (aka "Free Willy"). Arnarson was struck by the amount of cloud and christened the city "Smokey Bay", not knowing that the clouds were steam from the geothermal springs that now bespatter the travel brochures of "the land of Fire and Ice".

Before it became a destination Reykjavik was a gateway to the unique geological curiosities of an island with adolescent growing pains, none more famous than the Blue Lagoon, the capital's suburban swimming-pool of mud-bottomed, fluorescent blue thermal waters – set disturbingly in the backyard of a chemical factory. Now Europe's youngest capital is a wired pseudo-metropolis, a cross between a gadget-obsessed city that has bypassed the industrial age and a village with a local pond and

"Nice friendly place that it is, to describe Reykjavik as the new London is like describing Lego as the new sex."

Tim Moore, *Frost On My Moustache*

Arnarson, let the will of the laughing Viking Gods choose the city's location by casting overboard his ship's main seat to see where it washed up. A disenchanted slave quipped, "To no avail we have crossed fine districts to live on this outlying wilderness."

The impression is pretty much the same on arriving today – a treeless, pot-holed and lichenous landscape that W.H. Auden labelled "moon country". Only several barren miles inland from Keflavik airport does the Legoland of brightly-coloured, corrugated metal-clad houses appear in the bay, often shrouded in Stygian

geese. The city's main shopping street, Laugervegur, is achingly trendy and has an attitude to match. There's so little crime that – the joke goes – inmates of the city prison are allowed to fetch the football when it goes over the wall. Reykjavik's residents are a paradox: eccentric but aware of their own eccentricity, well-travelled but in-bred and obsessed with their own genealogy. But they know how to party, especially under the midnight sun when on a *runtur* (pub crawl) they fuel to excess their belief in the supernatural by getting well and truly wrecked.

> REYKJAVIK, ICELAND > LONGITUDE: 21°55' W > LATITUDE: 64°08' N > ALTITUDE: 53 feet/16 metres > POPULATION: 118,000 > TWINNED WITH: Brussels, Orlando FL, Seattle, Winnipeg (Canada)
> NATIVES: Björk, Vigdis Finnbogadottir, Eider Gudjohnsen, Magnus Magnusson, Unnur Birna Vilhjálmsdóttir

81

SALVADOR BRAZIL

PERCHED ON A PROMONTORY over a lagoon of white sand beaches harbouring 38 islands, Salvador da Bahia boasts a setting to rival Rio. Known to friends as simply Bahia, Brazil first capital is a true metropolitan version of paradise.

This is where Amerigo Vespucci, the Portuguese navigator, landed in 1501. Relieved no doubt to have arrived, but surely also stunned by the location, he called the place his saviour and the bay "the bay of all Saints". Here the Portuguese built what was to be the second city of the empire after Lisbon, a fortress of opulent churches – supposedly 365 of them in all, one for each day of the year – many filled with lavish golden altars, and ornate colonial houses painted in childish pastel colours, yellow, green and blue. In the upper, older half of modern Bahia around the Terreiro de Jesu and the old slave-market site Largo de Pelourinho, the Portuguese legacy is still perfectly preserved.

Bahia was built on slavery, the coalface of the triangle between Lisbon and the African colonies. Even today the population is mostly black, earning Bahia the soubriquet, "Africa in Exile". The invaders didn't have it all their own way in the beginning, though, and legend has it the first Portuguese governors were eaten by indigenous Indians.

The legacy of slavery remains in the combustive ethnic mix that is the soul of Bahia and which pervades its food, religion and music. As a melting-pot it is more mulatto than most. The flavours and scents of the street food that waft through the streets are from Senegal and Nigeria. The native *capoeira* dance is a foot-fighting martial art that Angolan slaves cunningly disguised as a dance. The rest are *mestizo*, Amerindians and progeny of white sexploitation, when in the last years of colonialism Bahia was a sexual playground and last refuge for cracked European minds.

Dance and music, pelvic and scantily clad, form the erotic beat of Bahia, birthplace of many famous Brazilian exports including Astrud Gilberto, the voice of the girl from Ipanema. In Bahia they have more saints' days than saints, every one of them an excuse for a party. Religion is fused with music in the local Afro-Brazilian dance religions of Candomble and Umbanda, known by many around the world through the Olodun and Timbalada bands, where frenetic drumbeats and movement transport reveller-worshippers to orgasmic epiphany. The greatest party of all though is Carnival, the biggest carnival in the world, more edgy and less cosmetic than Rio's, when for a whole week a city drunk on *cachaça* sugarcane liqueur is a deafening cacophony of drumming *afro blocos* processions of dancers and, thudding *trios eletricos* lorries with deafening sound systems, all draped in shimmering bikini-clad *bahianas*.

"The Bay of All Saints, and every conceivable Sin." Local Saying

> SALVADOR, BAHIA, BRAZIL > LOCAL NAME: Salvador da Bahia > LONGITUDE: 38°25' W > LATITUDE: 12°57' S > ALTITUDE: 3 feet/1 metre > POPULATION: 3,180,000
> TWINNED WITH: Los Angeles > NATIVES: Carlinhos Brown, Gilberto Gil, Astrud Gilberto, Sérgio Machado > RESIDENTS: Jorge Amado, João Gilberto, Caetano Veloso

"E sal, é sol, é sul."

("It's salt, it's sun, it's south.")

Ronaldo Boscoli and Roberto Menescal, "Rio"

> RIO DE JANEIRO, BRAZIL > LONGITUDE: 43°17' W > LATITUDE: 22°55' S > ALTITUDE: 36 feet/11 metres > POPULATION: 6,119,800 (metro: 10,556,000) > TWINNED WITH: Atlanta, Kobe (Japan), Warsaw
> NATIVES: Pierre Savorgnan de Brazza, Paulo Coelho, Chiquinha Gonzaga, Jairzinho, Antonio Carlos Jobim, Cildo Meireles, Marisa Monte, Vinicius de Moraes, Fabrizio Moretti, Milton Nascimento, Oscar Niemeyer, Hélio Oiticica, Nelson Piquet, Flora Purim, Ronaldo, Marcos Sacramento, Heitor Villa-Lobos
> RESIDENTS: Ronnie Biggs, Carmen Miranda, Baden Powell, Nana Vasconcelos

RIO DE JANEIRO BRAZIL

YOU CAN'T REALLY BLAME it on Rio. The city is blessed with so many natural benefits that it has unselfishly and assiduously devoted itself to the celebration of hedonism. Trapped between lush forest, granite mountains and beaches in a strip of land thinner than a Brazilian thong, Rio wisely uses all its available resources. Its inhabitants, the *cariocas,* either seek out the cool and shade of the hills, or shift their entire daily life out on to the sand where they can do a few business deals and a little flirting, or undertake some serious tanning work on the body beautiful that is the focus of Rio's unofficial religion.

Time was when Rio de Janeiro was the capital of Brazil (its advocates say it is still the spiritual capital). At one point it was even head of the entire Portuguese Empire, when Dom João VI was harried out of Europe by Napoléon and relocated to Rio. The Portuguese had come across this great natural harbour as early as 1 January 1502, thinking it must be the mouth of a major river. Though these first visitors did not linger, they did leave behind an enduring name for the site, Rio de Janeiro, the River of January. There then followed a tussle for control with the French, who wanted it to form part of a Calvinist Antarctic France: imagine, if they had won, the

girl from Ipanema would have been permanently encased in sackcloth and chastity belt...

The discovery of gold inland, and Rio's position as the closest port to the mines, guaranteed a couple of centuries of undisputed glory and prestige. With space at a premium the city blasted its way through the mountains to head south to Copacabana and beyond, and entered the 20th century with aspirations to become a tropical Paris. By the 1950s and 1960s, when São Paulo took over its mantle as Brazil's commercial hub, and the bureaucrats decamped to Brasilia, Rio shrugged and concentrated on its role as a party city. Rio's is undisputedly the biggest and most flamboyant carnival in the world. They even have their

own dedicated beachside stadium where the performers can strut their stuff and send their samba sounds out around the globe – the music of the poor black community converted into the national anthem of Brazil.

In a very Rio way the city has embraced the poor who live there, hardly marginalized, since the *favela* shanty towns are right in the middle of the city, and indeed have some of the best views in town. They are now an essential part of the landscape (complete with tours for tourists), alongside those two great, instantly recognizable, icons: the Sugar Loaf Mountain and Christ outstretched on the Corcovado, underneath the stonework doubtless grooving to a samba beat.

SÃO PAULO BRAZIL

LIKE THE ARGUMENT BETWEEN Sydney and Melbourne, São Paulo inevitably draw comparisons with Rio, and the debate polarizes natives and visitors alike. *Paulistanos* pride themselves on their city's work ethic, and decry the laziness and decadence of the Rio *cariocas*. The laid-back *cariocas* simply say people from São Paulo don't know how to enjoy life, especially not sex.

It is hard to believe that in 1870 this futuristic yet chaotic and labyrinthine megalopolis was a settlement of a few hundred thousand. Founded by missionaries in 1554 it was thought of little

For its Manhattan skyline and for its predominant immigrant communities São Paulo attracts comparisons with New York. With no unique origin to its name it is truly a city of the post-modern global world, modelled on and composed of other cities. Almost everyone here is from somewhere else. The Bixiga neighbourhood is home to over a million Italians, while Liberdade houses a bigger Japanese community than most Japanese cities. Beyond these choked districts of marble, glass and concrete (to avoid the traffic São Paulo has the

> "A city of towering skyscapers, kilometric avenues and constant chaos – think Bladerunner in the tropics."

DJ Suba, *São Paulo Confessions*

significance until the fertility of the area's *terra roxa*, red earth, was discovered and the coffee barons moved in. Since then the city underwent a meteoric rise in population, as the barons sought an ever-bigger workforce and the poor, in search of their fortune in the increasingly affluent city, were attracted to work for them.

Its speed of growth defines the São Paulo of today. If new arrivals and new industries were to be accommodated there was no time for intricate urban planning and florid aesthetics. What dregs of colonial coffee heritage the Italian, English and French had left in the way of art nouveau and art deco buildings were razed in favour of space-efficient vertical cities, although there is the odd survivor in the city's old core around Praça da Se and Praça de Republica.

world's largest fleet of private helicopters), lie sprawling *favelas* where people scratch a living in corrugated metal and mud huts. Such is the paradox that makes São, like its favourite son Ayrton Senna, one of the most intense and fearsome cities in the world.

But it is also said that São Paulo is a carousel where many people manage to rise, if only for the humbleness of their origins. For São Paulo is Brazil's financial, industrial and cultural capital, the city that makes the country tick for better or worse. In the Jardims district, São's answer to Beverly Hills, and along the posh avenues of Avenida Paulista, rua Augusta and rua Osario Friere, São Paulo's Fifth Avenue, are the banks, restaurants, boutiques and galleries that keep São Paulo at the forefront of global affairs.

> SÃO PAULO, BRAZIL > LONGITUDE: 46°43' W > LATITUDE: 23°35' S > ALTITUDE: 197 feet/60 metres > POPULATION: 17,711,000
> TWINNED WITH: Barcelona, Osaka, Tokyo > NATIVES: Rubens Barrichello, Alice Braga, Maria Bueno, Öyvind Fahlström, Emerson Fittipaldi, Alexandre Herchovitch, Fernando Meirelles, Rivelino, Ayrton Senna

"The truth is, the dream was smaller than the reality. And the reality was bigger and more beautiful than the dream."

Oscar Niemeyer

> BRASILIA, BRAZIL > LONGITUDE: 47°55' W > LATITUDE: 15°49' S > ALTITUDE: 3,543 feet/1,080 metres > POPULATION: 2,052,100 NATIVES:
> TWINNED WITH: Rabat (Morocco) NATIVES: Ricardo Izecson dos Santos Leite aka Kaká

47°55' W

IT SEEMED LIKE A MISSION improbable, if not totally impossible. In 1956 Brazil's new president Juscelino Kubitschek declared that a new Brazilian capital would be built from scratch – *"ex nihilo"*, in Unesco's phrase – on the dusty plains of the country's interior ... in less than four years. Yet a thousand days or so after work started, the city was inaugurated on 21 April 1960. Miracle, or madness?

Brasilia was no overnight wheeze. From the 1790s onwards Brazilian governments had been on the look-out for a replacement for Rio de Janeiro. By 1823 the name Brasilia had been chosen, by the end of that century its general location defined, and a foundation stone laid as early as 1922. Kubitschek's urgency stemmed from the fact he knew he had only one presidential term to make the dream happen. Architect Oscar Niemeyer, town planner Lucio Costa and landscape designer Roberto Burle Marx were the under-pressure triumvirate who helped him beat the odds.

Reactions to their Brasilia have always been mixed. Robert Hughes called it "a Utopian horror, a ceremonial slum". Yuri Gagarin said, "I feel as if I had stepped on to the surface of another planet." Post-modernists continue to complain that it is lifeless, soulless. Yet this ignores the upsides: awesome sunsets, some fabulously futuristic buildings – the Palácio do Itamaraty and the cathedral in particular – the extraordinary achievement itself. And of course there are the two million inhabitants who live there. After hours, when the offices and the parliament have shut down for the day, the bars are humming out in the residential areas.

The planners failed to envisage two things. They created a spacious administrative centre, where ministry buildings march in serried ranks alongside sweeping highways, and designed formal residential quarters for the bureaucrats, but totally overlooked the need to cater for such mundane creatures as support staff. Consequently Brasilia is surrounded by chaotic shanty towns. In a peculiar inversion, this inner-city slum is on the outside.

And nobody, but nobody, expected that the city would become a spiritual centre. Cults have sprung up all around it. Brasilia's shape – a bird, a plane, a dragonfly? – is endlessly analyzed for hidden meaning. Even the bus station has been seen as a symbol of mortal man. Followers of a 19th-century Italian priest, Dom Bosco, who determined that this was the site of the land of milk and honey, continue to wait in hope.

Amidst it all, the founder himself, Kubitschek, is celebrated in a mausoleum containing, in a glass cube, the tail-finned Ford Galaxie 500 in which he died, while muzak croons gently in the background. A surreal, kitsch monument that would surely have Brasilia's minimalist visionaries spinning in their own graves.

"THE WORLD'S SMALLEST CAPITAL", Greenland's tourist office states, "with all a capital city has to offer." The list then descends into unintentional irony – "People." Always a good start. "Modern houses." Note the epithet. "Cars." Maybe even a rush-hour? "Skiing and restaurants." An unusual combination not many world capitals can offer, especially not with seabirds on the menu. The average European ski-resort may be bigger than Nuuk but the city's importance is its place in the spectrum of very few other places. Indeed the question of what is visible and what is invisible is a fact of Nuuk life as the *fata morgana* effect of the northern light plays tricks on the eye creating arctic mirages of ships and islands.

Nuuk and Greenland obtained home rule from Denmark in 1979 (Norway had vigorously disputed Danish ownership since the 1600s) and set about a proud modernization. Consequently there are two very distinct Nuuks – the pretty colourful 18th- and 19th-century bungalows of the

> "The fantastic North of men's souls,
> the place of unbelievable desolation
> and final solitude… the last place." Jack Kerouac

humanity on our earth; that not just a few people choose to make this isolated, northern outpost home, but several thousand.

Pronounced "Nuke", the atmosphere of the city could be post-apocalyptic, but the name means "promontory" on account of the small peninsula at the end of which the city sits. That was a downscaling of the original christening, Godthaab, meaning "Good Hope", of its founding settler, the Norwegian missionary Hans Egede who arrived here in 1721. The hardy Viking Eric the Red had already passed through on this way to America and in a partially successful attempt to lure Norwegian farmers to migrate and settle here sent back reports of a green and fertile land – hence Greenland – an excellent piece of branding. It seems advertising runs in the Viking blood.

However, even the tourist office acknowledges that the city's beauties lie not in the concrete but in its extraordinary setting in a fjord filled with icebergs, its wildlife and eerie light and the chance to expand the mind and see things you can see in

Kolonishavnen colonial harbour, and the profoundly ugly blocks of the new town including the aforementioned capital attributes of parliament, concert and exhibition halls.

The arts are very much alive in Nuuk, and every March sees the international snow sculpture festival attended by would-be Eskimos from all over the world. The streets are alive with robust native hackers sporting ice-axes and anoraks – a Greenlandic word meaning "against the wind" – and the city sprouts huge and intricate ice monuments that would be ephemeral were it not so bitingly cold.

Something similar runs in the blood of these seemingly interchangeable northern peoples – Inuit, Eskimo, Kalaalit. Nuuk does not bear the scars of invasion, covetousness and vanity. Greenlanders have never waged war on anyone. Instead they live in peace among the fishes of a dreamscape on the confines of reality, a curiosity for cruise-ship stopovers, but laughing inwardly at gawping tourists in their own fish-bowl.

> NUUK, GREENLAND > LONGITUDE: 51°45' W > LATITUDE: 64°11' N > ALTITUDE: 0 feet/0 metres
> POPULATION: 13,700 > NATIVES: Jesper Gronkjaer

91

MONTEVIDEO

SQUASHED, LIKE A SALT-BEEF SANDWICH, between the imposing bulks of its neighbours Brazil and Argentina, Montevideo, the capital of Uruguay, has managed to carve out for itself a quirky character that remains pleasantly off the beaten track. There's a hefty tourist influx every summer, but most of the new arrivals are heading out to the groovy resort of Punta Del Este, giving Montevideo little more than a passing glance. That suits Montevideans just fine.

From its earliest days – the city was founded in 1726 by the Spanish governor of Buenos Aires as a bulwark against the Portuguese in Brazil – Montevideo has had to be judged in comparison to the Argentinian capital 155 miles (250km) away across the Rio de la Plata (so wide a river that it's called "El Mar"). Those comparisons have frequently been derogatory: "the Newark of Buenos Aires" or the "Cleveland of Latin America". More fool those who coined such analogies, since they have missed out on a city that has plenty to offer.

First of all, there's none of the traffic chaos of Buenos Aires –"BA without the LA", as it has been dubbed. In fact the trams, classic cars and Morris Minors that trundle round the city give the same sensation of travelling back in time to the 1950s as landing by plane in Southern India. Then there's the low crime rate. And the intellectual buzz about the place: more theatres per inhabitant and more intellectuals per square mile than anywhere else in Latin America, or so the statistics claim. This is an intimate place, its small old centre of museums, churches, theatres and opera house reminiscent of some provincial Italian city.

What Montevideans share with Buenos Aires is a love of beef, tea and tango. Amazingly, they eat even more meat and drink even more tea, the *maté* that is lovingly prepared with a whole paraphernalia of hot water flasks, drinking tubes, gourds and dried leaves. Music is equally ubiquitous, relayed by dozens of specialist tango radio stations alongside the homegrown *candombe*, developed by the descendants of enfranchised slaves, a samba-style beat that is part and parcel of the Barrio Sur. The mix in Montevideo is funky and cosmopolitan – Italian and Spanish immigrants abound – and the city's café-based hospitality has seduced travellers from Charles Darwin onwards.

The old town sits on a peninsula pushing out into the River Plate, alongside the Cerro, the landmark conical hill which is allegedly the basis for the city's name, from a Portuguese look-out's cry of "Monte Vide Eu" ("I see a hill"). Best of all, the string of urban beaches below are just perfect – absolutely no need to go out to Punta del Este at all.

"What makes Montevideo so alluring is its **sense of quiet confidence**."

Richard Hinzel, *Wallpaper**

> MONTEVIDEO, URUGUAY > LONGITUDE: 56°13' W > LATITUDE: 34°52' S > ALTITUDE: 95 feet/29 metres > POPULATION: 1,347,600
> TWINNED WITH: Barcelona > NATIVES: Delmira Agustini, Hugo Fatturoso, Diego Forlan, Jules Laforgue, Juan Carlos Onetti, Gustavo Poyet, Jules Supervielle, Joaquin Torres-Garcia, Marquesa de Varela

IN LATIN AMERICA THEY SAY "Mexicans come from the Aztecs, Peruvians come from the Incas, Argentinians come from the ships." Buenos Aires is a city of immigrants and outside influences, utterly distinct in look and personality from other South American metropoles.

Founded on the River Plate by 16th-century conquistadors, Buenos Aires was settled by the Genoese and virtually reinvented during the late 19th-century beef boom, becoming a world centre of culture in the early 20th when the rest of the world was in Depression. Introverted, obsessed with appearance and with an ability to source and reinvent – all age-old Italian qualities – they borrowed and creamed the best from various world-vogues, transplanting to their city a distillation of world architecture. BA grew Parisian boulevards, a baroque Spanish opera-house, Italian fountains, and a central Modernista grid like Barcelona. The Puerto Madero docks were styled on London and there are red letter- and phone boxes in the posh Recoleta district where Eva Peron rose up and is buried. It creates an odd impression – all the trappings of an imperial city but without the imperial history – a palimpsest.

Another jibe says, "An Argentine is an Italian who speaks Spanish, wants to be an Englishman and behaves like he's French." In polo-playing Palermo, the etiquette and blazers-and-brogues look are oh-so Savile Row. The swagger up and down the cat-walks of Florida's boutiques, and the Belle Époque café politico-intellectualism is all French. European aspirations contribute to BA's noted melancholy. The *porteños* have a sense of not belonging, referring to their city as *otro mundo*, another world, an island separate from the pampas plains of Argentina. At least the Falklands give them a European neighbour, sneer out-of-town Argentinians.

But for all its vulture culture BA is an erotic, sensuous place, if also rather Old World and a little scruffy. This is the city that invented the dance that is as close to penetration as it gets while standing up with your clothes on. It took the French to accept the tango before the plaintive *bandoneon* of this working-class dance took hold in upper class BA. The ritual of licit coitus intertango frottage is today alive and well in the arms of slick black-maned Julio Iglesias look-alikes. The city's other carnal pleasure is its famously tender meat, displayed everywhere in *parillas* steak-houses like abattoirs.

These dual pleasures sum up BA's paradoxical atmosphere: on one hand the nostalgic and decadent hedonism-in-exile of the southern European fleeing the rigours of the Old World. On the other a guilty yet vital sense of getting away with it, because the good times are mortal and one day, as so many failed currencies and dusty chandeliers show, it will be *Buenas Noches*. But until then, there is always time for one last tango.

"Buenos Aires is as eternal as air and water." Jorge Luis Borges

> BUENOS AIRES, ARGENTINA > LONGITUDE: 58°24' W > LATITUDE: 34°36' S > ALTITUDE: 89 feet/27 metres > POPULATION: 13,818,677
> NATIVES: Eileen Agar, Norma Aleandro, Martha Argerich, Hector Babenco, Daniel Barenboim, Bernard Blier, Jose Luis Borges, Esteban Echeverría, Adolfo Pérez Esquivel, Victor Grippo, Olivia Hussey, Mauricio Kagel, Diego Maradona, José Marmol, Baldomero Fernández Moreno, Astor Piazzola, Manuel Rojas, Gabriela Sabatini, Lalo Schifrin, Alfredo di Stefano, Soledad Twombly, Juan Sebastian Veron > RESIDENTS: Eva Peron

95

61°30' W.

TRINIDAD IS NOT QUITE the island paradise of popular imagination and travel brochures. It leaves the white sand, turquoise sea and palm trees thing to its northern partner, Tobago. But that's not to say Port of Spain doesn't function on island time. Locals here like nothing better than to kick back "ee-zee", with a Carib beer and catch of the day, and just "lime" – hanging around with friends.

Only a few miles off Venezuela, Trinidad is different from the rest of the Caribbean. Emphatically diverse in its ethnic mix, Port of Spain feels continental, industrial and worldly. The island has seen Spaniards, French, French Africans, Portuguese, Chinese and Indians, to name just a few diaspora who have settled here over the centuries. Consequently, Port of Spain is the most cosmopolitan of Caribbean cities, populated by exotic varied physiognomies that have given the planet its fair share of Miss Worlds. Statues around town commemorate anyone from Columbus to Gandhi, while street names such as Essex, Salazar, Tywang and Hyderabad evoke an itinerary of different cultures.

The blueprint for the city is definitely British, following the Victorian rulers who made the two islands one in 1889. The grid of neighbourhoods, Belmont, St Clair, St James and Woodbrook, have a colonial ring and are lined with heavyweight Victorian houses. The Magnificent Seven is a row of mansions like overblown Oxford colleges. Down near the industrial waterfront is the vast green chill-out space of Queen's Park savannah, containing the famous Oval cricket ground, sacred to all Trinbagians.

Trini's diverse roots are present in the mix of its musical rhythms, the fusion of a cuisine that includes curried conch and in the medley of religions and festivals that provide an almost constant excuse for a *bacchanal* ("par-tay"!). This is the spiritual home of the three C's – cricket, calypso and carnival. Originally a language of praise and derision among slaves, the calypso is the pulsating smiley and sexy beat of island life. Mixed in is the cheerful sound of the steel drums, or "pans", religiously practised in "pan yards", that were originally made from sliced 45-gallon oil drums. Add to that the "wine" (sexy hip dance) of *soca* and their many fusions such as the Hindu-based *Chutney*, the *Parang* (Christmas carols with maracas) and *Rapso* and the island is a delirium of music, never more so than at Carnival, known as "De Mas", which starts well before Christmas.

But there's no need to move too fast. Life's no less a beach here. Flip-flops are *de rigueur*, as are dental-floss bikinis and big Rasta hair. Bacardi time means more hours in the day. In the local patois, there's always time for a B'n'C on T'n'T – time to "take a dip in de salt" down Maracas Bay, site of the weekend party scene, or simply to lime in the Bounty-ad rock pools on Blanchisseuse beach.

"Liming? Don' worry. It ah' Trini t'ing."

Local T-shirt

> PORT OF SPAIN, TRINIDAD AND TOBAGO > LONGITUDE: 61°30' W > LATITUDE: 10°37' N > ALTITUDE: 0 feet/0 metres > POPULATION: 45,300
> TWINNED WITH: Atlanta, Morne-a-Lou (Guadeloupe), Richmond CA, St Catharine's (Canada) > NATIVES: Ato Boldon, Stokely Carmichael,
C.L.R. James, Brian Lara, V.S. Naipaul, Edmundo Ros, Dwight Yorke

THE SHARKS OF WEST SIDE STORY were typical Puerto Ricans in New York City. They retained a love for the pineapples and coffee blossoms of their home island, but were glad to have left behind the hurricanes and the overcrowding. Yet they were sassy enough to know that the American way of life was not all roses – though the pull of NY is such that there are allegedly more Puerto Ricans there than in PR itself.

Their ambivalence sums up the split personality of San Juan, the capital of the island. The city has a Spanish past and a Caribbean location, but links so close to the United States that referenda have been held on whether to become the 51st State of the USA; the locals turned down that particular option, but Puerto Rico continues as a Commonwealth voluntarily associated with the States.

who was cruising the Caribbean looking for easy pickings. The Spanish connection lasted for nearly 400 years, before San Juan was ceded along with Puerto Rico to the US in 1898 following the Spanish-American War. A political carve-up could not cauterize the Hispanic connection, so that San Juan still retains the wrought-iron balconies of the colonial days, and is dotted with patches of adequine, the bluestone cobbles that were transported as ballast in ships heading out from the mother country. The steep and narrow streets of pastel-coloured houses in Old San Juan are cool and shady; the settlers did well when picking the location for their city.

However, unlike many of its cash-strapped Caribbean neighbours, San Juan and Puerto Rico have benefited from – or been corrupted by, depending on your point of view – the Yankee dollar, with a healthy

> "I'll drive a Buick through San Juan."
> "If there's a road you can drive on."
> "I'll give my cousins a free ride."
> "How can you get all of them inside?"
>
> "America", *West Side Story*, Stephen Sondheim

San Juan is the oldest city over which the Stars and Stripes fly, though its age is more to do with Spain's imperial ambitions. Columbus popped by in late 1493 and not long afterwards San Juan was well established as a strategic bastion. The heart of the city is still known as the *ciudad amurallada*, the walled city, with the 18-feet (5-m) thick walls of the El Morro fortress testament to a fierce determination to repel anybody with evil designs on its gold, silver and precious gems – the likes of that old seadog Sir Francis Drake,

infrastructure, interstates and a rash of international fast food and retail chains. The two strains of influence merge in areas like the bohemian art gallery *barrio* of Santurce and the 1950s holiday resort of Condado.

In return San Juan has paid back the States with salsa greats (the spirit of Tito Puente and Celia Cruz hovers over the city), baseball stars, some very good rum – and, according to fashionista Donatella Versace, the world's best-looking men ...

> SAN JUAN, PUERTO RICO > LONGITUDE: 66°04' W > LATITUDE: 16°26' N > ALTITUDE: 8 feet/2 metres
> POPULATION: 434,400 > TWINNED WITH: Honolulu > NATIVES: José Ferrer, Giovanni Hidalgo, Raul Julia, Ricky Martin

99

CARACAS <small>VENEZUELA</small>

OIL IT WAS THAT brought wealth and sophistication to Caracas following the discovery of a major field in 1922. By the 1960s and '70s, when Caracas was regularly hosting meetings of the OPEC members, the country that the city reigns over was known by jealous and more impoverished neighbours as "Saudi Venezuela". And there's more than a touch of the Dallas of JR and Sue-Ellen about the place. Its six-lane motorways scooting through tunnels and beneath glistening glass skyscrapers are full of gas-gorging cars with chrome trim that would never be permitted in a post-catalytic converter kind of world.

Although the city was founded by the conquistador Diego de Losada in 1567, the area was never a major priority for the Spanish. Few remnants of its original colonial buildings remain; most, other than the area around the Plaza Bolívar, were bulldozed during the oil years. But there are plenty of Spanish-style houses to maintain the connection.

What Caracas has always had is a spectacular location, in a narrow valley above which the mountain of El Avila looms. At weekends the locals head out and up to the El Avila National Park to jog and cycle. During the week they have a wide range

> ## "I'd come from a country where we dress in grey and pretend to be British, to a place enjoying the oil boom, where there was an erotic charge on the streets."
>
> Isabel Allende, on moving from Santiago to Caracas

This is one of the most yanqui-fied cities in Latin America – not just the cars, but a love of baseball, early adoption of fast food habits and soap opera addiction have placed a distinctive Stateside stamp on the city. It has often been said that Caracas has turned its face to the USA and its back to the rest of South America, but in fact there is plenty of Latin style here. Although *nouveau riche* (and quite often when the oil boom crashed, *nouveau pauvre*) its inhabitants, the *caraqueños*, have a reputation for being charming, glamorous – possibly more glamorous than the city itself – and extremely good-looking. And, like Isabel Allende, writers, artists and actors from all over the continent have been drawn to its grace and culture.

of gardens and parks to choose from: the Parque del Este was designed by Robert Burle Marx, the landscape planner for Brasilia; the Hacienda Floresta was once a coffee plantation. All these oases in an extremely green city offer some escape from the congestion of Caracas. Although underground there is a light and efficient metro, above ground there is serious overspill.

The shanty towns, the *ranchitos*, teeter tenuously in the hillsides above Caracas. Earthquakes are a constant threat, mudslides in 1999 wiped out large tranches. Perhaps the shadow of this threat explains why people live life hard and fast – in the areas of Las Mercedes and Altamira the night-life is notoriously exhausting. The pace may be frenetic, but, this being Caracas, it is always gracious.

> CARACAS, TACHIRA, VENEZUELA > LONGITUDE: 66°59' W > LATITUDE: 10°28' N > ALTITUDE: 3,012 feet/910 metres > POPULATION: 1,975,800 > TWINNED WITH: Honolulu, San Francisco, Santiago de Cuba
> NATIVES: Andres Bello, Serge Blanco, Simon Bolivar, Chico Carrasquel, Oscar D´Leon, Rómulo Gallegos, Reynaldo Hahn, Carolina Herrera, Lauren Hutton, Ilich Ramirez Sanchez (Carlos the Jackal) >
RESIDENTS: Isabel Allende

ONLY IN THIS CONTINENT of extremes could you approach the world's highest capital city from land and still look down on it. The Altiplano plateau, stretching south from Lake Titicaca, suddenly falls away to reveal, like a lost world, a natural canyon, dominated by 20,000-foot (6,000-m) Andean peaks, along whose floor, all a mirage, are spread the orange-brick houses and gleaming skyscrapers of a toy-like, almost unimaginable megacity.

La Paz is an improbable place. Yet life has been going on here before and will carry on after you have left, only – it seems – in a parallel universe. Or maybe that's just what the locals call *soroche* – altitude sickness.

Down in the cauldron is the maelstrom of megacity life, the constant call of trade that knows no ebb or flow. All day and all night the *collectivo* minibuses rush up and down the main avenues, glittered banners across their windscreen and icons swaying under the mirror, their smiling but toothless adolescent conductors hanging on to the windows, shouting out the roll-call of district stopoffs. Packed inside are diminutive suited men in tombola hats and wide Indian women, high-cheeked, weather-worn and inscrutable, laden with wares and babies strapped on their back in the brightly striped blankets that are Bolivia's signature.

Almost every inch of pavement downtown is dedicated to business: street hairdressers and shoe-polishers, scribes with battered Remingtons and impromptu sell-it-all stalls with second-hand phones for phone boxes. Everywhere you look there are surreal sights: a suited man carrying an entire sofa strapped to his back, a group of yet more suited men moving a lorry-load of toilets. Here is the *chiaroscuro* of great wealth, modern beneficiaries of the Spanish rape of Bolivia's silver and tin resource, and the destitution of the continent's poorest nation.

Plaza San Francisco and Plaza Murillo are the nominal centres of this helter-skelter city. The atmospheric, steep cobbled streets around the calle Jaen offer the only respite from the confusion. If the scenes outside aren't at times bizarre enough, the stalls of the Hecheria witchcraft market sell superstitions to sway the most devout cynic. Buy a dried llama foetus to bury in the foundation of your new house and bring you luck. Alternatively sit at a booth and enjoy some fried trout from the world's highest lake, washed down with a papaya milkshake, or *chichi*, the potent fermented maize drink – definitely an acquired taste!

As graffiti slogans around the capital tell, in words of pure South American revolutionary idealism, Bolivia has been bruised and abused through the centuries, its mineral wealth torn out. The colonial mining villages have long been ghost towns and the 20th century bequeathed only a monotonous sequence of crackpot dictators. A new-born llama, the country's symbolic animal, represents what little hope they have.

> "The traveller arriving for the first time in La Paz experiences a sensation of awakening, of coming from the vast desolate desert, as if out of a nightmare, into the Garden of Eden."

Jean Manzon and Miguel-Angel Asturias, *An Undiscovered Land*

USHUAIA ARGENTINA

IN A BID TO APPEAL TO EXPLORERS and fans of Wim Wenders' films, Ushuaia calls itself "the city at the end of the world". Sitting at the coccyx of the South American continent it would also have itself be the place "where America is born". None of which really dispels the thought that the only inhabitants must be Antarctic researchers, intrepid hikers or the transient populations of cruise liners.

The answer is, no one went there voluntarily. They were sent there, as prisoners of the Argentine government, where they could do no harm. The convicts came on "the train to the end of the world", now a much-marketed journey in the global galaxy of train trips, to "the prison at the end of the world". Predictably where this ultimate gaol once stood there is now a museum, but it tells the fascinating story of a city whose economy and whole *raison d'être* revolved not around the trade in spices, minerals or slaves like any normal city, but around a prison. The prison ran workshops and was responsible for the city's whole production base for fabrics, furniture, machinery, you name it, for anything other than the basic supplies that arrived once a month by ship.

Nowadays Ushuaia is simply a slightly haunting place, little more than a port-town alongside the megacities of South America – set on the shores of the Beagle channel, surrounded by the white teeth of the Martial Mounts – a place of withering beauty. Founded in the late 19th century its predominantly neocolonial pastel-coloured architecture is still essentially untouched.

The soul of the place is the Casco Antiguo, the old port with the feeling of a fishing village but with an extreme edge. Here over recent years in the bars along Malvinas Argentinas Street (translated as "the Argentine Falklands!") has gathered a lively and alternative society of hardcore pseudo-explorers and backpackers, attracted to one of the world's ultimate finisterres as one is to the moon. They come to enjoy and sustain the disturbed and off-the-wall atmosphere that befits any place of former or desired exile.

Either that, or they come to enjoy the skiing and tax-free shopping of a city that is nominally the capital of Antarctica – not that there's a lot of competition.

Built on different levels, the town rises up steep and quaintly cobbled streets, the top of which afford breathtaking views across the moody glare and murkiness of "the bay entering into the west" from which Ushuaia takes its name in the native Famana Indian language. A similar view greeted Magellan's navigators when they first arrived here. They mistakenly interpreted the tricks of the glacial light as smoke and fire, whence they baptized this literal corner of the earth la Tierra del Fuego, the land of fire.

> USHUAIA, TIERRA DEL FUEGO, ARGENTINA > LONGITUDE: 68°19' W > LATITUDE 54°46' S
> ALTITUDE: 0 feet/0 metres > POPULATION: 57,300 > NATIVES: E. Lucas Bridges

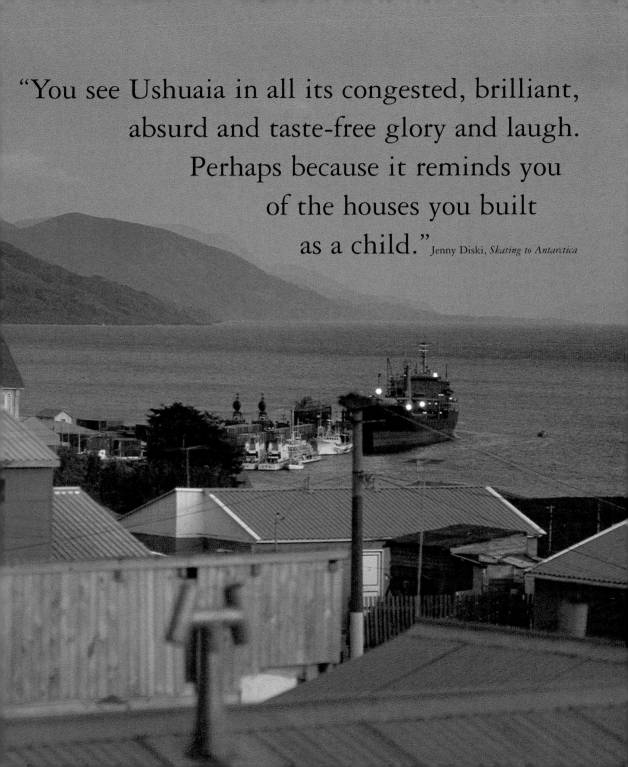

"You see Ushuaia in all its congested, brilliant, absurd and taste-free glory and laugh. Perhaps because it reminds you of the houses you built as a child." Jenny Diski, *Skating to Antarctica*

THE INHABITANTS OF SANTIAGO, the capital of that pipe-cleaner of a country, Chile, have often chosen to compare themselves to Londoners, perhaps because of a shared fondness for promptness, the love of fine art or the frequent rain. Although Londoners would not welcome Santiago's pollution or traffic problems (even worse than their own), they might trade that in for its geographical location, if not its wines. The city is only an hour or two away from top-class skiing in the snow-covered Andes, at resorts like Valle Nevado or Portillo, where both the American and Austrian skiing teams have training centres. Alternatively there is a choice close at hand of white water rafting, or luscious Pacific beaches where an impromptu relaxing day off can be taken without intensive pre-planning.

One of the aspects of *santiaguino* life that might spur the decision to head out is the smog that hangs over downtown Santiago, known as Sanhattan because of its raft of skyscrapers. The smog, a vicious brew of toxicity, rarely disperses, since few winds breeze by. Nevertheless, the city is a pleasant place to exist. The people are renowned as friendly, and consider themselves – sometimes in a snobby way – to be virtually European. Even within the city limits there are oases, either indoors at the exclusive gentleman's club, the Club de la Unión, or outdoors in the gardens of the Cerro Santa Lucia

and atop the city's other great hill, the Cerro San Cristòbal, at the feet of a mammoth statue of the Virgin Mary.

Santiago was built on fertile valley land by Pedro de Valdivia, who headed south from Cuzco in 1541, with a squad of Spanish soldiers and a posse of Peruvians to check out a land that Magellan had discovered but never explored. On the banks of the Mapocho River, Valdivia laid out the basic grid of streets that survives to this day, in a trapezium of land girded by the river and the hills. Later, along the river, the Alameda de las Delicias was created by Chile's liberator Bernardo O'Higgins – it's striking how many people in Santiago carry Irish, Scottish or English names.

O'Higgins is commemorated in a flurry of street names and monuments; the main thoroughfare is named after him, though known locally as the Alameda, and the square that bears his moniker is simply called the Plaza. His ashes reside there, in a marble urn within a monument erected by General Pinochet – Pinochet, a name that summons up the dark side of Santiago, the bad, bad days of the 1970s when Salvador Allende was gunned down in his presidential palace, and when in the National Stadium dark deeds cost the lives or minds of so many, including Victor Jara. At least the smog of Pinochet's reign has cleared, and Santiago can breathe more easily.

"I don't know what I had expected from Santiago, but it wasn't a city that, on the face of it at least, has more in common with Seville than with Lima."

Stephen Fry

> SANTIAGO, CHILE > LONGITUDE: 70°39' W > LATITUDE: 33°28' S > ALTITUDE: 1,713 feet/522 metres > POPULATION: 5,261,000 > TWINNED WITH: Miami, Minneapolis, Riga
> NATIVES: Alejandro Amenábar, Michelle Bachelet, José Danosa, Juan Davila, Eugenio Dittborn, Vicente Huidobro, Roberto Matta > RESIDENTS: Salvador Allende, Victor Jara, Pablo Neruda, Bernardo O'Higgins, Uwe Schmidt (aka Señor Coconut)

> BOSTON, MASSACHUSETTS, USA > LONGITUDE: 71°06' W > LATITUDE: 42°23' N > ALTITUDE: 21 feet/6 metres > POPULATION: 589,100 (metro: 3,406,800) > TWINNED WITH: Barcelona, Bordeaux, Hangzhou (China), Kyoto, Melbourne, Padua (Italy), Sekondi-Takoradi (Ghana), Strasbourg, T'ai-pei > NATIVES: Samuel Adams, Charles Bulfinch, Ralph Waldo Emerson, Arthur Fiedler, Benjamin Franklin, Joseph Kennedy, Jack Lemmon, Henry Cabot Lodge, Sylvia Plath, Edgar Allen Poe, Paul Revere, Jonathan Richman, James Spader, Donna Summer, James Taylor, Uma Thurman, Steve van Zandt > RESIDENTS: Alexander Graham Bell, Saul Bellow, Julia Child, Isabella Stewart Gardner, Mark Sandman, Derek Walcott, Malcolm X

MAYBE IT'S THE EARLY MORNING MIST that drifts across Boston Common like lingering wisps of revolutionary gunsmoke, or late October memories of assaults by the Red Sox on baseball's World Series, but Boston seems to be at its best bathed in a gentle autumnal light. Certainly the city is strongly evocative of a lengthy history at the very heart of the creation of the United States.

Stand on the northern edge of the Common, a location instantly familiar thanks to the exterior shots of the bar in TV's *Cheers*, and a handful of yards away is where the city's Puritan founders punished any transgressions of their unbending moral code via pillory, stocks and whipping-post. All around are remnants of the Revolution: the site of the Boston Massacre of 1770 (a significant

refinement. And anywhere that could produce the Lemonheads, Morphine and the spirit of Ally McBeal is far from conventional all the way through.

Boston was also the powerbase of the Kennedy clan. Though the family's brief shining moment is long gone, the John Fitzgerald Kennedy Library, overlooking Boston's harbour, captures a fragment of the charisma. At the Library's exit, architect I.M. Pei created a "great space", an atrium where a single bench, beneath a gigantic American flag and a quotation from JFK, allows contemplation of the skyline of modern Boston, under which the Big Dig is burrowing new tunnels, and above which Pei's own John Hancock Tower dominates like an unyielding obsidian obelisk.

"Boston is one of the few American cities that regret the past. Boston's like England. Up to its ears in yellowing photographs."

Penelope Gilliatt

turning-point in the hardening of anti-British feeling), the grave of Paul Revere, or the simple, dignified brick frontage of the Old South Meeting House, from where the Boston Tea Party raid of 1773 was launched.

Boston is proud of these early contributions to American history, and equally upfront about its litany of "firsts" – the first telephone call, the first subway, the birth of the Internet ... Maybe that's what gets under the skin of the rest of the nation. "I guess God made Boston on a wet Sunday," snarled Raymond Chandler.

The descendants of those original settlers, the self-appointed Boston Brahmins, still represent an important tone in Boston's character, characterized by a certain formality of dress, clubbable lunches and education at the Harvard campus in Cambridge over on the other side of the Charles River. But they are a minority. Their buttoned-up, townhouse manners are offset by the less precious energy of the city's black, Italian, Chinese, Vietnamese and particularly Irish communities – pro-Republican support used to be rife, and home games for the Celtics basketball team are guaranteed to raise the roof.

Never forget that Boston is also known as Beantown, offering a good strong dose of honest, plain fare as much as preppy

QUEBEC CITY CANADA

LOCATION, LOCATION, LOCATION – Quebec has it all. The upper town is perched high up on the cliffs of the Cap Diamant, where the wood-clad expanse of the boardwalk of the Terrasse Dufferin offers unbeatable vistas out over the St Lawrence River and beyond. Behind, the Château Frontenac, the steep-roofed hotel which is Canada's most photographed building, could easily be transported to the banks of the Loire, and hold its own against the châteaux of Amboise, Chambord or Chenonceau.

A cute funicular – should the steps of the alarmingly named Escalier Casse Cou not

appeal – descends from the Haute to the Basse Ville. This is the oldest permanent European settlement in North America, where the explorer Jacques Cartier dropped by as long ago as 1535, and where Samuel de Champlain founded Quebec 70 years later.

On the site of de Champlain's first fur trading post, the Place Royale, its bust of Louis XIV dating from 1686, is the epicentre of French Canada. Quebec City (technically Quebec is the province, PQ, which includes Montreal) is French through and through. The British might have gained control in 1759, after General Wolfe and his troops scaled the cliffs and caught the French literally napping on the plains of Abraham – losing his life, as did his opponent, the Marquis de Montcalm, in the process – yet there is little sign of any subsequent Britannic influence. Less than five per cent of the population count English as their first language. This is the heartland of the French presence in North America.

But whereas Montreal has moved on and discovered the modern world,

Quebec, for all its Gallic charm, is locked firmly in the past – and somebody threw away the key. The serried ranks of quaint shops, candle-lit bistros and horse-drawn carriages may pull in the tourists, but for any travel-hardened visitor, the incessant Frenchness can be twee to the nth degree, and although the buildings are authentic, it is still like finding yourself in a Disneyland fantasy of a French provincial town in Molière's day.

However there is one major plus point: the culinary skills of the mother country have been as well preserved as the austere architecture of the Séminaire de Québec. The results – including local specialities like *poutine* (fries doused in gravy with a curd cheese topping), pork ragoût, and a mean shepherd's pie – are served nightly in the restaurants of the rue St Jean and the Grande Allée. After dinner, it would be a mistake to say that Quebec rocks, but it might tap its foot discreetly to some jazz or gentle blues: after hours is as chilled as befits a city where the winter temperatures can drop to a teeth-chattering –25°C (–13°F).

> "Quebec is as refreshing and definite after the other cities of this continent as an immortal among a crowd of stockbrockers." Rupert Brooke

> QUEBEC CITY, QUEBEC PROVINCE, CANADA > LOCAL NAME: Québec > LONGITUDE: 71°15' W > LATITUDE: 46°48' N > ALTITUDE: 233 feet/71 metres > POPULATION: 169,000 (metro: 682,800)
> TWINNED WITH: Bordeaux, Calgary (Canada), Ouagadougou > NATIVES: Marc Garneau, Robert Lepage

OVER-VISITED AND LONG REVERED as a mystical Eden by backpackers in search of themselves, Peru's spiritual capital, for many people the embodiment of mythical Peru, remains one of the most impenetrable places in the world.

Already through its altitude of nearly 11,000 feet (3,350m) in a hidden valley in the Andean *cordillera* it still evokes something of the unattainable, an ultimate destination. As you make the tight landing on the city's tiny airstrip, the first glimpse of its terracotta roofs and lush terrace-farmed hills brings out the would-be explorer. Once out in the cool mountain air the altitude kidnaps you with its chloroform, simultaneously relaxing and sapping you. Giddy, the *collectivo* bus bounces past a blur of donkeys and brightly coloured weaves set against mountain scenery and, as if hypnotized, you are transported to the referential bandit world of *Tintin and the Temple of the Sun*.

> "An impalpable dust of other ages covers its streets, rising in clouds like a muddy lake when you disturb the bottom." Che Guevara

For all its bungled physical sacking by Pizarro's conquistadors and modern commercial sacking by tourism, the Inca civilization of which Cuzco is capital is still in this age of globalization a riddle to modern man. The local *kiwicha* and *quinua* corns may no longer be the currency, and local Indians are the first to want to relieve gringos of their green dollars in exchange for a ride on their boney donkey for "another" visit to their ancestors' ruins. Spanish may be the language of commerce but among themselves they still speak the Inca language, *quechua*. And who does not understand that distant language cannot really understand what goes on in the Quechua mind. We have seen and heard them playing "Hey Jude" on panpipes in the squares of European capitals, but their half-

Mongolian, half-Big White Chief faces remain as inscrutable as a poker player and we are left only with our own projections.

But even that is enough, to kick back on a terrace overlooking the scorched cobbled Plaza de Armas with a Cuzquena beer or Inca-Cola (in a firm cultural anti-US stance the red stuff is banned) and soak up the view of the beautiful cathedral with its massive gold bell and half-Indian, half-Christian carvings. It was built by the Spanish using some of the enormous made-to-fit stones from the nearby Inca fortress of Sachsayhuaman (known to backpackers as "Sexy Woman"). The rainbow colours of the Inca flag flutter above it and a relaxed, timeless atmosphere drones like a fly in the air.

Cuzco is no longer the awesome city it once must have been. But its legacy is thought-provoking and ever-present even as a modern staging post and gateway for unknowing secular pilgrims who come here to embark upon arguably the most famous 25-mile (40-km) walk on the planet – originally a humble messenger route – to the Inca sanctuary of Machu Picchu.

PORT-AU-PRINCE HAITI

THE SHORT HISTORY of this enigmatic land is populated by post-colonial black leaders with picaresque names straight out of Voltaire's *Candide*. Papa Doc Duvalier, his son Baba Doc and the Tontons Macoutes faction. Unfortunately the tyranny of these despots is a terrifying and bloody reality.

In 1804, half a century after the French had established themselves on the island, Toussaint L'Ouverture, self-styled Black Napoleon and early Luther-King of black rights, proclaimed the world's first Black Republic. Sadly his was just the first of a series of corrupt, bloodthirsty and trigger-happy banana republics which dragged the country through a continuous underlying civil war. Despite attempted elections, bullets have always ruled over ballot boxes.

Haiti occupies the western half of the Hispaniola island, south-east of Cuba, which it used to own wholly but, like a child in a Haitian divorce, now shares uneasily with Santo Domingo. In the native creole, distantly descended from French, "Haiti" means "land of the night mountains", and its capital, named after one of the vessels of the colonizing French fleet, sits on the west coast beneath the impressive mountain of Kenscoff. Here, in a horseshoe bay, under the unrelenting heat of the Caribbean sun, lies a vast sea

of sink-or-swim humanity. Throngs of people carry great burdens, who knows where, in some Sisyphean metaphor of human struggle, while street tradesmen of just about anything sellable sit alongside beggars waiting for accidental tidbits of charity.

Parting the crowd where possible are the *tap-taps*, the city's old buses, painted in garish stripes, decked in glitter and carrying political and religious slogans in eulogy of anyone from Jesus to Ronaldo.

There is no respite, no place to sit back, chill out and watch it all go by. The centre of Port-au-Prince is exhausting, the atmosphere highly charged and highly strung, the air asphyxiated by the smell of rum and open sewers. Yet amid this turmoil, among the Heath-Robinson electrics and mechanics of houses and businesses, is life-affirming improvisation and resilience.

The nervous centre is the Marché de Fer, a surprising French colonial building supposedly destined for French West Africa but shipped to the Caribbean by mistake. Nearby is the 18th-century colonial core of so-called white gingerbread houses with their turrets and verandahs which inspired the Hotel Trianon of Graham Greene's *The Comedians*.

Beyond, the city has sprawled like the bougainvillaea that carpets its sun-baked walls. Here is La Saline, the world's largest *bidonville* (or shanty town), but also Pétionville, the affluent quarter and haven of rest where galleries display the Haitian art that so influenced the French surrealists and the icons of vaudou. This is not the ersatz voodoo of Baron Samedi in *Live and Let Die* but a bonafide religion seeking mainstream legitimacy. Yet its piercing imagery and supernatural mood are the face and soul of this troubled people.

"Everyone is in some sort of prison in Port-au-Prince."

Graham Greene

MONTREAL CANADA

UNIQUE – A WORD to be used with caution under any circumstances. But there's a certain safety in using it about Montreal. North America has no other city like it, simple as that. Take the gutsiness of Chicago, the neatness of Denver and cross-pollinate them with the elegance and flair of Paris or Bordeaux – and that's Montreal. Chutzpah and chic. Street-smart sass meets *savoir-faire*.

Where Toronto has barely a flicker of Frenchness, and Quebec City runs the risk of being too chocolate-box French, Montreal gets the balance almost perfectly right. Although over half the population speaks French (this is the third largest French-speaking city, after Paris and … Kinshasa) and though this is where de Gaulle uttered his contentious proclamation, "Vive le Québec libre", the Anglo- and Francophone communities have rubbed alongside each other pretty well, though they might begrudge the very thought.

The two mirror each other neatly. The Université de Montréal is reflected by McGill University, named after one of the Scottish merchants who built themselves worthy Victorian piles up in Westmount. Westmount itself, the upscale Brit zone south-west of Mont-Royal ("the mountain") is diametrically opposite to Outremont, the upscale French quarter north-east of Mont-Royal. Tolerance is a Montreal characteristic. During the American Civil War, the city took in slaves and Southerners alike. Smoking in bars is still not considered a hanging offence, and the sexual liberation of an outrageous Mardi Gras gives a *frisson* – but a trouble-free one – to the night-time activities of the rues Crescent and St Cathérine.

Although it has not always been a story of love and peace – in the 1970s the separatists ran their own vicious campaign of terror – the cosmopolitan vibe of Montreal has generally had the upper hand. Humour is part of the city's fabric: the internationally renowned Just For Laughs/Juste Pour Rire festival is one aspect. The quirky surrealism of the Cirque du Soleil, which first raised its tent in Montreal, is another.

When a band of French pioneers arrived in 1642 with instructions from a missionary group to convert the natives (Algonquin and Iroquois), what really turned everybody on was not the word of God but the prospect of fur-trading. A peace negotiated with the Five Nations Indians in 1701 provided the base for prosperity, which went swimmingly for the French, until the Brits took over in 1763. Down in Vieux-Montréal, narrow, cobblestoned lanes capture a flavour of the 18th-century city, but Montreal in general feels like a modern place, stretching over man-made islands on the mighty St Lawrence. From the white water rafts that plunge into the rapids virtually in the heart of the city, Montreal looks relaxed and happy. Perfect. *Génial. Vive la différence.*

> "Some say that no one ever leaves Montreal, for that city, like Canada itself, is designed to preserve the past, a past that happened elsewhere."
>
> Leonard Cohen

BOGOTA IS IN EL DORADO COUNTRY, where adventurers and explorers journeyed in their quest to find the mythical "golden city". They never found it, but Bogota, high up in the verdant mountains of Colombia, does contain the nearest thing on earth, the extraordinarily opulent Museo de Oro, a museum dripping with over 34,000 items of gold, emeralds and precious stones.

Outside and all around the city, the rough and tumble of Colombia's recent history has tossed and turned. Four decades of civil conflict, cocaine wars, violence and corruption have laid siege to the country's capital. Amazingly, Bogotans have managed not only to survive but to flourish.

In fact their reluctance to leave the comparative safety of their city, because of the threat of kidnapping or guerrilla attack elsewhere (though Bogota is by no means immune from rebel incursions), has made them turn inwards to seek out their own

> ## "Bogota runs and lazes for miles across a sun-drenched, drizzly green mountain plateau… A mile-high city."
>
> Andrew Loog Oldham

pleasures within the city limits. Bogota may frequently be overcast and grey – it's a place that is full of umbrellas ready to unfurl – but its denizens provide their own colour, not least under cover of darkness, in the salsa-jumping nightclubs of 93rd Street. This headlong quest for enjoyment amidst the anarchy has created a special kind of energy, the headlong delirium that has given the whole country the nickname of "Locombia".

It's not all madness, though. Founded in 1538 by a law graduate and writer, Gonzalo Jiménez de Quesada, Bogota has long had a reputation for artistic credibility; its *tertulias*, literary salons held in cafés, were admired throughout the Spanish-speaking world.

"The Athens of South America", they called it. Christopher Isherwood remembered it as a "city of conversation" where endless discussion and debate was an essential feature of daily life.

Its most recent mayor, Antanas Mockus, has continued that tradition. A maverick academic, mathematician and philosopher, famed for once mooning a class of unruly students, the Abe Lincoln look-alike was swept to power on a platform of tackling the city's overcrowding, filth and crime. He halted alcohol sales after 1am, set up 125 miles (200km) of bike paths and hired mime artists to mock bad driving on the streets. Killings and petty theft fell. Microsoft boss Bill Gates's Foundation granted a million bucks to boost libraries in Bogota's slum quarters.

This hit a chord with the city's inhabitants, who, when rebel guerrillas attacked the presidential palace with rockets, kept queuing to see a Rembrandt exhibition at the National Museum in case they lost their place. They like to see themselves as a "parenthesis" in the troubles – the rebels on the other hand see the city's middle-class as self-satisfied and pampered. The truth, as ever, lies somewhere in between.

> BOGOTA, COLOMBIA > LOCAL NAME: Santa Fe de Bogotá > LONGITUDE: 74°04' W > LATITUDE: 4°35' N > ALTITUDE: 8,733 feet/2,620 metres > POPULATION: 6,545,200
> TWINNED WITH: Miami, Seoul, Toronto > NATIVES: Santiago Gamboa, Bruce Graham, Antanus Mockus, Catalina Sandino Moreno, Rafael Puyana, Doris Salcedo, José Asunción Silva
RESIDENTS: Simon Bolivar, Gabriel García Márquez, Andrew Loog Oldham, Shakira

119

NEW YORK USA

THE FIRST-TIME VISITOR TO NYC is struck immediately by a remarkable sensation of *déjà vu*, or certainly *déjà visité*. Stevie Wonder, in the song "Living For The City", got it 100 per cent spot on: "Wow ... New York, just like I pictured it". Nothing seems strange, everything is remarkably familiar – the yellow cabs, Broadway's lights, the steam rising out of the manholes in the street, the narrow skyscraper canyons, the joggers in Central Park, the curly-wurly Guggenheim Museum.

For the generations who grew up watching, variously, Woody Allen movies, *Kojak*, *Cagney and Lacey*, *Friends* and *Sex in the City*, New York's environment and etiquette is already deeply engrained, whether it be the technique of shutting out the incomprehensible chatter of the cab drivers or the ability to buzz an apartment bell with your nose while carrying two brown bags stuffed full of goodies from the local deli.

And New York does not disappoint: New York delivers. It also polarizes opinion quite swiftly. Although the first sight of New York City may figure high on the recognition scale, the first 24 hours of exposure can leave you totally exhilarated or bruised, bothered and bewildered. The brusqueness and energy of native New Yorkers is no front: their honesty can be brutal, but is more often than not refreshing. Following the World Trade Center attacks of 11 September 2001, the raw strength of New York and its determination to rise above the tragedy swamped the city in a wave of sympathy that it had never experienced before, and may never again enjoy. With its skyline forever altered – a skyline that was the most famous in the world – its psyche may also have changed for good.

But New York is not just Manhattan. The other boroughs – Brooklyn with its brownstones, Queen's (once the centre of the film industry until Hollywood won out), Staten Island and the much maligned Bronx – are part of the incredible variety of New York. There is so much here that it's easy to show New Yorkers a part of their own city that they have never seen. From Woodlawn Cemetery to McSorley's Old Ale House on East 7th Street, from brunch at Sylvia's on Lenox in Harlem to the jazz at the Village Vanguard, from Grand Central Station's oyster bar to the aisle of second-hand books lining the Strand Book Store, there are enough nooks and crannies, oddities, acronyms (current favourite: DUMBO – Down Under the Manhattan Bridge Overpass), eateries, museums, excitements and ethnic quarters in New York to fill a lifetime fuller than a salt-beef sandwich.

There's a bite of the Big Apple available for every taste, proclivity and expectation. And but for a quirk of history it could all have been "New Amsterdam, New Amsterdam".

> NEW YORK CITY, NEW YORK, USA > LONGITUDE: 73°59' W > LATITUDE: 40°41' N > ALTITUDE: 87 feet/27 metres > POPULATION: 9,314,235 > TWINNED WITH: Cairo, Jerusalem, Johannesburg, Liverpool, London, Madrid, Paris, Rome, Santo Domingo (Dominican Republic), Tokyo > NATIVES: Woody Allen, Diane Arbus, Lauren Bacall, Jean-Michel Basquiat, Humphrey Bogart, James Cagney, Maria Callas, Eamon de Valera, George Gershwin, Whoopi Goldberg, Michael Jordan, Fiorello La Guardia, Roy Leichenstein, Jennifer Lopez, the Marx brothers, Yehudi Menuhin, Al Pacino, SJ Perelman, Theodore Roosevelt, Sonny Rollins, Martin Scorsese, Jonas Salk, Neil Simon, Barbra Streisand, Fats Waller > RESIDENTS: Truman Capote, Alistair Cooke, O. Henry, John Lennon, Samuel Morse, Dorothy Parker, Gloria Vanderbilt, Diana Vreeland, Andy Warhol, Thomas Wolfe, Tom Wolfe

"The Rome,
the Paris,
the London
of the
20th century,
the dense
magnetic
rock, the
irresistible
destination
of all those
who insist on
being where
things are
happening."

Tom Wolfe, *Bonfire of the Vanities*

> PHILADELPHIA, PENNSYLVANIA, USA > LONGITUDE: 75°10' W > LATITUDE: 39°57' N > ALTITUDE: 46 feet/14 metres > POPULATION: 1,491,800 (metro: 5,100,900) > TWINNED WITH: Florence, Tianjin (China) > NATIVES: Eve Arnold, Frankie Avalon, Milton Babbitt, Kevin Bacon, Ethel, John and Lionel Barrymore, Alexander Calder, Noam Chomsky, Bill Cosby, Chubby Checker, Stanley Clarke, W.C. Fields, Richard Gere, Stan Getz, Eve Jihan Jeffers, Grace Kelly, Patti LaBelle, Mario Lanza, Harold Melvin, Lee Morgan, Man Ray, Dennis Rodman, Todd Rundgren, Will Smith, Jacqueline Susann, McCoy Tyner > RESIDENTS: Edgar Allan Poe, Sylvester Stallone, Walt Whitman

PHILADELPHIA USA

NOWADAYS A PROVINCIAL and genteel relative of North America's great cities, Philly was once the nation's capital. It was here that America's independence was declared and its constitution written, project and product of the great Philadelphian thinker, inventor, artist and statesman, Benjamin Franklin.

Founded by Quakers and given the name "city of brotherly love" it has always reflected the conservative liberalism at the heart of the American constitution. One of the expressions of this was to oppose the British slave trade, an attitude still symbolized by the famous Liberty Bell. Philadelphia was the first American city to be ethnically tolerant and mixed, proud of its Afro-American culture and

Society of Traders, are more quaint cobbled and gas-lit streets lined with early Federal and Georgian houses with, in their window frames, the keystones that are typical of Pennsylvania. Philadelphia wears its political history on its sleeve: historically significant ships are moored in its port, and a walk through the street of the INHP (Independence National History Park), dubbed "America's most historic square mile", is inevitable.

South Philadelphia is where the city's heart beats, by day and night, sparked by the large Italian community that lives here, epitomized by its enormous daily street market, America's largest and still furnished with the original wooden stalls. The most famous Italian to walk, or rather

"It's a handsome city, but **distractingly regular**. After walking about it for an hour or two, I felt I would have given the world for a crooked street." Charles Dickens

the first city to elect a black mayor for its majority black population. From Philadelphia out across America, Quaker conservatism may lie at the core but the things being conserved are often quite radical. You can read American civic pragmatism and even-handedness into the city's architecture. Philadelphia was laid out in the 18th century in a simple and democratic grid system, which was the blueprint for so many US cities.

Bound in by the Schuylkill and Delaware rivers, the streets of Walnut, Vine and Arch are the city's oldest quarter and home to perfectly preserved colonial red brick houses. You could almost be in England. Further up, on Society Hill, now full of posh residences but original named after the Free

run, these streets was Sylvester Stallone, aka Rocky, as he trained for his heroic comeback in the ring, running up and down the steps of the city's Museum of Modern Art, oblivious to its trove of European art treasures, up 26th Street, down Franklin Parkway and across the huge expanse of Fairmount Park.

Another of Philly's great contributions to civilization is its cheese, traditionally sampled in a local cheese steak – a boxer's protein heaven but a heavyweight in cholesterol. Then, for something lighter but no less cheesy there's always the famous easy-listening 1970s Philly sounds of Patti "Voulez-vous couchez?" Labelle, Harold Melvin, or Eve, the modern soft rap equivalent.

OTTAWA CANADA

OTTAWA – THE HAMLET that woke up one day and discovered it was a capital city. By the same kind of regal, random intervention that plucked the likes of Madrid and Yamoussoukro from previous obscurity, so too did the choice of Canadian capital come winging in out of the mighty blue skies of the North.

There was Ottawa, then known by the rather unassuming name of Bytown, minding its own business as a simple logging town. The people of Bytown were lumberjacks, and they were perfectly OK, working hard, drinking hard and doing their best to survive each harsh winter. Then the hand of politics intervened. Because of its location on the very border of Upper and Lower Canada, which were about to be united into one mighty dominion, the spotlight fell on Bytown in 1857. Within a matter of months, a certain amount of Victorian airbrushing had taken place. Out went the name Bytown and in came Ottawa, a politically correct piece of deferential reference to the original Algonquin sub-tribe, the Odawa or Outaouais. Then the constructors moved in, erecting some seriously Gothic parliament buildings – whose green copper roofs still gleam – boosting employment and the population. By the early 20th century Ottawa was more than passable for the ruling classes. The makeover was complete.

But Ottawa's selection as the capital of Canada put several noses (and, as far as the French of Montreal and Quebec were concerned, quite a few *becs*) out of joint: those cities with what they considered to be stronger claims were distinctly miffed. And they haven't let Ottawa forget it. The whispering campaign began; but Ottawa is characterless, the whisper ran, it's just a bureaucratic backwoods 'burb.

Ottawans are happy to dispute the slander. They revel in their setting in the countryside of Eastern Ontario. After the Second World War the Parisian landscape artist Jacques Greder was drafted in to help make the most of the city's parks – and his green legacy has helped make Ottawa a consistent representative among the world's top cities ranked by the quality of life on offer, as clean and crisp as a Mountie's best uniform.

And while the good folk of Montreal retreat into their underground walkways and shopping malls once the first snows of winter threaten, Ottawa bucks the trend and heads outdoors. They spend every February celebrating the coldest season in the Winterlude festival. When the Rideau Canal freezes over, Ottawans use it as a glacial motorway, skating in to work, treating it as a long, thin pleasure rink, encouraged by the council who arrange for the surface to be cleared on a regular basis, and kindly supply heated cabins for the use and comfort of their citizens.

124 > OTTAWA, ONTARIO, CANADA > LONGITUDE: 75°40' W > LATITUDE: 45°25' N
> ALTITUDE: 23 feet/75 metres > POPULATION: 326,800 (metro: 1,063,700)
> TWINNED WITH: Cairo > NATIVES: Paul Anka, Margaret Atwood, Dan Aykroyd, Angela Hewitt,
Alanis Morissette, Elizabeth Smart > RESIDENTS: Yousuf Karsh, Wilfrid Laurier, Matt Perry

"The Glory of the North alone is thine, O Ottawa my Queen."

James E. Caldwell

IT'S ALL TOO EASY to confuse a description of Medellin with a biography of its most infamous son, Pablo Escobar. The so-called "land of eternal spring" was for so long shrouded in the daily fear of imminent death. Medellin is rightly proud of its year-round temperate climate and ability to festoon itself perennially in brightly coloured flowers. Yet there was a time when flowers were mainly used in bouquets and wreaths to mark yet another killing in the guerilla drugs war conducted by "El doctor", Health Secretary of the Medellin cocaine cartel.

Escobar made Medellin one of the scariest places on the planet, conducting a policy of *"plata o plomo!"* – "accept my bribe or eat lead". In 1993 after being tracked by the Columbo-esque Colonel Hugo Martinez, it was Escobar's turn to taste death, gunned down in the los Olivos district trying to escape prison.

Escobar is an unlucky name in these parts. A year after his death, following an inadvertent own-goal that saw the Colombian national team eliminated from the 1994 World Cup, footballer Andreas Escobar was shot dead in the Las Palmas district.

But Medallo, as it is known affectionately to locals, is no longer the Wild West it was always considered from afar and, despite its cult status among war tourists, has gone to great lengths to reinvent itself to reflect the innate warmth, generosity and courtesy of its inhabitants, *las Paisas*.

Colombia's second largest city and capital of the Antioquia region, it is nestled in the enchanting Alburra Valley between two mountain ranges, El Penol – its own Rio-esque sugarloaf – and surrounded by gently sloping screens of coffee plantations. Coffee is Medellin and Colombia's second largest export – or first if you only count legal ones – and a morning cup of gold roast tasted at source makes you feel like you're in a sun-kissed TV coffee commercial.

Medellin is a modern city with few buildings remaining of its pre-Spanish or colonial heritage. Republican skyscrapers stand spaced out between plazas abounding with fountains, statues and flowers. Every year in August the city shows off its floral distinction in the Desfile de los Silleteros, a unique parade of intricate tapestries of woven flowers. Yet despite its big town architecture, Medallo exudes a relaxed small town atmosphere. Cafés are as central to life as to be expected in this Costa del Coffee, and by night the bars in Poblado come alive with the city's young university population, steaming up with the sweat of bodies coming together in the salsa dance born not far away in Cali.

Escobar's presence may still haunt the city and cartel memorabilia be hawked to tourists, like Lenin badges in 1990s Moscow, but in a fable for the rest of the drug world, Medellin is getting on very nicely without him, thank you.

> "The only law which holds true on the hillsides of Medellin is gravity."
>
> Victor Galvira, film maker

"You'll never discover a stranger city with such extreme style. It's as if every eccentric in the south decided to move north, ran out of gas in Baltimore, and decided to stay." John Waters

THERE IS A STRONG MARITIME TANG about Baltimore, a salty nip in the air that is both bracing and captivating. The city's revived inner harbour area is still very much the focus of activity, where water taxis criss-cross the water linking the old seamen's boarding-houses of Fells Point with the Orioles' old-style baseball stadium over at Camden Yards or the extraordinary folk art collection of the waterside American Visionary Art Museum. At night, the glowing red sign of the Domino Sugars building at Locust Point acts as a surrogate lighthouse.

And from the Chesapeake Bay come fleets of crabs, destined to be tipped in steaming, spicy bucket-loads onto the brown paper-covered tables of Obrycki's Restaurant. Eating crab Baltimore-style is a no-holds-barred activity, armed with a hammer and plenty of gusto.

Often considered one of the most blue-collar cities in the United States, Baltimore started life as an attempt by Cecil Calvert, Lord Baltimore, to re-create the blue-blooded life of the English gentry. He had a vision of rolling estates for hunting and fishing (and a little slave trading), but it was a doomed vision, swept away in revolutionary zeal, which the city embraced with the same fervour that led them to support Napoleon. During the war of 1812-1814, the city's Fort McHenry was attacked by British warships. The sight of the young nation's flag fluttering bravely aloft under the siege inspired the onlooking Francis Scott Key to pen "The Star-Spangled Banner".

A sense of the elegance of Baltimore in the 19th century remains in the houses of Mount Vernon and the Walters Art Museum, but it was as a hard-working port that Baltimore survived, before being plunged in a decline in the 1960s that saw the harbour warehouses abandoned and the wharves decaying. "Hard times in the city, in a hard town by the sea", sang Randy Newman in "Baltimore", although he admitted he had only passed through on the train, and by the time he wrote the song in the late 1970s the city was already making efforts to revive itself.

The revival was achieved, but without losing Bawl'more's charm, as captured by the movies of Barry Levinson. In Little Italy the descendants of the immigrants from the old country still sit outside and chat on summer evenings. The bars between the painted houses and bijou galleries of Fells Point heave of a night. It's an honest, though quirky charm, as befits the city of Frank Zappa, John Waters and long-time resident Edgar Allen Poe; the city boasts the world's only light bulb museum (the Museum of Incandescent Lighting). Protected through geographical luck from the spotlight glaring on its neighbour Washington DC, a half-hour's drive inland, Baltimore is holding its own, and doing it with panache.

> BALTIMORE, MARYLAND, USA > LONGITUDE: 76°37' W > LATITUDE: 39°17' N > ALTITUDE: 0 feet/0 metres > POPULATION: 652,400 (metro: 2,553,000) > TWINNED WITH: Alexandria, Cádiz (Spain), Cardiff, Genoa, Kawasaki (Japan), Luxor (Egypt), Odessa, Piraeus (Greece), Rotterdam, Xiamen (China) > NATIVES: Larry Adler, Spiro T. Agnew, Eubie Blake, John Wilkes Booth, Martha Clarke, Divine, Adam Duritz, Mama Cass Elliott, Anna Faris, Philip Glass, Alger Hiss, Billie Holiday, Barry Levinson, Jerry Lieber, Morris Louis, H.L. Mencken, Babe Ruth, Henry Segrave, Pam Shriver, Upton Sinclair, Jada Pinkett Smith, Leon Uris, John Waters, Frank Zappa > RESIDENTS: Cab Calloway, Mary E Frye, David Lynch, Edgar Allen Poe, Mother Elizabeth Seton

KINGSTON JAMAICA

KINGSTON IS ONE OF THOSE CITIES that has become overgrown with myth and mystique. Although it stands on the edge of a beautiful natural harbour on Jamaica's south coast, set against the misty heights of the Blue Mountains to the north, this is not the Jamaica of the tourist posters, nor a kind of *Dr No* come to life, full of country clubs and cheery locals getting on down in a beachside lean-to. Kingston has always had a harder, tougher edge to it than that. Yet equally, it is not the gangland, ratchet-swinging danger zone that expatriate Yardie activities might suggest. Like any major conurbation, from Washington DC to Johannesburg, there are areas of deprivation and anger, "badman territory" that keeps itself to itself unless some unwitting tourist starts sticking a nose into other people's business.

The music, however, is completely real. Out of Kingston, either home-grown talent or incoming musicians "from country" have had an extraordinary impact on the aural awareness of the rest of the world. That international explosion was fronted in the 1970s by the reggae of Bob Marley, aided and abetted by the white Kingstonian Chris Blackwell of Island Records. But "No Woman No Cry" is just one gem in a rich seam of Kingstonian music, from the pre-war native-influenced mento, via ska, rock steady, dub, roots to the in-your-face attitude of dancehall. In the 1950s the battles on the streets were not between dealers or political factions, but between the massive mobile sound systems of Duke Reid and Coxsone Dodd. The bass beat of their "tons of houses of joy" is still informing Kingston.

The city was run by the British for three centuries; the harbour was settled by a group of plantation owners in 1692 when the nearby town of Port Royal was destroyed by an earthquake – natural disasters (especially hurricanes), fire, disease and, in the 20th century, town planning, have left modern Kingston with few reminders of its early past. The rifts caused by the earthquakes were replicated in the class divisions along racial lines, and not surprisingly Kingston was the centre for resentment and unrest – with Marcus Garvey just one of its great nationalist leaders.

The class divisions remain: the middle classes are in the outer suburbs, and up in the foothills of the Blue Mountains (themselves home to the ganja-heightened soul of rasta consciousness). In the heart of downtown, near the ocean, Trenchtown remains a hot cauldron, rarely touched by the breezes from the mountains. Once a posh colonial

> "I remember when we used to sit, in a government yard in Trenchtown. In this great future you can't forget your past."
>
> Bob Marley, "No Woman No Cry"

address, where Noel Coward would watch Louis Armstrong at the Ambassador's Theatre, the area was created in the 1950s from old slave "yards", the intense feeling of community a way of surviving the low times. Uptown is slightly less intense, but wherever you are in Kingston the energy is palpable.

> KINGSTON, JAMAICA > LONGITUDE: 76°47' W > LATITUDE: 18°00' N > ALTITUDE: 177 feet/54 metres > POPULATION: 590,500 > TWINNED WITH: Coventry (UK) > NATIVES: Beenie Man, Louise Bennet (aka Miss Lou), Chris Blackwell, Dennis Brown, Desmond Dekker, Clement 'Sir Coxsone' Dodd, Garth Fagan, Gregory Isaacs, Bunny Livingstone, Michael Manley, Augustus Pablo, Errol 'ET' Thompson, Alfred Valentine > RESIDENTS: Bob Marley, Lee "Scratch" Perry

"Washington is a city of Southern efficiency and Northern charm."

John F. Kennedy

JFK, ONE OF THE UNITED STATES' WITTIER PRESIDENTS, had his tongue firmly in his cheek when delivering his dig at the nation's capital, but he touched on the very reason why the newborn republic chose the banks of the Potomac as an acceptable site in the 1790s. It was neatly positioned between the Yankee towns of the north and the rural states of the south, just above the Mason-Dixon Line; the Civil War was decades away, but already the battlelines were being drawn.

The overall design for the new city was conceived by a Frenchman, Pierre l'Enfant, in the 1790s. Construction, however, was sluggish. Charles Dickens, on a visit to the city in 1842, remarked on "spacious avenues that begin in nothing and lead nowhere". The majesty of l'Enfant's vision eventually came to fruition, wide avenues cutting diagonally across a grid of alphabetical streets, with the heart of

government, Capitol Hill, standing on a bluff from which the stately procession of the Mall marches down towards the river.

Along the way, the procession passes the Smithsonian's rich collections, the White House, a monument to George Washington. At the far end, beyond the engraved black marble walls of the Vietnam Veterans memorial, beyond the 19 life-size figures of soldiers on a recce through the grass in memory of the dead of the Korean War, sits Abe Lincoln, nobly looking right back up to the Hill. Just across the Potomac, in the state of Virginia, the Arlington National Cemetery – where JFK, RFK, Jackie and nearly a quarter of a million servicemen and women lie – rises next to the citadel of the Pentagon.

This is impressive stuff, but Washington is not only a city of sombre and uplifting monuments, or of politicians and bureaucrats. There is room to have fun as well, in the funky jazz bars of Adams-Morgan, or amongst the town houses and cafés of Georgetown, which has emerged from too much yuppification in the 1980s as a calmer, collegiate quarter. Washington also has its own right-on punk scene: harDCore. The Watergate complex is still down on the riverfront (something of a surprise to find it there; it feels like a relic from ancient history) with its memories of the less ethical side of politics.

Washington has its problem areas, of course. Black workers seeking tolerance flooded in during the late 19th century, but the city could not cope with their numbers, and the ensuing poverty and disappointment led to extreme inner-city strife. "Don't try to find no home in Washington DC," sang Leadbelly, "Lord it's a bourgeois town." The worst is past (the one-time highest murder rate in the States, Mayor Marion Barry's 1990 crack cocaine bust) but the inequalities within the city which was built to implement the principle that "all men are born equal" will take a long time to mend. Martin Luther King's dream – he gave the speech on the steps of the Lincoln Memorial – is not yet fulfilled.

> WASHINGTON DC, USA > LONGITUDE: 77°01' W > LATITUDE: 38°54' N > ALTITUDE: 150 feet/46 metres > POPULATION: 572,000 (metro: 4,039,000) > TWINNED WITH: Bangkok, Beijing, Dakar, Havana, Paris
> NATIVES: Edward Albee, Carl Bernstein, Pat Buchanan, Tim Buckley, Tracy Chevalier, Duke Ellington, Ahmet Ertegun, John Foster Dulles, Marvin Gaye, Nan Goldin, Al Gore, Goldie Hawn, J. Edgar Hoover, William Hurt, Armistead Maupin, Henry Rollins, John Philip Sousa > RESIDENTS: Katharine Graham, Sugar Ray Leonard, Bob Woodward

"At the core of the city lies the decaying hulk
of a great colonial shipwreck.
In flaking baroque these relics gaze,
stained and weary, over the tin and concrete
and electric wires." Matthew Parris

> LIMA , PERU > LONGITUDE: 77°03' W > LATITUDE: 12°04' S > ALTITUDE: 354 feet/108 metres > POPULATION: 7,060,600 > TWINNED WITH: Austin TX, Bordeaux > NATIVES: Isabel Allende, Alberto Fujimori, Mario Vargas Llosa, Meredith Monk, Javier Perez de Cuellar, Nolberto Solano, Mario Testino > RESIDENTS: Nobu Matsuhisa

PERU'S CAPITAL SUPPOSEDLY CAME ABOUT as the result of a practical joke. Legend has it that, having laid waste to the Inca civilization, Pizarro and his fellow conquistadors were looking for a good place to make the military and political capital of the Spanish New World. They sought the advice of a vanquished Inca chief, who jumped at the opportunity to take revenge, and so brought them to a place at the delta of the River Rimac, no doubt facetiously highlighting the strategic value of such a trickle, where it never rains and where the sun rarely shines.

It seems far-fetched that the Spanish swashbucklers could have fallen for such a ruse, and the story is probably more the result of an ironic post-colonial Spanish imagination looking to undermine the achievements of their forebears. The truth is, Lima is generally considered a disappointment, a one-night stand in the foreign love affair with traditional, darkest Peru, quickly jilted in favour of the seductions of Cuzco and the country's Inca past.

Nestled on the Pacific coast, against the distant backdrop of the Andean cordillera, it is a mournful place, almost constantly shrouded in a milky veil of mist known locally as *la garua*. The rainforest air meets the cold air coming up from the Antarctic Humboldt current and condenses, but, trapped by the mountains, simply lingers above Lima year-round, becoming almost a personality in the city. A series

of earthquakes between 1535 and 1746 ensured that little remains of the original Lima, although what has survived of the timbered mansions of the old and dilapidated colonial centre is now a Unesco heritage site. Lima is a symbol of modern Peru, blazing a shining path into the 21st century while tourists ply the Inca Trail; it is a city with its own distinct urban poetry.

Away from the imposing central square of Plaza de Armas, where, behind the shoeshine boys, the country's military can be seen conducting their version of the "Changing of the Guard", the city spreads out into a collection of varied neighbourhoods. Across the river is the Rimac quarter, old Lima, where football is played in the streets, home to the former aristocratic residences of the conquistadors. Barranco is an old bathing station full of cobbled streets, romantic promenades lined with marble statues, gardens and complete with its own Bridge of Sighs. It was here that the veiled *tapadas*, the femmes fatales of 19th-century Lima society, used to turn male heads. Chic Miraflores is where every Peruvian wants to live. This is the *City of Dogs* of Lima novelist and presidential candidate, Mario Vargas Llosa. Animated at night, its streets are teeming with "made in Peru" VW Beetle taxis, echoing with the wistful sound of the Peruvian waltz and bolero; and the bars of the Avenida Grau, packed with *pisco*-sipping urbane Peruvians, are a far cry from their ponchoed relatives in the mountains.

ECUADOR IS SOMETIMES referred to as the Switzerland of South America. It might have something to do with the chocolate-box views of snow-capped volcanoes, Amazonian rainforest and the unique riches of the Galapagos Islands – although Switzerland would be flattered to think so. But it is most likely to do with the fact the country, and Quito as its capital is no different, offers a refreshing and relaxing respite as an island of mellowness in the whirlwind clamour of the continent's other conurbations.

The first democracy to emerge from the South American military cancer of the 1970s, Ecuador has always been relatively calm and stable,

of this region, the streets of calle Cuenca are lined with pastel-coloured façades with twirly white baroque decorations. Calle Ronda is a perfectly preserved cobbled alley of colonial residences from the 16th century. As if the modern rest of the city were excluded, life carries on here in a provincial time-capsule, the bells of the church of San Francisco in placa de la Independencia daily calling *quiteños* to the spiritual heart of their city. But these are no museum streets. In the slogan-less walls, and soldierly daily import and export of green bananas and potatoes, there is still a sense of *miga*, the compulsory ethic of community labour inherited from the Incas.

> "Quito, the oldest city of the New World, is seemingly built over a sunken rollercoaster. It is at once like Tunis and like Bruges, and its nearby background of mountains reminds one of Innsbruck." Ludwig Bemelmans, *The Donkey Inside*

keeping its head while surrounding countries were losing theirs. Fifteen miles (24km) south of the girdle of the world, Quito is a quiet, beautiful city of whitewashed houses with blue railings and green-tiled roofs, the legacy of Spanish colonization. When the Spaniards arrived, though, they found a city razed to the ground. Considering her beauties to be pearls before Spanish *jamón*, its proud Inca fathers, rulers of the Kingdom of Quitu, couldn't bear to see their city wasted on the invaders. So they laid waste to it themselves.

Quito was refounded by Benalcazar in 1534, and the imprint of its old centre is of the purest Spanish colonial elegance. Despite the attempts of the numerous earthquakes that are characteristic

As its democracy has borne fruit the city has oozed into every nook and cranny of the valley, but is ultimately contained by the Pichincha and Cayambe volcanoes. Covered in flowers like an Alpine spring, the fertile volcanic plateaus between the peaks feed the world's demand for roses and carnations. To continue the Swiss analogy, the El Panecillo sugarloaf is as much the city's trademark as the Matterhorn on a box of Caran d'Ache crayons.

The country took its name from the nearby equator. Calm, cool and unassuming, the city with its head in the clouds, that calls itself *un hueco en el cielo* (an opening into heaven), has one foot in the past and one in the future, just as it has a foot in both hemispheres.

> QUITO, ECUADOR > LONGITUDE: 78°30' W > LATITUDE: 0°14' S > ALTITUDE: 9,068 feet/2,764 metres > POPULATION: 1,578,700
> TWINNED WITH: Coral Gables FL, Louisville KY

IT HAS BEEN CALLED "the greatest liberty Man has ever taken with Nature" yet the Panama Canal remains a towering example of the triumph of man's will and ambition as a result of which the world's cargo ships can pass between the Pacific and the Atlantic Oceans, entering the canal mouth in the western suburb of Panama City to emerge from 50 miles (80km) of irrigation at Colon on Panama's northern coast.

Built between 1904 and 1914 by French labourers, the canal's width and the size of its many locks define the dimensions of ships built worldwide. Passage is charged by weight, and in 1928 an

between the oceans", and to see freighters nudge their way between tracts of jungle down one of the most significant waterways on earth is an amazing sight.

But Panama City existed before the canal. Situated on the southern pacific coast of the Central American isthmus, the Spanish conquistadors used it as a base for their looting of Bolivia and Peru, and all the gold, silver and treasures plundered from South America were brought here. With their appropriated riches they constructed a baroque city of which little but the sea wall and the decaying grandeur of the San Felipe district on the Casco Viejo headland

"A hot blue evening sky was disappearing into night but its heat remained behind because in Panama City it always does. There is dry heat, there is wet heat. But there is always heat."

John Le Carré, *The Tailor of Panama*

American swimmer paid 36 cents for the pleasure of swimming through. Being of such strategic importance the Canal Zone was inevitably the subject of much international tussling. In 1989 the US, owners of the original railroad via a treaty with Colombia, invaded to depose the military dictator Noriega, who had brought the Canal to the centre of his pseudo-nationalist cause. He was famously forced into submission in the Vatican embassy, his eardrums having been relentlessly pounded by the best in American rock music. In 1999 the Panamanians were handed back control by a munificent Jimmy Carter.

The canal, which, but for the city's greater ability to withstand frequent regional earthquakes, could have been the Nicaraguan Canal, is bizarrely but undoubtedly one of the city's attractions, even for non-cargo-ship-spotters. The city itself claims to be "the bridge

survives. Panama was a prime target for bounty hunters, and the English pirate Henry Morgan all but laid waste to it.

Today the city that gave its name to the eponymous hat (the hats are actually from Ecuador) is a cosmopolitan frontier city and transit town. Indian, Caribbean, mestizos, Chinese, Middle Eastern, Swiss, Yugoslav and North American residents cohabit in a cabaret-loving cultural melting pot born of the coffee and shipping industries.

Surrounded by a thick rainforest singing with *quetzal* birds and palm-shaded beaches and islands home to leatherback turtles, locals pride themselves that in Panama City you can see the sun rise and set on the same beach and swim in two tropical oceans on the same day. The ultimate in continental and oceanic crossroads, perhaps Panama, not Greenwich, should be the real prime meridian on our planet. But then that would mean setting our clocks by P.M.T.

IN THE VERTICAL-GLASS HEAVEN of modern America, Charleston is a perfectly preserved piece of the Union's colonial history. Instead of skyscrapers, Charleston has church spires, almost one at every corner; instead of apartment blocks, detached Georgian and Italianate porticoed villas with cool and shady verandahs, decorative iron gates and long, wide gardens. Along its narrow streets are lantern posts not streetlights, and by night there is hardly a neon sign to be seen. The Empire aesthetic is everywhere.

Charleston is a colonial, almost West-Indian city, *par excellence*; however, what meets the eye today is the product of a miracle of restoration. The USA's first preservation project, the city has been reborn as a museum to a bygone era of style. In its slavish detail and cleanliness it might even be a film-set. In fact one of the great dashing gentlemen of the silver screen, epitome of the chivalry of yesteryear, hailed from these parts: Rhett Butler, Mr Brylcreem himself, was from Charleston, although the object

"Charleston is a beautiful memory, a corpse whose lower limbs have been resuscitated."

Henry Miller

> CHARLESTON, SOUTH CAROLINA, USA > LONGITUDE: 79°58' W > LATITUDE: 32°48' N > ALTITUDE: 7 feet/2 metres > POPULATION: 549,000 > TWINNED WITH: Berlin-Tempelhof, Spoleto (Italy)
> NATIVES: Lauren Hutton, Henry Laurens, Alphonse Mouzon, Robert North, Joel Robert Poinsett

of his attentions, Scarlett O'Hara, was apparently not impressed with the place. "Scarlett did not like the people who called, with their airs and their traditions and their emphasis on family." And therein lies the rub. For all its antiquated ante-bellum architecture and the politeness of its upstanding citizens, restoration goes hand-in-hand with conservatism, and Charleston is a place where you can sense the reign of moral authority on the sultry air of the Carolina low country. "Death on the Atlantic," as someone once said.

Set on a swampy peninsula, surrounded by a coastal plain of sparkling beaches, spacious marshes and palmetto trees Charleston (originally named Charles Town in homage to King Charles II) was originally built like a medieval fortress. The ramparts were removed in 1717 to make room for expansion. The city grew rich on rice and rice lords built the grand 18th-century mansions that survive today. They could not have

done so without the sweat of slaves, and there is little left in the aesthetic beauty of the exterior to hint at the city's dark past. The wharves along Cooper River and the sea wall south of Broad Street, now a Waterfront Park and promenade, are where the slaves were auctioned. On Chalmers Street the old slave-market still stands. Blacks were rigorously segregated, many of them forced to live on Catfish Row, most famously Dubose Heyward of *Porgy and Bess* fame. Black children would dance in the street for pennies giving rise to the gay, leg-cocking, hand-waving dance so popular in white high society in the 1920s.

In 1860 Charleston found itself the cradle of secession, the centre of the American Civil War; but apart from being the country home to the Bloomsbury Group, that was its last grand entrance. Since then it has stayed in the wings, shunned the limelight, a jewel of American history, "Gone with the Wind" like the cinema classic – an easy, mellow and conservatively glamorous city.

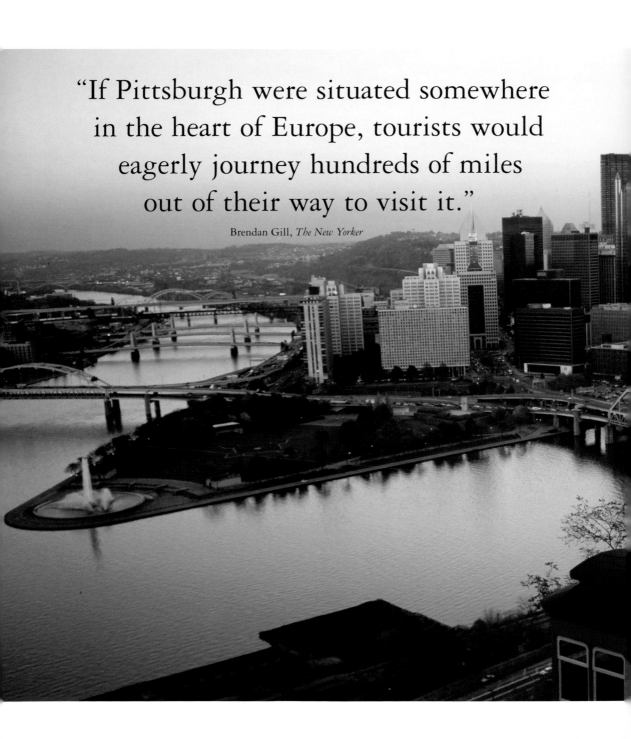

"If Pittsburgh were situated somewhere in the heart of Europe, tourists would eagerly journey hundreds of miles out of their way to visit it."

Brendan Gill, *The New Yorker*

79°59' W

PITTSBURGH IS ONE OF THE great American cities whose glass, iron and steel industries helped forge the nation's expansion and economic growth.

Engine-room, coalface and furnace of the American industrial age, it could not also be fussy about its looks – and the city has always been much maligned by the clinical modern eye which projects on it a gloomy Dickensian image of belching steam and smoking towers. It's not surprising therefore to find Pittsburgh brushing itself down, printing tourist brochures and entering the leisure market. The city's heritage of warehouses, factories and furnaces is now sought-after by interior designers, bar and restaurant empires and cultural development officers. Alongside the great Pittsburgh and Lake Erie Railroad whose freight juggernauts still rumble and reverberate through the city, the bandwagon of the post-industrial age is in motion.

Formerly known as Fort Duquesne by its French founders, Pittsburgh's strategic position at the meeting of the Allegheny and Monongahela rivers meant it was keenly fought over – and wrested from the French by the British, who rechristened it Fort Pitt. Pittsburgh is city of bridges, 15 of them in total, its heart sitting on the so-called Golden Triangle at the confluence of two rivers. Emerging from underneath the majestic cream and blue Smithfield Street Bridge the view is so impressive, one *New York Times* journalist remarked that the smoky city is "the only American city with an entrance". Its heart is Station Square; on the north side are the small battered wooden houses of the Mexican War Streets, while on the south is the Strip District; and around East Carson Street are the onion domes of the Polish and Ukrainian immigrant steelworkers' district – centre of Pittsburgh's resurgent night-life, lubricated by the local Pious Monk Dunkel Ale.

Before the yuppies came, it was a Scot, Andrew Carnegie, steel baron and philanthropist, who picked the city up off its knees. He introduced the Bessemer furnace and built the steel empire that made him the world's then richest man, defining the city's image right down to its football team, the Steelers. He was also a man of great culture, and, with the charity that comes easier to millionaires, bequeathed to the city a legacy of cultural institutions, none greater than Pittsburgh's Carnegie Museum of Art, containing many Van Goghs among its resident collection. In Pittsburgh there is a Carnegie everything.

No less immense is the legacy of another Pittsburgh son, Andy Warhol, whose Campbell's Soup cans and printing techniques are surely born of a fascination with the industrial over the effete. Warhol was born in the leafy Oakland district, and his birthplace and dedicated Museum, a Pittsburgh version of Glasgow's Mackintosh, are the flagship of Pittsburgh's drive to reinvent its harsh industrial past and turn its collar from blue to white.

> PITTSBURGH, PENNSYLVANIA, USA > LONGITUDE: 79°59' W > LATITUDE: 40°26' N
> ALTITUDE: 1,223 feet/372 metres > POPULATION: 334,600 (metro: 2,358,700) > TWINNED WITH: Bilbao,
Donetsk (Ukraine), Matanzas (Cuba), Omiya (Japan), Saarbrucken (Germany), San Isidro (Nicaragua), Sofia, Wuhan (China), Zagreb > NATIVES: George Benson, Art Blakey, Roy Eldridge,
Nancy Friday, Erroll Garner, Jeff Goldblum, Earl Hines, Henry John Heinz, Gene Kelly, Dan Marino, Mary Roberts Rinehart, David O Selznick, Paul Taylor, Stanley Turrentine, Johnny Unitas, Andy Warhol

CAPITAL OF THE SUNSHINE STATE, Miami is a land of swaying palms, roller-skating bikinis and soft-top sports cars, where the sun really does shine like on TV.

Miami is more laid-back latino than American and the predominant lingo is Spanish. In the 1950s the Cuban middle class sought refuge from the Batista and Castro regimes, and the city has been a virtual suburb of the Caribbean island ever since. In the bars of Little Havana, don't expect men playing dominoes and chewing on fat cigars, but ask for a *cafecito* (Cuban coffee) or a *batido* (milkshake) made from one of the myriad fruits of this smoothie heaven – papaya, lychee, tamarind, mango. The first Cubans have moved up and out to the richer suburbs but they have been replaced by latinos from Nicaragua and the poorer *marielito* Cubans (so named after the infamous 1980 Mariel boatlift of refugees from Castro's regime). Miami's downtown Freedom Tower ironically acted as the refugee centre.

Despite its idyllic setting at the end of the Florida prong, Miami was until 1896 an underpopulated, swampy and mosquito-ridden outpost. Then the railroad arrived and within a few decades the peninsula had undergone a real estate boom. The boom coincided with the art deco movement, which in Miami received its own, candy-coloured dialect. Miami's gentrified South Beach along Ocean Drive is known as the Deco district, lined with pastel mansions, glowing with wavy neon lines like old-fashioned cinemas. It feels jokey, theatrical and camp, and the preserve of Florida fashionistas. No surprise that here is Florida's unofficial gay community, and the Casa Casuarina was the former home of Gianni Versace, on whose steps he was so brutally gunned down. Yet the Beach – actually a meticulously sculpted and manicured piece of reclaimed land – might be all six-packs and chic but it is not the exclusive area it might seem. Here also is a resident population of sun-wrinkled retirees come to finish their days in trousers hitched high over portly bellies.

As if the name Miami Beach was not evocative enough, the city abounds with neighbourhoods whose names seem as familiar as the Florida TV sun: the boulevards of Coral Gables, lined with Hispanic and Italianate architecture, the dream of local aesthete George Merrick, and the Miracle Mile, lined with bridal shops the dream of eloping couples; Coconut Grove, the former artists' and intellectuals' colony now a hi-rise haven for the city's jet-setters; and across the many causeways that are the Miami signature, the secluded island havens of the Keys – Key Biscayne, Key West and Key Largo.

The drug scene that plagued the city in the 1980s may have been cleared up, but in the breeze of the neon-striped balmy night air Miami is every bit the baggy linen-suit, pumps, T-shirt and stubble city of Don Johnson.

"A lot of us say we like living in Miami because it's so close to the United States. We are the capital of Latin America, a very exotic place, a very dangerous place, a very strange, weird and unusual place." Carl Hiaasen

> MIAMI, FLORIDA, USA > LONGITUDE: 80°18' W > LATITUDE: 25°41' N > ALTITUDE: 20 feet/6 metres > POPULATION: 362,500 (metro: 2,253,400) > TWINNED WITH: Agadir (Morocco), Amman (Jordan), Bogotá, Cochabamba (Bolivia), Kagoshima (Japan), Managua (Nicaragua), Montes De Oca (Costa Rica), Murcia (Spain), Nice, Palermo, Ramat-Hasharon (Israel), Santiago, Santo Domingo (Dominican Republic), Varna (Bulgaria) > NATIVES: Fernando Bujones, Steve Carlton, Patricia Cornwell, Debbie Harry, William H. Macy, Sidney Poitier, Janet Reno, Craig Robins, Ben Vereen > RESIDENTS: Harold Danhackl (aka Holly Woodlawn), Gloria Estefan, Mary Joe Fernandez, Andy Garcia, George Merrick, Tito Puente, Gianni Versace

145

TORONTO

ALTHOUGH IT IS BRIMMING with all the multicultural energies supplied by a major influx of ethnic communities during the second half of the 20th century, Toronto is still having to work hard at putting to rest its one-time reputation as one of the dullest places in Christendom, let alone Canada. Peter Ustinov's one-liner – "Toronto is a kind of New York operated by the Swiss" – was a typical view: of a soberly industrious, far too worthy, one-dimensional Anglophone city which sat, like a prim Chicago, on the north shore of Lake Ontario.

Reassuringly, Toronto, despite its primness (or because of it) has always been able to produce a good crop of spiky and one-off personalities, including the reclusive pianist Glenn Gould, Neil Young, film-maker David Cronenberg and Mike "Austin Powers" Myers. Nonetheless, the immigrants who arrived in the city gave it a massive and much-needed kickstart, like the arrival of some bubbly new guests at a sterile drinks party.

As the French Canadians in Montreal and Quebec grew increasingly nationalistic, English-speaking companies and residents moved out and south to Toronto, bringing in further fresh blood and money. A key moment was the realization in 1970 that the population of Toronto now outstripped that of Montreal; with its new role as the unofficial capital of Canada, a resurgence of confidence and pride followed.

The next thing you know, the Maple Leaf hockey team will rediscover its former, long-faded, glories and win another Stanley Cup.

The new Toronto is not some great big melting-pot; its various communities have remained discrete. Their names are self-explanatory: Chinatown, Greektown, Little India, Little Poland, Little Italy (in fact the largest of the communities) and Caribbean Village are typical. Cabbagetown does need an explanation: it's the recently gentrified and now very desirable old Irish quarter. With such diversity, the personality of the city is difficult to pin down. It's still in a state of evolution, just as the old 1960s counter-culture area of Yorkville in the city centre reinvented itself as a bijou enclave of bars and galleries.

The physical layout of the city is equally wide-ranging, lying along the flat city shoreline, but does have one clear focal point: the CN Tower, the spindly needle that is the world's tallest freestanding structure. Around the Tower and the next-door Sky Dome, the downtown area that responded to the economic upswing is predictably formed of glass and steel, but hints of its Anglo-Canadian 19th-century past (before that it was a French trading post on the site of a native lake village) can still be discovered. A prime example is the Holy Trinity Church just next to the Eaton Centre Mall, where the Cowboy Junkies recorded their *Trinity Sessions*.

"It's a city where almost everyone has come from elsewhere… bringing with them their different ways of dying and marrying, their kitchens and songs."

Anne Michaels, novelist

> TORONTO, ONTARIO, CANADA > LONGITUDE: 80°36' W > LATITUDE: 40°28' N > ALTITUDE: 348 feet/106 metres > POPULATION: 650,000 (metro: 4,682,900) > TWINNED WITH: Amsterdam, Bogota, Chicago, Eilat (Israel), Kiev, Warsaw > NATIVES: John Candy, Jim Carrey, David Cronenberg, Gil Evans, Frank Gehry, Glenn Gould, Norman Jewison, Beatrice Lillie, Erik McCormack, Lorne Michaels, Rick Moranis, Mary Pickford, Christopher Plummer, Robbie Robertson, Ann Rutherford, Kwame Ryan, Miriam Schapiro, Jane Siberry, Roy Thomson, Linda Thorson, Neil Young > RESIDENTS: Margaret Atwood, Frederick Banting, Cowboy Junkies, Robertson Davies, Nelly Furtado, Mike Myers

"Hello Cleveland...
Rock and Roll!"

Spinal Tap

LIKE MANY A ONCE GREAT industrial city that fell down on its luck in the 1960s, Cleveland has done well to pull itself up by its bootstraps. The thing is, in Cleveland's case there was an awfully long way to get back up.

The nadir in its fortunes was the moment in 1969 when an errant welder's spark set fire to an oilslick on the Cuyahoga River, which worms its way through the city to Lake Erie. Although the blaze lasted but a matter of minutes, the image of the polluted, flaming river stuck. Randy Newman thoughtfully perpetuated it with his song "Burn On Big River", comedians chortled about it in their stand-up routines – and when, in 1978, Cleveland became the first city since the days of the Great Depression to default on its municipal debt, the tag "The Mistake on the Lake" looked like it would be hard to shake off.

Cleveland tackled the problem by playing to its strengths – even perversely proud of its image ("The Burning River City" is now a local brand of beer). City pride was at stake, pride that had been strong from the Civil War to the Second World War, when it produced steel and ships for the rest of the nation. Rockefeller was only one of the millionaires who made a fortune here. But by the beginning of the 1980s the grand mansions that he and the others had built were too often standing abandoned and boarded up.

One potent symbol of a return to old times is Jacob's Field, the Cleveland Indians' ballpark slap bang in the middle of town, adjudged one of the most successful new old-style stadiums in the country. Over on the west bank of the river, the old warehouses of the Flats became a slightly over-hyped night-life quarter (locals reckon the Warehouse district is more authentic, and the Ohio City area hipper). The city also turned its attention to the waterfront of Lake Erie, sprucing it up with a Great Lakes Science Center, a new stadium for the Cleveland Browns – and, since its grand opening in September 1995, the Rock'n'Roll Hall of Fame.

The city's determination to secure the Hall of Fame saw it beat off the challenge of Memphis, even though Cleveland's claim was based primarily on the activities of Alan Freed, the pioneering D.J. who was at the forefront of pushing and marketing rock'n'roll as a viable teen product. After he departed for New York in the mid-1950s, Cleveland's rock'n'roll heritage was patchy to say the least – apart from the Raspberries, Joe Walsh and Devo, there was nothing of real note until Trent Reznor created Nine Inch Nails. Never mind, the I.M. Pei building has boosted local business and regular arrivals of limos ferry the aristocracy of the music business there to be inducted into the Hall of Fame. Cleveland, as they say, rocks!

> CLEVELAND, OHIO, USA > LONGITUDE: 81°41' W > LATITUDE: 41°30' N > ALTITUDE: 850 feet/259 metres > POPULATION: 478,400 (metro: 2,908, 400) > TWINNED WITH: Alexandria, Bangalore (India), Brasov, Bratislava, Gdansk, Ibadan (Nigeria), Klaipeda (Lithuania), Ljubljana, Segundo Montes (El Salvador), T'ai-pei, Volgograd (Russia) > NATIVES: Albert Ayler, Halle Berry, Drew Carey, Renée Green, Don King, R.B. Kitaj, Henry Mancini, Paul Newman, Harvey Pekar, Glen Tetley, Debra Winger, Bobby Womack > RESIDENTS: Alan Freed, John D. Rockefeller

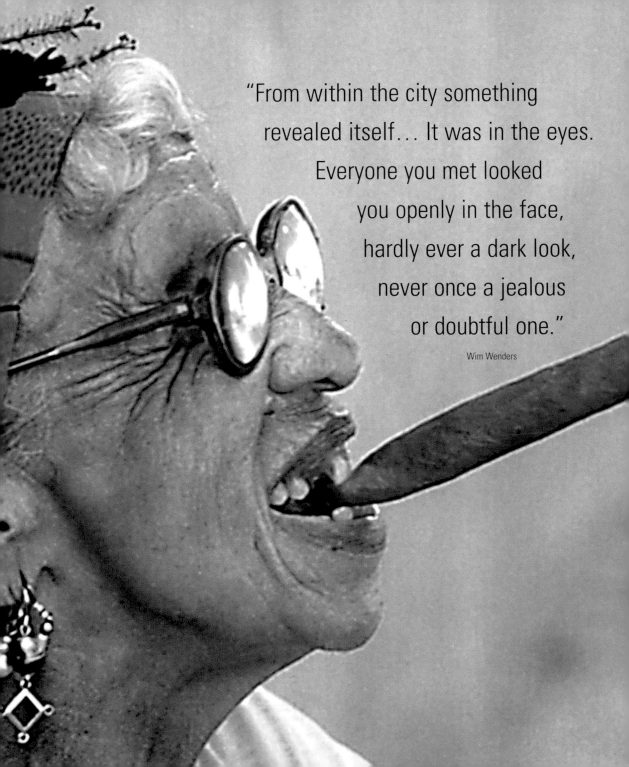

"From within the city something revealed itself… It was in the eyes. Everyone you met looked you openly in the face, hardly ever a dark look, never once a jealous or doubtful one."

Wim Wenders

CARS, CIGARS, BOXERS AND BALLERINAS ... just some of the things synonymous with Cuba that have given Havana a magical ring over the last decades. At least to outsiders it is an Eldorado, a cross between haven and nirvana.

A geographical and emblematic island, Cuba remains one of the last utopian experiments of the 20th-century cult of ideology. It would be nice to think that it worked and that there is an alternative to what the rest of the world has accepted.

Communism certainly had a better chance of working in a warm climate, and there are not many places on earth whose unswerving pride verging on arrogance combined with a pure *joie de vivre* can make sense of what it means to be alive and what a gift that is. And yet with so little. Virtually every day one of Havana's dilapidated buildings collapses, power cuts are a routine and sanctions still ensure that there is little food in the shops save the vast surplus of tooth-decaying sugar the country has nowhere left to export to.

It's a shamefully seductive dilapidation, an exotic war zone stuck in a decaying golden age, which we can look back on with a Cuban version of Baudelaire's *nostalgie de la boue*. The salty buildings of Habana Vieja are a mixture of baroque, neoclassical and Moorish, with sculpted façades and wrought-iron balconies. *Boteros*, big old American cars from the age of Elvis, bounce and lollop along the dusty streets between children

kicking footballs, purposefully trotting dogs and bikini-clad girls in hair-curlers. On street corners old men play dominoes while prostitutes and rent-boys play another game, and in the bars and backyards rings out the sensual soundtrack the island has become famous for: but not just the mournful *son de cuba* of Buena Vista Social Club fame, humble hybrid of African and Spanish tunes, but also the upbeat mambo, chachacha and rumba. Rock, jazz and hip-hop also have their own indigenous forms here, fruit of a people whose daily improvization with their limited means finds its ultimate expression in music and for whom song, sex and dance is the very essence of life.

Havana has a better claim that most to Hemingway's soul and in the bars of Habana Vieja, downtown, in leafy Vedado or in the cool brine of the Malecon sea front it's hard not to imagine yourself in Ernest's company, over a *mojito* or a *daiquiri* – two cocktails that are proof of Cuban inventiveness. That was all pre-Fidel and Che and no one knows what Hemingway would have thought of la Revolución. He'd no doubt applaud 100 per cent literacy, taxi-drivers with PhDs, the health system and lack of homelessness. The poverty is undeniably a problem, but, as often, its hardships inspire rare warmth and passion. In Havana resilience seems to be the lifeblood. It may be an island whose time is nearly up, but for now, in Cuba, if in doubt shout *"Quero bailar la salsa!"* and you'll never be alone.

> HAVANA, CUBA > LOCAL NAME: La Habana > LONGITUDE: 82°22' W > LATITUDE: 23°07' N > ALTITUDE: 16 feet/5 metres > POPULATION: 2,189,700
> TWINNED WITH: Glasgow, Mobile AL, Washington DC > NATIVES: Alicia Alonso, Jose Canseco, José Raul Capablanca, Alejo Carpentier, Celia Cruz, Gloria Estefan, Abilio Estévez, Andy Garcia, Horacio "EL Negro" Hernandez, José Martí, Leonardo Padura
> RESIDENTS: Fidel Castro, Che Guevara, Pedro Juan Gutiérrez, Ernest Hemingway, Tony Pérez

IN A SECLUDED BAY on the western Gulf Coast side of Florida, Tampa – and its close neighbour St Petersburg – has been offering an alternative to the Atlantic attractions of Miami, Palm Beach and Daytona since the 1880s. This was when the railroad and steamship magnate Henry B. Plant brought his twin commercial interests to a perfect union on the shores of Tampa Bay: a propitious meeting between the narrow-gauge South Florida railroad and steamers plying to Havana and back.

He built the Tampa Bay Hotel, a lavish recreation of the marvels of the Alhambra in Granada, complete with 13 silvered minarets, crescents and cupolas. Guests could take advantage of its own racetrack, "natatorium", golf course and railroad terminus; each room offered electricity and a telephone. Sadly, Plant's grand project faltered after only a few years, although its very presence had boosted the population (from 700 to over 10,000 people) of what up until then had been an unremarkable backwater. Wisely, the city decided to rescue the hotel from imminent decrepitude, and the building survives in much of its former glory as part of the University of Tampa, and adds its own off-beat contribution to Tampa's infectious charm.

About the same time as construction work on the Alhambra look-alike was under way, a Cuban cigar manufacturer, Vincente Martinez Ybor, opened a cigar factory in Tampa that quickly became the biggest in the world. Ybor City, the block of cobbled streets where the factory stood, has kept its expat vibe. The neighbourhood buzzes with Cuban bakeries, restaurants and fantastic coffee, although, sadly, there is no longer any cigar production.

It was in the bars of Ybor City that baseball players in Florida for spring training would come to let their hair down during the Prohibition years: the sound of bat on ball is still part of Tampa's annual ritual. And it was in the city's Plant Field that Babe Ruth nailed his longest home run, recorded at 587 feet (179m). The New York Yankees have had a long relationship with the city, as did the Phillies and Cardinals with St Petersburg. Football fans finally got their moment of glory in 2003, when the Tampa Bay Buccaneers won their first ever Super Bowl.

You can't mention Tampa without St Petersburg. Just as Minnesota has Minneapolis-St Paul, so West Florida has Tampa-St Pete. And like the Twin Cities, they are divided by water and united in their rivalry. St Petersburg, on the peninsula to the west of Tampa Bay, represented the vision of John Williams, a Michigan farmer, whose partner Peter Demens, a noble Russian émigré, supplied the name for their dream city from his home-town. It has its own signature hotel (the pink 1920s Don Cesar Beach Resort), is just about overcoming its reputation as a retiree heaven, and boasts the world's largest private collection of Salvador Dalí's work.

> "A big city with a small town feel. The strong Cuban influence adds another dimension. And the weather is perfect – except for the occasional tropical storm."
>
> M. Diane Vogt, novelist

> TAMPA, FLORIDA, USA > LONGITUDE: 82°29' W > LATITUDE: 27°57' N > ALTITUDE: 26 feet/8 metres > POPULATION: 303,500 (metro: 2,396,000) > TWINNED WITH: Agrigento (Italy), Boca Del Rio (Mexico), Córdoba (Argentina), Granada (Nicaragua), Izmir (Turkey), Le Havre (France), Oviedo (Spain), Veracruz (Mexico) > NATIVES: Cannonball Adderley, Dwight Gooden, Butterfly McQueen > RESIDENTS: Tampa Red

IT IS ALMOST IMPOSSIBLE to escape the influence of the motor car in Detroit. The city – Motor City, no less – was founded in 1701 by the French soldier and settler Antoine de la Mothe Cadillac. Just to the north of Detroit is the town of Pontiac (named after a local native American chief). Berry Gordy enshrined the city's automotive heritage in the name of his record label, Motown. Much, to be honest virtually all, of that heritage is down to the vision and, appropriately, the drive, of one man – Henry Ford.

He, along with other local entrepreneurs like the Dodge brothers, capitalized on Detroit's late 19th-century reputation as a centre for building horse-drawn carriages and bicycles. Its location on the Great Lakes (in a geographically disturbing inversion, the tip of Canada actually lies south-east of the city) and the Erie Canal provided freight routes, and nearby iron- and coalmines the raw materials. What Henry Ford brought to the nascent motor car was practicality, reliability and, above all, the concept of the assembly line – which revolutionized the whole of industry.

After decades of growth producing one of the great symbols of America's sense of freedom and opportunity, Detroit's car industry slammed into reverse in the late 1960s and 1970s – and the city suffered. Ethnic tensions and the discrepancy between the very rich and the very poor erupted in 1967 in some of the nation's worst riots. The middle class upped and headed out to the suburbs of Royal Oak or Grosse Pointe, leaving behind a decaying, abandoned urban wasteland where there was precious little dancing in the streets and that became a byword – a caricature – of depression, deprivation and danger.

Detroit has, like Cleveland, striven to overcome those dark days and the bad reputation. Bill Ford, the new heir to the company, is an environmentalist with green plans. The gardens of the inner-city island of Belle Isle are still a haven for Detroiters. The Detroit Institute of Arts houses a top-class, if not world-class, collection, with rackloads of Rembrandts, Picassos and Matisses and Diego Rivera's massive mural tribute to Detroit Industry. And the downtown areas of the Theater District and Rivertown have seen a renaissance of night-life and activity, tucked between the warehouses of old.

Music remains a vital part of the city. Berry Gordy – a one-time automotive worker – applied Ford's assembly line principles to pop music; his team of writers and producers created a superlative product range in the 1960s, from Marvin Gaye and Diana Ross to Stevie Wonder and Smokey Robinson. In the '70s MC5, the Stooges and Bob Seger provided its rock resilience, and George Clinton's Parliament the funk. And now Eminem – especially with his gritty portrayal of Detroit in the movie *8 Mile*, named after the eight-lane highway north of downtown that marks an unofficial border between the inner city and the 'burbs – is proving that the hard-headed business and marketing skills of Detroit are as potent as ever.

"You've got the East Coast and you've got the West Coast. Detroit is in between both of them. So when you mix the two, you get something crazy." Eminem

> DETROIT, MICHIGAN, USA > LONGITUDE: 83°04' W > LATITUDE 42°19' N > ALTITUDE: 581 feet/177 metres > POPULATION: 951,300 (metro: 5,456,400) > TWINNED WITH: Dubai, Toyota City (Japan)
> NATIVES: Nelson Algren, Anita Baker, William Boeing, Sonny Bono, Jerry Bruckheimer, Avery Brundage, Harry Callahan, Francis Ford Coppola, Alice Cooper, John DeLorean, Maria Ewing, Berry Gordy, Charles Lindbergh, Lene Lovich, Ted Nugent, Freda Payne, Suzi Quatro, George Peppard, Smokie Robinson, Diana Ross, Tom Selleck, Lily Tomlin, Robert Wagner, The White Stripes, Jackie Wilson
> RESIDENTS: Aaliyah, Eminem, Henry Ford, Aretha Franklin, Elmore Leonard, Kid Rock

"When I pray,
'Thy kingdom come on earth',
I mean I want Atlanta to look
like heaven." Andrew Young

> ATLANTA, GEORGIA, USA > LONGITUDE: 84°22' W > LATITUDE: 33°46' N > ALTITUDE: 1,010 feet/307 metres > POPULATION: 2,689,000 (metro: 4,112,200) > TWINNED WITH: Brussels, Bucharest, Fukuoka, Lagos, Montego Bay (Jamaica), Newcastle, Port of Spain, Rio de Janeiro, Salzburg, T'ai-pei, Tbilisi, Toulouse > NATIVES: Mary J. Blige, Kirstin Hersh, Bobby Jones, Martin Luther King, Gladys Knight, Spike Lee, Margaret Mitchell, Mary Lou Williams > RESIDENTS: Alonzo Herndon, Ted Turner, Andrew Young

AT THE CNN HEADQUARTERS IN ATLANTA, Ted Turner, so rumour had it, used to have on display the Best Picture Oscar awarded to David O. Selznick for *Gone With The Wind*. It neatly sums up Atlanta: that old celluloid image of the ante-bellum city, burning to the ground in 1864 courtesy of General William Sherman's troops, is very much a past to be polished and consigned to the trophy cabinet. The global success of CNN is much more typical of the attitude of aggressive regeneration adopted by the city's leaders to rebuild Atlanta after the ravages of the Civil War. Back then, before satellite, before TV – hell, before radio – it was the newspaper owners who joined forces with the bankers and politicians (collectively known as "boosters") to get the city back on its feet and on the road to becoming the unofficial capital of the New South. When Atlanta won the 1996 Olympics, it proved that the "booster" spirit lived on.

The city's industrial and business clout – Coca-Cola was born in Atlanta and stayed; the likes of Delta and UPS are based here – is somewhat at odds with the rest of the still mainly rural Georgia. Although Atlanta is blessed with its fair share of dogwoods, oaks, hickory and magnolia trees, its rather un-Southern energy and pace has created a downtown cityscape that is more Toronto than Tara; as one popular bumper sticker used to proclaim, "Where's Sherman when you need him?"

There is little of the original Atlanta left. The city was founded in 1837, for no other reason than as a railroad junction where the line from Chattanooga coincided with other main routes. In fact, its first name was the decidedly unpoetic though undisputedly precise Terminus; the Zero Mile Post that marked the point is preserved, along with a few other remnants of the old city, in the Underground Atlanta mall. Elsewhere a few memories survive: the extravagantly Moorish 1920s Fox Theater, some rusting mills along the Chattahoochee River.

Perhaps the most significant older part of Atlanta is Auburn Avenue – Sweet Auburn – which was a bustling centre of black enterprise in the 1920s. After the Civil War, Atlanta tried hard to work for reconciliation. In this birthplace of Martin Luther King, Alonzo Herndon, founder of Atlanta Life Insurance, became one of the USA's first black millionaires. And during the early 1960s Atlanta made a conscious decision to desegregate at a time other cities and other states were doing their damnedest to obstruct even a hint of civil rights. It became known as "the city too busy to hate".

Still energetic, still striving, Atlanta is neither free of urban tensions, nor the usual big-city problems. But the phoenix that emerged from the ashes is still flying high and proud.

CHARMING, CHARACTERFUL, TIMELESS... Granada has often been dubbed "the Charleston of Nicaragua", a favourite destination for the well-travelled, because the city's relaxed and tourist-friendly atmosphere provides a welcome respite to the overcrowded, oven-hot, off-putting freneticism of the country's capital, Managua.

Granada is one of the oldest colonial cities in Latin America, named by Don Francisco Hernández de Córdoba, who founded the city in 1524, in tribute to the Spanish city of Granada. He also founded León (Nicaragua's second city) setting up an intense rivalry between the liberal academics of León and, surprisingly given its current laid-back appeal, the much more robustly conservative inhabitants of Granada. The bitterness spilt over frequently into violence, capped off when the people of León invited the American adventurer and chancer William Walker to take over the country. Walker appointed himself dictator and general panjandrum, occupying Granada in the 1850s until an army of Nicaraguans and their central American allies forced him out.

As Walker retreated he razed Granada, so that the city that remains is mainly late 19th century, although a few pre-Walker buildings survived. The Casa de Leones is a 1724 labyrinth of courtyards and corridors – the stonework of the original church and convent of San Francisco dates from 1529 – and the walls of the cathedral and the Church of La Merced (Granada was, and is, a devout city) both carry the scars and fire-blackened memories of Walker's destruction. Once the transit point for the country's gold, the Spaniards had grown fat on the proceeds and built churches rather than defences. Previous invaders included the pirates Henry Morgan and William Dampier, who had also uncaringly torched the place.

To end the rivalry between León and Granada, Managua was invented, and with the consequent shift in power Granada could develop its special sense of timelessness. Of an evening, the breeze comes off the shoreline of the massive Lago Nicaragua soothing away the heat and humidity of the day, while the inhabitants rock gently on wicker *mesedora* chairs on their porches, surrounded by pastel houses, dilapidated mansions, huge doors, wrought ironwork and cobbled roads. *Fritanga* stalls dispense curd, grilled plantain, richly lacquered barbeque chicken, pork rind and yucca salads – the market also offers turtle or armadillo for those in search of an aphrodisiac gourmet menu.

The pace is slow (the *diligencia* horse-drawn carriages are not just put on for the tourists), and the energy gentle and meandering. Granada has become a destination for artists and burnt-out Silicon Valley escapees, and the property prices of those dilapidated mansions are on the rise. For the moment at least the restful spaces of the Plaza Colon and the citrus-shaded central park are served by cooling guava juice-sellers rather than Starbucks.

> GRANADA, NICARAGUA > LONGITUDE: 85°58' W > LATITUDE: 11°56' N > ALTITUDE: 154 feet/47 metres > POPULATION: 127,000
> TWINNED WITH: Tampa, Terrassa (Spain) > NATIVES: Ernesto Cardenal, Dennis Martinez

"It was just what I needed.
Here in Granada we saw these kids playing.
And even though they had nothing,
they were all having a really good time."

Joe Strummer, on location for *Walker*

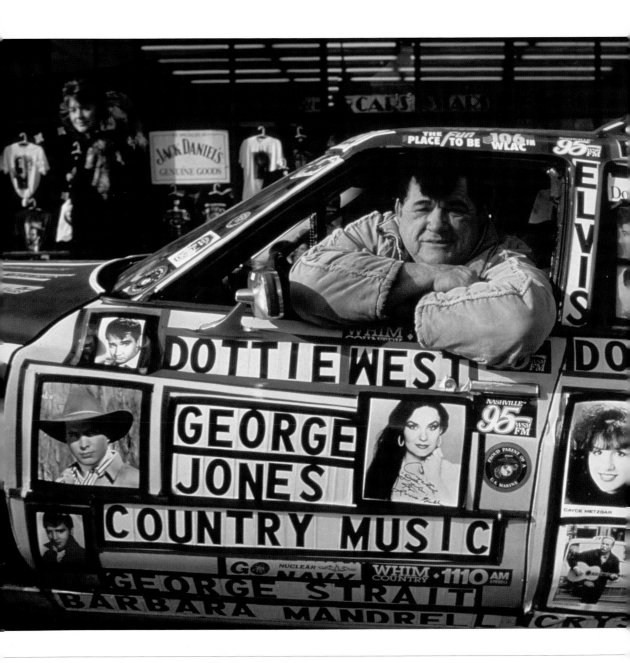

NASHVILLE HAS BECOME such a fabled place, the El Dorado of country music, that it would be easy to believe the place never actually existed. Yet it does, among the rolling and fertile hills of mid-Tennessee, a living, breathing city, with as many faces as there are ways of singing about heartbreak and hardship.

There is, of course, for those who want to experience it, any amount of yahoo countryism available. The out-of-town tourists who get bussed in to see the Country Hall of Fame, Opryland or Dolly Parton's Dollywood are handsomely catered for. And wannabe Garth Crooks and Shania Twains still pitch up in the record and publishing company offices of Music Row, hoping to earn that lucky break.

The city's country credentials are undeniably impeccable, right from the time that the WSM radio show started broadcasting the *Grand Ole Opry* show in 1927, first from its own studios and after 1943 from the Ryman Auditorium, where the pews and the gallery of the former tabernacle were graced for 30 years by the high priests and priestesses of country. Nashville, though, like its Tennessee cousin Memphis, has plenty more music history to offer. Slim Harpo sang the blues; Gene Vincent recorded "Be Bop A Lula" here. In RCA's studios Elvis cut "Heartbreak Hotel" and Roy Orbison "Only The Lonely". In their wake the likes of Bob Dylan (starting with "Blonde On Blonde") and Elvis Costello ("Almost Blue") have come into town in search of a little magic.

Beyond the sequin-studded jacket, Nashville – founded in the late 18th century as Fort Nashborough – sports both a blue collar and an academic gown. There is a strong manufacturing presence (including Nissan and Saturn) and an impressive academic tradition (the Vanderbilt and Fisk Universities are but a couple of the institutions of higher learning dotted throughout the city). The latter earned Nashville the name "the Athens of the South". Rather sweetly, the city built a full-scale replica of the Parthenon for its first centennial, which still stands.

There is, too, the Nashville of winter rain flooding relentlessly down the city streets before the dogwoods flower in spring; of religion, where Bible printing is bigger business than music; of grand ante-bellum mansions and quiet trails wending across Edwin Warner Park; of the Van Vechten Art Gallery, whose intimacy and richness is reminiscent of New York's Frick Collection.

But, hell, this is also Music City USA. And maybe the gimcrack and sentiment of the George Jones Gift Shop, and the "Nash Vegas" razzamatazz, is as valid and authentic as ham and gravy at the Loveless Café, or the young no-rhinestone, no-stetson bands playing nightly at the Bluebird on Hillsboro Road.

"There's **thirteen hundred and fifty-two guitar pickers** in Nashville, and they can pick more notes than the number of ants on a Tennessee ant hill."

The Lovin' Spoonful, "Nashville Cats"

> NASHVILLE, TENNESSEE, USA > LONGITUDE: 86°46' W > LATITUDE: 36°11' N > ALTITUDE: 825 feet/251 metres > POPULATION: 524,700 (metro: 1,231,300) > TWINNED WITH: Belfast, Caen (France), Edmonton (Canada) > NATIVES: Duane Allman, Greg Allman, Rita Coolidge, Robert Ryman, Edwin Starr, William Walker, Reese Witherspoon > RESIDENTS: Alfred Leland Crabb, Jay McInerney, Dolly Parton, Ann Patchett, Robert Penn Warren, Tammy Wynette

CHICAGO USA

CHICAGO IS A CITY LOVER'S CITY – that is, if your prerequisites for a city are that it should be big, bold, brash, beefy and broad-shouldered. Chicago feels as if it is standing four-square, ready to take on all comers. The fact that its towering buildings were constructed on swampy land on the Western shoreline of Lake Michigan just proves the self-belief (or arrogance, if you're a detractor) of the place.

Given all its assertiveness, it's reassuring to find that Chicago has a sensitive soul, able to be a little prickly about its "Second City" sobriquet, and slightly paranoid that everything groovy is happening in the cities on America's two coasts. However, Chicago does not lack for culture – in the lakeside Art Institute of Chicago alone, there are a host of iconic American images, including Edward Hopper's *Nighthawks* and Grant Wood's *American Gothic.*

The lakeside is Chicago's most striking, in fact its only striking geographical feature. The totally urban skyline comes to a dramatic halt, then there's just... a lot of lake. From the waterfront the architecture of the city rises, topped off by the Sears Tower. Around it – within the Loop circumscribed by Chicago's rackety, elevated railway, the El – is a master-class in urban architecture: the late 19th-century strength with elegance of the Reliance Building and the Carson Pirie Scott department store; Mies van der Rohe's modernist

masterpieces; while a little further west in Oak Park, Frank Lloyd Wright and his acolytes created the Prairie School style. And Wrigley Field, the Cubs' home, is one of the last grand, original city ballparks.

What gave Chicago the wherewithal for all this real estate was hogs and cows. When the Erie Canal opened in 1825, Chicago became a conduit and clearing-house to the East Coast. From the vast Mid-West came wheat, pigs and cattle: and in an inversion of the techniques Henry Ford would use on his model T, Chicago ("Hog Butcher for the world," in Carl Sandburg's phrase) systematically stripped down and de-constructed the animals. An Italian beef sandwich is still essential fare – forget the namby-pamby pizza.

With wealth went jobs, and among the flood of immigrants came the bluesmen of the Mississippi Delta. They amplified their acoustic guitars with an electric pick-up, spawning Chicago blues, fronted by the likes of Muddy Waters, Howlin' Wolf and Willie Dixon, and its delinquent offspring, rock'n'roll. Chicago has been home to plenty of music – including the birth of house music, the indie rock of Liz Phair and the Smashing Pumpkins, even the AOR of Chicago – but the blues, whether in the tourist-friendly North Side clubs or the grittier South Side venues, is the perfect sound-track for the Windy City, the nickname nothing to do with gusts off the lake, but a New York journalist's take on the boasts of the city.

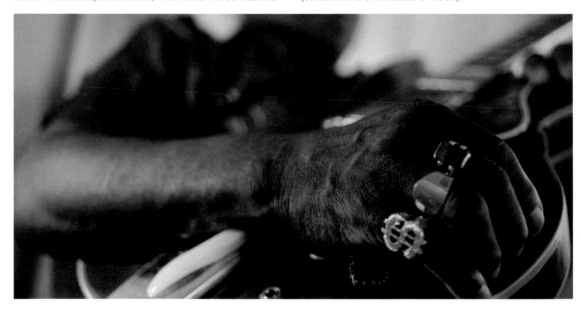

"Chicago is a great American city.
Perhaps it is the last of the
great American cities." Norman Mailer

> CHICAGO, ILLINOIS, USA > LONGITUDE: 87°38' W > LATITUDE: 41°55' N > ALTITUDE: 579 feet/176 metres > POPULATION: 2,895,000 (metro: 8,272,800) > TWINNED WITH: Accra, Athens, Birmingham (UK), Casablanca, Delhi, Dresden, Durban (S. Africa), Galway (Ireland), Gothenburg, Hamburg, Kiev, Lucerne (Switzerland), Mexico City, Milan, Moscow, Osaka, Paris, Petach Tikva (Israel), Prague, Shanghai, Shenyang (China), Stockholm, Toronto, Vilnius, Warsaw > NATIVES: John Belushi, Jack Benny, Raymond Chandler, Hillary Clinton, Sam Cooke, Philip K. Dick, Walt Disney, Bobby Fischer, Harrison Ford, Bob Fosse, Benny Goodman, Herbie Hancock, Hugh Hefner, Ernest Hemingway, Ray Kroc, Ring Lardner, David Mamet, Curtis Mayfield, Eliot Ness, Patti Smith, Gloria Swanson, Scott Turow, Raquel Welch, Robin Williams, Florenz Ziegfeld > RESIDENTS: Nelson Algren, Louis Armstrong, Saul Bellow, Al Capone, Buddy Guy, Sara Paretsky, Liz Phair, Muddy Waters, Oprah Winfrey, Frank Lloyd Wright

NEW ORLEANS USA

W.03.06

SOME CITIES ARE defined by a sight, New Orleans is defined by a sound - jazz, that quintessential American art form, with all the cool, the colours and the deep southern drawl that word conjures up. The sound of Buddy Bolden's horn echoes around the globe and the ciy has long blown its trumpet on a ticket of Big Easy intrigue, romance and decadence. That was until August 2005 when Hurricane Katrina and her waves breezed into town, sounding a different note of blue, flooding and destroying 80% of the city, including the prized French quarter of streetcars, filigree iron balconies and colonnades. The city's setting in the swampy bowl of Lake Ponchartain below sea level had conspired both to give birth to a music revolution and be the city's undoing.

Music had been the ultimate bridge between black Africans and the Creoles, descendents of the French settlement of 1717. As they interbred, creating quadroons and octaroons like semi-quavers and demi-semiquavers, a quarter or an eighth black, the forms and fugues of European music fused with the cake-walk, spirituals and worksongs of African slavery. As if by fate, a flurry of diverse instruments arrived in their lap, courtesy of the Spaniards fleeing the Spanish-American war in 1898. With the arrival of the Americans law put Black and Creole together but gave them rights enjoyed by Blacks nowhere else in America. In 1897 city leader Sidney Story declared an area of legalised prostitution known as Storyville, an earthy and licentious, vital yet suicidal place of seedy bordellos and honky-tonk bars that was heaven and deathbed to many jazzmen.

Storyville was closed in 1917, a victim of its own hedonism, and destroyed in the 1940s to make way for ill-advised urban housing projects. But once these too were all but swept away New Orleans had a chance to create a new blueprint for its own rebirth and to ensure that post-Katrina the city could once again walk on sunshine. Amid recriminations of neglect by the Bush administration, New Orleans and Katrina became a political football with every new plan hotly debated by the Bring New Orleans Back Commission. Quarters that are not repopulated will be turned into extra flood defences, while the current mayorship proposes to recreate a sanitised Storyville complete with jazz museum, recording studios and live music venues (but without the prostitution). Congo Square, which had become a sad minor seventh of a square may once again recall, more than a lone statue of Louis Armstrong, the meeting place of the great brass bands. The streets Bourbon, Basin, Burgundy, Canal, Decatur and Perdido may again do justice to their former nocturnal heroes, Ferdinand "Jelly Roll" Morton, Joe King Oliver and Leon "Bix" Beiderbecke.

The New Orleans spirit is unbroken. That delirious, most carnal of carnivals, with its masks, drag-divas, aptly-named Hurricane cocktails and prescient, world-is-nigh Baptists will rise again like Baron Samedi to resume the mantle of creative debauchery. New Orleans, like the best jazz, will always represent life in all its exuberance, mortality and tragedy.

> NEW ORLEANS, LOUISIANA > LONGITUDE: 90°03' W > LATITUDE: 29°58' N > ALTITUDE: 35 feet/11 metres > POPULATION: 484,700 (metro: 1,288,900) > TWINNED WITH: Innsbruck (Austria), Juan-Les-Pins (France), Liverpool, Matsue (Japan), Merida (Mexico), Pointe-Noire (Congo), San Miguel De Tucumán (Argentina), Tegucigalpa (Honduras) > NATIVES: Louis Armstrong, Sydney Bechet, Willie Birch, Buddy Bolden, Truman Capote, Harry Connick Jr, Johnny Dodds, Fats Domino, Thomas Dolby, Lillian Hellman, Mahalia Jackson, Dr John, Wynton Marsalis, Jelly Roll Morton, King Oliver, Neville Brothers, Randy Newman, Lee Harvey Oswald, Andrew Young > RESIDENTS: Professor Longhair, Trent Reznor

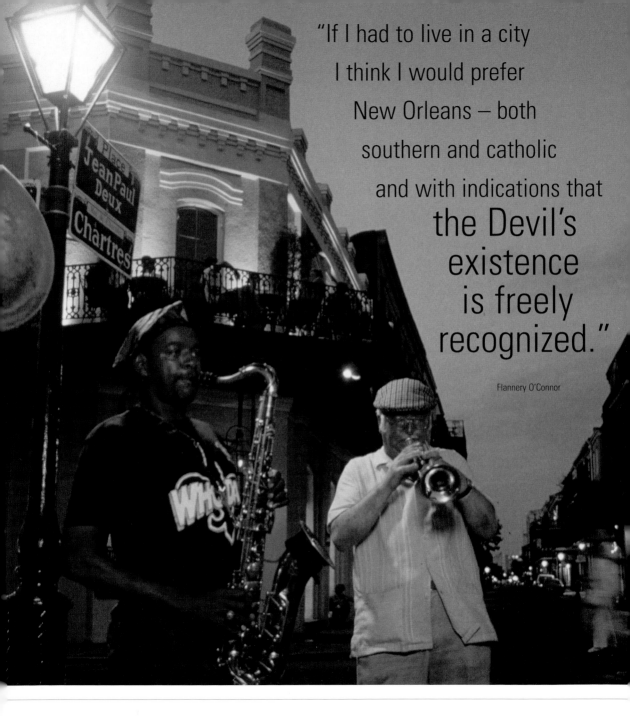

"If I had to live in a city
I think I would prefer
New Orleans – both
southern and catholic
and with indications that
the Devil's
existence
is freely
recognized."

Flannery O'Connor

165

TO THE QUEUES OF VISITORS snaking round the house and gardens at 3734 Elvis Presley Boulevard, Memphis is the home and the final resting-place of the King, a world of shag carpets and gigantic TVs. Graceland is one of America's top three tourist destinations, but what it is *not* is a summation of the parts of Memphis, although Graceland is a reminder of the city's remarkable contribution to the musical heritage of the world. And the Presley estate's commercial nous is an appropriate accompaniment to the Memphian record of entrepreneurial activity: home of Fedex and Holiday Inn, birthplace of the supermarket (Clarence Sanders's Piggly Wiggly, which opened in 1916).

white boys – Elvis, Carl Perkins, Jerry Lee – turned it into rockabilly and rock'n'roll. In the 1960s Booker T's mixed-race rhythm section at Stax Records (Soulsville USA) was there for Otis Redding, Isaac Hayes and Sam and Dave. As befits one of the most church-heavy cities in the States, gospel came courtesy of Al Green and Mahalia Jackson. There is country music besides, just less big hair and fewer rhinestones than in Nashville.

Apart from the music, Memphis has much else: the steamboats, cotton mansions, magnolias, iced tea and barbequed ribs; the legacy of Martin Luther King's gunning down outside Room 306 at the Lorraine Motel – now a museum to civil rights; and the looming

"I don't know of a better place to be on this Earth." Sam Phillips

Before the blues, before Elvis, before Piggly Wiggly, there was the Mississippi, the mighty Muddy, the "strong, brown god" of T.S. Eliot's description. Memphis sits up on a bluff above the river, and it seems to have much more in common with the delta state of Mississippi than the rolling hills of Tennessee, the state in which it actually falls. The river and its trading potential kept the city alive when, after the Civil War, waves of yellow fever threatened to wipe it out (the War had left it relatively unscathed, unlike Atlanta). And from the delta came the black migrants heading north away from poverty – those who stayed in this cotton city left an indelible mark, especially in their music.

Music and Memphis are indissoluble. The great W.C. Handy codified the jug band blues at the beginning of the last century. In the 1920s and '30s Beale Street was thick with bars and theatres and the blues of Robert Johnson and Will Shade. There are fewer gin-soaked bar-room queens these days, but Beale Street still runs up from the river and presents its music in a safely packaged way. Then postwar, B.B. King led the way to R'n'B, and the

32-storey Pyramid building (a deliberate nod to the home country of Memphis's Egyptian namesake), which stands in stark contrast to a city that still has more than a hint of the 1950s about it.

> MEMPHIS, TENNESSEE, USA > LONGITUDE: 90°04' W > LATITUDE: 35°09' N > ALTITUDE: 331 feet/101 metres > POPULATION 650,100 (metro: 1,145,000) > TWINNED WITH: Memphis (Egypt)
> NATIVES: Kathy Bates, Dee Dee Bridgewater, George Coleman, Donald "Duck" Dunn, William Eggleston, Aretha Franklin, Morgan Freeman, Al Jackson Jr, Booker T. Jones, Cybill Shepherd, Memphis Slim, Justin Timberlake, Junior Wells > RESIDENTS: W.C. Handy, John Lee Hooker, Albert King, B.B. King, Sam Phillips, Elvis Presley

167

"It fuses northern and southern qualities, perhaps native and foreign ones rendezvous the whole stretch of the Missouri and Mississippi rivers, and its American electricity goes well with its German phlegm." Walt Whitman

ST LOUIS SITS AT THE CROSSROADS of America's two great roads, route 66 and route 61 (known to jazz aficionados as the Blues Highway), along which the history and development of modern American music can be traced.

St Louis always was something of a transit town, both for musicians and traders. Just south of the confluence of the Mississippi and Missouri rivers, the city was founded by the French fur trader Pierre Laclede, who named it after the Crusader King, Louis IX. The city was built on fur and then, after President Thomas Jefferson had negotiated from Napoleon the Louisiana Purchase of the vast, uncharted expanse to the west, the city became the great staging post for the discovery and expansion of the United States. The achievement of the two explorers Lewis and Clark, who set off from St Louis, is

> ST LOUIS, MISSOURI, USA > LONGITUDE: 90°14' W > LATITUDE: 38°43' N > ALTITUDE: 500 feet/152 metres > POPULATION: 334,000 (metro: 2,603,600) > TWINNED WITH: Bologna, Donegal (Ireland), Galway (Ireland), Georgetown (Guyana), Lyons, Nanjing, St Louis (Senegal), Samara (Russia), Stuttgart, Suwa (Japan), Szczecin (Poland), San Luis Potosí (Mexico) > NATIVES: Maya Angelou, Josephine Baker, Yogi Berra, Linda Blair, William Burroughs, Kate Chopin, Charles Eames, T.S. Eliot, Walker Evans, Joe Garagiola, John Goodman, Betty Grable, Spike Jonze, Kevin Kline, Michael McDonald, Vincent Price, Clark Terry, Shelley Winters > RESIDENTS: Chuck Berry, Jimmy Connors, Miles Davis, Scott Joplin, Jackie Joyner-Kersee, Stan "The Man" Musial, Joseph Pulitzer, Ike & Tina Turner

commemorated by the huge futuristic arch, which has dominated the city's skyline since 1956. From a small community of around 1,000 inhabitants St Louis bulged with fortune-seekers and frontiersmen, in thrall to the myth of the West.

Now that the city had become a transport hub for rail freight and steamboats, St Louis became a port of call for musicians migrating from down south in search of their fortune in the cities of the north. "Meet me in St Louis, Louis" goes the lyric, and the city was born musical when in the early 1900s it was home to Scott Joplin – he of "The Entertainer" and "Maple Leaf Rag", and undisputed king of ragtime. Cornet-player and band-leader W.C. Handy then composed his "St Louis Blues", one of the great jazz standards that has probably been played and rearranged more often and by more jazz musicians than any other twelve-bar. Miles Davis was born across the river in East St Louis, and in the 1950s Chuck Berry pioneered his unique fusion of blues, country and R'n'B here. St Louis was a city open to all the influences that passed through and in turn became a haven for the improvisation at the core of jazz music.

Other than a name that evokes the roots of jazz, modern St Louis has all but said toodle-oo to its musical heritage, and the city now has to play second horn to the great soloist-cities of jazz and blues. The "Deep Morgan" part of town where the greats used to blow hot and cold is run down and deserted, and the city has a classic Marriott-Hyatt-dominated skyline of a business centre that belies the soul that once was its beat – legacy of the 1904 Olympics Games and World Fair. But in the funky Soulard district and loft-warehouse heaven of Laclede's Landing it is still a spirited and congenial city, especially when lubricated by a can of the locally-brewed, original "Bud".

"The difference between St Paul and Minneapolis is the difference between pumpernickel and Wonder Bread." Garrison Keillor

MINNESOTA'S TWIN CITIES are conjoined – Minneapolis on the west side of the Mississippi, St Paul immediately opposite on the east – but they are far from identical. While St Paul is more conservative ("more venerable", its inhabitants would say), Minneapolis, the larger of the two cities, is the bolder, more inquisitive of the pair. St Paul draws on a German, Irish, Catholic tradition; Minneapolis has a Scandinavian, Lutheran heritage. But what they share is a reputation for friendliness, inventiveness and extremely cold winters, and a sense of civic pride that other American cities either envy or find irritatingly smug.

Here at the confluence of the Minnesota and Mississippi rivers, French traders and trappers first set up their posts, before the US acquired the land as part of the Louisiana Purchase of 1803. Just west of the Great Lakes and with the prairies rolling further westward for hundreds of miles, Minneapolis in particular became a hub for the grain industry (as well as for the lumber camps upriver).

Its agricultural heritage is prominent – General Mills and Pillsbury are still based in the city – but though the Mississippi location was what first attracted settlers, the great river here is not the feature it is downstream in St Louis, Memphis or New Orleans. Jonathan Raban, tracing the course of the river, was disappointed to find that the cityscape had effectively canalized and cannibalized the river. "Once, the Mississippi had provided Minneapolis and St Paul with the reason for their existence. Now it wasn't even an impediment. The twin cities went about their business as if the river didn't exist."

To make up for that, Minneapolis – which means "water city" in its Sioux/Greek neologism – has a string of over 20 lakes within its city limits, and each July celebrates its watery traditions with the parades and events of the Aquatennial. The other overriding natural feature, the severe winter colds, it has dealt with through practical Nordic ingenuity. This is, after all the city that invented the post-it note (at 3M, Minnesota Mining and Manufacturing). So glass-clad walkways protect shoppers and commuters from the great chill, and in the suburb of Bloomington, the Mall of America, a gigantic shopping metropolis, complete with its own amusement park, shields visitors from inclement climes.

Minneapolis is far from chilly in personality, though. While St Paul is perhaps more reserved and literary (Scott Fitzgerald was born there), Minneapolis has hot and controversial shows at the Walker Art Center, saw Prince explode onto the scene at the First Avenue club – as well as His Purpleness, the city spawned Hüsker Dü, the Replacements and Soul Asylum – and more theatres and dance companies per capita than New York City. Small wonder they call it the Minnie Apple!

> MINNEAPOLIS, MINNESOTA, USA > LONGITUDE: 93°18' W > LATITUDE: 44°55' N

> ALTITUDE: 3,130 feet/954 metres > POPULATION: 354,590 (metro: 2,968,800) > TWINNED WITH: Eldoret (Kenya), Harbin (China), Ibaraki City (Japan), Kuopio (Finland), Novosibirsk (Russia), Santiago (Chile), Tours (France), Uppsala (Sweden) > NATIVES: The Andrews Sisters, Patty Berg, Jean Paul Getty, Peter Graves, Prince, Charles Schulz, Mike Todd, Anne Tyler, Jesse Ventura, Paul Westerberg, Minor White
> RESIDENTS: Hubert H. Humphrey, Garrison Keillor, Charles Pillsbury

171

HOUSTON HAS A PROBLEM. It may have been the first word ever to be spoken on the moon, but since 1969 the city hasn't really come down to earth. Houston remains an inflated city with a monumental skyline of concrete and glass born amid the certainty of the oil boom, but which, following the 1980s slump, finds itself overweight and outsize, a leviathan with an uncertain purpose.

Mind you, size has never been a worry for Texans. In Texas, size matters. Big hats, big flares, big trucks… in this county big is beautiful. Every year Houston's Reliant Astrodome hosts big-wheel truck championships, and the world's largest livestock and rodeo shows, all fanatically followed with typical Texan zeal and pride by locals dressed in ten-gallons and Stetsons.

But it is Texan excess that makes Houston endearing. Texans are well aware of their own appetite for exaggeration and do not take themselves totally seriously. Like the city's most famous son, millionaire Howard Hughes, it is all part of an eccentric, overbearing and sleazy attitude that is curiously appealing.

For all the glimmering glamour of its skyscrapers, Houston had inauspicious beginnings. In 1837 two brothers arrived from New York with the typically eccentric idea of building the capital of the new Republic of Texas. Barely a river, no obvious natural attributes, just a barren, muddy plateau, but somehow the city developed into a mediocre commercial centre until oil was struck in 1901, feeding a real estate boom – and the rest is history.

Year-round Houston chokes under the combination of heat, humidity and traffic pollution, which sends most of its inhabitants underground into the surreal world of the tunnels – seven subterranean miles (11km) of shops and restaurants. If, outside, the skyline is already futuristic, this brave new world is like a post-apocalyptic bunker universe, a labyrinth of malls and lost souls.

Above ground, in the reflected sunlight, Houston has a surprising artistic heritage. The sidewalks are dotted with modern sculptures, including many by Joan Miró, and there is a whole district devoted to museums containing collections as diverse as Magritte and Malinese African art.

The human face of the city, though, is Montrose, at the junction of Smith and Elgin. Here are retro boutiques, tattoo parlours and weird boutiques selling experimental art or tex kitsch, according to your point of view. This is the heart of Houston's flamboyant gay community, counter-balancing the vertical rigidity of the city's skyscrapers.

The vertical challenge – that metaphysical desire to build immortal monuments in measurement to human vanity – is strongly evident in Houston, from the world's tallest stone column monument that permits a view over the San Jacinto Battleground (where, in 1836, two months after the Alamo, the Texans defeated the skilled Mexican Army), to the Johnson Space Centre, from where all space flight is controlled. Maybe, deep down, Houston's architectural megalomania has always been about reaching for the sky.

"In Houston the air was warm and rich, with a suggestion of fossil fuel…" Joan Didion

> HOUSTON, TEXAS, USA > LONGITUDE: 95°19' W > LATITUDE: 29°43' N > ALTITUDE: 25 feet/8 metres > POPULATION: 1,857,500 (metro: 4,177,600) > TWINNED WITH: Abu Dhabi (UAE), Baku, Cairo, Chiba (Japan), Guayaquil (Ecuador), Huelva (Spain), Istanbul, Leipzig (Germany), Nice, Perth, Shenzen (China), Stavanger (Norway), T'ai-pei, Tyumen (Russia) > NATIVES: Paul 'Red' Adair, Lois Chiles, Shelley Duvall, George Foreman, Lightnin' Hopkins, Howard Hughes, Beyonce Knowles, Lyle Lovett, Eva Mendes, Johny Nash, Billy Preston, P.J. Proby, Dennis Quaid, Randy Quaid, Kenny Rogers, Mike Singletary, Johnny "Guitar" Watson, Jo Beth Williams > RESIDENTS: George W. Bush

DALLAS _{USA}

"If there's a place that nurtures the American Dream,

a city that congratulates you for your fabulous success,

rather than perceive it as a threat, it's Dallas."

Clare de Vries, *I & Claudius*

> DALLAS, TEXAS, USA > LONGITUDE: 96°48' W > LATITUDE: 32°46' N > ALTITUDE: 463 feet/141 metres > POPULATION: 1,188,600 (metro: 3,519,200) > TWINNED WITH: Brno (Czech Republic), Dijon (France), Monterrey (Mexico), Riga, T'ai-pei > NATIVES: Edie Brickell, Charlie Christian, Morgan Fairchild, Don Henley, Michael Johnson, Justin Leonard, Meat Loaf, Robin Wright Penn, Anne Rice, Aaron Spelling, Stephen Stills, Sly Stone, Lee Trevino, Stevie Ray Vaughan, Doak Walker > RESIDENTS: Dick Cheney, Peri Gilpin, Blind Lemon Jefferson, Norah Jones, David "Fathead" Newman, Jack Ruby

FOR A WHILE, during the 1980s, the skyline of Dallas was one of the most famous cityscapes in the world, thanks to the 357 episodes of the soap that was a quintessential product of its era, where the arts of money-making, ruthlessness and revenge went hand in hand. Dallas, a city built on the proceeds of commercial success – first cotton, then oil, and home of the original Neimann-Marcus store – glinted and gleamed in the relentless Texas sunshine like a beacon of prosperity. The glitter of the '80s was as specious in Dallas as elsewhere, but the TV show was a brilliant piece of PR.

Dallas needed it. On 22 November 1963, the city took a massive knock when John F. Kennedy was assassinated in Dealey Plaza. It is bizarre – given the natural inclination of Dallas to eradicate the stain – that the Plaza, a tiny cockpit of a space almost designed for drama, remains recognizably the same four decades on. The underpass of Houston Street still swings down under the railroad bridge. The grassy knoll bobs up stage left. And the Book Depository is now a museum which invariably jerks tears from all but the most hardened anti-Kennedyite. A couple of blocks away, the Conspiracy Museum hardly lessens the scar...

But the TV series, as well as the 1970s success of the Dallas Cowboys – helped no end by their lithe-limbed, ultra-healthy cheerleaders – restored much of the city's pizzazz. The neon Pegasus on top of the 1921 Magnolia Building took flight again. In the year after the railroad arrived in 1872, 725 buildings had risen – Dallas likes to demonstrate its ambition through construction. And no little hubris: the city is disdainful towards the pretentions of Houston, and distinctly superior to what it sees as the cowtown of Fort Worth, the city to which it is joined in the massive Metroplex area. "Dallas," wrote John Gunther, "is a baby Manhattan. Fort Worth is a cattle annex." Fort Worth was the final stop on the old Chisholm Trail to Kansas, and although it has stayed more "Western" than its neighbour, is less full of itself.

That's not to say that Dallas is a horrendously self-centred oil-rich ignoramus. In a throwback to some of its first settlers – a group of French artists, the Réunion collective, who couldn't quite hack the climate in Texas, and eventually moved on – the city is wealthy in artistic enterprise. The extensive Dallas Museum of Art is close by the home of the Dallas Symphony (comfortably cosseted in some 80 million dollars' worth of purpose-built luxury). A tad less ostentatious is the old warehouse district of Deep Ellum, east of downtown, whose bohemian antecedents stretch back to the jazz and blues clubs of the 1920s.

SAN ANTONIO USA

IF HOUSTON IS ALL George Dubya bombast, big architecture and big statements in search of a meaning, San Antonio is the opposite of the Texan stereotype. It's still big, but it's not puffed up like its neighbour. A small-town warmth and assurance about its place in American heritage combine to make it more chilled-out and at one with itself – and a far cry from the skyscrapers, nodding oil pumps and tumbleweed of popular imagination.

That doesn't make San Antonio any less Texan, though. The stubbornness that defines the people of this state is nowhere better enshrined than in the memorial of the Alamo, the mission building from which in 1836 a band of 189 Texan volunteers sought to defend themselves against the Mexican General Santa Anna and 5,000 of his soldiers keen to curb the Anglo expansion. They failed and were wiped out, but the names of Davy Crockett and Jim Bowie passed into American folklore as testament to Texan resilience. What ensued were ten years of independence which Texans feel sets them apart from the rest of the US and for which San Antonio proudly claims the title "birthplace of the revolution".

Originally a small fortified town, the Alamo had been established by Spanish missionaries as a base from which to convert the Coahuiltecan people whose

native American word *tejas*, from which Texas is derived, means "friend". Although it went through an adolescence as a rodeo and oil sin city after the Civil War, the Hispanic influence is still predominant in San Antonio, seen through its Spanish billboards, prevalent Catholicism and Tex-Mex restaurants. It contributes also to the city's laid-back and festive Latin atmosphere and a more passionate Mexican take on country music that floats on the air in the lazy heat of the day. The romantic cobbled promenade of the Paseo del Rio along the San Antonio River is the soul of the modern city, crossed by hump-backed bridges and scented by swathes of pine, cypress and willow. Here for ten days every April San Antonians celebrate the Texan victory at the Battle of San Jacinto with concerts, parades and "cookouts" in the streets.

The rest of the city has grown up with the 20th century but with the maturity of a more self-assured older brother to brattish Houston. Drastic floods in 1920s virtually wiped out the original settlement, whose only remnants are still visible in the district of la Villita, with its plain-walled white adobe houses straight out of a Western film. In the centre of downtown, only the chapel survives of the Alamo, but in its ruined state, especially at night, it still echoes with the ricochets of a gunfight and images of a last stand.

176 > SAN ANTONIO, TEXAS, USA > LONGITUDE: 98°27' W > LATITUDE: 29°22' N > ALTITUDE: 650 feet/198 metres > POPULATION: 1,490,100 > TWINNED WITH: Guadalajara, Kaohsiung (Taiwan, ROC), Kumamoto (Japan), Kwangju (South Korea), Las Palmas (Canary Islands), Monterrey (Mexico), Santa Cruz de Tenerife > NATIVES: Joan Crawford, Christopher Cross, Flaco Jimenez, Oliver North

"The San Antonio River is wound cunningly through the town like a pattern on a Valentine. You have the sensation in San Antonio by day of the world being deliciously excluded." Graham Greene, *The Lawless Roads*

"It is a stunningly grand centre with a scatter of abysmal squalor around its hems, like a mother who keeps herself in style at the expense of her children." William McIlvaney

MEXICO CITY IS A PLACE of superlatives. It is the world's most populous city, a state in its own right. The airport is in the middle of the conurbation, so that, looking down from a plane gliding in, the sensation is that it will touch down right on top of the roofs stretching away apparently to infinity.

The main square, the Zócalo, where each day a clockwork corps of soldiers fastidiously raises a vast Mexican national flag, is claimed to be the largest public space in the world. On one side, the Catedral Metropolitana oversees the world's biggest Catholic diocese. The size of the city can take the first-time visitor's breath away to an almost scarily suffocating extent. Once the initial panic attack has passed, though, a sense of excitement arrives, as the pace and the energy of the place takes over.

Underfoot there is much history: in another of those superlatives, the site of Mexico City has been continually inhabited for two millennia. This was where the Aztecs built Tenochtitlan, the lake city of Montezuma II. When the conquistador Hernando Cortés saw it in 1519, he reported that it was "so great and beautiful that I can hardly say half of what I could say about it, and this part alone is practically unbelievable". However, the Spaniards then razed Tenochtitlan (much to Cortés's regret, by all accounts), reusing the destroyed stonework to rebuild a city in their own vision, and the National Palace on the Zócalo is built not only on the ruins of Montezuma's Palace but on the residence erected by Cortés. Montezuma, of course has had his revenge on travellers ever since.

For centuries Mexico City has been unchallenged as the capital of its country, through centuries of colonial control, through the upheavals of revolution. To the rest of the population, the city swallows up vast amounts of taxpayers' money – allowing its efficient metro system to offer good, cheap fares – but, they grumble, gives very little back in return. The magnet effect of so much centralization has brought an ever-swelling, census-defeating influx of new *chilangos* – as the residents are called – and the cars, taxis and buses that serve them leave a pallor of terracotta-brown smog hanging over the city built on the flat lakebed.

Among the 350 *colonias*, or neighbourhoods, that make up the city, there are retreats from its enormity, or from the commercial freneticism of the Tepito district, "the Wall Street of the black market". The woody Bosque de Chapultepec is Mexico's equivalent of Madrid's Retiro, and the upmarket area of Coyoacán is a tranquil arty community, where the great muralist Diego Riviera and his wife Frida Kahlo once lived. Each *chilango* has to find his or her personal space, just like the fire-eating kids and stilt-walkers blithely performing amid the profusion of green and white VW Beetle taxis that scuttle about inches away.

> MEXICO CITY, MEXICO > LOCAL NAME: México > LONGITUDE: 99°12' W > LATITUDE: 19°24' N > ALTITUDE: 7,287 feet/2,221 metres
> POPULATION: 18,327,000 > TWINNED WITH: Chicago, Los Angeles, Nagoya (Japan) > NATIVES: Rosario Castellanos, Carlos Chávez, Alberto Gironella, Frida Kahlo, Juan O'Gorman, Octavio Paz, Pedro Rodriguez, Alejandro González Iñárritu, Alfonso Cuarón > RESIDENTS: Luis Buñuel, Sergei Eisenstein, Carlos Fuentes, Tina Modotti, Diego Rivera, Léon Trotsky, Gabriel García Márquez

179

ACAPULCO MEXICO

AT NIGHT-TIME, as the lights of Acapulco sparkle beside the waters of the bay below the old coastal road that heads down from the mountains of the Sierra Madre del Sur, it is easy to appreciate what captured the imagination of the famous and the wealthy during the city's golden age in the 1950s.

During the period immediately after the Second World War, while Europe was still in the process of rebuilding itself, Acapulco was exotic and glamorous, a Pacific alternative to the Riviera. Liz Taylor married Mike Todd (husband number two) in a hillside villa; JFK and Jackie honeymooned here – as later, did Bill and Hillary Clinton. They were following in the footsteps of the Duke of Windsor, who had visited Acapulco as Prince of Wales in the 1920s, and of Orson Welles, John Wayne and Errol Flynn, who had headed south from Hollywood.

The same attractions remain. The temperature stays at 31-32°C (88-90°F) almost all year round. There are plenty of soft, sandy beaches, from the original Caleta to the current favourite, Condesa. The sunsets are spectacular, although since the horizon at sea level is blocked by the hills to the west of the horseshoe bay, dedicated aficionados of the crepuscular head along the coast to the beach at Pie de la Cuestra. The tequila sunrises, on the other hand, still go down a treat all night long.

And then there are the cliff divers of La Quebrada, the *clavadistas* whose death-defying leaps into the Mexican waves pulsing 130 feet below have been astonishing visitors since the 1930s, the difficulty quotient increased exponentially by the need to dive outward several feet, since the drop is not vertical, as well as co-ordinating the jump to the split second with the incoming swell. After dusk, the final dive – with torches – is, not surprisingly, a star turn.

Acapulco, of course, contains more than the hotel and beach strip, even if few visitors step outside their comfort zone. Only a few streets away from the seafront lies the real Acapulco: the shady rubber and mango trees of the main square, dirt paths, local bars, and nary a tourist to be seen.

Elsewhere, the old fort of San Diego is a reminder of the first uninvited visitors to this site: the Spaniards arrived in the 1520s. From here they could sail west to Asia, but the return journey proved difficult until the existence of the north trade winds were discovered. Thereafter, for centuries, the so-called Manila Galleon would head off every other year and return from China and the Philippines laden with riches. But once the Mexican War of Independence ended this lucrative shuttle service, Acapulco went into an extended siesta until tourism resuscitated its fortunes.

"If you've seen *Fun in Acapulco* you know the drill for the cliff divers. Climb to the top of the cliff, bless yourself at the shrine of the Virgen de Guadalupe, and jump."

Peter Moore, *The Full Montezuma*

GUADALAJARA IS THE MOST MEXICAN of Mexican cities. Resting on a plateau in Mexico's western Jalisco region just north of the vast pristine inland Chapala Lake it is surrounded by the peaks of the middle Sierra Madre. By day it breathes with the slow post-prandial snore of a sated moustachioed *hombre* asleep in a hammock under the shade of his sombrero.

But for all its siesta feel in the heat of the midday sun, by the Mexican moon Guadalajara transforms into a potently energetic city fuelled by a turbo-charged student population. The rocket fuel that drives them is that most disgusting, beloved and hated of party jump-starters – tequila, distilled from the maguey plant just up

the road in the town of the same name. The bars of downtown Guadalajara are shrines to the spine-shuddering extract of the peyote cactus, with regulars and tourists alike locked in the daredevil lick-slam-wince elbow dance that seems to be the obligatory purgatory on the way to drunken bliss. And if, woe betide, you should desire something a little longer, there's always the comparative soothing sweetness of a Sol beer, topped naturally with a slice of lemon.

But Guadalajara is neither wild nor, for all the 50 per cent proof of its liquor, emancipated. It is, rather, a conservative and traditional place, its trees, flowers and friendliness, and the plethora of colonial architecture and picturesque little plazas lending it an air

"I sat in a square and hired a wandering orchestra to play for me.

For about 50 pence

I got a heartrending song

accompanied by four fiddles, three guitars and a trumpet."

Laurie Lee

of provincial elegance and old-world atmosphere. The 19th-century mansions around the Plaza Tapatia exude patriarchal moral authority while the proud yellow-tiled twin towers of its cathedral dominate the centre-piece Plaza de los Laureles and the old centre, as a sign of the city's profound Catholicism. The energy in the air is the nervous energy of frustrated youth wanting to taste the forbidden fruit (and we're not talking lime here). As Ramon said in D.H. Lawrence's *The Plumed Serpent*, "It is a country where men despise sex, and live for it ... which is suicide."

The southern suburb of Tlaquepaque is the home of the *mariachi* band whose Los Lobos ponchoed imitations are the curse of

seaside restaurants in the Mediterranean but who here still manage to evoke not *la cucuracha* but the uplifting communal spirit of songs round the campfire. Tlaquepaque is something of an artists' colony: residence of artisans and craftsmen working artifacts in a guacamole of native Mexican and Spanish colonial styles; impromptu stage for colourful Mexican *guignol* street theatre productions and blank canvas for painters seeking to be the next Orozco, the region's famous artist-son. One day the worm will turn but, until then, despite the modern trappings of an industrial and commercial hub, Guadalajara will be the guardian of the nachos-and-tacos Mexican tradition.

DENVER REALLY IS THE MILE HIGH CITY. On the fifteenth step of the Colorado State Capitol building a plaque marks a spot precisely 5,280 feet (1,609m) above sea level. But its elevation has not made Denver or its residents high and mighty. Perhaps that's because the city itself is always aware that it is only a stepping-stone to the Rocky Mountains, whose foothills are only 15 miles (24km) away to the west. First-timers in Denver are often surprised that the city is not perched in the mountains themselves. In fact it sits on flat plains – hence its other, and less well known nickname, the Queen City of the Plains.

Just like the residents of Santiago in Chile, Denver's citizens can enjoy outdoor activities right on their doorstep. The wilderness is latticed with cycle trails, and the mountains offer some of the best skiing in North America, if not the world; nearby is Aspen, the legendary resort of "the haves and the have mores". With so much great environment on tap, and blessed with a dry, mild and sunny climate (300 days of sunshine a year, easily competing with the likes of San Diego and Miami Beach), Denverites take full advantage of these wide-open opportunities, and consistently top polls as America's leanest, thinnest citizens. Even their rock'n'roll is healthy and outdoors: the Red Rocks Amphitheatre is a majestic arena, pinioned between two massive outcrops of sandstone, and made famous by U2's *Under A Blood Red Sky*.

Denver is unusual because the city was not created on a major trading and transport route. It is not near a lake, a major river or a natural harbour. It stands where it does simply because the location is where a few flakes of gold were found in 1858; the city's name was a bit of blatant schmoozing towards the then governor of the Kansas Territory, one James W. Denver. Subsequently the city's fortunes were boosted through the lottery of encountering precious mineral resources – silver in the Victorian era (discovered at the inaptly named Leadville), gold again at the end of the 19th century, oil and coal in the 1980s.

The wealth that ensued was wisely spent: Denver is full of elegant parks and fountains, adding a civilized veneer to the original prospector-cum-desperado mood of the city. This blend created a vibe that attracted Jack Kerouac and the beat boys in the 1950s. They liked the "Western" feel of Denver (although it's actually the most central city in the USA after Kansas City) – and probably the beer. This is the home of Coors and myriad micro-breweries, especially in LoDo, the lower downtown area, which retains something of that down-home, bohemian feel amid the hi-tech glass of the *Dynasty*-style skyscrapers along 17th Street.

> "Here I was in Denver.
> # I stumbled along with the most wicked grin of joy in the world,
> among the bums and
> beat cowboys of Larimer Street."
>
> Jack Kerouac

> DENVER, COLORADO, USA > LONGITUDE: 105°02' W > LATITUDE: 39°45' N > ALTITUDE: 5,280 feet/1,609 metres > POPULATION: 554,600 (metro: 2,109,300) > TWINNED WITH: Aksum (Ethiopia), Brest (France), Chennai, Cuernavaca (Mexico), Karmi'el (Israel), Kunming (China), Nairobi, Potenza (Italy), Takayama (Japan), Ulan Bator > NATIVES: Tim Allen, Douglas Fairbanks Snr, James McDonnell, Ruth Mosko Handler, Paul Whiteman > RESIDENTS: "Unsinkable" Molly Brown, Neal Cassady, Gary Hart, Jack Kerouac, Linda Lovelace, Golda Meir

SANTA FE USA

SANTA FE HAS SURVIVED its most challenging test, when, during the 1980s and 1990s, it became *the* desirable destination for the upwardly mobile and artistically aspirational of the United States, a "sagebrush Shangri-La", as *People* magazine announced. Santa Fe Style – a mixture of pueblo chic and hippy New Mexicana – was made tangible by chains of red chile *ristras*, native American rugs and beehive fireplaces. The smell of *piñon* and cedar and the tinkling of wind chimes drifted in the air. Chef Mark Miller created a distinctive, spicy local *haute cuisine* at his Coyote Café. There was even a Ralph Lauren Santa Fe paint range.

The city has got through the most pretentious excesses of those times and settled back into a more tranquil life, where the best of its individuality can emerge in a gentle and relaxed way. Up on a high plateau against the backdrop of the Sangre de Cristo Mountains, and bathed in a sharp desert light, its scenic attractions have been charming a group of artists and writers since the beginning of the last century, amongst them D.H. Lawrence, Ansel Adams and the patron saint of Santa Fe art, Georgia O'Keefe.

There is a warmth and intimacy about the centre of Santa Fe, a small-town scale which is enhanced by the low level of the curvaceous adobe buildings, none of which can rise higher than the towers of the St Francis Cathedral which dominates the east side of the main Plaza. Even the McDonalds is strictly adobe-clad. Nearby, the rounded walls and timber beams of the Museum of Fine Arts are some of the finest examples of pueblo revival architecture, built in 1918 at a time when Victorian elements were being stripped back to what was already being called the Santa Fe style.

The Spanish heritage of the city of the Holy Faith (founded in the 1590s, the city became part of Mexico in 1821 before the US Army occupied it in 1846) is best reflected by the original Palace of the Governors. The original inhabitants of the area, the Navajo and Apache tribes, retain something of their culture and their dignity in the pueblos scattered north of Santa Fe, of which Taos is the most renowned, but the smaller settlements like San Ildefonso and Santa Clara are less touristic, where the latest generations of potter-artist families produce exquisite geometric designs.

Los Alamos, where Robert Oppenheimer and his Manhattan Project colleagues devised the atom bomb, squats up in the mountains above the pueblos (managing to be simultaneously banal and sinister), but back down in Santa Fe, the *mañana* pace and dream-catcher vibe of life eases away such painful and mass-destructive memories – such is the soothing and addictive effect of the self-styled "City Different".

105°57' W

> SANTA FE, NEW MEXICO, USA > LONGITUDE: 105°57' W > LATITUDE: 35°42' N > ALTITUDE: 6,989 feet/2,130 metres > POPULATION: 147,600
> TWINNED WITH: Bukhara, Holguin (Cuba), Parral (Mexico), Sorrento (Italy) > RESIDENTS: Mary Austin, Witter Bynner, Tom Ford, D.H. Lawrence

"The moment I saw the brilliant, proud morning shine high over the deserts of Santa Fe, something stood still in my soul." D.H. Lawrence

SALT LAKE CITY USA

SUCH WERE THE WORDS of the Mormon founder of Salt Lake City, who obviously found something appropriately austere in this windswept corner of the world to call it home. The towering rocks of the great Wasatch Mountain front – towering even in this most outsize and Blefuscan of landscapes – form a divide between Utah's lush valleys to the east and the great dry alkaline basin of the Salt Lake to the north-west, the largest inland body

night, beneath the rather soulless stalagmites of skyscrapers, the highway-wide streets reminiscent of Moscow, are deserted. The place is as dead as the Dead Sea.

But Salt Lake City is all about the great outdoors. Not far from the city are the great ski-resorts of Alta, Snowbird and Park City, permanently cloaked in virgin powder snow that won the city the 2002 winter Olympics. In January each year, high up in a location

"This is the place."

Brigham Young

of salt water in the world, which Cecil Roberts deemed to be "of no use, even for suicide". That was in the age before land-speed record attempts, but his words paint a picture of how big the sky is in these parts. And yet on this plain, flatter than the pristine but uninhabitable expanses of canyon country that define the rest of the state, is where, like a mirage in a desert, Utah finds its capital.

Salt Lake City is no oasis to the traveller seeking a thirst-slaking beer. Almost as dry as its setting, this is the world headquarters of the Mormon Church. Originally arriving in 1847, the Mormons still account for 70 per cent of the population. Their strict drinking laws all but forbid the liberal consumption and public display of alcohol: beer here is served only in private clubs that charge a nominal membership for a pleasure less profane than that normally served up by establishments of such description. And so Salt Lake City is probably not the place to come on a stag weekend – the streets at

that knocks the spots off Hollywood and Cannes, Park City hosts the prestigious Sundance Film Festival.

From Temple Square the startling, tall granite spires of the Mormon answer to St Peter's towers above all other buildings, acting as the focal point of the city. From here the church administers its agrarian family values, which in recent years have created a fiercely pro-mining and anti-conservationist population at odds with the beauty of their environment.

While not supporting alcohol consumption, the Mormons did, until recently, believe polygamy a more constructive use of one's time. But Oscar Wilde felt that in so doing, Salt Lake City, along with its "execrable architecture", rather robbed life of romance – "for the romance of life is that one can love so many people and marry but one". An opinion to be taken with more than a pinch of the local mineral…

> SALT LAKE CITY, UTAH, USA > LONGITUDE: 111°54' W > LATITUDE: 40°42' N > ALTITUDE: 4,330 feet/1,320 metres > POPULATION: 181,700 (metro: 1,333,900) > TWINNED WITH: Matsumoto City (Japan)
> NATIVES: Roseanne Barr, Frank Borzage, Neal Cassady, Paul McCarthy, Loretta Young > RESIDENTS: Brigham Young

"A week in Vegas is like stumbling into a time war a regression to the late 1950s. This was Bob Hope's tur Frank Sinatra's. Spiro Agnew's." Hunter S. Thompson

LAS VEGAS USA

IT WOULD BE UNWISE – not to mention medically inadvisable – to encounter Las Vegas whilst loaded with as much tequila, amyl and mescaline as Hunter S. Thompson's Raoul Duke, but it is certainly best to clap eyes on it with as open a mind as possible. For maximum anticipation, the flight in at night is hard to beat, when, after mile upon mile of pitch-black Mojave Desert, the lights along the fabled Strip burst into view like the most garish fairground ride ever invented.

Down on the ground the pace is unrelenting (though in daylight the casinos just look tatty and tawdry). The city is literally explosive – and not just thanks to the nearby nuclear test site – with the most dynamic growth of anywhere in America: a mere 6 out of 100 inhabitants are natives. Seventy years ago Las Vegas – Spanish for "the meadows" – was a sleepy railroad siding of 8,000 people. What turned its fortunes around was the decision by the US government to dam the Hoover River. Construction work and a wartime air force base provided human fodder in need of amusement. Nevada's legislators provided legal casino gambling. By the tail-end of the 1940s the bootleggers and gangsters were in situ, led by Bugsy Siegel, whose Flamingo hotel set the tone of neon and plush velvet. Vegas was ready to rock, and the Rat Pack were heading into town. By the end of the 1960s Howard Hughes was in residence at the Desert Inn, and Elvis at the Hilton.

The Mob connections have been apparently cauterized, and the focus now is on family leisure. The casinos, taking their cue from the first themed venues – Circus Circus and Caesar's Palace in the 1960s – have taken folly to new heights. The surreal faux cityscapes of the Venetian, Paris and New York, New York have irrevocably changed the skyline. Only the vacant stare of the out-of-town innocents robotically working the one-armed bandits remains the same. The rest of old Vegas is gone, apart from an occasional glimpse: the neon sign at the Stardust, or Glitter Gulch downtown.

Beyond the entertainment and the gambling, there are glimpses of fine culture and some classy buildings like the neoclassical Clark County Library. Yet even the treasures of the Guggenheim Hermitage gallery seem less real here than the bejewelled quail's eggs on show at the Liberace Museum. In Las Vegas reality should be checked at the door. Nowhere else can you roll up to Miss Charolette's Little Wedding Chapel – 24-hour drive-up marriages a specialty (as Britney Spears found to her cost!) – before booking into the Tropicana, blowing your life savings at craps, and hightailing it out of town with your reputation and bank balance in tatters. Vegas, Lost Wages, the greatest Gonzo city in the world.

> LAS VEGAS, NEVADA, USA > LONGITUDE: 115°09' W > LATITUDE: 36°10' N
> ALTITUDE: 2,030 feet/619 metres > POPULATION: 1,563,300 > TWINNED WITH: Banes (Cuba),
Huludao (China), Phuket (Thailand) > NATIVES: Andre Agassi, Jenna Jameson, Jack Kramer
> RESIDENTS: Howard Hughes, Liberace, Benjamin "Bugsy" Siegel, Siegfried & Roy

"Welcome to Tijuana
Tekila, Sexo y Marijuana
Welcome to Tijuana
Con el Coyote no hay Aduana."

Manu Chao, *Clandestino*

> TIJUANA, BAJA CALIFORNIA, MEXICO > LONGITUDE: 117°02' W > LATITUDE: 32°29' N > ALTITUDE: 125 feet/38 metres > POPULATION: 1,210,800
> TWINNED WITH: Inglewood CA, Pusan (South Korea), San Diego CA

ACCORDING TO LA MIGRA, the Mexican-US border patrol police, Tijuana is the most visited city and largest consulate in the world – an ironic reference to the city's transitory population of desperadoes and fortune-seekers trying to cross the "Tortilla curtain" into the United States.

Here the American Dream is big business, organized like a parallel, underworld civil service. Here are the *pollos* (migrant chickens) – merchandise without documentation – and the *coyotes* – selling them dreams in the form of passports visas and employment in LA or San Diego. Everybody here wants or needs to be someone else – a new identity for a new life. The state archives of Baja California are full of people who have never died, their identities taken on in perpetuity by a series of impostors and new incarnations. Then there are the *polleros*, employers who take a cut of the *pollo's* salary, and the opportunist bounty-hunters who pick off the night-time border raiders, knowing they are carrying their worldly possessions as they attempt to cross the toxic Tijuana River Canal. This is the real Wild West.

The flight north is not the only migration here. TeeJay, as the city is known to young Americans, symbolizes coming of age. At weekends, under-21s pile south from San Diego in their Recreational Vehicles to get drunk, get laid and "get primitive". It is a rite of passage. They flock into the bars, clubs and brothels of Avenida Revolución – El Main Street – in search of margaritas, both the liquid and lithe varieties, returning, or being returned, north in the early hours of the morning, slammed on tequila and with Mexican wrath at their backs pealing inwardly "Yanqui go

home!" TeeJay is also a convenience store for older Americans who come here for anything from drugs and divorces to teeth, car parts, Aids cures and orphans to adopt. Tijuana's registers are full of mysterious weekend "births".

Strangely, Tijuana's tequila-and-brothels reputation has turned this ultimate frontier town into an artists' muse. As a meeting-point for chancers it's an experimental and liberating place. The combination of San Diego glitz, factory life and extraordinary mixture of architecture – Moorish, Spanish colonial, Chinese and art deco rolled into one – has attracted installation artists, photographers and musicians. TeeJay D.J. Ramon Bostich pioneered the Nortec sound here, a fusion of traditional Mexican and electronic rhythms.

But this cannot take away from the bizarre waiting-room-cum-party zone atmosphere that will define Tijuana as long as it remains a Mexican version of the Cold War, on the cusp of two worlds. There are millions who never make it, condemned to live among the piles of tin, tyres and rusting cars of shanty towns all along the chain-link fence. While others, by a matter of miles more fortunate in their birthplace, return home merry, having lost their virginity and their childhood to the real world.

BELOW THE CACTUS GARDEN OF THE Getty Museum up on the crest of the Hollywood Santa Monica Mountains, Los Angeles spreads – yes, sprawls – across the flatlands below, drifting off into the unconsciousness of the outer suburbs somewhere beyond the haze, rubbing up against the inviting blue of the Pacific Ocean just to the right. The city lies there, semi-naked, on display for all to see. Depending on your point of view, LA is vulnerable, confused, and an easy target for cheap jibes, or a leathery, hardened pro, constantly hustling another trick.

The critics have always had a field day here – mostly along the lines of a lack of intellectual and cultural substance. Dorothy Parker wrote that the only "ism" here was plagiarism; Neil Simon, another inveterate East Coaster, that "it's like paradise, with a lobotomy". "A big hard-boiled city with no more personality than a paper cup," contributed Raymond Chandler. Los Angeles rides these punches because it knows that most of the critics are desperate to come and sign a deal here. Hollywood is not all of LA, not by a very long chalk, but it dominates the spirit of the place. The star-struck kids from Iowa and the languid script-writers from London (always "in development") have all been drawn by the prospect of glamour, fame, wealth – and a generally fabulous climate.

Hollywood Boulevard, despite a recent wash and brush-up, is still a little tawdry and disappointing, like seeing the back of a set on the Universal Studios tour, but the sign is still an unmistakeable and strangely thrilling landmark. What the movie industry has done is give the world a vague, befuddled impression of familiarity with Los Angeles – its streets, condos, tar pits and empty watercourses always a handy location – but on arrival no sense of geography or place.

And that, in a funny way, is the city's undoubted charm. Each area, each suburb – spinning like a mirrorball to refract LA's multiple personalities – offers up a new experience waiting to be discovered, bit by bit: Marilyn Monroe's neat grave near relaxed Westwood Village; the small downtown with its clutch of skyscrapers (as if a location director had been told to "give me a downtown"); Beverly Hills, where Rodeo Drive is surprisingly cute; the much-maligned South Central; and the lesser known, lesser visited – little Tokyo, the Hispanic markets of East LA, the grittier portside of San Pedro, Pasadena's low-key gentility.

There is no better way, the only way in truth, to discover LA than in an open-topped car, cruising the city designed for automobile life, arm out, shades on, Sheryl Crow or a latino station cranked up on the system, driving down Santa Monica Boulevard to where the city stops and the surf begins, as far west – or so it feels – as you could ever wish to go.

"It's the place where the sky is always blue and so are the screen-writers."

Maureen Lipman

> LOS ANGELES, CALIFORNIA, USA > LONGITUDE: 118°15' W > LATITUDE: 34°01' N > ALTITUDE: 297 feet/91 metres > POPULATION: 3,694,800 (metro: 9,519,300) > TWINNED WITH: Athens, Auckland, Berlin, Bordeaux, Eilat (Israel), Giza (Egypt), Guangzhou, Jakarta, Kaunas (Lithuania), Lusaka (Zambia), Makati (Philippines), Mexico City, Nagoya (Japan), Mumbai, Pusan (South Korea), Salvador, Split, St Petersburg, T'ai-pei, Vancouver > NATIVES: Herb Alpert, Drew Barrymore, Beck, Busby Berkeley, John Cage, Ry Cooder, David Crosby, Leonardo di Caprio, Mia Farrow, Jodie Foster, Dustin Hoffman, Angelica Huston, Ice Cube, Etta James, Florence Griffith Joyner, Diane Keaton, Liza Minnelli, Marilyn Monroe, Isamu Noguchi, Ryan O'Neal, Bonnie Raitt, Robert Redford, Sally Ride, Charlie Sheen, Adlai Stevenson > RESIDENTS: J. Paul Getty, Alfred Hitchcock, David Hockney, Hugh Hefner, Richard Neutra, Mary Pickford, Simon Rodia, Phil Spector, Igor Stravinsky, Gloria Swanson

SEATTLE USA

> SEATTLE, WASHINGTON, USA > LONGITUDE: 122°20' W > LATITUDE: 47°36' N > ALTITUDE: 14 feet/4 metres > POPULATION: 540,000 (metro: 2,414,600) > TWINNED WITH: Beer Sheva (Israel), Bergen (Norway), Cebu (Philippines), Chongqing (China), Christchurch (NZ), Galway (Ireland), Gdynia (Poland), Haiphong (Vietnam), Kaohsiung (Taiwan, ROC), Kobe (Japan), Limbe (Cameroon), Mazatlán (Mexico), Mombasa, Nantes, Apolo Ohno, Pécs (Hungary), Perúgia (Italy), Reykjavik, Sihanoukville (Cambodia), Surabaya (Indonesia), Taejon (South Korea), Tashkent > NATIVES: Paul Allen, Carol Channing, Judy Collins, Frances Farmer, Bill Gates, David Gutenberg, Jimi Hendrix, Robert Joffrey, Gypsy Rose Lee, Mary McCarthy, Duff McKagan, Mark Morris, Apolo Ohno, Jessica Stockholder, Jennifer Warnes, Minoru Yamasaki

"You gotta understand Seattle. It's grungy. They're building airplanes all the time, and there's a lot of noise, and there's rain and musty garages. Musty garages create a certain noise." Duff McKagan, Guns N' Roses

SEATTLE ALWAYS HAD A HISTORY of boom and bust, of chancers and entrepreneurs acting on a hunch and riding the crest of some short-lived wave. Founded by pioneers after the Duwamish native Americans had been chased out (the city is named after the native American chief Sealth) it became the staging post for dollar-eyed gold prospectors rushing to plunder the minerals of Alaska. The age of flight saw the birth of the local Boeing dynasty. Local boy Bill Gates founded his Microsoft empire here, giving a new meaning to the word "windows" and silicon paving the way for the birth of the Internet and a thousand Seattle-based dot-coms, including, most famously, Amazon.

These modern-day pioneers grew rich in the early 1990s and the city with it, but the 30-year-old millionaires are few these days, and the city is experiencing a relative trough. But never mind, the locals can always fall back on the couch counsel of the world's most famous radio psychologist, local doctor, Frasier Crane.

Failing that there is always the caffeine tiramisu of "lah-tey", cappuccino and frappaccino; tall, skinny, regular or half-shot – frothed up just about any way you could want and from any variety of bean. This is the home of the caffeine craze currently keeping Seattle sleepless and captivating the noses and taste buds of commuters every morning from Seattle all the way to Beijing.

Sometimes referred to as an urban creek, Seattle lies on the Puget Sound on America's West Coast just south of the Canadian border. Behind the city rise Mount Rainier and other peaks of the Olympic Mountains, a backdrop Seattle shares with its up-coast Canadian neighbour, Vancouver. The two cities also share the same copious rain-clouds, and the joke that the locals don't tan, they just rust, is as good as interchangeable. More cheerfully both cities share a love of the outdoors, fitness and sport. Rude health is a religion and Seattle-ites generally have flush complexions. They are never knowingly without backpacks, fleeces and sneakers ready for the next hike, bike-ride or sail.

It's not all greedy entrepreneurs and tanned (or rusted) sports pros, though. Here equally there is art and above all the sound of creative discontent and disaffected youth. Birthplace of Jimi Hendrix, Seattle is also the cradle of grunge music and the flannel-and-jeans Seattle Sound of Nirvana and the Pearl Jam. In Fremont is Seattle's eccentric artists' colony, while downtown, amid Pioneer Sqaure and the iconic Space Needle observation tower of the *Frasier* credits sequence, is Frank Gehry's Experience Music Project, inspired by the shape of drums and rock guitars. Like many cities Seattle is rediscovering its neglected urban spaces: the bizarre underground district of basement houses, the original Skid Row, created by the 1889 fire, is now a tourist attraction. The centre-piece Pike Place Market is one of America's great markets. Along the reborn Elliot Bay waterfront and in Belltown, Seattle's new generation of pioneers are plotting the next American Dream.

SAN FRANCISCO USA

SAN FRANCISCO HAS A PERVERSE individuality all its own. Its liberality and tolerance has often been at odds with the prevailing moral tone of Middle America. Its climate, with sudden fogs and chills (Bob Hope once quipped that the city had four seasons… all in one day) is resolutely out of kilter with the traditional perception of California's sunshine. And across the hills which switchback up and down next to the waters of the San Francisco Bay, the streets do not wind around the contours like those of Lisbon or Marseilles – instead a grid system that Manhattan would be proud of was imposed, regardless of the gravitational implications.

The hills are one of San Francisco's trademark elements. Since 1873, when Scots engineer Andrew Hallidie created the concept of the cable-car after seeing a horrendous accident when a horse-drawn carriage slithered out of control, the bell-ringing cars have continued to haul themselves and their passengers – or rather have been hauled – at 9½ miles (15km) an hour up and over the downtown streets. In fact, the cable cars are a luxury. San Francisco, unlike LA for example, was built not for automobiles but for human beings, and, like old European city centres, is immensely walkable, whether in the original Mission quarter or along the waterfront promenades.

There is a lot of waterfront, as with the hills goes the Bay: within it lies the squat lump of Alcatraz, above and over it arches the rust-red Golden Gate Bridge, which finally opened in 1937 following years of debate about its practicality in an area of high winds and currents, and promptly became a symbol of success during an era of depression. It also formed part of the great rebuilding of San Francisco, which – after the end of a great age when the Gold Rush and later silver discoveries had padded the fortunes of the grandees on Nob Hill – was flattened by the earthquake and fire of 1906. "San Francisco is gone", Jack London had written in sadness after the disaster; but the city bounced back.

Its resilience is matched by its inclusiveness. This is a city of neighbourhoods, each of which is not only tolerated but celebrated (though even in funky SF they have not always been). One of the largest Chinatowns in the world is balanced by the lesser-known Japantown. North Beach was the haunt of Lawrence Ferlinghetti and the beat generation. Haight-Ashbury and the Fillmore Auditorium hosted peace and love, the Grateful Dead, Jefferson Airplane and Ken Kesey's Merry Pranksters. And the Castro has been the city's gay centre since the 1960s – "in this town," wrote Armistead Maupin, "the Love That Dare Not Speak Its Name almost never shuts up". With so many options, so many facets, it is truly little surprise that so many people have lost their heart to (or left it in) the vertiginous streets of San Francisco.

> SAN FRANCISCO, CALIFORNIA, USA > LONGITUDE: 122°25' W > LATITUDE: 37°45' N > ALTITUDE: 63 feet/19 metres > POPULATION: 776,700 (metro: 7,107,100) > TWINNED WITH: Abidjan, Assisi, (Italy), Caracas, Cork, Esteli (Nicaragua), Haifa (Israel), Ho Chi Minh City, Manila, Osaka, Paris, Seoul, Shanghai, Sydney, T'ai-pei, Thessaloniki > NATIVES: Ansel Adams, Dorothy Arzner, David Belasco, Rosie Cazals, Isadora Duncan, Clint Eastwood, Robert Frost, Jerry Garcia, William Randoph Hearst, Lonnie Johnson, Steve Jobs, Paul Kantner, Bruce Lee, Monica Lewinsky, Jack London, Courtney Love, Johnny Mathis, Richard Serra, O.J. Simpson, Christy Turlington, Natalie Wood > RESIDENTS: Maya Angelou, Lawrence Ferlinghetti, Bill Graham, Dashiell Hammett, Armistead Maupin, Harvey Milk, Carlos Santana, Robert "Birdman of Alcatraz" Stroud

"San Francisco put on a show for me. The afternoon sun painted her white and gold – rising on her hills like a noble city in a happy dream. A city on hills has it over flat-land places."

John Steinbeck

"Nobody's really sure what the pot laws are, but there seem to be an awful lot of very funky-looking people roaming the streets."

Doug Coupland

> VANCOUVER, BRITISH COLUMBIA, CANADA > LONGITUDE: 123°08' W > LATITUDE: 49°16' N > ALTITUDE: 9 feet/3 metres > POPULATION: 545,700 (metro: 1,986,965)
> TWINNED WITH: Chiba City (Japan), Edinburgh, Los Angeles, Odessa, Yokohama (Japan) > NATIVES: Michael Bublé, Hayden Christensen, Doug Coupland, Karl Urban, Jeff Wall > RESIDENTS: William Gibson, Jessica Stockholder

SET BETWEEN AN ARCHIPELAGO of Pacific islands and snow-tipped mountains cloaked in cedar trees, to most people Vancouver is a city of scenery.

The city coasts quite shamelessly on what's on its doorstep: you can ski Whistler in the morning, sail the Strait of Georgia in the afternoon and be back to groove in downtown Vancouver after sundown. Every third car is a Winnebago, has a trailer with a boat, or boards on top. This is the ultimate Tommy Hilfiger city where everyone walks around in vulgar health wearing deck shoes and polo shirt or fleece, Vancouver's official and ubiquitous fabric.

So far from its centre, Vancouver considers itself different from the rest of Canada. Founded at the dawn of the 20th century as a sawmill settlement called Gastown, it was renamed after its discoverer, Captain George Vancouver. Today the capital of BC is one of the world's youngest cities.

With youth comes freedom from historical baggage, and the city has always had a bit of a rebellious streak. A Vancouver basement saw the birth of the Greenpeace movement in 1971. General mistrust for corporations secured a strong Vancouverite attendance at the 1999 Seattle WTO demonstrations. Vancouver's green lobby (virtually every citizen) is protective of its vast and beloved Stanley Park, a symbol of post-logging rebirth. The city still has no freeways.

Vancouver was always the country's alternative, experimental city with a thriving hippy and gypsy culture. Local government tolerates the mass cultivation of pot, earning it the affectionate sobriquet, Vansterdam. Like a Generation X kid, it may not know what it wants to be when it grows up, but right now it's just happy being young.

Maybe it was so as not to deflect from the setting, but Vancouver is a city of concrete, glass and cedar brutalism, its identikit skyline doubling as New York, New Orleans or Denver in the city's thriving film industry (nicknamed Brollywood on account of the excessive local rainfall).

But the quality of life in this green city is regularly deemed to be the highest in the world. Stanley Park is the world's largest urban park where you can lose yourself and not know you're in a city at all. Framed by the Lions Gate Bridge the harbour of Burrard Inlet is home to love-boats and seaplanes, its sea wall a rush hour of rollerbladers and joggers. North Van's beautiful sculpt themselves on the beaches of residential Kitsilano, while South Van's bohemians muse and celebrate the city's First Nations history under the bridge on Granville Island. Vancouver's dominant Asian and Indian populations ensure a varied Pacific-rim fusion cuisine to go with the blueberry jam and syrup of the Japanese maples that set the city on fire in Fall. And just over the horizon under the arched back of leaping orcas is the silhouette of Vancouver Island, just a BC ferry ride away.

ALASKA DOES NOT conjure up metropolitan images. "The great land of the west" – as the word Alayeska translates from the native American Athabascan language – is supposed to be the last frontier, perhaps the last great wilderness between the earth's two poles, a blank canvas on which to paint dreams of adventure and hallucinations – not the kind of place where you want to linger among city values and claustrophobia.

But Anchorage has always been just as much a frontier land in itself. The city was attracting frontiersmen long before Alaska became a playground to cruise ships, heli-skiers, bear tourists and salmon fishers wrapped in the latest Gore-Tex® and Berghaus protection.

The first settlers were Russian fur-trappers from across the Bering Sea who came to trade their minerals for valuable coats with the Native Americans. Captain Cook paid a visit in 1778 while in search of the north-west passage, naming the narrow strip of water in whose bay the city lies after himself. A series of other booty attracted more and more prospectors: first gold-diggers, then logging companies and most recently oil speculators. In its early years, Anchorage was a windswept one-horse town in a cold version of the Wild West.

Wedged underneath the imposing flat-top Chugach Mountains the modern city was founded in 1915 as a tent city for construction-workers building the Alaska Railroad. Today it is as functional as it was intended to be. No aesthetic ambition has ever been projected onto this city to try to turn it into a piece of urban heritage. The city is laid out on a grid like a microchip, a mixture of old 1930s brownstone-like town houses and the faceless blocks of global homogeny.

Like Panama and Istanbul, Anchorage is one of the world's real crossroads cities, set at the edge of the American continent, equidistant between Tokyo and New York. A noticeable legacy and influence from Japan and Russia lends the place a strange cosmopolitan air and, down the uniquely named Northern Lights Boulevard, a surprising night-life and varied cuisine.

Anchorage seems to be set up to service the requirements of loners and adventurers returning after a period in the mind-altering wilderness in search of restoration and home comforts, the conveniences, fun and services of urban reality. Often, as in the Wild West, this means that the apparently innocuous hotels, bars and clubs have a none-too-hidden louche pay-by-the-hour side.

The city is "just half an hour from Alaska", so the joke goes, and down the inlet are indeed the awesome fjords of the Kenai peninsula, the chance to see the outsize grizzly Kodiak bear and be bitten by Alaska's state bird, the mosquito. Anchorage may not be what people come to see, but the capital of America's 49th state is still a pretty unusual, at times surreal, place. Where else is the traffic regularly held up by a gormless moose crossing the road?

> ## "Anchorage isn't Alaska – but you can see it from here."
>
> Local saying

> ANCHORAGE, ALASKA, USA > LONGITUDE: 149°52' W > LATITUDE: 61°12' N > ALTITUDE: 114 feet/35 metres > POPULATION: 260,300 > TWINNED WITH: Chitose (Japan), Darwin (Australia), Inch'on (South Korea), Magadan (Russia), Tromsø (Norway), Whitby (UK) > NATIVES: Irene Bedard, Nina Kemppel > RESIDENTS: Byron Birdsall, Dana Stabenow   203

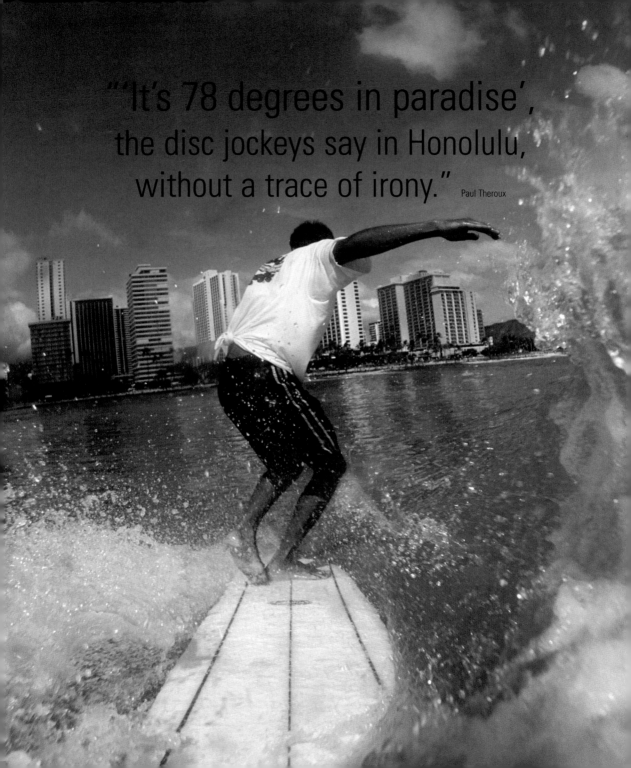

"'It's 78 degrees in paradise', the disc jockeys say in Honolulu, without a trace of irony." Paul Theroux

HONOLULU USA

HONOLULU IS BY FAR the most exotic city in the whole of the United States. The most traditionally exotic, that is: it is the only US city located in the tropics and the only one which can claim to contain a genuinely royal palace. After the Second World War, when the attack on Pearl Harbor, just to the west of Honolulu, had brought swarms of US conscripts to Hawaii, the victors headed back to their hometowns throughout the States and unleashed a fad for all things Polynesian. Ukulele-playing, surfing, gaudy *aloha* shirts, hula hoops and bamboo-clad clubs offering dodgy coconut-flavoured cocktails all created an ersatz but enticing vision of the delights to be found in Hawaii and its capital Honolulu.

The visitors are still flying in. At times, the strip of beach and sand along the front at Waikiki, Honolulu's tourist enclave, is reportedly one of the most dense concentrations of human beings in the world. What they have come for is not difficult to work out. Like Acapulco, Honolulu offers the virtual guarantee of sun, sea and sand (plus surfing) in a sumptuous natural environment on the shores of the Pacific. The whole chain of Hawaiian islands are the residues of volcanic activity: two extinct volcanoes rise above Honolulu. The trademark Diamond Head, to the south-east of the city, is a grass-

lined cone of 762 feet (232m) down which the locals slide on *holya* land-sledges; the Punchbowl is a military cemetery.

Below them, the city is split into two clear sections. Honolulu proper, the compact downtown area, includes Victorian-style houses and the Puritan churches erected by missionaries arriving to proselytize the relaxed Hawaiians with their stern religion. Next to a plaza on King Street, the Iolani Palace, constructed in 1882 by King David Kalakaua, is a reminder of Hawaii's indigenous royal family (who were great ukulele-players well before the 1950s revival, by the way), and contains the room that acted as a set for Jack Lord in *Hawaii Five-O*.

Right next door to downtown, but somewhat isolated by the Ala Wai Canal, is Waikiki. Since 1901, when the first hotel went up on this reclaimed swampland, the quarter has been 100 per cent dedicated to tourism: the area was a favourite retreat of the royals, since it was rich in coconut groves yet free of the dreaded mosquito. The patronage of the Rockefellers and the Roosevelts, who stayed at the 1920s Royal Hawaiian Hotel, known as the Pink Palace, and which is still right on the beach, helped add the necessary kudos and glamour. The tales of the GIs returning from the Pacific theatre of war did the rest.

> HONOLULU, HAWAII, USA > LONGITUDE: 157°52' W > LATITUDE: 21°19' N > ALTITUDE: 7 feet/2 metres > POPULATION: 876,200 > TWINNED WITH: Caracas, Hiroshima (Japan), Hue (Vietnam), Manila, Mumbai, San Juan, Seoul, Tokyo > NATIVES: Hiram Bingham, Yvonne Elliman, Nicole Kidman, Barack Obama, Michelle Wie > RESIDENTS: Q'Orianka Kilcher, Bette Midler, Sun Yat Sen 205

"Sailing mad Auckland.

Everyone sailed here.

Maoris in vast canoes that rode the currents with stars and gods for guidance, then Captain Cook who discovered it for the western world." Matthew Brace

PERCHED ON A NARROW ISTHMUS of land barely a mile wide, Auckland is almost completely surrounded by sea and it is no surprise that life in the city is dominated by water and wind. It's as if every Aucklander owned a boat of some description. To the west is the natural harbour of Manukau, bristling with the tinkling masts of sailing-boats, and beyond, the Tasman Sea. To the east, facing the Pacific horizon, Waitemata harbour is a virtual marina of super-yachts and gin palaces. Further out, in the Hauraki Gulf beyond the span of Harbour Bridge, lies moored a flotilla of islands. This is truly the city of sails.

As landmasses go, the bony spine of the New Zealand archipelago is pretty young. The city's seven underlying volcanoes have long since vented their wrath but Auckland is built on the resulting lava field. Atmospheric vents like New York alleyways are still visible in outlying areas and the cone of Mount Eden provides a Fuji-esque backdrop and reminder of the city's foundations.

The city also has a new pride in its Pacific roots. Auckland has the world's largest Polynesian population and the influence of the aboriginal Maori population is visible in the onomatapoeic names of the districts of which Auckland is composed – Waitekere, Manukau – and in the powerful physique and physiognomy of their descendants. Once the marginalized people of the Auckland-shot *Once Were Warriors*, subjects of a post-colonial white regime, the Maoris have been welcomed into New Zealand's culture. If they are still left out it is, like Jonah Lomu, usually on the wing of the rugby field where their power and athleticism is used to devastating effect. In recent years Maoris have provided the All Black New Zealand rugby team with a supply of withering playmakers and battering rams, and the fearsome *haka* war dance – all penetrating eyes, foot-stamping and threatening arm gestures, performed before each international clash – remains a unique ritual in the sporting world.

Despite losing its status as capital to Wellington in 1865, Auckland is today New Zealand's largest city – in a land where there are supposed to be more sheep than Kiwis – the main gateway to the country and its commercial centre. Spiritual home of the America's Cup the city has plotted a new course of late in search of a vivid international profile. Once the domain of commercial fishermen and shipping companies, Viaduct Harbour, complete with its own bridge, has reincarnated itself as a mini-Sydney. Ponsonby district is café central. The city has similarly white-sanded beaches. And despite the calm, understated level-headedness of their accent, the natives have an innate ability to let themselves go – especially on one of the bungee-jumps that were first invented here. Perhaps it's one way to make the world look upright again from Down Under.

> AUCKLAND, NORTH ISLAND, NEW ZEALAND > LONGITUDE: 174°46' E > LATITUDE: 36°52' S > ALTITUDE: 20 feet/6 metres > POPULATION: 372,500 (metro: 1,158, 891) > TWINNED WITH: Brisbane, Fukuoka, Guangzhou, Los Angeles, Pusan (South Korea) > NATIVES: Peter Blake, Russell Coutts, Russell Crowe, Sean Fitzpatrick, Edmund Hillary, Rachel Hunter, Lucy Lawless, Jonah Lomu, Arthur Lydiard Bruce McLaren, Pamela Stephenson, Hugh Walpole RESIDENTS: Witi Ihimaera

"Wellington doesn't have a magic formula. I just think it's a great place to live."

Peter Jackson, director

WELLINGTON IS THE OTHER Windy City. But whereas Chicago was given its nickname by a disgruntled New York journalist who was mocking what he saw as the bombastic claims of Chicago's politicians, Wellington's is pure Beaufort scale stuff. The winds come gusting in along the Cook Strait which separates Wellington, perched on the southern tip of New Zealand's North Island, from the top of South Island. But rather than ignore them, the turbine on top of Brooklyn Hill gathers up their forces and converts it into a contribution to the power requirements of the city.

From the turbine – or from the nearby Mount Victoria Lookout – the topography of Wellington sweeps around. The city centre lies on the Western edge of a spectacular harbour, gripped tightly between the pincers of two peninsulas. When the first European

settlers managed to make a landing in the 1840s (something neither Abel Tasman nor James Cook had been able to achieve courtesy of those afore-mentioned winds), they had first settled further round the bay at the mouth of the Hutt River, but when the river flooded they shifted anti-clockwise some 90 degrees, and named their new site after the victor of Waterloo.

Almost immediately they began reclaiming land from the harbour, because of the steepness of the hills heading up from the water. This has been the pattern ever since: eking out more and more land to enhance the narrow shoreline strip, with expansion constantly hampered by the difficulty of building on the hillsides. As a result of its striking setting, the city has been forced to remain compact; the downside is that its suburbs sprawl ever outwards.

In 1865, only a couple of decades into its life, Wellington took over from Auckland as the capital city of New Zealand. Wellington's position as a linchpin between the two islands and its excellent harbour gave it the edge over its rival. The current parliamentary buildings include the Beehive, housing the executive wing, which was designed by Sir Basil Spence, Lutyens's assistant in Delhi and architect of Coventry Cathedral. It is not Wellington's only architectural landmark: New Zealander Ian Athfield has left his playful stamp on at least half a dozen buildings within the city. And now Wellington has become the unofficial capital of Middle Earth, thanks to local boy Peter Jackson, who shot the *Lord of the Rings* movie trilogy in the city's surrounding woodlands.

For relaxation, Wellington's functionaries have plenty to choose from. They can ride or hike through upland terrain, relax on wild beaches, sail in the harbour waters, check out the biennial International Festival of the Arts (where revenues can be higher than Edinburgh's) or chill out in Courteney Place. But if Wellingtonites get too big for their boots, they will happily be brought back down to earth by Aucklanders, who consider that their city, free of "stuffy politicians", is where the real action is.

BRISBANE AUSTRALIA

JUST SOUTH OF THE Tropic of Capricorn, which cuts right through Queensland, Brisbane possesses a laid-back, sub-tropical attitude that suits the sunny daytimes and balmy nights of its summer. The image of the city evoked by Bill Scott, its "sleeves rolled up, casually sprawling across its 37 hills", suggests to some a sluggish indolence that Brisbane has tried hard, however, to belie. It doesn't mind being friendly, relaxed and informal, but it does not want to be seen as lazy.

As one of Australia's fastest-growing cities – incomers attracted by its climate, the attitude and the proximity to the Gold Coast, the Sunshine Coast and the Great Barrier Reef – Brisbane made its intentions clear by hosting the 1982 Commonwealth Games and the 1988 Expo. For a long time, it had been seen by the rest of Australia as a backwater, a philistine, red-neck kind of place. Now it was keen to dispel that image, and establish itself as worthy of more respect.

In CBD, the central business district on a peninsula surrounded by the deep curve of the Brisbane River, which heads sluggishly 20 miles (32km) or so east to the coast, a wave of construction threatened to wipe out much of the city's 19th-century core, but in the end sense prevailed, and key buildings like the original Commissariat Stores and the twin spires of St Stephen's Cathedral survived the voracious appetite of the bulldozers.

Further out in the leafy suburbs the traditional "Queenslander" houses, raised weatherboard cottages with leisurely verandahs, have also remained intact and distinctive. And beneath the Old Government House and Parliament House, the planners sensibly preserved the Botanical Gardens, first set out in 1855 in the very curve of the river's arc, so that at its very heart the city's modern aspirations are softened by an abundance of jacarandas, oleanders and bougainvillaea.

The Gardens offer a hint of the lush vegetation that first attracted the settlers of the 1820s, when Sir Thomas Brisbane, an administrator and astronomer, and Governor of New South Wales, was instructed by the British government to explore the region for possible sites for yet another penal colony. This was a time when Britain was offloading most of its undesirables on ships heading to the Antipodes, conveniently on the other side of the world.

The rigours of that life now seem far distant. On the South Bank of the river, which is home to Brisbane's cultural and performing arts centres, the man-made lagoons and beaches mean that swimmers can relax late into the night, the sand and the water still warm from the oppressive heat of the day, and, with fruit foxes buzzing overhead, contemplate the cityscape on the far side of the river. Little surprise that Brisbane is now one of Australia's favourite cities.

"I grew up in Brisbane in the '30s and '40s. It seems to me now a mini metropolis, then it was a big sprawling weatherboard town, a wonderful place to come to terms with that old Australia." David Malouf

> BRISBANE, QUEENSLAND, AUSTRALIA > LONGITUDE: 153°03' E > LATITUDE: 27°33' S > ALTITUDE: 83 feet/25 metres > POPULATION: 1,591,300 > TWINNED WITH: Auckland, Kaoisiung (Tiawan, PRC), Kobe (Japan), Semarang (Indonesia), Shenzen (China) > NATIVES: Diane Cilento, Mick Doohan, Shane Gould, Michael Lynagh, David Malouf   211

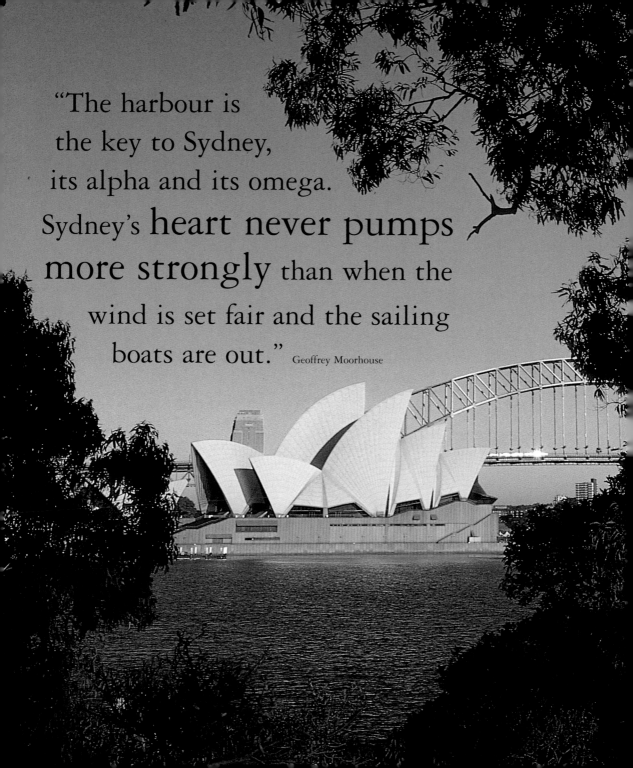

"The harbour is
the key to Sydney,
its alpha and its omega.
Sydney's **heart never pumps
more strongly** than when the
wind is set fair and the sailing
boats are out." Geoffrey Moorhouse

SYDNEY GOT THE LOOKS. In the great "Miss World" competition of cities, Australia's spiritual capital can be touched only by Rio. Sydney spends an equal amount of time parading in a swimsuit, greased with suntan oil and sporting a synchronized swimming smile worthy of the Olympic pool. Like Rio, Sydney is often mistaken for Australia's capital (that'll be Canberra!): in Bondi she has a beach as famous as Copacabana and during gay-lesbian Mardi Gras hosts one of the world's great parties, albeit more red-blooded than the Brazilian carnival.

Completed by the double-act of the bridge and opera-house, the glistening deep-blue harbour, bristling with yachts and criss-crossed by old-fashioned green and yellow ferries, is one of the world's great views. Sydneysiders are proud of the single arch that spans Port Jackson, visible from almost everywhere, dubbing it "the coathanger". Built on the site of an old municipal tramshed, Jørn Utzon's opera-house has attracted more equivocal opinion: inspired by sailing-boats, the surprise competition winner was half-built before they realized the complete design was impossible. But the potential white elephant which Clive James described as "a portable typewriter full of oyster shells" is a modern victory for flair. Now the opera-house is as familiar as if it had always been there.

Sydney was founded as a penal colony in 1788 by Captain Arthur Philip and would have been called Albion had not Philip decided to defer to the then Home Secretary to the Empire, Thomas Townsend, first Baron Sydney. Expelling the Eora aborigines, the new arrivals made their centre in cottages and alleyways in the Rocks district on Miller's Point, whence the city expanded in countless suburbs along the coves of the Parramatta Estuary, importing names (Hyde Park, St James, Paddington) from "the home counties". The aboriginal conscience lives on in names such as the Woolloomooloo wharf development of trendy restos and frappaccino cafés.

Sydney's would-be Priscillas and exuberant AC/DC population put the city on the party map long before the Olympic tide. Oxford Street in Darlinghurst (nicknamed Darlo) is the "pink strip" of this Queen of gay cities. The art deco Little Italy of Leichhardt (or Dyke Hart) is navel of the lesbian scene, and for carnival when the two persuasions come together, led by the Dykes on Bikes set piece, the sight is a fearsome feast of fetishwear and flesh – like Ann Summers on heat. It's so INXS; but just s-oo Sydney.

Beloved to all creeds in Sydney are her beaches. Be it on the competitive topless strip of Bondi, laid-back Coogee, or among the gay glamazons of Tamarama (Glamarama) Bay, the world is full of Quicksilver-clad surf dudes sporting six-packs and swigging four-packs, would-be Russell Crowes, Nicole Kidmans and Dame Ednas. In Oz, these are the golden sands at the end of the rainbow. This is *Baywatch* Aussie-style.

> SYDNEY, NEW SOUTH WALES, AUSTRALIA > LONGITUDE: 151°11' E > LATITUDE: 33°54' S > ALTITUDE: 3 feet/1 metre > POPULATION: 3,997,300 > TWINNED WITH: Florence, Guangzhou, Manila, Nagoya (Japan), Portsmouth, San Francisco, Wellington > NATIVES: Jack Brabham, James Clavell, Russell Crowe, Dawn Fraser, Lew Hoad, Paul Hogan, Michael Hutchence, Nathalie Imbruglia, Clive James, Thomas Keneally, Harry Kewell, Nicole Kidman, Baz Luhrman, Elle Macpherson, John Newcombe, Kerry Packer, John Pilger, Ken Rosewall, Bob Simpson, Joan Sutherland, Jeff Thomson, Ian Thorpe, Mark Waugh, Stephen Waugh, Peter Weir > RESIDENTS: Richie Benaud, Jane Campion, Jelena Dokic, Miles Franklin, Mel Gibson, Patrick White

MELBOURNE AUSTRALIA

TIME WAS WHEN MELBOURNE was the centre of things Down Under. But since Melbourne got the Olympics in 1956 the rivalry between Victoria's capital and Sydney has been the stuff of soap operas, each doing it all it can to keep up with the neighbours. Right now you could say that Melbourne is suffering from harbour-envy, living in the eclipse of Sydney's iconic bridge, opera-house, Millennium celebrations and Olympic 2000 afterglow.

But sights, Melburnians would say, are for museums, and despite not having any sight or monument to speak of (other than the hanging place of favourite national villain, Ned Kelly) theirs is the ultimate lifestyle city where a diverse, energetic yet relaxed outdoor life is championed above all things. Melbourne shares with London its composition from distinct suburban villages, each home to different ethnic groups. Lebanese, Turkish and Asian populations, added to a predominant Italian and Greek community (Melbourne is sometimes mocked as the third largest Greek city after Athens and Thessaloniki) ensure that since 1950s the city has a 24-7 café culture.

Ethnic diversity also makes Melbourne a foodie's paradise in a country whose menu, like a spit, seems to revolve around the native barbeque. Beneath the skyscrapers, goldrush Victorian façades, trundling 1930s trams and Milanese arcades of the Central Business District, Melbourne throbs with a cosmopolitan bar and bistro culture. By day they are full of men at work enjoying short-sleeve business lunches, by night they are populated by young Sheilas and Bruces burning the midnight oil.

Melbourne is capital of Australian sport: home of the Australian Open, the Australian Grand Prix, the Melbourne Cup horse-race and HQ of Aussie Rules Football – still the nation's number one game. Nothing gives an Aussie more pleasure than thrashing the Poms (as Brits are known), especially at cricket when the Ashes are at stake. And where better than amid the vast cauldron of partisanship that is the 100,000-seater Melbourne Cricket Ground.

Yet laden with galleries, Melbourne combines its love of sport with culture, its summer festival the antipodean equivalent of Edinburgh. On location here in 1959 filming *On the Beach*, Ava Gardner was reputed to say, "It's a story about the end of the world and Melbourne sure is the right place to film it." How wrong she would be now. The centre has recently reconciled itself with the Yarra that flows through its heart, sprouting an Oceanarium and leisurely waterfront renovation. The docklands area has been earmarked for Gehry-style gentrification. Meanwhile the city's outlying districts have developed their own brands of flair: Brunswick Street in Fitzroy, residence of the local fringe, the espresso culture of Carlton providing the caffeine for heirs of the beat generation, and the beach and esplanade of St Kilda's supplying the changing rooms for the city's red light district. Melburnians wouldn't give a XXXX for Miss Gardner's thoughts.

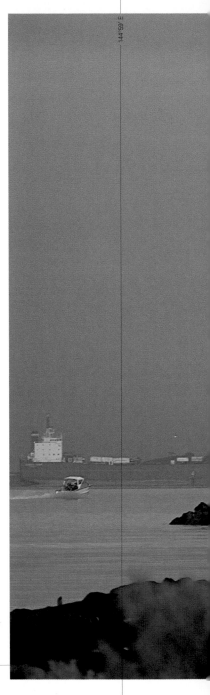

214 > MELBOURNE, VICTORIA, AUSTRALIA > LONGITUDE: 144°59' E > LATITUDE: 37°49' S > ALTITUDE: 115 feet/35 metres > POPULATION: 3,203,100 > TWINNED WITH: Boston, Osaka, Thessaloniki > NATIVES: Michael Balzary (Flea), Cate Blanchett, Raelene Boyle, Pat Cash, Neale Fraser, Germaine Greer, Percy Grainger, Alan Jones, David Helfgott, Barry Humphries, Nellie Melba, Kylie Minogue, Rupert Murdoch, Sidney Nolan, Mark Philippoussis, Helen Reddy, Barry Tuckwell, Shane Warne, John Williams > RESIDENTS: Juan Davila, Cathy Freeman, Rachel Griffiths

"If Queen Victoria were still alive,
not only would she approve of Melbourne,
she would probably feel more at home there
than in any other city of her former Empire."

Jonathan Aitken

TOKYO JAPAN

ON THE SURFACE, Tokyo might seem to be very Western: the fast food chains, the teenage punks, the Burberry umbrellas, the love of Americana. But looks can be deceptive. The beauty of Sofia Coppola's movie *Lost in Translation* was her exquisite pinpointing of the sense of surreal dislocation experienced by every Western visitor at some point during their first trip. Tokyo feels Western simply because it is modern. A massive earthquake in 1926 and the Allied bombs of the Second World War between them wiped away much of the old city. There are relatively few historical sites, but an unlimited amount of brand-new, constantly changing energy in Tokyo to spark up even the most jaded soul.

Its citizens have absorbed many of the brand values of the West, but in return dispatched their own flurry of left-field inventive creations. You give us McDonalds, we'll give you sushi, the convenience food invented on the streets of old Tokyo. You send us Disney films, we'll make *Manga* movies. From karaoke machines to Sony Walkmans, SuperMario and the robot dog, Tokyo's imaginative export department has achieved an almost ubiquitous level of penetration.

And so, just as first-timers in New York City find themselves in what seem like remarkably familiar surroundings, much of Tokyo (the heavily-photographed Ginza Yon-Chome pedestrian crossing, for example) taps into a similarly deep-rooted pre-memory. But

although the neon, the sardine-like metro trains and the shoebox houses crammed cheek by jowl are all expected, the cleanliness of Tokyo's streets is a shock, and a realization that, at one level, there is an obedience to rules and regulations and civic duty that underpinned Japan's economic miracle. For the city's dodgy underbelly, you have to peek into the loner's bars and hostess clubs, past the *yakuza* "security consultants".

Tokyo has no obvious centre. Each area has a strong personality, and rather than being some quaint quarter is usually city-sized in its own right. So Ginza is shopping heaven, West Shinjuku the corporate headquarters, East Shinjuku where the workers of West Shinjuku look for fun at night. In Shibuya the teenagers follow the fads and fashions of the latest idol, or *idoru*. Their older brothers and sisters head to the all-night music clubs of Roppongi.

There is some history though, at the Senso-ji Temple, originally built in AD645 – and restored after bombing – or the Imperial Palace, which marked the return of the imperial capital to the city in 1868 (when it was named Tokyo, or "Eastern Capital", having previously been Edo) and the end of eight centuries of introspective, closed-door shogun rule. And for a moment of peace and quiet, the garden at Chinzan-so or the pagodas and shrines of Ueno Park provide the necessary pause before hitting Tokyo's fast forward button once again.

> TOKYO, JAPAN > LONGITUDE: 139°48' E > LATITUDE: 35°41' N > ALTITUDE: 16 feet/5 metres > POPULATION: 11,823,000 > TWINNED WITH: Beijing, Berlin, Cairo, Honolulu, Jakarta, Moscow, New York, Paris, Rome, São Paulo, Seoul > NATIVES: Kobo Abe, Nobuyoshi Araki, Sushako Endo, Tsuguharu Foujita, Olivia de Havilland, Emperor Hirohito, Katsushika Hokusai, Rei Kawakubo, Takeshi Kitano, Akira Kurosawa, Yukio Mishima, Miyuki Miyabe, Tatsuo Miyajima, Hayao Miyazaki, Yoko Ono, Yasujiro Ozu, Tatsuhiko Shibusawa, Kei Takei, Toru Takemitsu, Yoshio Tanaguchi, Liv Ullmann, Kitagawa Utamaro, Yohji Yamamoto > RESIDENTS: Saleeva Atisanoe (Konishiki), Issey Miyake

"For me, Tokyo is like one long film trailer — one of those quick-cut, fast-moving, highlight teasers for a noisy action flick, in molar-shaking, heart-pounding surround sound." Anthony Bourdain

"It feels rather like an urban version of
a gentlemen's club – comfortable,
old-fashioned, quietly grand, slightly drowsy
by mid-afternoon, redolent of another age."

Bill Bryson

YOU COULD EASILY VISIT AUSTRALIA and not know Adelaide was there. With the vast expanse of Australia's outback to the north and west, and to the south only sea, the city does not come in for the same attention as her siblings Mel and Syd further east.

Virtually deserted at night, impatient city-slickers won't want to get delayed in Adelaide, viewing the city as a gateway to the country's great back of beyond. But this city of spires, encircled by parks, has an all-Australian relaxed and healthy attitude, where every day seems like a Sunday afternoon. Set on the east side of the boomerang-shaped bay of Gulf St Vincent, with the rolling hills of the Mount Lofty Ranges rising up behind it, South Australia's capital is the driest city in the country, as remote from the gardens of Victorian England as could be. So it is a measure of the homesickness of the city's founders that they struggled so valiantly to recreate the idyllic image of their homeland. The city abounds with solid, classic Victorian town houses and gardens dripping with jacarandas, built in the local sand- and bluestone, more reminiscent of Bath or Shakespeare country in the UK. The city has so far largely eschewed big-city concrete and glass, and feels more like a large country town with a country club, tea-and-cucumber-sandwiches atmosphere, especially during a cricket match at the city's famous Oval ground, where St Peter's Cathedral stands at long leg.

That's not to say there's no spirit here. Adelaide was reportedly laid out in the image of Catania in Sicily, and the significant Italian community gives the city its sunny and artsy café life. Around Rundle and Hindley Streets the clink of cappuccinos mixes with the sound of the outback as musicians entrance passers-by with the hypnotic drone of their didgeridoo pipes. North Terrace along the banks of the River Torrens, with its serene population of cruising pelicans and black swans, is home to Adelaide's cultural district of museums and universities, the legacy of the 1960s when this was the hippest city in Oz, a haven for artists and intellectuals. Adelaide's Arts Festival and the biennial Womadelaide are two of Australia's most important festivals. The South Australia Museum houses an extraordinary collection, from the world's largest dinosaur skeleton to the world's second largest nugget of gold – and next to these the collected memorabilia of Australian national hero and probably the greatest cricketer of all time, Sir Donald Bradman.

But the great outdoors is what Adelaide is really about, whether lounging about with a glass of South Australian wine in central Victoria Square or the expanse of Montefiore Park in the prosperous leafy North Side, or cycling along the river banks, or heading for the nudist beaches of Glenelg suburbs.

> ADELAIDE, SOUTH AUSTRALIA, AUSTRALIA > LONGITUDE: 138°40' E > LATITUDE: 43°56' S > ALTITUDE: 141 feet/43 metres > POPULATION: 1,061,200 > TWINNED WITH: Austin TX, Christchurch (NZ), Himeji (Japan), Matsumoto (Japan) > NATIVES: Judith Anderson, Robyn Archer, Wayne Arthurs, Greg Chappell, Ian Chappell, Lleyton Hewitt, Alicia Molik > RESIDENTS: Don Bradman

KYOTO IS BOTH the anagram and antithesis of Japan's capital. Where Tokyo is the voracious sampler of modern world fads, Kyoto is the bastion of tea-and-temples traditional Japan. From Buddhist temples – over 1,600 of them in total – to Zen gardens, and pavilions seemingly taken from the set of *Madam Butterfly*, here are all the iconic images and totems of classic Japan, legacy of the city's 1,000-year reign as Japan's imperial, spiritual and cultural capital.

Kyoto lies contained in a broad sloping valley astride the Kamo-gawa River, surrounded by impressive hills and dominated by the snow-capped Mount Hiei. Although today it is a living city central to Japan's industrial sector, Kyoto is, for locals and visitors alike, the proud custodian of a centuries-old culture, a city preoccupied with conserving the past. At almost every turn in the centre are reminders of yesterday's Japan: in the east-side Higashiyama hills are the winding cobbled lanes of traditional *machiya* wooden houses. Here is also the Gion entertainment district, traditionally associated with geishas, photogenic by day and seductive by the lantern-lit night. In the north-east is the beautifully understated Ginkaku-ji Silver Pavilion, less extravagant than its Golden brother in the north-west (actually a 1950s reconstruction), both originally commissioned under the great Ashikaga shogun warrior dynasty of the 14th century. In the southern suburbs are laid out the ethereal imperial gardens of Saiho-ji and Katsura Rikyu, which during the April *sakura* (cherry blossom) season and equally with the autumn incandescence of their maple trees, reach a nirvanaesque zenith of beauty.

"Kyoto, or for that matter any Japanese city, is a barfly's Valhalla."

Truman Capote

Their inheritance has an effect on the locals, who among Japanese are known to be conservative, snobbish and exclusive, and as private, reclusive and inaccessible as the city's many hidden gardens. Proud of their high culture, the locals consider themselves in turn less showy and more subtle than Tokyo. The city is laid out on a rigourous grid which, as elsewhere, implies logic, but which in Kyoto also smacks of the orthodoxy and introspection at the core of the Japanese psyche. The streets are easy to navigate but they give very little away.

We can thank the cultural conscience of 1945 American Defence Secretary, Henry Stimson, for keeping Kyoto from the top of the list of targets for the A-bomb. However, Kyoto is more than a mausoleum. Not as far under the surface as it might appear, the reserved hospitality of dignified Japanese ceremony is there for all to enjoy. Behind the fans and screens, amid the backstreets even just off the main thoroughfares of downtown Kyoto are the city's famous traditional *ryokan* (inns) where the subtle flavours of *kaiseki*, Japan's most refined cuisine, is a feast both for the eyes and taste buds.

"In trade it is a Chicago. In situation it is a Venice."

John Foster Fraser, *Round the World on a Wheel*

> OSAKA, JAPAN > LONGITUDE: 135°30′ E > LATITUDE: 34°42′ N > ALTITUDE: 0 feet/0 metres > POPULATION: 2,598,800 > TWINNED WITH: Budapest, Chicago, Copenhagen, Hamburg, Manila, Melbourne, Milan, St. Petersburg, San Francisco, São Paulo, Shanghai > NATIVES: Tadao Ando, Junichi Inamoto, Yasunari Kawabata, Michiko Koshino, Yasumara Morimura, Hideo Nomo, Naoko Takahashi, Osama Tezuka, Jiro Yoshihara

NOT FAR SOUTH-WEST of the frosty fragile beauty of Kyoto is Japan's big bad city, with all the relish those words imply – Japan's ugliest, second-largest and much-maligned city, but a beautifully sinful Gomorrah of unashamed capitalism, hedonism and epicurean *joie de vivre*.

Osaka's not pretty but what it lacks in stone beauty it makes up for in supercharged life. Largely razed to a heap of rubble in the Second World War Osaka has picked itself up with a work hard, play hard culture that has turned it into one of the most affluent cities in the world. The local greeting translates as "Are you making any money?" and the nights might as well finish with the salutation, "Have you tried singing in tune?" as Osaka's tone-deaf boozy businessmen fall about in the city's alfresco karaoke bars in Tennoji-Koen.

Osaka's eyes are firmly set in modern times, with a sports stadium seemingly transplanted from outer space and a Universal Studios theme park that sums up the nation's sampling psyche. The city is one of Japan's most cosmopolitan, its port welcoming a large population of Koreans and also *gaijin*, the Japanese equivalent of *gringo*, "foreigner". Osaka's emancipated mind enables its Liberty Osaka human rights museum to confront some of Japan's elsewhere most taboo subjects, such as its Burakumin "untouchable" caste, ethnic minorities and sexism.

The city does however retain some links, albeit refabricated, with a more glorious past. The centre is dominated by Osaka-jo, the city's famous castle, originally built in the 16th century on the site of a temple then subsequently ravished and rebuilt several times. Unlike most of the rest of the city, the current 1868 restoration survived the Allied bombings, and now it is used affectionately by Osakans as a concert venue for their own particular brand of rock music. Given its unchained young citizens it is hard to think now that Osaka was once an important religious centre. The two noble temples of Shitenno-ji and Sumitoshi Taisha are all that remain of the city's former civic restraint.

Osaka was always "the kitchen of Japan", a foodies' paradise home to specialities such as *udon* noodles that have made a name for themselves internationally. But the city really lives for the night. The neon fairground world of Ebisu-bashi is the shadowy area of wild and dazzling fashion and nightclubs where *Black Rain* was filmed. Osaka's miniskirted girls are notoriously easy-going and fiery, and to see them flirt with likely Japanese lads, dressed in their dyed techno-punk fusion in downtown Shinsaibashi and along the Amerika-mura strip of trendy bars, seems at odds with the traditional rigours of Japanese society seemingly in force in other parts of the country. Here in Osaka the made-in-Japan love hotels are in constant demand.

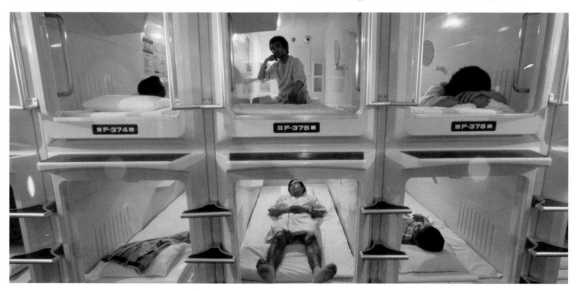

"Vladivostok is far away –
but it's ours." Vladimir Ilyich Lenin

> VLADIVOSTOK, RUSSIA > LONGITUDE: 131°56' E > LATITUDE: 43°07' S > ALTITUDE: 0 feet/0 metres
> POPULATION: 626,400 > NATIVES: Yul Brynner

FOR GENERATIONS VLADIVOSTOK will have been "that other city" of the Soviet Union they had heard of but weren't quite sure where it was. Only that it was a "vladi" long way away. Vladivostok was synonymous with Soviet remoteness, cold and suspicion, a city whose alliterative name rolled off the tongue and lent itself delightfully to mocking clipped-vowel and pursed-lip Russian accents.

To a certain extent the stereotype was justified. Until its "liberation" by the Bolsheviks post-1917, Vladivostok had been an exciting cosmopolitan Tsarist city that lived up to its name – Lord of the East.
It was home to French hoteliers, German store-owners and merchants and sailors from the four corners – even birthplace to would-be King, Yul Brynner. Then Stalin cleansed Vladivostok of an Asian population who had built the place and at one stage made up four-fifths of its inhabitants. As the war got colder the life, soul and significance of the city seeped away. In 1948 the American consulate up and left, and in 1958 the city was officially closed to the outside world, to become a not-so-secret naval compound, home to the Soviet Union's Pacific fleet of warships and Red October submarines. The famous railway station, inaugurated by Tsar Nicholas II, with its exotic cocktail of architectural styles and bright pre-1917 murals, became the end of the line for dissident deportees of the Soviet regime, a waiting-room for the archipelago of gulags and gold mines to the north. A less lordly place was hard to imagine.

Now that the curtain has been opened a new dawn has greeted the city. Vladivostok finds itself in a fascinating part of the world, nestled in the Amursky Gulf bound in by China to the west and the next piece of land to east, Japan. Rusting relics of the Pacific fleet are mere museum curios of perverse Cold War nostalgia and, like the statue of Lenin outside the station, the city now looks firmly eastwards. The streets are full of Nissans and Toyotas and lined with trendy sushi bars – Alka-Seltzer to its post-Soviet hangover. Barring the odd power shortage, Vladivostok has become Russia's money-making, fast-spending, high-living nouveau riche financial centre in Asia – something akin to what it was under its Tsarist founders. The station is one again beloved of scenery-starved travellers arriving aboard the Trans-Siberian *Rossia* train and the city an ironic party town for thrill-seeking backpacker *arrivés*.

Laid out in tiers around the finger of Golden Horn Bay, Vladivostok is one of Russia's physically most attractive cities, its downtown waterfront parallel with Svetlanskaya Street, and Aleutskaya Street lined with grand 19th-century Tsarist mansions built by the Japanese. From the succinctly-named "Bortsov Square of the Fighters for Soviet Power in the Far East" a quaint funicular railway plies the steep hillside up to Sukhanova, with a view from the end of the Eurasian continent to the East, the horizon and the future.

"The curious thing about your ignorance regarding Fukuoka is that this city probably invented Japan.

But say Fukuoka outside Asia and people expect you to **break into the 'Shaft' guitar riff.**" Stephen Armstrong, *Wallpaper**

CLOSER TO SEOUL, the Korean capital, than to Tokyo, the capital of its own country, Fukuoka has for centuries been very much the gateway city into Japan for both Korea and China. As a result, it possesses a significantly more diverse cultural buzz than places like Kyoto, Osaka and Tokyo itself, which have been somewhat hermetically protected within Japan's main island, Honshu.

Down in the south-west, on the coast of the island of Kyushu, Fukuoka is definitely not some backwater port, a charge which is sometimes levelled at it by other Japanese, who find the local dialect, Hakata-ben, frequently difficult to follow. Fukuoka is a breezy, thriving seaside centre with one district, Nakasu, jam-packed with so many restaurants, bars and clubs that it has attracted the attention of the extremely hard-to-please ranks of the self-appointed style magazines.

Divided by the Naka River, Fukuoka is a city of two halves, which merged in 1805: Fukuoka was the samurai fortress, Hakata the merchants' town. The joint resources of the two communities secured the city's future. When the Mongol hordes, aware of Fukuoka's strategic importance, attacked twice in the late 1200s, they were repelled first by the resilient defence of the locals, and then – at the second time of asking – by a combination of a freshly constructed 10-foot (3m) wall and the intervention of a typhoon, thereafter known to posterity as the "divine wind" or *kamikaze*. The merchants of Hakata then provided the trading base for the region's prosperity, and the links to the neighbouring countries were acknowledged by the gold seal presented by the Chinese Emperor, which is still on display in the City Museum.

The past is present throughout Fukuoka. One of Japan's oldest Zen Buddhist temples, Shofuku-ji, is in the old Hakata quarter. There are shrines and temples dotted around. Ohori Park in the middle of Fukuoka is the model of traditional lakes, pavilions and bridges. But modernity is the dominant impression. On the waterfront area of Momochi, the Fukuoka Tower points the way onwards and upwards, just near the futuristic Fukuoka Dome, home of the Daiei Hawks, the local baseball team.

Noted for its food, local specialities include *yatai* stalls, where, on the street side, a passer-by can squat down and savour noodles and stews which owe more to Cantonese cuisine than the conveyor belts of Yo Sushi!

> FUKUOKA, JAPAN > LONGITUDE: 130°24' E > LATITUDE: 33°35' N > ALTITUDE: 15 feet/4 metres > POPULATION: 1,315,800 > TWINNED WITH: Atlanta, Auckland, Bordeaux, Guangzhou, Ipoh (Malaysia), Oakland CA, Pusan (South Korea) > NATIVES: Aska, Tamori, Misia, Lucia Shiomitsu > RESIDENTS: Chage

EVERY DAY AT 11.02am a bell tolls in Nagasaki. It marks one of the defining moments in the city's history, the exact moment when, on 9 August 1945, Nagasaki became the second – and so far the last – city to be attacked with an atomic bomb. Three days after Hiroshima had suffered this fate, the US Air Force dropped "Fat Boy" on a city which had not, until the final minute, even been on the short list of targets. Nagasaki's fate was determined by climatic considerations, a decision not to obliterate the old Japanese imperial capital Kyoto and the presence of the Mitsubishi arms factory; Nagasaki, the rumour went, was where torpedoes used at Pearl Harbor had been manufactured. And so the Fat Boy fell.

Over 75,000 perished immediately; no one knows how many died from the effects in the aftermath. Nagasaki has rebuilt itself, and committed itself to the cause of world peace, but it has not hidden the hurt or the scars. In the Peace Park, at ground zero, the remains of walls still carry the silhouettes of irradiated victims. The museum there, although objective, pulls no punches, and leaves a sense of pensiveness and sadness that such an exhibition need even exist.

Nagasaki is not locked in this past, however. On the far western edge of Japan's most westerly island, Kyushu, it is a pleasant port built on a strip of flat land along the waterfront. The rest of the city spreads up into the steep hills behind the harbour, with, in the words of travel writer Josie Dew, "a topsy-turvy audience of old wooden houses ... like the stepped tiers of a grand amphitheatre encircling the harbour".

Up in those hills, too, is Glover House, the one-time residence of the energetic 19th-century Scot Thomas Glover, whose résumé included stints as an arms trader, railway entrepreneur and founder of Kirin Beer. The stone dragon featured on Kirin labels is inside his house, which provided the setting for the story of Puccini's *Madam Butterfly*, and

which is now part of a preserved group of stone and weatherboarded houses reminding visitors of Nagasaki's trade with the West.

Originally a small fishing village, the city was always a window to the outside world, initially via the Portuguese and Chinese. The latter bequeathed the 17th-century stone "Spectacles" Bridge which has become the city's most photographed image. Even when that window was slammed shut for two centuries during Japan's self-imposed isolation between 1638 and 1854, Dutch merchants managed to maintain a small enclave on the island of Dejima. Consequently Nagasaki is a relaxed, open and more culturally diverse place than many other Japanese cities – despite all the atomic reasons not to be.

"The Lourdes of the Atomic Age."

Murray Sayle

> NAGASAKI, JAPAN > LONGITUDE: 129°52' E > LATITUDE: 32°45' N > ALTITUDE: 0 feet/0 metres > POPULATION: 436,000 > TWINNED WITH: Fuzhou (China), Middelburg (Netherlands), Oporto, St Paul MN, Santos (Brazil) > NATIVES: Kuzuo Ishiguro > RESIDENTS: Thomas Glover, Philipp Franz von Siebold

229

IN RECENT YEARS SEOUL has become the perfect host city, its innate hospitality extending to first the Asian Games in 1988, the Olympics in 1988 and then the World Cup in 2002, when half the football circus rolled into town, shared with traditional foes and serial invaders, Japan.

These events have marked a significant upturn in the fortunes of a city that has lived most of its life

adorned in brightly painted wooden masks and animal-symbol sculptures, still stand, as do the old city gates, Tongdaemun in the east and Nandaemun to the south, all laid out according to the geomantic superstitions of feng shui. To the north of the Namsam sugarloaf peak at the city's fulcrum, the traditional tile-roofed courtyards area, former residence of noblemen is once again

"The city is as grey as a parking garage and cleaner than a living room." P.J. O'Rourke

as a rape victim of Japan and China and battered wife of its northern Korean neighbour. First, in 1592, it was sacked by the Japanese shoguns who looted almost the entire cultural treasures of the imperial Yi dynasty of which it was capital (Seoul means "capital" in Korean). They were swiftly followed by the Manchu Chinese warriors who installed and fed the Qing dynasty in Beijing. By the 17th century Korea had retreated into itself, a Hermit Kingdom, its capital an introspective centre furrowed by seoul-searching. Worse was to follow in its turbulent history. Freedom seemed to beckon with Japanese defeat in the Second World War, only for North Korea to march in under the new ideological banner of communism in 1948. Thereafter, each half backed by NATO and the Warsaw Pact respectively, Korea became an Asian mirror for the Cold War, its civil war the subject of many films, a country split along that most notorious of latitudes, the 38th parallel.

Of the two kin, Korea's southern brother was born in the right place and Seoul developed in tandem with the West to become one of the movers and shakers of the Asian economy and one of the world's largest cities.

Amid the traditional bland clothes of fast-paced technological development are some vestiges of the city's past, more noble, glory. The picture-book royal palaces of Toksugung and Kyonghiogung,

prized property, while the lively backstreets of the Insa-dong district are lined with the city's art galleries, teahouses, traditional homes and inns.

Deep down, underneath the apparently homogeneous fast-food and department-store consumerism, Seoul is very Korean. Suited commuters still stand at street stalls, slurping bowls of silkworm soup and dried squid. Ginseng wafts through the air of market streets where crowds of heads still teem through the streets in hats like a thousand umbrellas. After centuries of pillaging, this southern tip of the Korean peninsula is being allowed to express itself again. Facing the yellow sea the sun is shining again on the Costa del Seoul.

SHANGHAI CHINA

THE SHANGHAI THAT ALDOUS HUXLEY visited was the pre-Second World War, pre-Communist Shanghai, a rumbustious, fast-paced, glamorously seedy city of free trade and expensive love, where gangsters, prostitutes and traders commingled in a port that was open to the West and moulded to no little extent by the European merchants whose enclaves lay at the city's heart. Then, for 50 years, Shanghai was drained of that vitality, starved of its dynamism by the constrictions of the party regime, but once the official go-ahead had been given by Deng Xiaoping for a new economic revival, all of Shanghai's pent-up energy erupted.

Throughout the 1990s construction cranes sprouted, creating a mushrooming forest of new buildings, especially on the once deserted east bank of the Huangpu River (a tributary of the great Yangtse) in the area called Pudong. Of all these the Oriental Pearl broadcasting tower shot up highest, its space-station looks beaming out a futuristic message back to the curving embankment of the Bund Promenade opposite, where in the early morning spirit-conscious Shanghainese rise to practise *t'ai chi* in the dawn light.

The peaceful exercises offer but a brief respite. Whereas Beijing is still rather ordered, and sometimes spookily quiet, in Shanghai all is boisterous, rumbling, tumbling and organic, with all the bustle, sounds and smells - surprisingly - of Mumbai. Even the apparent oasis of the Yu Yuan gardens and teahouse in fact only offers the tiniest of diminuendos. This is, nevertheless, a Chinese city, and despite its long exposure to the influences, good and bad, of the West and its fashionable internationalism (*Vogue China* launched here in 2005), there are still the temples and pagodas that make it clear Shanghai was a prominent settlement long before the British swung by in the 19th century.

The British were joined by the French, then the Americans and later the Japanese, each nation setting up its own area, or concession, where they could live within their own laws and in their own culture. The riverside Bund was their workplace and their playground, lined with clubs, bars, trading houses and banks behind the protective screen of warships along the waterfront. Many of the colonial buildings remain, and the Peace Hotel at the Bund's northern end is an art deco reminder of Shanghai's jazz age as the "Paris of the East", although it was equally known as "the whore of the Orient". But it was a whore with a golden heart, its open door policy welcoming not only those with a past to hide, but also 20,000 Jews fleeing first the Bolsheviks, then the Nazis.

Back into the 21st century, Shanghai is ready to keep on expanding (though it's far too crowded already) and to continue moving and shaking as the largest city in the world's largest country. As is often observed, Shanghai's present will be China's tomorrow.

"Life itself. Nothing more intensely living can be imagined."

Aldous Huxley

> SHANGHAI, CHINA > LONGITUDE: 121°30' E > LATITUDE: 31°14' N > ALTITUDE: 13 feet/4 metres > POPULATION: 1,471,100 > TWINNED WITH: Barcelona, Chiang Mai (Thailand), Chicago, Dubai, Gothenburg, Hamburg, Liverpool, Osaka, San Francisco, Yokohama (Japan) > NATIVES: J.G. Ballard, Eileen Chang, Chen Gang, Wong Kar-Wei, Sun Li, Soong Mei-Ling, Yao Ming, Zhu Rongji, T.V. Soong, Fou Ts'ong, An Wang, Jian Wang, Yang Wei, Liu Xiang, Wang Xiaoshuai, Edward Yang, Lou Ye, Terence Young
> RESIDENTS: Soong Ching-Ling, Zhou En Lai, David Sassoon, Lu Xun, Sun Yat Sen

"We went to Manila as champions, Joe and I, and we came back as old men."

Muhammad Ali

WHEN MUHAMMAD ALI and Joe Frazier battled out the "Thrilla in Manila" in 1975, they returned home from their grudge match in the Philippine capital bruised, bloodied and battered, yet somehow still standing – rather like Manila itself.

Modern-day Manila contains relatively few physical reminders of its past. Fought over between US forces and Japanese invaders during World War II, the city was basically bombed out of existence. While the destruction of Hiroshima, Nagasaki, Warsaw and Dresden has passed into universal awareness, the levelling of Manila seems to have been forgotten.

As a result, much of Manila's 19th-century Hispanic splendour is long gone. Founded in 1571 on the site of a Malay town called Maynilad, the city was a Spanish colonial powerhouse, heady with Catholicism. In 1898, a dispute over Cuba allowed the US to side with Filipino rebels, leading to half a century of US domination. Consequently, Manila's history has often been compared to three centuries of cloistered convent life followed by fifty years on a Hollywood backlot.

The American influence – this was the Seventh Fleet's stamping ground, an R&R destination for jaded GIs – is always visible in Manila's streets in the iconic *jeepneys*, originally recycled from old US Army jeeps, transformed not only into long-wheelbase taxis, but also mobile works of art, collections of buffed chrome and lovingly painted billboards, topped off by all manner of streamers and decorations (Filipinos love flamboyant festivals). Traffic remains one of Manila's big problems – despite the valiant attempts of the MRT metro to alleviate the problem. Squeezed into an isthmus between two bays – like a corset trying to contain the uncontainable – this is a city formed from eight other cities and nine townships, a sprawling city in a sprawling archipelago, a city where "cacophony" rules and which hums in all senses of the word.

Such is the amount of smouldering refuse around that one semi-permanent pile of garbage, in the slum of Tondo, was granted the name "smoky mountain". Which, sadly, is the image that has stuck, along with a reputation for heat, monsoons and corruption. That, and the excess characterized by Imelda Marcos's legendary shoe collection. And the nudge-nudge jokes made unavoidable when the country's religious head was called Cardinal Sin.

So the fact that Manila – and the Philippines in general – is noted for its friendliness ("the land where Asia wears a smile", according to one slogan) is a refreshing surprise. There are oases amid the tumult. Rizal Park is a green corner of calm in the centre of the city. Within the old Spanish colonial quarter of Intramuros, the restored Casa Manila offers a glimpse of the shuttered windows, bleached façades and hardwood floors of the past. The calm is a temporary respite, though. In Manila things are rarely quiet – and rarely dull.

T'AI-PEI TAIWAN

IN THE 1990s "MADE IN TAIWAN" became a familiar inscription on clothes labels and electronics equipment, synonymous with byte-size and cheap technological innovation. And yet Taiwan only gained independence from Japan in 1949, in the aftermath of the Second World War. The economic significance and prodigious productivity of this little state on the isle of Formosa, within striking distance of China and Japan, is testament to the industriousness of the Taiwanese.

Physically, T'ai-pei (meaning "North Taiwan") reflects Taiwan's strengths. Inelegant, it is laid out like a massive circuit board of skyscraper chips and broad tarmac avenue conductors, criss-crossed with neighbourhood loops of fuse-box apartment blocks and wire nexuses of solder-coloured streets. Japanese concrete, glass and aluminium have all but replaced the traditional 18th century homesteads, although one beautiful example, Lin Antai, still survives, moved painstakingly brick by brick, Abu Simbel-like, to avoid being flattened by a motorway. Above it all soars T'ai-pei 101, at 509m (1,670ft) currently the world's tallest building. Yet despite its macrochip order, close-up the city is organized chaos, its streets possessing some four names, one Cantonese the other Roman, neither connected in meaning or sound yet both mistranslated into the other alphabet.

At the turn of the 19th century this flat northern corner of the island was home to a few thousand rice and vegetable farmers. The provinces were attracted by the gold-paved streets of the industrial and technological explosion, some of them creating multinational success stories, others ending up in the sweatshops that shod the trainer empires of the West.

Taipei's weather makes no distinction: the perennial smog and humidity here make sweat a by-word for all forms of work. But for all its industry and mini Hong Kong capitalism, T'ai-pei is also a cultural centre, its National Palace Museum a centre for Chinese art, accidental home to the vast and priceless collection of the Chinese imperial Song dynasty, including so many pieces of prehistoric pottery that fragments are only exhibited on a rotational basis.

Away from the wired technocrats, T'ai-pei chills to the slow grace of t'ai chi slow-mo shadow boxing and the serene lotus ponds in its botanical gardens. Nightime revolves around markets, specializing in jade, flowers and, more unusually, snakes. Down louche Huahsi St. (branded Snake Alley) locals perform with live cobras, slurp snake soup and worship the eastern viagra of snake bile and penis pills.

People of intoxicating energy, the locals are famous for their *renao* (liveliness) and this boisterous 24-hour spirit ensures that among the fibroptic alleyways of its nightmarkets the city is a neon-eating orgy of smiling students high on serpentine aphrodisiacs, brothels and the joy of a thousand karaoke bars.

"T'ai-pei is still as Chinese as a spring roll – with barbecue sauce on top." Peter Biddlecombe

> T'AI-PEI, TAIWAN > LONGITUDE: 121°33' E > LATITUDE: 25°04' N > ALTITUDE: 26 feet/8 metres > POPULATION: 2,707,800 > TWINNED WITH: 46 cities including Atlanta, Boston, Cleveland, Dakar, Dallas, Ho Chi Minh City, Houston, Jeddah, Johannesburg, La Paz, Los Angeles, Manila, Panama City, San Francisco, Ulan Bator, Warsaw > NATIVES: Cho-Liang Lin, Kaku Morin

"Nanjing has had a horribly chequered past.
And yet on the surface you would
never know it. Her image is
relentlessly upbeat." Simon Winchester

THE CITY OF NANJING has a credible claim to be the authentic capital of China. For centuries, under a host of dynasties, but most notably during the Ming dynasty, it was the country's capital, but eventually lost out to Beijing. The etymology of the two names says it all: Nanjing means "southern capital", Beijing "northern capital". Since losing the struggle for supremacy, Nanjing (which the West used to call Nanking) has been able to concentrate on its role as one of China's most attractive cities, with a more countrified air than Beijing, and a less frenetic pace than Shanghai.

Located at the meeting of the Qinhuai River and the Yangtse, which heads on towards the coast of the East China Sea some 70 miles (113km) away, Nanjing is surrounded on three sides by hills and mountains, with lakes and rivers watering its greenery. Its position as the gateway of the Yangtse made the city a much prized site, over which extensive amounts of blood have been spilt.

In the Stone City area in the west of Nanjing, traces of the red rock walls built 2,000 years ago are still visible, as well as the extensive remains of the Ming dynasty brick wall which follows the contours of the Qinhuai River and which attempted, often in vain, to protect the city from onslaughts. These came from all sides. In 1864, the Qing dynasty swept down from the north and wiped out the Taiping Rebels who had been based in Nanjing for over a decade, eradicating them and almost all the Ming dynasty buildings. British warships threatened the city during the Opium Wars of the mid-19th century, and, nearly a century later in 1937, the Japanese captured Nanjing, inflicting a massacre of such barbarity and ferocity (an estimated 300,000 people were killed) that it has become known as "the other Holocaust" and continues to exacerbate tensions between the two countries.

Despite the grimness of its past, Nanjing has an agreeable feel. As well as its artisanal heritage (textiles, especially brocades, and the cotton known as "nankeen") the city has a strong intellectual and academic reputation – one of the earliest great dictionaries was compiled here – that has attracted a strong Western student community. Its broad boulevards are frequently lined with multiple rows of plane trees, and to the east of the centre is Zijin Shan (the Purple Gold Mountain) which offers a cooling retreat from the fierce summer heat down in the city. Here lie the tombs of Ming emperors, and the mausoleum of Sun Yat-Sen, China's first, and increasingly revered, post-imperial president: the marble stairway which ripples up the hillside to the white granite, blue-roofed mausoleum, surrounded by pine trees, has become one of China's most visited sites.

ARCHETYPAL SYMBOL OF REVOLUTION, equality and self-propelled individuality, the bicycle has long reigned supreme in Beijing. But now, with the city in a constant state of transition as it gears up for the 2008 Olympics, even this icon of popularism is under threat from the 4x4s and Mercs now cruising Beijing's freeways.

Beijing is China's seat of power – moved here from Nanjing in 1421 – and the country's showcase for the Western world. Here is Utopia writ large. The faded China of Bertolucci's *The Last Emperor* survives in the red walls, palaces and courtyards of the Forbidden City, stately pleasuredome of the Ming and Qing dynasties of China's imperial past, right in the heart of Beijing. Immediately alongside lies the vast eulogy to control, order and harmony that is Tiananmen Square, the largest public space in the world, and in 1989 the scene of one of modern history's most iconic moments: the student David defying the Goliath tank. Like many Beijing landmarks – the Gate of Supreme Harmony, the Hall of Literary Glory, the Hall of Martial Valour –

Tiananmen's name, "The Gate of Heavenly Peace", is abstract and absolute, an appellation bequeathed by Mao Zedong, "The Great Helmsman", whose cult still lives on in his mausoleum in the square, and in the sale of kitsch Maomorabilia.

Order lives hand-in-hand with superstition and symbolism. Feng Shui and Taoism – those opiates of Western interior designers and psychoanalysts – find their ultimate expression here in the north-south layout of pavilions, city gates and squares, New Age fashions that have done much to open up China to the West (that, of course, and the ubiquitous Peking duck, available here as on Chinatown menus worldwide). Beijing people take time out to search for those elusive universal forces of *qi* and *ling*, staring at trees in meditation, conducting slow-motion *qigong* gymnastics or therapeutic street calligraphy. Huge and busy city though it is, Beijing has an air of calm.

But it's not all *yin*. There's some *yang* as well. A handful of Beijing's *hutongs* have survived – the narrow, nearly impassable lanes of the city's old merchant districts, named as if by a child: Rain Lane, Luck Lane, Happiness Lane. A hubbub of reckless rickshaws, and the impromptu business of street barbers and dentists, still provide a flavour of old Beijing, just as the parks, the quiet courtyards and the

colonnades of the Summer Palace provide a counterbalance to the stern concrete order of the grey flats marching across the suburbs.

In the silicon valley zone of Zhongguancun, intent on finding the Chinese Bill Gates, blue-suited Maoist conformity has been replaced by the polo-necked millionaires of a start-up city. Hi-rise has superceded the traditional horizontal living plane, and massive post-modern hotels give the main east-west artery, Chang'An Avenue, a distinctly Vegas feel. Beijing may not yet be a reflection of the rest of China, but this crouching tiger is confident of a golden age not known since Kubla Khan, the Silk Road and pretty vases.

"The people coming here to plant trees are fewer, but the people coming here to pick fruit are more and more."

Xu Hong, professor at Beijing University

> BEIJING, CHINA > LONGITUDE: 116°27' E > LATITUDE: 39°52' N > ALTITUDE: 170 feet/52 metres > POPULATION: 6,643,900 (metro: 12,845,00)
> TWINNED WITH: Bangkok, Belgrade, Berlin, Cairo, Canberra, Tokyo, Washington DC > NATIVES: Cui Jian, Emperor Kangxi, Chen Kalge, Jet Li, Lao She, Mei Lanfang, Wang Meng, Tz'u-His, Faye Wong, Xinran, Zhang Ziyi > RESIDENTS: Cao Xueqin, Empress Cixi, Pu Yi (the Last Emperor), Matteo Ricci, Soong Qing-Ling, Mao Zedong

PERTH AUSTRALIA

THERE WAS A TIME, in 1987, when Australia launched its defence of the much-prized America's Cup trophy off the coast of Perth's port of Fremantle, that – for the first time in a long while – global attention was firmly turned to what is always called the most isolated major city in the world. The most telling statistic is the one that reveals that the distance from Perth to Sydney, on the far side of Australia, is as far as London to Beirut, with really nothing in between. Perth is in a bubble all of its own – a very pleasant bubble, it has to be said. Perthians love their home city, but some escapees will remark that's only because they have nowhere else to go. Even along the West Australian coast, the nearest place of note northwards is an eight-hour drive away.

Consequently, Perth has learnt to live off its own resources, which it has a-plenty. Half a dozen miles inland from the Indian Ocean, it lies on the shores of the delightfully clean Swan River, which swells to form what is effectively a lake in the middle of the compact city. King's Park, up on Mount Eliza next to the river, provides 1,000 acres (405 hectares) of bushland right in the heart of Perth. The ocean shores offer surfing and bodyboarding, or a chance just to chill out.

Other resources, of the mineral variety, provided the city's wealth. After Captain James Stirling dropped anchor in 1826, the British, in very short order, expelled the native aboriginal people and imported hulk-loads of convicts to build the infrastructure. However, the future did not look especially bright until the 1890s, when gold was discovered at Kalgoorlie and Coolgardie.

The Mint building, Government House and St George's Anglican Cathedral all reflect this upswing in Perth's fortunes. They lurk in between the new buildings that shot up during the city's second mineral boom (this time bauxite, nickel and iron ore), which started in the 1960s, creating some less than aesthetically pleasing constructions, dubbed "down-under Dallas".

As word about Perth's lifestyle spread, so too did its LA-style suburbs, mile upon mile of malls, villas, pools and gardens, reaching out and engulfing Fremantle, which had always been a separate port town in its own right (and which retains many original penal colony buildings). The affluent headed to the ocean at Cottesloe and Peppermint Grove, the arty to Northbridge, and the cappuccino ladies to Subiaco, just next to King's Park. Natural fun-seekers headed out to Rottnest Island for snorkelling and bird-watching, while more nocturnal creatures now prefer Onyx, voted Australia's sexiest bar.

Isolation has its advantages, although Perth possesses a few quirks (abortion is illegal, prostitution legal) and the extraordinary cleanliness and ubiquitous niceness can feel a little bit Stepford Wives. But, small matter, the lifestyle is suitably seductive…

> PERTH, WESTERN AUSTRALIA, AUSTRALIA > LONGITUDE: 115°47' E > LATITUDE: 31°56' S
> ALTITUDE: 32 feet/10 metres > POPULATION: 1,315,900 > TWINNED WITH: Houston,
Kagoshima (Japan), Rhodes (Greece), San Diego CA, Vasto (Italy) > NATIVES: Judy Davis,
Herb Elliott, Rolf Harris, Stan Lazarides, Dennis Lillee > RESIDENTS: Robert Holmes à Court

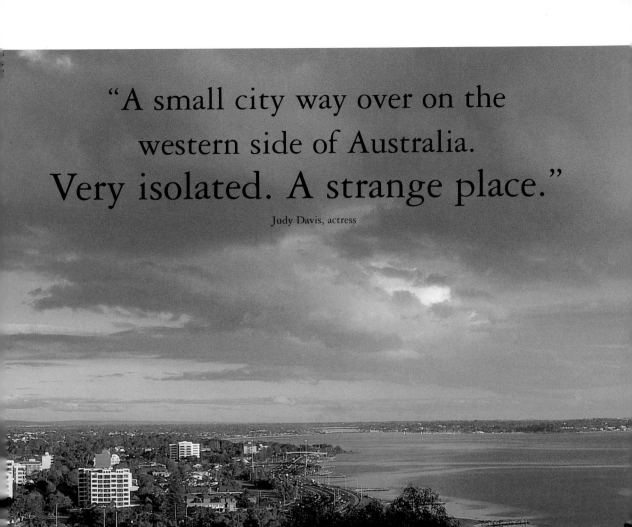

"A small city way over on the
western side of Australia.
Very isolated. A strange place."

Judy Davis, actress

AN OUTPOST OF THE WEST on the underbelly of the sleeping Chinese giant, Hong Kong always was an exception – a peninsula out on a limb, a paean to capitalism and sign to the East of the way the world was going.

That it existed at all was testament to the outrageous manoeuvring of colonial times. In 1771,

return to its neighbours. Enter the dragon in 1997 for the "handover" amid apprehension as to whether Beijing would curb the island's freedoms and the glitzy lifestyle they brought.

But China, it seems, is addicted to Hong Kong as much as its inhabitants are to the fluctuations of the Hang Sheng Index. Across the dotted

"You may not like it. We don't ask you to like it. We don't expect you to like it. But you must admit it works." Jan Morris

seeing themselves increasingly overcharged for silk and their beloved tea, the British decided to drug the local Chinese with 154,000lbs (70,000kg) of Bengal opium. The Chinese became so addicted that when the Emperor banned the trade in "foreign mud" the British could always find corrupt Chinese officials to keep it going – at least until 1839, when harsher imperial punishments stamped it out. At this point the British decided to invade, and in 1841 claimed control of Hong Kong Island. Control of the Kowloon peninsula was granted under the Convention of Peking, and in 1898 they secured a 99-year mortgage-free lease on their New Territories.

The successive conflicts of Chinese civil war, Japanese invasion and trade embargoes during the Korean War forced Hong Kong to move from trade to manufacturing and eventually the service industries, transforming it over the years into a banking paradise with vertical glass temples to the worship and pursuit of Mammon – a dynamic, free-wheeling hedonistic Vegas of a city, all the racier for its stance at odds with its future landlord next door.

No city is an island, and it was written in Hong Kong's green tea leaves that it would one day

border is the Special Economic Zone of Shenzhen, China's free-market experiment – a Chinese Silicon Valley of homegrown dot coms, new engine of the economy. Hong Kong may officially now be called Xianggang but the walls of capitalism seem impregnable to fading Maoism. The expat British community still waft through their world of cricket, hobycats, rugby tournaments and private clubs, retiring to their mansions around Repulse Bay on "the Island". Bankers, lawyers and brokers still come out to work hard, play hard on rites-of-passage, live-it-up placements. And the Cantonese follow suit, sashaying (or satAying!) through the shops and markets of Tsim Tsa Tsui.

Perhaps there always was a thin seam of Chinese tradition beneath the glitz – in the noodles, dumpling soup, floating restaurants and the enclave of fishing junks in Aberdeen. But looking down into the volcano of lights and dramatic architecture from the steep cliff of Victoria Peak, Hong Kong is one big market of giddy consumerism, fake and real at the same time. Hong Kong is not a city but a brand, territory, time zone, attitude and way of life.

> GUANGZHOU, GUANGDONG, CHINA > LONGITUDE: 113°12' E > LATITUDE: 23°09' N > ALTITUDE: 16 feet/5 metres > POPULATION: 3,998,000 (metro: 10,110,000)
> TWINNED WITH: Auckland, Durban (South Africa), Fukuoka, Honolulu, Kwangju (South Korea), Linköping (Sweden), Los Angeles, Oita City (China), Sydney, Vancouver
> NATIVES: I.M. Pei

JUST SOUTH OF THE Tropic of Cancer, Guangzhou – better known in the West as Canton – is diametrically opposed in spirit as well as location to Beijing, far up in the north of China. The view from Guangzhou is that the capital is uptight, bureaucratic, emotionally and climatically chilly. For the residents of Beijing, Guangzhou is just chaotic, unregimented and far too obsessed with business and gluttony. In fact, the saying goes, the people of Guangzhou will eat anything that flies, apart from a plane, and anything with four legs except a table.

And it's hard to disagree down amongst the street markets and the restaurants, where the products on offer belong less on a menu than a list of endangered species: serpent gall, salamanders, turtles, monkey brain, bear's paws, even whole owls. Although Cantonese cuisine – stir-fries and dim sum – is what most of the rest of world imagines when it thinks of Chinese food, these more recherché dishes are probably not what it has in mind.

The awareness of Cantonese cooking is a side effect of the vast diaspora of Guangzhou's population to create the Chinatowns of Europe and the United States. That millions of emigrants were able to do this is because of Guangzhou's historical position, for long tranches of time, as the only Chinese port allowed to have any trade or truck with the rest of the world, while the rest of the country had sternly slammed the doors shut.

In the curve of the slow, gentle Pearl River (pollutants, sadly, have diminished the nacreous suggestion of its name), on a fertile delta opening up into the South China Sea, Guangzhou flourished as a trading centre under a variety of dynasties since the 7th century. Eventually the Europeans arrived, and Britain began a lucrative trade shipping in opium from Bengal in exchange for (all the) tea in China. A dispute led to the Opium Wars of the mid-19th century, which the Europeans won, giving them the chance to secure their presence, after which the British and French established a firm foothold in Shamian Island in the heart of the city: the island's cathedrals and grand houses still lend it the genteel air of Kensington or Bordeaux.

Apart from the Orchid Gardens (Guangzhou is known as the City of Flowers) and the temples – there is little peace or gentility to be had. Bikes, cars and taxis clog the narrow streets and lanes of the main city, dodging the traders and stalls occupying every available space. The sounds of Hong Kong soap-operas and Cantonese pop compete with each other. Speech patterns are not the crafted diplomatic Mandarin of the north, but guttural, rough, street patter. And the owls just keep their heads down.

"It is at once the flashiest and most traditional of the great cities. Whereas Shanghai grew sudden and unnatural from its origins, Canton remains rooted in a long, commercial past." Colin Thubron

"Please don't laugh but would you like to **buy a wolf?**"

Tiziano Terzani, *A Fortune-teller Told Me*

> ULAN BATOR, MONGOLIA > LOCAL NAME: Ulaanbaatar > LONGITUDE: 106°58' E > LATITUDE: 47°48' N > ALTITUDE: 4298 feet/1310 metres > POPULATION: 754,000
> TWINNED WITH: T'ai-pei, Tianjin (China), Yinchuan City (China) > RESIDENTS: Genghis Khan

TO THE INHABITANTS OF Outer Mongolia's capital, the proverbial middle of nowhere is the centre of the world. Situated on a windblown steppe surrounded by four holy peaks on the edge of the Gobi Desert, this planet's largest, the city is the country's only metropolitan area.

The concept of a city is at odds with the fundamentally nomadic nature of the Mongol people. As their main camp, a collection of *gers*, or felt- or skin-covered tents, Ulan Bator moved around as they foraged, changing name with each change of location. And they foraged quite a bit: in the 12th century under Genghis Khan, the world's best-known Mongol, they boasted an empire that stretched from the Danube to the Pacific, still the largest ever to have existed on earth.

It was not until 1788 that Urga (the city's former name) was established, the encampment having grown so large that finally it had to stay put. Chronicles tell of a rich, luxurious and cosmopolitan centre of commerce, teaching and religious tolerance. The smooth-textured *gers* gave the impression of a "City of Felt", then home to Russians, Tibetans and Chinese and interspersed with Byzantine cupolas, Buddhist temples and monasteries thronging with orange-clad *lamas*. The *yurt* of the last *khan* – who went by the nickname of Batman – was said to be covered in the luxuriant skin of a snow-leopard.

The name Ulan Bator means "Red Hero", which gives an idea of the visitation that was shortly to befall the Mongol capital. The Soviets invaded and swept aside the Mongols' medieval ways. As Tiziano Terzani writes, "the symbol of modernity was the city, and so even the Mongols – nomads, shepherds, men of the steppe – used to living in yurts – had to have one". The city was given the Soviet imprint,

complete with the standard Lenin and Stalin Streets. The Zil limos of *apparatchiks* replaced the camels, cold grey apartment blocks sprang up in place of the *gers*, and the *lamas*, along with private enterprise and freedom of learning, incompatible with Communism, were chased out of town.

The Soviet Empire has collapsed and Mongolia is again independent, but Ulan Bator will probably never recover its original oriental character and mystique; the concepts of statehood and modernism are irreversible, the Soviet influence too concrete and indelible. Amid the dusty building site they left behind, though, the fortune-telling *lamas* are returning and the Mongol identity is being re-established. Mongols are newly proud of Genghis Khan. Every July in the central Sikhbatar Square they celebrate the brawn at the core of his methods in the Nadaam festival of wrestling, a Mongolian version of *Gladiators*.

Although these rites exist there is the sense that the collective consciousness of a people is gone. But Ulan Bator is no longer a mere tourist curiosity along the Trans-Siberian railway, or Outer Mongolia a mocking metaphor for being lost; it is once again a destination.

JAKARTA INDONESIA

IF SINGAPORE IS A PARADIGM of urban planning, of a city conceived with almost excess thought, its near neighbour Jakarta is its antithesis, the epitome of urban impetuosity, of buildings thrown up with little or no thought at all.

Jakarta is a teeming and unwieldy hotchpotch of upwardly mobile skyscrapers next to downtrodden *kampung* huts, of exposed sewers, smelly canals, congested expressways and lingering smog. North to south the city becomes progressively more modern, poverty gradually hidden by penthouses and golf courses. Jakarta is an all-too-typical image of destitution and excess.

Jakarta, the largest port on the island of Java, is the capital of the archipelago of islands and jigsaw of ethnic groups that make up the state of Indonesia. Java, Bali, Makasser… exotic names that adorn the canisters of musky Western deodorants, until recently a byword for paradise and escapism. But like the terrorist bomb that so rudely shattered these visions in Bali, Jakarta is a rude awakening.

The history of Jakarta is a tale of exploitation and transient colonial interest. The city was founded by Pajajan Indians at the port of Sunda Kelapa and christened Batavia. The Portuguese were the first to invade, purloining the port as a valuable stopover for their incursions into the Spice Islands. When they left, the opportunity to take over was seized by the Sultan of Banten. Successful in his conquest he made the city part of his Muslim sultanate and rechristened it "Jayakarta", meaning "City of Victory". And so it remained, decimated by cholera and known as the "white man's grave", gently sliding into decline, until, in the great colonizing era of the 19th century, the Dutch arrived. In a token gesture of colonial awareness they restored the city's original name and made the city an administrative hub of the Dutch East India Company. At its apogee Batavia was the most important port of the Dutch Empire.

The only legacy of the Dutch colonial area is Jakarta's prettiest feature. Kota district is a mini-Amsterdam of tall, thin timbered houses with porthole attic windows, sloping red-tiled roofs, canals and locks, straight out of a Rembrandt landscape. While there may be no other competition for scenic spots, Kota is as beautiful as it is surprising.

The final straw for this troubled port was the Japanese invasion of 1942 when the city's name was shortened to its current appellation. While the inevitable push for independence from Holland gained momentum, Jakarta and Indonesia had been left with little infrastructure or identity. When independence came in 1949 centuries of instability revealed a vacuum into which only a dictator could step. The last of the Suhartos resigned amid student riots in 1998, leaving this sultry and humid country and its capital on the verge of combustion and threatening to boil over.

"Jakarta is a bizarre rijsttafel of a city, as if served by a trainee anarchist Dutch waiter who has no more idea of the proper way to serve an Indonesian meal than how to survive without drugs for a whole afternoon."

Peter Biddlecombe

> JAKARTA, INDONESIA > LONGITUDE: 106°48' E > LATITUDE: 6°07' S > ALTITUDE: 33 feet/10 metres > POPULATION: 9,815,000 > TWINNED WITH: Berlin, Casablanca, Los Angeles
> NATIVES: Mohammad Husni Thamrin

"Three years, how quick they moved – look how the world's improved. Saigon, that queen of sin, re-named for Ho Chi Minh!"

Alain Boublil, *Miss Saigon*

> HO CHI MINH CITY, VIETNAM > LOCAL NAME: Hồ Chi Minh > LONGITUDE: 106°42' E > LATITUDE: 10°45' N > ALTITUDE: 26 feet/8 metres > POPULATION: 3,934,000
> TWINNED WITH: San Francisco, T'ai-pei > NATIVES: Richard Cocciante, Marguerite Duras, Le Van Duyet, Thich Quang Duc > RESIDENTS: James Fenton, Graham Greene

106°42' E

come through decades of French colonization, after all. So, 20 years further on, when the clamp of Communism relaxed, private enterprise resurfaced with a vengeance.

As a result, the Ho Chi Minh City of the 21st century shows the impact of a building boom unleashed in the 1990s. The loss of French influence is inevitable (although tree-lined avenues, some fine façades and the grand Hôtel de Ville, the old city hall, have escaped), but the eradication of the old-style, communal Vietnamese houses is a much sadder loss. The Sai Gon River has seen it all and rolls on down towards the South China Sea, recalling the original Khmer city built on swampy forest land, the Saigon that became a major trading post, then the leading city of French Cochinchina, and – once the UN's cartographers had bisected Vietnam at the 17th Parallel in 1954 – capital of the South.

It is still possible to see the traceline that links present back to past. Cyclists carry massive loads in baskets on simple shoulder poles as they have done for decades. Tricycle-taxis provide a roller-coaster ride past cell-phoning businessmen and women (the latter sporting either "now girl" miniskirts or the traditionally elegant *ao dai* combination of slit silk tunic and trousers) buzzing purposefully on their scooters. Hungry pedestrians squat on low stools at the street side, filling themselves up with *pho*, the traditional broth of noodles, herbs, bean sprouts, lime juice and whatever meat is to hand.

This is a city still in regeneration. The neon, nightclubs and discos are aglow once more, the shops on the Dong Khoi and in the Chinatown of Cho Lon are full of activity, but it takes more than some consumer bullishness to forget what was. The Museum of War Remnants, with its foetuses deformed by Agent Orange, or the massive Cu Chi complex of Viet Cong tunnels (which makes the Great Escape's efforts look positively amateurish) pull no punches. Look into the eyes of a Ho Chi Minh citizen and there's a wariness, a memory of past pain…, but within seconds they'll still be offering a deal on some Buddha cigarettes and a Zippo lighter.

FOR MUCH OF THE WORLD the overriding memory of Ho Chi Minh City (aka Saigon) is the footage of choppers airlifting the last Americans out of the US Embassy as the Vietnam War imploded. The Embassy is no more, though the legacy of the war – and the progeny of GIs on R&R in the city – lives on. The foreign journalists enjoying cocktails and the view from the verandahs of the Rex or the Majestic (as Graham Greene's Quiet American did) made their excuses and left. With a weary shrug, the people of Saigon watched the helicopters depart and got on with their daily existence. They'd

COMPARED TO THE BRASHER, flashier, easier-going Saigon (or Ho Chi Minh City as we must now call it), the Vietnamese capital Hanoi is less crowded, more reserved and conservative, more traditional. Precisely because of that, its frequently rainy, muted, discreet charm is beguiling. Although Hanoi is resolutely proud to embrace Communism – the black-suited, goateed Ho Chi Minh, installed in perpetuity in his hushed mausoleum, is still revered – there is no forbidding Stalinist architecture or oversized public square.

Hanoi did not call in the wrecking balls, but preserved its old medieval quarter, Pho Co, the area of "36 Streets", a jumble of 13th-century lanes where each street, or pho, was named after a different guild, and the business conducted there, from coffin-making to the horse hair trade.

In many cases the businesses, bursting out of the tiny frontages of long, narrow, tunnel-like stores, have not changed. In Pho Hang Bac, gemstones are still the principal business; in Pho Hang Gai, the rolls

> HANOI, VIETNAM > LOCAL NAME: Ha Nôi > LONGITUDE: 105°51' E > LATITUDE: 21°01' N > ALTITUDE: 20 feet/6 metres > POPULATION: 2,871,000
> NATIVES: Bao Ninh > RESIDENTS: Ho Chi Minh

of silk are as fresh and soothing to the touch as ever. A few of the *phos* have evolved. Hang Hanh, Onion Street, now offers a wider choice of fare, full of cafés and restaurants. And in medieval times, there was no street dedicated to the sale of calculators or "Swiss" watches. Hanoi is surrounded by fertile land irrigated by the Red River (Hanoi means "city within the bend of the river") and fresh produce, fruits, flowers, vegetables, flourishes. Water is plentiful too; as well as the river there are canals and a couple of dozen lakes, especially Hoan Kiem, where senior citizens practise t'ai chi alongside vendors, photographers and puppeteers who perform waist-deep in the lake.

A *cyclo-pousse* ride west from the lake, the quarter of Ba Dinh contains boulevards of French villas with wrought-iron railings; the city's restored Opera House is a miniature version of Charles Garnier's Opéra National in Paris (Hanoi's nickname was "the Paris of the Orient").

As Tonkin, this was a French protectorate city for 50 years, before defeat in 1954 at the siege of Dien Bien Phu put the kibosh on France's presence, and started the domino effect which led to US involvement and the whole débâcle of the Vietnam War. Three-quarters of the city's population was evacuated to avoid the US bombing; "Hanoi Jane" Fonda made the journey the other way to protest.

When the French took over in the 1880s, the city had only been known as Hanoi for half a century: its first name (the first of many) was Thang Long, the City of the Soaring Dragon, after a vision experienced by the Emperor Ly Thai To, who founded the city in 1010. Behind the changes inevitably brought about by increasing construction and capitalism, Ly's dragon is still making sure Hanoi doesn't forget its past.

"The spirit of Hanoi is strongest by night, even stronger in the rain."

Bao Ninh, *The Sorrow of War*

PHNOM PENH CAMBODIA

THERE IS STILL BEAUTY TO BE FOUND in Phnom Penh: in a stroll down past the restaurants and hotels on Sisowath Quay, the broad promenade along the west bank of the Tonlé Sap River, or on entering the Royal Palace, beneath tiered roofs and gables which help to enhance the turrets and spires that – rather than hi-rise office blocks – punctuate the skyline of the Cambodian capital deep in the jungle. The compound of the Palace contains the Silver Pagoda with its many Buddhas (including one of emerald and another of gold and diamonds) and its floor made of 5,000 blocks of silver.

But, like a scar across a beautiful face, the short, savage four-year regime of the Khmer Rouge from 1975 to 1979 rearranged the physiognomy – and permanently damaged the psychology – of the city that was once hailed as the most beautiful city in Indo-China. The Khmer Rouge was methodical in its brutality, keeping detailed audits of the tortures and killings. The memory of the atrocities carried out behind the closed doors of the S-21 prison and on the killing fields of Choeung Ek, 15 miles (24km) away from the city, is preserved both in the chilling Museum of Genocide and a glass memorial filled with skulls of the victims.

Phnom Penh emerged from that nightmare a tougher, hardened place, where many of the secrets of those years remain sealed, and where the rule of law is under strain, especially following the coup of 1998. Weapons are visible and plentiful, likewise prostitution and drug abuse, and the physical damage caused by landmines. But far from all of the old Phnom Penh was destroyed – the Khmer

Rouge never harmed the fabric of the Palace, for example – and when the moon rises over the Mekong, the dominant river of the three that converge here, it is still possible to imagine the erotically sugared romance of the pre-Khmer Rouge city.

The Cambodian King Ponhea Yat, abandoning Angkor, moved his capital in 1432 to the site of a temple, Wat Phnom, built 50 years earlier by one Lady Penh, who had experienced a vision involving a tree and a number of Buddhas. However, the city slid back into obscurity a century or so later and it was not until the 1860s, when one of Ponhea Yat's successors, King Norodom, moved the court back there that Phnom Penh's fortunes revived.

The French helped King Norodom construct his palace and supplied city planners to add canals, boulevards and a river promenade – the usual Indochine colonial look. It is a vista that can still be enjoyed from an armchair in the old Foreign Correspondents Club overlooking the quayside, with an iced coffee to relieve the humidity.

"It was a city
of twists,
a town of
secrets,
a wonderfully
lawless place,
a good city
for a motorbike."

Robert Bingham, *Lightning On The Sun*

> PHNOM PENH, CAMBODIA > LOCAL NAME: Phnum Pénh > LONGITUDE: 104°57′ E > LATITUDE: 11°33′ N > ALTITUDE: 39 feet/12 metres > POPULATION: 1,133,800
> TWINNED WITH: Tianjin (China) > NATIVES: Norodom Sihanouk

AN APPARENT PARADIGM OF SOPHISTICATION and arty aristocracy, Paris would seem to have a relative in every part of the world; but the one in the heart of Siberia is perhaps its least known. Siberia may not be associated with cities, but Irkutsk is Siberia's urban soul.

The city sits astride the Irkut River on the shore of Lake Baikal, the largest freshwater lake in the world, famed for its purity and brittle ecosystem and *cause célèbre* of ecologists. The presence of the lake has largely eclipsed the fame of the rather surprising and pretty minor metropolis and quasi spa town of 18th- and 19th-century wooden architecture and flamboyant cupolas by which it is reached. And yet Irkutsk occupies a unique and transitional place in Russian history.

This is where the 1905 Decembrists, young officers of the Tsar's army, were exiled after their failed attempt to overthrow the Romanov regime. They were Russia's first revolutionaries and a sign of things to come, but finding themselves so remote from the injustices of St Petersburg these parvenus forgot their revolutionary views and grew instead rather fond of the status they were granted and the respect with which they were viewed by the peasant population of their new home. Their sophistication and civility of accent granted them aristocratic status and so they became the world's original champagne socialists – *flâneurs* and *boulevardiers*, perfecting the art of highfalutin conversation and guardians of local *bon ton*.

Unravished by Soviet planning, the Gogolian confused identity of that era is still very much part of the city's magic and character. Originally little more than a trading post that benefited from the cross-current of wealth from the gold and sable-fur trade, Irkutsk is still essentially a provincial town. The old-world humble, higgledy-piggledy architecture of wood houses, some of them like Chekhovian summer-houses, smell of the forest and give the impression of quiet rural retreat. And yet here and there are signs of an imposed form and the greater ambition of a regional capital. The writer Colin Thubron noted the "outbursts of pomposity and fuss" that leap out among the dachas, determinedly European but with tell-tale flamboyant oriental touches such as the turquoise cupolas of the Zvarovsky Monastery, sparkling against the snow like a Fabergé egg and reminding one of bygone Tsarist opulence.

A little-known jewel at the heart of the pristine landscape of the Siberian taiga, frozen in the snow as if in time, Irkutsk is set to experience a new boom as the ecologists and conservationists are joined by the gaudy new tsars of a newly rich nation rediscovering domestic tourism.

> "A provincial dowager living in two ages, frontier entrepôt and minor metropolis, Tsarist boom town and plaything of Soviet directives."
>
> Bartle Bull, *Around the Sacred Sea*

103°51' E

THE ULTIMATE STOPOVER CITY, long
derided as bland and boring, Singapore
is trying to shake off its image as an
intolerable dictatorship of hygiene and order
and to find reasons to make people stay.

If ever a city embodied Huxley's *Brave
New World* then surely it was Singapore.
A model of urban planning, its skyscrapers
are glass monuments to a roll-call of the
world's leading architects. A heaven of IT
efficiency, its taxi cabs are all GSP-linked.
A subservient work ethic has built an
unparalleled independent economic prowess.

But all this is implemented with draconian
rules. Singaporeans are spoonfed endless
social campaigns. There are ubiquitous
commandments (even the obvious: "no
urintaing in lifts"!), while other weaknesses
of the 20th-century city-dweller such as
littering, spitting and jaywalking are virtually
capital offences.

It was not ever thus. A natural harbour next
to lush fertile farming land, Singapore grew
up as a haven for pirates on the East-West
trade route. Founded in the 14th century, its
Hindu Majapahit rulers christened it
"Singapur" – Sanskrit for "The Lion City" –
and under their rule the city-state was a lively
home to a rich mix of faiths and their
festivals. Under subsequent Muslim rule the
city was undergoing a middle-age malay-se,
when, in the 19th century, it was single-
handedly revived by an official of the East
India Company, whose name has become
synonymous with the hotel named after him
and the only thing most people appreciate
about the city, Sir Thomas Stamford Bingley
Raffles, the founder of modern Singapore.

Raffles found a pretty city full of fine
pastel-coloured Chinese-baroque houses.
He switched the city's industry from farming
to trade and set about an urban generation
which led Roland Braddell in 1934 to describe
the city as "so George Fifth, a kind of tropical

cross between Manchester and Liverpool". His vision of a tapestry-city organized according to its ethnic communities is still in place: South Street is the core of Chinatown, Serangoon Road the heart of Little India and Kampung the glamorous Muslim district. Raffles House itself lies in the heart of the financial district and the famous hotel, where the Singapore Sling cocktail was first concocted, in the Civic District.

Capitulation to the Japanese in 1942 (after which the city was briefly renamed Syonan, "Light of the South") undermined the Singaporean reverence for its British masters. After the war, independence became inevitable, eventually achieved in 1965.

Today Singapore's Pernaham cuisine and tax-free boutiques on Orchard Road make it a haven for foodies and one-stop shoppers. The smiling Singaporeans with their quaint "Singlish" dialect have found a new sense of history through the conventions of their benevolent dictatorship. Censorship laws are being relaxed, and with its newfound liberalism the city is undergoing an arts explosion. But as one writer observed, it is still "like a big desk, full of drawers and pigeon-holes, where everything has its place, and can always be found".

"Even the chaos is planned chaos."

Rem Koolhaas

BAGUETTES, *CAFÉ AU LAIT* AND CROISSANTS – not the commodities you might expect to find in the capital of Laos. But Laos was once part of French Indo-China and the French influence is as palpable today in the taste of its wines and delicate patisserie as it is in its architecture, which, with its yellow-wash, shuttered villas and red-tiled roofs, exudes a Mediterranean air that is "toujours Provence". A small and quiet city, it underpins a mellow, almost lethargic post-colonial atmosphere that makes Vientiane one of the most agreeable cities in South-East Asia, a far cry from the techno and jungle music hustle and hustling of Bangkok.

Founded in the 10th century along the banks of the Mekong River, the city was originally called Vieng Chan (from "Wiang", meaning "fortified city"). Under King Setthathirat, the city was at the heart of the 14th-century Lan Xang kingdom (meaning "the Kingdom of a Million Elephants", and from which Laos is derived). But it was not until 1566 that the status of capital was moved to Vientiane from Luang Prabang.

The small kingdom could not escape the intentions of its neighbours across the river in Thailand and in 1827 the city was sacked by the Siamese. The cessation of hostilities eventually led to the construction of the Friendship Bridge that now joins the two countries; however, after the sacking Vientiane was effectively abandoned.

It was only *grâce à* the French explorer, Auguste Pavie, that the city was rediscovered and resurrected. A keen linguist, he was able to form alliances and wrest the city back from the Siamese, in 1893 declaring Laos a French protectorate. Up went the tree-lined boulevards and villas, in came the coffee culture and Michelin tastebuds. Lan Xang Avenue is still Vientiane's Champs-Elysées while the river-front Fa Nguan Road is a tropical *quai de la Seine*.

In the kitchen of ideological power-mongering, 20th-century Vientiane became a stir-fry of influences. On top of the French, Thai and Vietnamese *ménage* came 25 years of Soviet rule and architecture, while the US residence during the war in neighbouring Vietnam abetted the opium dens and contributed sex shows. Yet despite this *mélange* Vientiane still retains a strong Lao identity. The golden spire of That Luang is still the holiest Buddhist monument in the country, and Wat Sisaket monastery the country's pride, spiritual home and symbol of nationhood.

But for the time being at least, a visit to Vientiane is also a delightful trip back in time to a kind of tropical version of *Jean de Florette*. Among the seductive colonial decay a slow bicycle-ride along the Mekong River is a delightfully bucolic experience, like a *paysan* pedalling through Provence, and it would appear that here too, in the heat of the tropical afternoon, a Stella Artois is just as hard to come by.

> "Vientiane is exceptional, but inconvenient. The marijuana is cheaper than pipe tobacco, and opium easier to find than a cold glass of beer."
>
> Paul Theroux, *The Great Railway Bazaar*

> VIENTIANE, LAOS > LOCAL NAME: Viangchan > LONGITUDE: 102°37' E > LATITUDE: 17°58' N
> ALTITUDE: 525 feet/160 metres > POPULATION: 555,100 > RESIDENTS: Auguste Pavie   263

KUALA LUMPUR MALAYSIA

THE CITY'S NAME IS, FRANKLY, UNINSPIRING. Kuala Lumpur is a
Malay phrase for "muddy confluence", hardly a glowing description.
At the meeting of two sludgy rivers – the doleful-sounding Gombak
and Klong – there was little to get excited about in the early days,
when a handful of shacks made up the mining community created in
the 1850s by Chinese tin prospectors. Yet, despite these unpromising
origins, Kuala Lumpur has grown up full of confidence, and ready to
take on all comers.

Witness the Petronas Towers, Kuala Lumpur's instant icon, two
slender, tapering steeples, linked by a skyway halfway up, which rise
like overextended minarets from the city's Golden Triangle, and
which, at their topping-off in 1998, snatched, with a certain amount
of impudence, the "tallest building in the world" title from Chicago's
Sears Tower (a title subsequently acquired by T'ai-pei). Cesar Pelli's
structure finally reached 1483 feet (452m) from toe to tip, outstretching
even Kuala Lumpur's other giants (the KL telecommunications tower,
though shorter, stands on higher ground and, its fans claim, offers
the better view). There was no more assertive way to declare Kuala
Lumpur's achievements and ambition. Likewise, the city underwrote
the Malaysian Grand Prix while other races like the classic Austrian
GP at the A-Ring would fall by the wayside; it successfully hosted the
1998 Commonwealth Games. And its abbreviation, KL, grants it
membership of that select club of cities who need only a few initials
for recognition – LA, BA, NYC, DC – high company indeed.

The original, pre-Petronas, version of city lies round Dataran
Merdeka, Independence Square, a splash of green overlooked by
elegant buildings, where the Union Jack finally fluttered down in
1957. British hangovers include the Carcosa Hotel, where Queen
Elizabeth II liked to stay, and two Moghul-style extravaganzas
designed by A.B. Hubbock: the onion domes of the Masjid Jame, or
Friday Mosque (completed in 1909 at the very point where the two
rivers converge), and the train station, a colonial fantasy that looks as
if was transported direct to Kuala Lumpur from Fatehpur Sikri.

New Kuala Lumpur is the KL of air-conditioned shopping centres
like the self-proclaiming Mid Valley Megamall, and the cappuccino
cafés of Bangsar. Old Kuala Lumpur persists in the hibiscus and
orchid gardens of the 1880s Lake Gardens, or out in the Batu
complex, north of the city, where vertiginous steps lead up to vast
caves, one of which has housed a temple for over a hundred years.

Together with an ethnic mix of Malay, Chinese and Indian,
Kuala Lumpur's blend of old and new is the glue that holds the
city together, like the coconut milk which coagulates the sticky
rice, *nasi lemak* – along with satay sauce, the staple of every
KL street stall.

> KUALA LUMPUR, MALAYSIA > LONGITUDE: 101°42' E > LATITUDE: 3°05' N > ALTITUDE: 164 feet/50 metres
> POPULATION: 1,427,300 > NATIVES: Jenny Seagrove

"'Kuala L'Impure',
we had misnamed
it. There was an
atmosphere of
a over-rapid
luxury, of a city
that had sprung
up overnight,
like a mushroom
too specious, too
gaudy to be
wholesome."

Jean Cocteau

THAIS HAVE A PHRASE, "*JAI YEN*", which means "cool-heartedness" or "keeping your cool". It's a quality they admire, this ability to remain light-hearted but dignified while all around is swirling bedlam. *Jai yen* is a handy asset for anyone spending time in Bangkok. In this tropical city sweltering temperatures of 30°C (86°F) prevail, day and night, for nine months of the year. Walking around works up a hefty, sticky sweat, which is why so many people resort to hiring *tuk-tuks*, the nippy three-wheeled taxi cabs which swell the overall mass of traffic.

This impression of gridlock, pollution and heat was exacerbated for many years by overheated male fantasies. Tales relayed by Vietnam vets of bar girls performing gynaecologically gymnastic tricks with ping pong balls and hundred dollar bills fuelled the legend of Bangkok as Sex Central. The days of the city's sex industry are, if not numbered, then at least, in an Aids-aware world, being counted, and though bar girls are still around to entertain foreign visitors, lonely *farangs*, in quarters like Patpong, there is more sadness than eroticism in their displays.

Any whiff of excess testosterone is more than balanced by Bangkok's softer side: the smiles and charm of its residents, the exotic orchids which thrive in its hothouse climate, and the beautiful silks brought to world notice in the 1950s and '60s by American entrepreneur Jim Thompson, Bangkok's most renowned foreign resident.

And if Bangkok became known externally for the profane, then internally it has always celebrated the sacred. Tucked beneath the highrises, billboards and flyovers of its congested centre are the shrines and spires of temple complexes known as *wats* (most famously, the theatrical, colourful Wat Phra Kaeo housing the Emerald Buddha, and the ancient Wat Po). Alongside the city's buildings, little spirit houses seek to pacify volatile supernatural spirits. The chants of saffron-robed Buddhist monks and the temple chimes provide a welcome, harmonizing note of serenity.

Tradition and devotion are part of the city's way of life. Underneath everything lies a strong sense of Thai pride, both in the country's monarchy and in their capital Bangkok, or Krung Thep as locals call it (a drastic abbreviation of its full and record-breaking 62-syllable version). The city was built in the 1780s by King Rama I of Siam to replace his former capital Ayutthaya, razed by the Burmese. On the Chao Phraya river, a few miles inland from the Gulf of Thailand, the old royal city of Ratanakosin island was ringed by a system of canals, or *khlongs*; this was the "Venice of the East". Although virtually all have been infilled in the centre of Bangkok, plenty are extant in Thonburi, across the river, where a trip through the *klongs* by longtail boat provides one means of escape from the freneticism of the city.

> BANGKOK, THAILAND > LOCAL NAME: Krung Thep Manakhon Bovorn Ratanskosin Magintharayutthaya Mahadilokpop Noparatratchathani Burirom Udomratchanivetmahasathan Avatartsathit Sakkathattiya Visnukarmrasit > LONGITUDE: 100°33' E > LATITUDE: 13°44' N > ALTITUDE: 6 feet/2 metres > POPULATION: 7,753,000 > TWINNED WITH: Beijing, Manila, Moscow, Washington DC
> NATIVES: Adam Osborne, Paradorn Srichaphan, James Wattana > RESIDENTS: H.N. Andersen, Anna Leonowens, Khunying Pornthip Rojanasunan, Tamarine Tanasugarn, Jim Thompson

"I was charmed by Bangkok. Its character is complex and inconsistent. It seems at once to combine the Hannibal, Missouri of Mark Twain's boyhood with Beverly Hills, the Low Countries and Chinatown." S.J. Perelman

FOR THE LAST FEW DECADES of the last century, it seemed as if the march of time had completely sidestepped Yangon, once known as Rangoon. The Myanmar authorities had banned the importation of new foreign cars, so the old Wolseleys and Second World War trucks – remnants of the city's British days – which constituted the bulk of Yangon's automotive population pottered around, patched up and cobbled together. In recent years, spanking new Japanese models have been allowed to appear, but the requisite driving skills have not been upgraded in parallel. Myanmar still holds the dubious honour of having the highest road fatality rate in the world.

a host of smaller temples cluster either side of the walkways, framing its burnished central dome.

When the small village of Dagon was conquered by the Burmese king in 1755, it was renamed Yangon, burned down in 1841 and rebuilt, before the British took control in 1852, renaming the city Rangoon and adding a grid system town plan. But despite the predictability of its street layout, Yangon is definitely a maverick city. In the 1970s and '80s this was primarily due to the influence of its military ruler Ne Win, a man for whom numerology, particularly the number 9, became something of an obsession. Consequently, in the mid-1980s,

"The Shwe Dagon rose superb, glistening with its gold, like a sudden hope in the dark night of the soul of which the mystics write."

W. Somerset Maugham

Yangon, like Phnom Penh, is something of a rarity among major Asian cities, as it has not yet thrown up a forest of radically modern buildings like those at Kuala Lumpur, Shanghai or Singapore. In fact, it just feels like a real forest, with a mass of shady groves, lush foliage and teak trees, a mini-Eden which gave rise to its nickname, "the Garden City of the East" (although that rather mundane phrase makes it sound rather too like a piece of 1950s civil planning).

Above the greenery, the spire of the reputedly 2,500-year-old Shwe Dagon Pagoda pokes through. The temple is the most sacred site for all Myanmar Buddhists, and visually it lives up to that expectation. Approaching the main *stupa*,

the existing decimal currency was cancelled and replaced by a system based entirely on root 9. Likewise a national holiday was designated on 9 September every year. Disappointingly for Ne Win, by 9/9/99, a date which surely would have had him in raptures, he had been out of power for seven years.

But the eccentricity has stayed on, in a new generation of teenage Yangoners who have created their own quirky form of rebellion: Buddhist punks who won't touch alcohol because of their beliefs – and there are no nightclubs in Yangon. In a world that is increasingly globalized, it is bizarrely reassuring, despite its ruling regime, to know that, for now, somewhere like Yangon exists.

> YANGON, MYANMAR > LONGITUDE: 96°08' E > LATITUDE: 16°49' N > ALTITUDE: 20 feet/6 metres > POPULATION: 3,576,500
> NATIVES: Harry H. Corbett, Nick Drake, Daw Aung San Suu Kyi, Annabella Lwin > RESIDENTS: Pablo Neruda, U Thant

"If the palace had exceeded my expectations,
the town as far fell short of them…
even the mirth and laughter of the inhabitants
I thought dreamy and ghostly."

Thomas Manning, *Journey of Mr Thomas Manning to Lhasa*

TIBET HAS BECOME THE GLOBAL SYMBOL of repression and desire for freedom, adopted, as was Spain by artists and writers in the 1930s, by hippies, filmstars and comfortable Westerners in search of a cause. A mythical snowy country in the clouds, a fairy tale from the pages of *Tintin*, invaded and robbed of its sovereignty by a giant next door, a scar of injustice on this happy Americanized planet, ripe for rescue by Richard Gere and a host of Hollywood heroes.

Ironically, Tibetan culture is arguably now more often found outside Tibet than within the shrunken Tibetan Autonomous Region (TAR) that has, since the 1950s, been a province of China. It is perhaps found even less here in its nominal capital, where the population is said to be less than one-third Tibetan, and which as a showcase for Chinese tolerance is all but artificial.

Nevertheless, Lhasa – from the Tibetan "Lha Sa", meaning "Sacred Earth" – is still a sacred city, the seat of the Buddhist faith; and with its breathtaking setting, wedged into the side of a mountain beside the Kyi-hi River and surrounded by a crown of 16,000-feet (5,000-m) Himalayan peaks, it's no wonder it has always inspired in its inhabitants an awareness of the powers and harmonies of a greater natural force.

As a sacred seat devoted to worship Lhasa was never big or conceived along the practical lines of a city, and visitors expecting all the trappings of a metropolis have invariably been disappointed, in the same way as visitors to Timbuktu. Beyond the spectacular sight of the Marpon (red mountain) and the 13-storey fortress of the Potala and Norbulingka Palaces, winter and summer residences of the Dalai Lama, an infinite appreciation of monks and monasteries is required. And this was true even before the Chinese arrived, when travellers sent back reports of a small and dismal town.

Enter the dragon in the 1950s and the city grew hi-rise apartment blocks, karaoke bars, neon signs and hotels acting as fronts for brothels. A strong military presence allows a watered-down form of worship, controlled by the Chinese Religious Affairs Bureau, making a buck out of showcase Buddhism for the coach-loads of Beijing tourists who come for a dose of Tibet chic.

It is a further irony that Buddhism and Communism are both non-theistic systems. But the Chinese are apparently paranoid about resurgent Tibetan nationalism through Lhasa's monks. Like Judaism, Buddhism has almost acquired a sense of nationality. However, it also seems to be fair game to the interior designers and footballers who have colonized it in trendy disenchantment with warring Western values.

But bad karma and Baggio Buddhism cannot take away from Lhasa and Tibet's enduring magic. The prayer flags and saffron-orange robes may be sino-cinema, and the Dalai Lama, that ancient title bestowed by the Mongol Khans, still not at home, but this reclusive pacifistic city continues to inspire adventure and stir the most atheistic soul.

> LHASA, TIBET (XIZANG), CHINA > LONGITUDE: 91°02' E > LATITUDE: 29°39' N > ALTITUDE: 11,975 feet/3,650 metres > POPULATION: 230,000
> TWINNED WITH: Boulder CO > RESIDENTS: Heinrich Harrer

271

"Calcutta is the most **intellectually exciting** place in Asia. I wish I could divert some of the intellectual emphasis onto films, but most of it stays in the coffee houses." Satyajit Ray

ALTHOUGH THE MARXIST GOVERNMENT that has run the city once known as Calcutta for a quarter of a century would doubtless prefer not to admit it, Kolkata would not have existed without the British Raj. One Job Charnock arrived on the banks of the Hooghly River in 1690 to establish an outpost of the British East India Company in West Bengal. Eighty years later it was the capital of British India, a role it served for a further 140 years.

Not unnaturally, remnants of British pomp are still visible, though many visitors find them the least interesting parts of the city; Kolkata's vitality lies elsewhere: after all, grandiose imperial edifices – and Lord Curzon's empire-glorifying Victoria Memorial is

the most grandiose of the lot – can be found in most places where British empire-builders flexed their muscles.

In any case, the Raj is not what Kolkata is primarily known for. This is a city saddled with a serious image problem. It may be the "City of Joy", but the deserved spotlight on Mother Theresa's mission for the destitute and the dying only highlighted the city's overcrowding and areas of poverty. In the monsoon season the rain is relentless, and Kolkata's low-lying topography encourages floods and torrents of mud. Worse, the notorious Black Hole of Calcutta has become lodged in the English language as a byword for squalor, overcrowding and inhumanity. The reality is that

in 1756, when Siraj-ud-Daulah, a local nawab, briefly managed to wrest control of the city, a number of British were arrested. One of the survivors went on record afterwards to say that of 146 incarcerated in a tiny airless dungeon, 123 had died over the course of one night. Historians now believe the account to have been at best embellished, at worst invented – but the damage, as far as Kolkata is concerned, was done. With that background, the termini of the subcontinent's first metro, Tollygunge and Dum Dum (as in the bullets) sound disturbing rather than quaint.

But Kolkata has got on with its life, as the city is blessed with resilience and a good deal of "cussedness", in Geoffrey Moorhouse's term. Yes, it is chaotic, noisy and bewildering – so are most Indian cities, that is one of the charms of the country – but there is plenty of soul and attitude. In the city of Rabindranath Tagore (India's first literary Nobel laureate) and Satyajit Ray, there is also a strong and important tradition of Bengali culture, literature and film-making, but here the latter is a get-on-and-do-it craft, rather than the all-dancing, all-singing spectaculars of Bollywood – not glitzy, but definitely self-confident. In the Maidan parkland running alongside the river, the lungs of Kolkata, there is even a chance to take a breather and watch the cricket at Eden Gardens, while the rest of the city wheezes.

> KOLKATA, WEST BENGAL, INDIA > LONGITUDE: 88°21' E > LATITUDE: 22°32' N > ALTITUDE: 17 feet/5 metres > POPULATION: 4,580,544 (metro: 11,020,000)
> NATIVES: Sri Aurobindo, Victor Bannerjee, Fenner Brockway, Alec Broers, Julia Margaret Cameron, Kaushiki Chakrabarty, Amit Chaudhuri, Chitra Divakarun, Sourav Ganguly, Amitav Ghosh, Bharati Mukherjee, Meera Mukherjee, Satyajit Ray, Vikram Seth, Rabindranath Tagore, William Makepeace Thackeray > RESIDENTS: Mother Teresa

"What a loveable little city this is!
No one could call it a lovely city,
yet there is **an abundance
of beauty** to be found
here." Dervla Murphy

85°18' E

THE SPIRITUAL TREKKIES heading out to Kathmandu are always easy to spot at any international airport: their hiking boots and cagoules are accessorized with prayer bracelets and a slightly disturbing evangelistic zeal in their gaze. Kathmandu is the doorway to the Himalayas and/or enlightenment, and a vibe of hippie promise (as dated, but still as potent, as patchouli oil and joss-sticks) draws those travellers in search of their personal nirvana.

Some find the experience completely liberating, a total release from the pressures of modern life. On a purely geophysical level, the prospect of Nepal's Himalaya region – the "abode of snows", squeezed between Tibet and India, with eight of the world's top ten peaks, including Everest and Annapurna – is literally uplifting. For others the release is more spiritual. Here in a high fertile valley, Kathmandu and its surrounds are studded with all manner of prayer-wheels, temples, pagodas, stupas, shrines and monastic communities, both Hindu and Buddhist.

The only word of Nepali which everyone knows is *namaste* – "I salute the god in you". In Kathmandu there are a myriad deities to salute, thousands of incarnations derived from Brahma the creator, Vishnu the preserver and Shiva the destroyer – and one living deity, the Kumari Devi, a young girl (aged between four and puberty, chosen on the basis of a rigorous horoscopic and physical selection process) who lives in downtown Kathmandu. To celebrate all this spirituality, there is a rich variety of temples. The Newar Pagodas feature multiple-tiered roofs on a stepped plinth; the Buddhist stupas combine domes, spires and 13 tapering stages; Shikhara temples are mountainous, like small St Paul's Cathedrals.

The Shangri-La dream can prove to be disappointing. A miasmic mist of pollution caught in the bowl of the surrounding mountains often shrouds Kathmandu. And the reality is a dusty, clangorous, full-on, senses-working-overtime city full of backpackers, callow youths gathering in Jochne, or "Freak Street", to swop gap-year tales

and barter for incense sticks, saris, *kukris*, Buddhas and statues amongst the beggars for which the city is now renowned. Nepal is also volatile. Maoist insurgent attacks break the peace from time to time, and the shock wave sent out by the death of the royal family was up towards the higher end of the Richter scale when Crown Prince Dipendra took a machine-gun and blew away most of his relatives and himself in 2002.

Away from the masses, the rickshaw *wallahs*, the hustle, fast food and tat around Durbar Square, the central zone of Kathmandu full of courtyard *chowks* and yet more temples and shrines, there is an escape out into the valley or to the old and relatively unchanged city that is set apart to the west. And, as Dave Allen used to conclude, "May your God go with you".

VARANASI INDIA

VARANASI – BENARES AS WAS, an attempt by the British to pronounce its name – can rightly claim to be India's holiest city. Here is the most sacred place of pilgrimage for every Hindu: like the *hadj* for a Muslim, a visit to Varanasi, and the stretch of the Ganges which runs through it, is a once-in-a-lifetime must.

This is the Samarkand, the Mecca or Jerusalem of Hinduism, the epicentre of its knowledge. Temples and monasteries are as prolific here as they are in Kathmandu. It is believed that Shiva resides in the Tarakashevra Temple. There are two essential beliefs: that the sacred waters of the Ganges will cleanse and wash away your sins, and that to be cremated in Varanasi and your ashes poured into the Ganges will give you a get-out clause from *moksha*, the otherwise endless cycle of birth, death and renewal.

The river is the defining feature of the city (although its name is in fact derived from two other rivers, the Varuna and the Asi). Curving like a crescent alongside the city, which sits on its left bank, the Ganges is where all the action takes place. And the action is endless. A million pilgrims a year spill out of the trains that rumble and screech across the Dufferin Bridge. They pour down to the *ghats*, some 100 flights of steps, next to the river, against a backdrop of crumbling old houses, which once belonged to Hindi nobility but are now somewhat decrepit.

Behind them lies a maze of incredibly narrow alleyways. The visual effect is extraordinary, and uniquely Indian.

This is where the pilgrims act out their daily and eternal lives. Prayers are made facing the sun. *Sadhus* meditate. Clothes and bodies are washed, beards shaved, begging bowls proffered and cricket matches played. The senses are constantly stimulated, by the aroma of incense, camphor or iodine, by the sounds of dogs barking, cymbals and drums, and the chanting of the mantra "Ram Ram, Satya He".

In preparation for cleansing, men strip to their briefs for the dip in the river (women wear saris). Five of the *ghats* are for ritual bathing, others are reserved for the cremation of the dead, of which one – Manikarnika – is the most revered. A boat trip along the Ganges to Manikarnika, where tourists can watch from a distance, has to navigate past the odd bits of sewage and floating remains, on which the wheeling vultures keep a careful eye.

It's not all religion: Varanasi is famous for its brocade silks, the more mundane business of diesel locomotives and – in the city where Ravi Shankar was born – musical instruments. There is a business area, but it is merely a sideshow to the spectacle on the Ganges. At night, when the butter-oil candles flicker, the river and the *ghats* feel unreal and primeval, a direct nexus to ancient Varanasi and, despite the cacophony, to eternal peace.

> "Benares is older than history, older than tradition, older even than legend, and looks twice as old as all of them."
>
> Mark Twain

> VARANASI, UTTAR PRADESH, INDIA > LONGITUDE: 83°04' E > LATITUDE: 25°20' N > ALTITUDE: 265 feet/81 metres
> POPULATION: 1,125,600 > NATIVES: Rajul Mehta, Ravi Shankar

STILL BETTER KNOWN to the rest of the world as Madras, India's fourth largest city and southern hub was rechristened in 1996. Grand colonial buildings remain a dominant feature of the city, but it would appear that the old name is about as palatable here as the medium-hot curries named after the city, but most likely the invention of the curry houses of England.

That's not to say the city has no local speciality. Even within India's panoply of varied and celebrated cuisines, the vegetarian dishes of Chennai, such as *dosi* pancakes, *sambar* vegetable rice and *idli* steamed dishes are greatly appreciated. Chennai is one of the few places in India where coffee – a vestige no doubt of the Portuguese settlement – replaces the ubiquitous *chai*.

Chennai is the stronghold and spiritual centre of the Tamil Indians, a conservative and deeply religious city where men are clad in *lungi* wraparound cloths, women are rarely seen in western dress and rickshaws are draped in effigies of divine iconography. Chennai academics are custodians of classical Tamil traditions in music and dance, which are in constant performance in festivals and throughout town in the city's many *sabha* or music halls.

Chennai is also a celluloid city, producing more films than anywhere else in the world, including Bollywood. But these are less often popular music love stories than political films or films with a political end. For no one is anyone here in politics unless they have a film or two under their belts and are paraded around town adorned on one of the city's hundreds of surreal cut-out cardboard effigies. You thought America had it bad… here fame *is* politics.

The city was founded in 1639 by the British East India Company, north of an original Portuguese settlement, ousting the French who settled in the suburb city, Pondicherry. There is no natural harbour, and legend has it that the motives for founding a staging post here were most likely amorous. Some stout remnants of Raj architecture remain, most notably in the banking district of Georgetown and the imposing Fort St George along the sea front with its *chunam* finish, a sort of pebbledash of limestone and crushed seashells. The St Andrews Kirch appears to be a virtual facsimile of London's St Martin-in-the-Fields. In contrast, the Muslim district of Triplicane is secretive and atmospheric.

The modern city has brought both the light industry of weddings and the heavy industry of the Ford car plant that has had Chennai dubbed the Detroit of India. But among this Chennai has

all the surreal and paradoxical elements of classic India: constant, vivid colour, glittering elephants waiting outside shops, monkeys, mangos and wandering cows. And when the sun goes down the argy-bargy moves to the city's Kamaraj Salai beach, one of the longest in the world, where Chennai girls dare to hitch up their saris.

> "I miss the heat of India, the house lizards on the walls, the musicals on the silver screen, the cows wandering the streets." Yann Martel, *Life of Pi*

"I would wake and just smell things for the whole day;
it was so rich I had to select senses.
And still everything moved slowly
with the assured fateful speed of a coconut falling
on someone's head." Michael Ondaatje

79°50' E

ACCORDING TO MARCO POLO it was "for its actual size, better than any other island in the world". For its abundant natural riches the island of "Lanka", originally settled by the Sinhalese from northern India, was always coveted among explorers and entrepreneurs, undergoing many name changes as invaders came and went. When the Portuguese were fortunate to stumble upon it in 1505 it went by the Muslim name of Serendib, from which the word "serendipity" (coined in Horace Walpole's *Three Princes of Serendib*) is derived.

The Muslim settlement was the district of Colombo known as Pettah, still home to a cacophonic Arab-style bazaar and the city's most religious quarter. The Portuguese rechristened the island Ceilao and founded the port of Colombo. Ousted by the Dutch in the 17th century, Colombo became an important port of the Dutch East India Company, a valuable stopover en route to the spice islands of Indonesia but also a major trade centre in its own right. For Ceylan, as they rechristened it, was a land rich in valuable resources and in particular cinnamon, coconuts and coffee. The Cinnamon Gardens, now the city's most affluent district, with its overgrown mansions, museums and galleries, was once covered in cinnamon plantations. The Dutch influence is still very much in evidence in the town hall, police station and post office in Pettah, and Colombo still has a small resident diaspora of Dutch burghers.

It was not, however, until 1815, after the British Navy had defeated the Dutch, that Colombo really became a city and was installed as the capital of British Ceylon. The British were the first to hold sway over the whole island, controlling even the unruly Indian Tamil population of the north. By the time they departed following Indian independence in 1948 they had bequeathed a culture of tea, the cricket which would-be Muralitharans play in the street throughout Colombo, a Victorian transport network and the English language.

Reaffirmed as Sri Lanka (the "Sri" being a post-colonially proud word meaning "resplendent"), the country has undergone considerable turmoil, not least a bloody civil war with the Tamil Tigers, frequent political assassinations and some of the most devastating damage wrought by the 2004 Boxing Day tsunami. This chaos is reflected in the malodorous street jungle of humanity that is downtown Colombo. From the commercial centre of the former Colombo Fort the city descends down Galle Road along a strip of coastline sclerotic and polluted with a beehive of crazy three-wheel taxi cabs.

If Sri Lanka is often described as a teardrop off the continent of India, it could also be a giant drop of sweat. But remedy from the madness is at hand, in the local elemental spice medicine of Ayurveda, "the science of life", or simply on the palmed calm of beaches to the south around Mount Lavinia, where the outsize jackfruit and breadfruit trees grow straight out of some Edward Lear nonsense poem.

> COLOMBO, SRI LANKA > LONGITUDE: 79°50' E > LATITUDE: 6°56' N > ALTITUDE: 22 feet/7 metres
> POPULATION: 1,221,700 > NATIVES: Solomon Bandaranaike, Aravinda de Silva, Mahela Jayawardene, Michael Ondaatje > RESIDENTS: Arthur C. Clarke, Pablo Neruda

77°17' E

SLICE DELHI THROUGH THE MIDDLE and, like an archaeologist's dream, the strata of the city's, and India's, history are revealed. William Dalrymple has tellingly described this discovery as peeling away the layers of an onion, removing each of the city's seven incarnations before reaching its core – the site of the ancient Pandava city of Indraprastha, founded in the millennium before the birth of Christ; and, even before that, to a sacred legend in which the god Brahma recovered the sacred knowledge (which he had absent-mindedly mislaid) at the very site of Delhi on the River Yamuna.

Of all those eras Old Delhi is dominated by the legacy of the Mughals, who ruled India from the 1520s for three centuries before; as with all dynasties, later descendants proved to be enfeebled versions of their noble predecessors. The sweeping red sandstone battlements of Shah Jehan's 17th-century Lal Qila, the Red Fort, overlook Jami Masjid, the largest mosque in the subcontinent, also built by Jehan, down the steps of which a flood of worshippers spills after prayers. Further afield the symmetrical tomb of Humayun, dating from 1565, was the template for the Mughal garden tomb; the Taj Mahal in Agra, constructed (again by the prolific Jehan) some 80 years later, took the form to an exquisite new level.

Old Delhi's tight streets and bazaars provide a stereotypical Indian feel, yet alongside the Mughal monuments, it is New Delhi that also gives the city much of its character. Though the British Raj is little more than a blip in Delhi's history, its architectural heritage is highly distinctive. For Edwin Lutyens, the creator of the Cenotaph in London's Whitehall, Delhi was his chance to emulate L'Enfant's Washington DC or Haussmann's Paris. He gave it his best shot. The majesty of Rajpath (the King's Way) heading west from the India Gate – Lutyen's own Arc de Triomphe – to the former Viceroy's House (now the President's residence) is breathtaking; each January its two-mile length hosts India's Republic Day parade.

Many of the twists and turns of the republic have been acted out against the backdrop of the capital's colonial buildings. The calm, leafy quarter of New Delhi is full of tidy bungalows and manicured lawns. In the gardens of the Gandhi Smriti, where water sprinklers play, a sequence of brick footprints recreates the final walk of Mahatma Gandhi before his assassination in 1948. At the entrance to one neat bungalow is the glass memorial at the very spot where Indira Gandhi was gunned down by two of her Sikh guards. And in the Teen Murti Bhavan, which could double for a country house in the Home Counties, Indira's father, Pandit Nehru, oversaw the transition of India from colony to republic – in a neat loop back through time, independent India's new flag first flew above the Red Fort.

"Delhi was a city of djinns. Though it had been burned by invaders time and time again, millennium after millennium, each time it rose like a phoenix from the past." William Dalrymple

> DELHI, INDIA > LONGITUDE: 77°17' E > LATITUDE: 28°38' N > ALTITUDE: 741 feet/225 metres > POPULATION: 9,817,000 > TWINNED WITH: Chicago > NATIVES: Vikram Chandra, Deepak Chopra, Gulshan Grover, Madhur Jaffrey, Sharukh Khan, Padma Lakshmi, Pervez Musharraf, Virender Sehwag > RESIDENTS: William Fraser, Indira Gandhi, Mahatma Gandhi, Gita Hariharan, Jawaharlal Nehru

ALMATY KAZAKASTAN

TRUE TO ITS NAME, which in the native language means "father of apples", in the vast steppe that is Kazakhstan, Almaty is the country's one real "big apple".

Fundamentally nomadic, Kazakh culture never had a definable urban expression. Almaty is essentially a Russian creation. The original Kazakh settlement was laid waste by rampaging Mongols, and it was not until 1854 that the Russians laid the foundations of the modern city, christening it "Vernyi", after wresting control of the fertile territory of Kazakhstan (then called Jetysu, meaning "land of seven rivers") from the Muslim Kokand Khanate, which had for centuries been its vassal.

Whatever its identity and whoever its owners, a stronghold here had long been valued due to the prosperous conditions and propitious climate. Almaty sits at the foothills of the Tien Shan range, on the cusp of steppe and mountains. To the south the city is fenced in, like an Asiatic Denver, by a backdrop of perennially snow-laden peaks whose gorges run with rivers that feed the cattle-breeding plains of Siberia, with their unique singing dunes, that stretch to infinity to the city's north. The rivers in turn become brooks that babble and murmur by the side of the streets throughout Almaty, watering the poplars, pines and acacias that line its avenues and parks, and make the city the greenest in the arid world of Central Asia. The trees provide shade from the searing heat of the shelterless Asian summer sky, while the cool streams also nourish the bountiful natural orchards of fruit trees that encircle the city in a veritable Garden of Eden – apricot, pomegranate, plum cherry and, most abundantly, the apple from which the city takes its name.

Were it not for this verdant screen Almaty would not be much to look at. Two devastating earthquakes – a regional hazard by all accounts – took care of most of the original Russian architecture, except for the wooden stucco of the Zenkov Cathedral. What replaced this was the traditional Stalinist classicism of the museums and government buildings around the showcase Novaya Ploshad Square.

As Kazakhstan's cultural and commercial centre Almaty has become Central Asia's most cosmopolitan city. Always an important stopover for the desert caravans of the Silk Road, the city now lives off the Turkestan-Siberia railway, and is engine of the most progressive of the so-called "Stan" states whose weekenders go skiing at the resort of Shymbulak, or skating at the Medeu ice-rink. The orderly bazaar is replete with supplies and the bars full of Russians and Kazakhs enjoying pints of *kumis* (fermented mare's milk).

Kazakhstan may have moved its capital (to the cardboard city of Astana), but the blooming city of Almaty, the new apple of oil prospectors' eyes, will always be the country's Alma Mater.

"I looked across parklands where the spire of a cathedral hoisted gold crosses against the mountains… **the air blew up sharp and pure."** Colin Thubron

KOCHI INDIA

WAY DOWN SOUTH from the holiday beaches of Goa, Kochi (formerly known as Cochin) sits on the coast of Kerala, a gateway to a lush interior where canoes and barges glide quietly through the canals and lagoons of the Backwaters. The city itself is a mix of the big and bold and the timelessly old, spilling over a clutter of islands and peninsulas, from where ships are dispatched into Kochi's excellent and safe harbour, a salt-water lagoon lying just off the Arabian Sea.

Kochi's spice trade appealed to travellers and raiders from Europe and the Far East. They all left their traces. Early arrivals were the Portuguese, touching down on Christmas Eve 1500. The *rajah* of the region granted a *feitoria* to the incomers, a franchise for trading that they were quick to exploit. No less a voyager than Vasco da Gama arrived: he later died in the city and was for a while buried in the tiny church of St Francis, the oldest church in India, which still stands near the water's edge in Fort Kochi, though Vasco himself is long gone, transported back to his homeland.

Not far from the church stands Kochi's most celebrated sight, another reminder of foreign visitors, this time heading east to west: the Chinese fishing nets, great cantilevered constructions of bamboo and billowing mesh, bow down like a row of wading birds into the harbour water before surging back up to reveal the squirming victims in their maw.

In the straightforwardly-, rather than disparagingly-, named Jew Town, a luminous synagogue lined with blue and white Chinese tiles – no two alike – recalls the influx of Jewish immigrants in the 16th century. Although the synagogue is lovingly maintained, the ageing Jewish population has dwindled to low double figures; sadly this little gem may shortly become a preserved museum rather than the living place of worship it now is. The Dutch and then the British – of course – also came to Kochi for its spices: the commercial area of Willingdon Island was built in the 1920s from the residue of Lord Bristow's dredging of the harbour.

But it is not really for the legacy of the incomers that this area is the one most Indians say they would like to visit. It's the slow, relaxed Southern Indian quality of Kochi and Kerala that appeals. To the east, a day or so's drive up into the highlands of the interior are rolling tea estates and the elephants and tigers roaming free in the Periyar National Park. South are the backwaters and coastal villages where an Ayurvedic massage will soothe away the dust and hubbub of the city. And in Kochi itself, under the flickering lights of the arts centre, traditional Kathakali dancers beam audiences straight back into the legends of the past.

"Cochin was the site of the first contact between India and the West, a kind of science fiction moment, a meeting of two species." Salman Rushdie

KASHGAR CHINA

SOUNDING APPROPRIATELY LIKE an English budget superstore, Kashgar is the world's most ancient and famous market town. Set at the foot of the Pamir Mountains in the far west of China, between burning deserts and treacherous high-glacial passes, Kashgar is a centuries-old strategic junction on the famous Silk Road, offering access to Central Asia, India and Persia. For 2,000 years it has been a place to thaw out, rest, stock up and trade, the collection and distribution nexus of the ancient world.

In this kingdom of bazaars Kashgar was, and still is, Central Asia's largest – a teeming mêlée of ethnic interaction and human variety: Tadjiks, with dark, coarse skin, Kazakhs with aquiline noses and moustaches, Uzbeks with pork-pie hats, green-eyed Uigurs, Indians, Persians and Chinese… a timeless tableau of robes, beards, turbans, veils and hats. This was the Wall Street of the Middle Ages, and the Uigurs the usurers of the East, the traders dealing in stocks of wood, wool, carpets, tea, squawking chickens, donkeys and camels. When Marco Polo passed by this plateau he wrote of "grass so lush that a lean beast will fatten in ten days". Known as "the Land of Fruit and Melons", the stalls of Kashgar dripped with figs, grapes, apples and apricots.

Sadly only a small fraction of this Kashgar remains, its bazaar a collection of rebuilt backstreets, of shacks, tarpaulin and brick. Market Sunday has not lost its energy and still evokes the timelessness of old; but despite a history of occupation by successive invaders – Indians, Persians, Turks and Mongols all had their time – it is 20th-century Chinese ownership that has transformed Kashgar indelibly.

Capital of its Xinjiang province, China implemented a "modernization"

programme, razing the Uigurs's traditional huts and most of the bazaar, replacing dusty, atmospheric alleyways with car-less two-lane expressways, statues of Mao and a Ferris wheel. The beautiful garden of Chini Bagh palace, former home of Britain's consul George Macartney during the 19th-century three-way "Great Game" with China and Russia, has been supplanted by a luxury hotel. "Kashi" as they call it, is part of China's "Go-West" policy, the spanking new marble railway station linking Kashgar to southern Urumqui seemingly the final nail in the coffin of all hopes of independence that had been inspired by other Central Asian states following the break-up of the Soviet Union. Uigurs still make up 90 per cent of the population but the signposts, the rich and the employed are all Chinese. The muezzin prayer call of the Imam from the hulk of the Id Kah Mosque, still a feature of Muslim Kashgar, is a foreign and rare sound in China.

"Kashgar has taken on a new look. Silk Road [sic] is even more shining," reads a city billboard. But now even the famous route is tarmacked, and the spectacular 196-mile (1,300-km) ancient KKH (Karakoram Highway) through precipitous fang-shaped mountains is more of a motorway.

> KASHGAR, XINJIANG, CHINA > LOCAL NAME: Kashi > LONGITUDE: 76°03′ E > LATITUDE: 39°29′ N > ALTITUDE: 4,442 feet/1,354 metres > POPULATION: 240,000
> NATIVES: Mahmud Kashgari > RESIDENTS: Yusuf Has Hajip, George Macartney, Katie Melua, Nikolai Petrovsky

"Over the sacks of ground cumin, turmeric and coriander hung the background smell of Kashgar, a perfumed mix of warm dust, curling wood-smoke, charred mutton, the local tobacco and the tang of freshly cut kidney." Liam D'Arcy Brown, *Green Dragon, Sombre Warrior*

"Will you come home soon?
Waiting for you is
like waiting for spring.
We are waiting for the
almond blossoms. And, if God
wills, O! Those days of peace
when we were in love and the
rain was in our hands wherever
we went." Agha Shadid Ali, *The Country Without a Post Office*

IN A WORLD OF FEW remaining Shangri-las, Srinagar and the valley of Kashmir, at whose heart it sits, lie like a promised land tantalizingly inaccessible to the travelling world which has been selfishly awaiting a cessation in the hostilities that imprison the Kashmiris who actually live there.

Kashmir — the very word, soft and whispered, evokes all the luxuriance and Eastern mystery of the prized goat's wool, like a golden fleece, for which it is famed. Kashmir is not a valley but a vale, as if from some tale told around a campfire, as much imagination as fact: high up and hidden among the highest mountains, a land of seven cantilevered wooden river bridges over Venetian waterways and crystal-clear lakes where mermaids might live, sprinkled with a blossom of lotus flowers and water lilies, where the *shikara* gondola-boats float by as lazily as punts on a Cambridge summer's afternoon, of deep green rice fields and lush meadows, castles and the symmetrical gardens of a mythical dynasty of Emperors.

The Mughals ruled India from the early 16th century, constructing here under the ever-white Pir Panjal range of the lower Himalayas a legacy of imperial and imperious buildings such as the fortified sacred mount of Hari Parbat, built by Emperor Akbar, surrounded by fragrant almond orchards, the wooden mosque of Shah Hamdan Masjud and the great mosque of Madani Masjid, built by the poet-musician-ruler Zain-ul-Abidin.

Set on the banks of the Dal and Hagni lakes and bled by the River Jhelum, Srinagar was for centuries one of the great cultural and philosophical centres of Asia. It was also exposed to successive Muslim and Hindu rule, and in 1819, at the end of the first Sikh war, was annexed by Gulab Singh, the Hundu raja of the Jammu region.

Kashmir had always regarded itself as autonomous, but now was forced to accede to the Indian Union. In 1793 Srinagar had already become summer capital of the Singh Empire and also a holiday resort for the British Raj. The British were not allowed to build on Srinagar land, and so took to the water, where they built the luxurious wooden houseboats that still furnish the lakes with a bohemian air.

Following the British withdrawal in 1947, Kashmir was split in two and Srinagar found itself on the Hindu-Muslim fault-line. Since then Kashmiris who want their *azadeh* (freedom and independence) have found their land coveted and fought over by the nuclear powers of India and Pakistan.

The city whose name means "Happy City of Beauty and Knowledge" has for over half a century been a sad bastion of destruction and ignorance. And yet this is still surely one of the most romantic and romanced places on earth, an Eden of such eternal innocent beauty that no notion of nation or transient war could ever destroy.

RUDYARD KIPLING'S FATHER was the curator at Lahore's Central Museum, so father and son would have had a plentiful knowledge of Lahore's Mughal past. Present-day visitors to the Punjab city where Kipling's Kim played do not have to look too hard to be conscious of that heritage, as rich as that of Jaipur, Agra or Delhi. Standing right beside the central Hazuri Bagh Square is the Fort of Lahore, built by a succession of four Mughal Emperors (each adding their own choice of extensions and additions) in order to protect Lahore, otherwise relatively defenceless on its flat alluvial plain, against the attentions of passing armies. Opposite, the Badshahi Mosque – modelled on Delhi's Jami Masjid – is one of the world's largest, with a courtyard that can cater for upwards of 60,000 worshippers.

If that was not enough, the Fort itself contains the Shish Mahal, a marvel of mirrored mosaics, while just behind the Fort's walls the fresco-filled Begum Shati Masjid, or Ladies' Mosque, is another of Lahore's Moghul masterpieces. A few miles outside the city centre, the Shahdara site gathers together a collection of mausoleums to the Emperor Jahangir, his brother-in-law Asif Khan (father of the Taj Mahal's Mumtaz) and Jahangir's wife, the Empress Nur Jahan, who once said of the city, "By giving my life for Lahore, I have purchased another Paradise".

Pakistan's recent history, less paradise than paramilitary, is enacted every day at Wagah on the Indo-Pakistan border 18 miles (29km) east of Lahore, when crisply uniformed Pakistani and Indian troops mutually attempt to outdo each other in the precision with which they perform a solemn flag-lowering ceremony each dusk. As the independence of Britain's Indian Empire grew imminent,

"The growling, flaring, creed-drunk city." Rudyard Kipling

> LAHORE, PAKISTAN > LONGITUDE: 74°23' E > LATITUDE: 31°33' N > ALTITUDE: 699 feet/213 metres > POPULATION: 6,040,000 > NATIVES: Wasim Akram, Subrahmanyan Chandrasekhar, Shah Jahan, Shakar Kapur, Ved Parkash Mehta, Saqlain Mushtaq, Abdur Razzaq, Yousuf Youhana > RESIDENTS: Rudyard Kipling, Khushwant Singh

Muslims demanded a separate state from predominantly Hindu India, and – despite Gandhi's and Nehru's protests – Lord Mountbatten, overseeing the division, created West and East Pakistan (the latter now Bangladesh). Immediately after partition in August 1947, a huge transhumance occurred, with millions of Hindus fleeing east, and new Muslim migrants trekking west, an event accompanied by copious bloodshed. Riots split Lahore asunder, shops were looted, houses burnt, atrocities committed. The subsequent relationship between India and Pakistan has rarely been cordial, and often dangerously inflammatory.

In a country constantly in a state of flux and fervour ever since its creation, and sometimes described as unfriendly to outsiders, and in a city whose own past has been volatile and confrontational, Lahore's current reputation for a more relaxed and outgoing lifestyle than, say, the coastal city of Karachi is something of a relief. The city has a thriving tradition of art, film, fashion and music, and in the shopping arcades, cafés and boutiques of the Gulberg and Defence quarters, a new generation of Lahoris are enjoying the city's renaissance as the cultural capital of the region.

MOST CITIES, especially in India, bustle, but Mumbai can out-bustle pretty well anywhere else. Stand at one of the city's major road junctions – Horniman Circle or Nagar Chowk – and the colour and clamour will be in full spate. The energy is exhilarating: an energy that has propelled Mumbai to the top of the Indian fashion and film industries. There is money aplenty here too, but concentrated in the bank accounts of a tiny percentage of inhabitants, who live in the cool, restful residences up on Malabar Hill, a good place to survey the rest of the city. A significant proportion of the other 13 million inhabitants survive in shanty towns, vast labyrinthine mazes covered by acres of shimmering tin roofs.

Originally a group of seven islands, Mumbai has been formed, by man as much as by nature, into a long teardrop of an island dipping into the Arabian Sea. The sea is never that far away from anywhere in the skyscrapered downtown area – though a dip in the water is not recommended. On the west coastline, the causeway to Haji-Ali's tomb loops out to an offshore mosque. Marine Drive sweeps alongside Chowpatty Beach, both a playground and trysting point, with flamboyant wedding parties in full flow inside special marquee areas facing the water's edge.

When the constant activity gets too much, there are various lines of escape – to the Hanging Gardens on Malabar Hill, or the caves and carved temples of Elephanta Island (mind the *guano*), although the Towers of Silence, where the small Parsi community leave their dead for the elements and wildlife to erase, are not accessible. Or north of Mumbai, there is the celluloid escapism of Film City: after protracted negotiations that even John Le Carré might find far-fetched, it is possible to be ushered into the presence of a Bollywood star. Not Mollywood, note – while the city is now officially Mumbai, even the locals still call it Bombay.

The city was constructed to serve the mercantile needs of the British in the 1600s. The Raj has been left far behind by Mumbai's own exuberance, but remnants linger. Under the gaze of grandiose Victorian Gothic buildings, cricket matches are played all day long on the Oval Maidan, a wide and elegant swathe of grass cutting through the heart of the city. At the Breach Candy Club, waiters offer cool drinks next to manicured lawns which look out over the Arabian Sea in a *Heat And Dust* moment. Tellingly, though, the Gateway of India, a stately archway built to commemorate George V's visit in 1911 and only completed in 1923, served its main purpose as an exit point for the last active British regiment to leave in 1948.

"Quite sensibly, Bombay takes its cues from Hollywood. And what is today in India is tomorrow around the world."

Pico Iyer

> MUMBAI, MAHARASHTRA, INDIA > LONGITUDE: 72°51' E > LATITUDE: 18°56' N > ALTITUDE: 10 feet/3 metres > POPULATION: 11,900,000 > TWINNED WITH: Durban (South Africa), Honolulu, Los Angeles, Yokohama (Japan) > NATIVES: Madhuri Dixit, Rajiv Gandhi, Sunil Gavaskar, Trilok Gurtu, Douglas Jardine, Anish Kapoor, Kareena Kapoor, Karisma Kapoor, Aamir Khan, Salman Khan, Rudyard Kipling, Zubin Mehta, Ismail Merchant, Sania Mirza, Rohinton Mistry, Kajul Mukhajee, Merle Oberon, Juliet Prowse, Salman Rushdie, Sachin Tendulkar, T.H. White > RESIDENTS: Amit Chaudhuri, Yukta Mookhey

TASHKENT UZBEKISTAN

CULTURAL CENTRE OF THE SILK ROAD and industrial giant of Central Asia – few modern cities can be so distant, their myth from their reality, their present from their past, as Tashkent.

Predating the dawn of Christianity, this ancient city, situated in a valley where the Chrichiq River unravels like silk to the west of the Chatkal Mountains, was always an important junction on the famous trade route linking Middle Europe, the Caucasus, Byzantium and the Levant. Through its gates passed caravans of merchants bartering the sought-after spices of the East and, above all, the priceless and mysterious thread of the Chinese silkworm.

Conquered by the Arabs in the 8th century, it was not until the rule of the all-conquering Mongols and under their ancestor Amir Timur, better known to the West as Tamerlane, that Tashkent experienced its true halcyon days in the 14th century. Previously called Dzhadzh and Binkent – such was its morphing mythological status in the imagination – Tashkent now arrived at its final name, meaning "stone fortress", and became the cultural centre of Central Asia with the best Timurid architects, craftsmen and calligraphers building wonders under Tamerlane's patronage
and for several centuries after his death. Still stands the defiant squat fortress-like mosque of Kukeldash Madrasa with its turquoise cupolas and almost disproportionate main arch, the traditional blue tile-work and mosaics of the Khast-Imam mosque complex and the sleepy studious atmosphere of the Iman Bukhair Madrasah with its courtyard of poppies, apple and persimmon trees, and home to the oldest Koran in the world.

These are some of the few buildings that withstood the 1966 earthquake of which Tashkent was the epicentre and which all but wiped away any trace of the city's glorious past. The disaster completely destroyed the elegant mansions of a European city that had sprung up alongside the ancient walled town when the Russians had made the city capital of the Turkestan region of their empire in the mid-19th century.

On this *tabula rasa*, and as capital of Uzbekistan since 1930, Soviet urban planning imposed a utopian imprint of six-lane avenues, of trams and trolley-buses, parks and fountains, and vast, eerie and almost abstract open spaces, including the largest square in the Soviet Union with, at its centre, the now-vanished biggest

statue of Lenin in the world. Tashkent was the only Central Asian city to receive an underground railway, typically gleaming and complete with triple-chandeliers and socialist bas-reliefs.

Poised to emerge from its cocoon and reclaim its Uzbek identity, Tashkent's shimmering roots are still very much alive. Silkworms are still one of the city's major exports, and across the canal on the line that divides future and past, the old city on the hill overlooks the modern. Here in the Shahristan citadel the warps and wefts of the bazaar's myriad narrow alleys still weave the subversive and secretive atmosphere of a centuries-old place of human interaction.

> "The city's heart seemed numb with lessons and memorials, hesitating, as if waiting for something new to think."
>
> Colin Thubron

> TASHKENT, UZBEKISTAN > LONGITUDE: 69°15' E > LATITUDE: 41°16' N > ALTITUDE: 1,575 feet/480 metres > POPULATION: 2,117,500
> TWINNED WITH: Berlin, Karachi, Seattle, Tripoli > NATIVES: Mirza Muhammad Haidar RESIDENTS: Sevara Nazarkhan

KABUL AFGHANISTAN

AFGHANISTAN'S CAPITAL HAS BLAZED from oblivion to the forefront of global consciousness. The sight of the BBC's John Simpson, the self-appointed liberator of Kabul, barging peasant Afghans out of the way to be first in the queue back in has been one of the most striking news images of the post-9/11 world.

A diaspora of an estimated 1.5 million Afghans has followed, returning from Pakistan, Iran, Europe and the United States, where they have been keeping their country's culture and traditions alive. Among them are film-directors, painters and novelists (famous booksellers aside) who have sparked a fertile atmosphere of ideas-exchange that some are likening to 1920s Paris. Schools are reopening, even for girls, the bazaars are teeming and overflowing with produce while daily camel markets ensure a constant tumult of commercial activity amid streets lit up by shiny new yellow taxis. In the Deh-Afghanan commercial district shops stock Russian fridges while the latest music blares out from the *chaikane* tea-houses and satellite dishes are tuned into Indian movie channels. Traditional Afghan sports of kite-flying and *buzkashi* (polo with a calf's headless carcass) are being enjoyed once again. Many Kabulites have cast off their robes in favour of suit-and-tie modernity, and Gillette has probably seen a sharp rise in razor exports. There is even a weekly humour magazine, *Zanbel-e-Gham*.

Most of the above were until recently "tali-banned". Students from southerly Kandahar who subscribed to strict *sharia* law

and viewed Kabul as a pariah of liberalism, the Taliban ruled Afghanistan with a creed of the Koran and Kalashnikov. Appealing to an illiterate and embattled populace they were credited with stopping the civil war that had done more damage to the city than any of the previous invaders, Sikhs, Persians, Victorians, Tsars and Soviets, who had failed to govern Afghanistan's volatile mix of tribes. But with their Monty Python-esque Ministry for the Propagation of Virtue and Prevention of Vice they drove the city culturally from 1996 to 1396 and in so doing became a convenient image of Islam for the Western media.

After 23 years of war Kabul is experiencing the chaos of freedom, the boom not of bombs but of a frenzied backlash that has inflated salaries and expectations of lasting peace, and stretched to breaking-point a city short on water and hygiene, whose sewers are barely able to cope with the sudden population growth.

Kabul has something of a Dresden look, a once attractive city of crumbling building-shells beloved of blitz-chic reportage photographers, its chequered history the specialized subject of overnight pundits. Under the Loya Jirga, interim Grand Council leader Hamed Karzai has established a brittle but invaluable peace. Political violence is an ongoing threat, the political landscape as flagged with mines as the rocky terrain, and the city still the domain of NGO and UN vehicles. But Kabul is once again a dynamic city. *Inshallah*!

> KABUL, AFGHANISTAN > LONGITUDE: 69°11' E > LATITUDE: 34°30' N > ALTITUDE: 5,876 feet/1,791 metres
> POPULATION: 1,923,800 > TWINNED WITH: Omaha NE

"If the people of Afghanistan take the Almighty a little more seriously than most, they could argue that this is where He's done some of his best work." Andrew Mueller, *Rock and Hard Places*

KARACHI _{PAKISTAN}

ALTHOUGH GOVERNED FROM the puppet capital of Islamabad, Karachi is Pakistan's commercial centre, its former and still unofficial capital, a potent mix of subcontinental bazaar chaos and gleaming hi-tech.

Capital of Sindh province, Karachi lies at the mouth of the Indus River, washed by the Arabian Sea. A century ago it was a small fishing community spread across the three islands of Manora, Bhit and Baba, home to the Kalachi fishermen from which the modern city takes its name. It wasn't until the creation of the Muslim state of Pakistan in 1947 that the city's population exploded as the then capital (until 1959) welcomed an influx of immigrants from the Hindu south and east. Pakistan had first been the idea of a group of

Cambridge undergraduates who dreamed of a land incorporating the provinces of Punjab, Afghanistan, Kashmir, Sindh and Baluchistan, whose names would provide the acronym of the new country (another school of thought interprets "Pakistan" as meaning "land of the pure"). Karachi's white marble Quaid-e-Azam Mausoleum is a place of pilgrimage among Pakistanis to the resting-place of their country's founder, Mohammed Ali Jinnah

Karachi is anything but pure. It suffers all the blights of a dirty, overpopulated industrial city built in haste and still running too fast to keep up with itself. Karachi is a major port and the centre of Pakistan's automobile and oil industries. In the heat of day the smell of petrol can congeal with the whiff of open sewers to form air as

"Karachi is always dual. Pollution makes you gasp at the beauty of unnatural sunsets; dismissive of everyone outside its boundaries, embracing and accepting of outsiders; and yes, selfishness is the consequence of love."

Kamila Shamsie, *Kartography*

liquid as molten tarmac. Its saving grace is its coastline, whose beaches act like valves. There are precious few bikinis on display, and Karachi may not often be associated with the seaside, but the beaches of Sandspit, Hawkes Bay, Paradise Point and the old British haunt of Clifton provide welcome respite from the urban turmoil. This is, after all, birthplace of that resort connoisseur *par excellence*, the Aga Khan.

Downtown Karachi has a few remaining old colonial buildings, such as the incongruously out-of-place Holy Trinity Cathedral and St Andrew's Church, drafted in unmistakable Victorian Indo-Gothic style. Lined with messy, electronics shops full of unboxed hi-fis, the boulevards of Saddar city centre are reminiscent of London's

Tottenham Court Road, while other shops sell local carpets, snakeskin wallets, pashminas and that distinct type of fishy-smelling leather jacket. Anywhere where there's room, spontaneous cricket matches are played by budding Imran Khans and Wasim Akrams. And in the city's famous bazaar behind Boulton Street are to be found typically glittering Asian displays squeezed in aisles full of jostling camels and donkey carts.

And then by night, as if the noise of the day were a passing storm forgotten and from outside the city, the whole place mysteriously shuts down. Night-life here is an oxymoron, but then like a googly bowled by one its famous sorcerer leg-spinners, Pakistan is unreadable, mercurial and enigmatic.

> KARACHI, PAKISTAN > LONGITUDE: 67°03' E > LATITUDE: 24°51' N > ALTITUDE: 13 feet/4 metres > POPULATION: 9,269,300 > TWINNED WITH: Tashkent > NATIVES: Saeed Anwar, Benazir Bhutto, Mohammed Ali Jinnah, Imran Khan, Jahangir Khan, Shah Aga Khan, Margaret Lockwood, Sadhana, Kamila Shamsie > RESIDENTS: Charles Napier

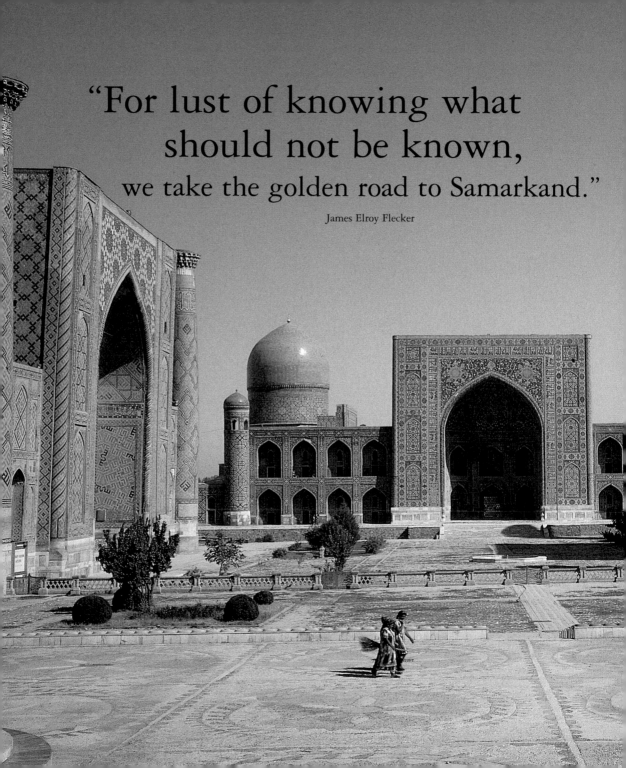

"For lust of knowing what should not be known, we take the golden road to Samarkand."

James Elroy Flecker

67°01' E

SAMARKAND UZBEKISTAN

LIKE BUKHARA, 140 miles (225km) to the west, Samarkand was one of the great links in the chain of the Silk Road. Both have a Registan Square surrounded by *madrasahs* where scholars studied; both have their mighty mosques. But while Bukhara is intense, infertile, essentially monochrome, Samarkand shimmers, a well-watered oasis overlaid with mosaic tiles and gold leaf.

As old as Babylon, Rome and Athens, the city has been receiving rave reviews for centuries. When Alexander the Great reached, and captured, Samarkand in 329 BC, he found that its PR was no idle hype. "Everything I have heard about the beauty of Samarkand is true," he wrote, "except that it is even more beautiful than I could have imagined." Later visitors, from Milton to Oscar Wilde, were inspired to poetic heights; it is still the major tourist destination in Central Asia. The beauty of its buildings has not faded. Its turquoise and azure tiles, the green jade, the burnished oranges and golds shine on.

In the 10th century Samarkand was already a major city, with 100,000 inhabitants, rich in canals, pools and gardens. But it was Timur (aka Tamerlane), the wandering warmonger, a local boy from a few valleys away, who added dynamism and established the Timurid dynasty here in the 1370s. Tamerlane may have left torrents of spilt blood in the wake of his career as all-conquering warrior, but he also had the vision to construct the massive and extraordinary buildings for which Samarkand is famous.

At his Gur Emir Mausoleum (itself magnificent), the inscriptions runs, "If this grave is disturbed the earth will rumble." The one time this dire warning was ignored, when a Russian anthropologist gingerly opened the tomb in June 1941, Hitler invaded the Soviet Union; days after the grave was resealed, the Nazis capitulated at Stalingrad.

That Samarkand is so spectacular does not mean it is a brainless bimbo next to Bukhara's academic rigour. Indeed, it was particularly noted for its scientists. Tamerlane's grandson, Ulug Bek, was an astronomer of the stature of Copernicus: the giant brick sextant from his observatory is still visible. But even when learning and studying were the business of the day the surroundings were sumptuous. The vast Registan Square with its three great *madrasahs* is monumentally and coolly beautiful, a Timurid La Défense. The construction of the next-door Bibi Khanym Mosque was personally overseen by Tamerlane. The necropolis of Shah-I-Zinda ("the Shah lives") contains mausoleums where the art of ceramic decoration reached its apogee.

That so many monuments are extant is largely thanks to the Soviets, who put in place a programme of restoration. Unfortunately they also built dreary housing blocks outside the centre. Modern Samarkand is large and industrialized, which in conjunction with the city's overwhelming sites, means that for many people Bukhara, the apparently humbler city, is actually the more human place of the two.

> SAMARKAND, UZBEKISTAN > LONGITUDE: 67°01' E > LATITUDE: 39°39' N
> ALTITUDE: 2,644 feet/806 metres > POPULATION: 374,900
> TWINNED WITH: Olympia WA > RESIDENTS: Alisha Navoi, Tamerlane, Ulug Bek

BUKHARA UZBEKISTAN

A LITTLE PIECE OF THE ANCIENT WORLD preserved in the 21st century, Bukhara guardedly offers up its antiquity and its secrets for those who make their way into the heart of Uzbekistan. It is one of the three fabled Central Asian cities of the Silk Road – the triad (or triopolis, perhaps) of Samarkand, Bukhara and Khiva – that feel as if they have existed since before memory began.

Bukhara has an especially primordial feel. Its buildings are mud-coloured, as though they sprouted directly from the unforgiving,

(or Islamic seminary) are reminders of Bukhara's greatness. For if Bukhara lacked the beauty of Samarkand, it made up for it in brains. Religion and learning were its great strengths – under the Samanid dynasty, the city flowered in the 10th century, as capital of their empire, which included Persia and Afghanistan, and as one of Islam's great seats of knowledge and study. With some 360 mosques (one for every day of the year, it was said), and dozens of *madrasahs*, Bukhara shone bright. This great period was cut short by Genghis Khan and his Mongol forces,

unyielding desert that surrounds the city. Apparently windowless, they have huddled down to protect themselves from the winds of change and the threat of invasions and earthquakes, of which there have been many.

But close up, the lack of feature reveals itself to be deceptive. Though the predominant colour of the city is one of khaki-brick, the actual brickwork is rich in detail. On the tapering cone of the Kalyan Minaret, constructed in 1127, masons created patterns as intricate as the finest lace, and to offset the potential monotony of the brick, a ring of turquoise and peacock blue around its neck adds a flash of colour. Beneath the tower, a beckoning sign to caravans crossing the desert (and also whence bagged-up criminals were dropped to their doom), the monumental Kalyan mosque and Mir Arab *madrasah*

who razed and burnt and plunged Bukhara into darkness, although they never fully extinguished the light of learning.

Under Uzbek rule, and later Russian and then Soviet control, Bukhara survived, sometimes against the odds, as thankfully and plentifully did its buildings. There has been a fortress on the site of the Ark Citadel in the Registan Square for 2,000 years. The Ulug Bek *madrasah* of 1417 is Central Asia's oldest. Though remarkably intact, Bukhara is not a dead museum. Around the calm pool of Liabi-Hauz, weather-beaten locals sit on raised *topchan* platforms, drinking tea, jousting at chess, beneath mulberry and plane-trees. The storks, Bukhara's symbol, which used to haunt the mulberries and the minarets, have flown (driven away by the chemicals needed to fertilize the area's oversalty land), but their spirit lives on.

"Samarkand is the beauty of the earth, but
Bukhara is the beauty of the spirit."

Traditional saying

"There was a little of Jerusalem to its mystique, a little of Charleston, a touch of the backstreets of Oxford, of one of those little fishing ports on the Gulf of Venice – welded and illumined by an overpowering sense of the old Arabia." Jan Morris, *Sultan in Oman*

JUST AS ITS NAME EVOKES the mysterious rich woody scent of the Orient, so frankincense exudes from every sinew of Oman's capital. Sometimes imperceptible until caught on a draught, it is everywhere, in the taxis, on clothes, as if between the very sheets of the city.

Muscat was built on frankincense. In the 19th century, when Oman's capital was still Zanzibar – that ultimate byword for spicy exoticism – frankincense was the pot-pourri of choice from Luxor to London and its presence on the air gives Muscat its smooth, sensual, laid-back and almost hypnotized air.

Muscat sits on the Straits of Hormuz at the most easterly point of the Arabian peninsula. The city is draped out along a 19-mile (30-km) corniche of beaches and bays, a palm-lined strip-city interconnected by expressways, a kind of Florida Keys of the Middle East, except that the architecture is Islamic-Eclectic, with villas purloining a riot of influences from Parisian to flat-pack pseudo-fortress (Muscat used to be a walled city and having a retro wall, to keep up with the Omars, is the current trend). To the east is the Indian Ocean, to the west only desert and a spectacular backdrop of razor-sharp mountains and 60-feet (200-m) dunes.

Strange to think that in 1970 Muscat had no electricity, no running water, virtually no schools and boasted only six miles (10km) of surfaced road. Ruler of the state for 38 years, the hermit-king Sultan Said bin Taimur effectively kept Muscat and Oman in 13th century. In 1970, following a bloodless coup, he found himself shoved upstairs and propelled rudely into the 20th century (or, specifically, into the suite they seem to have at the Dorchester, London, for exiled sultans). Meanwhile his son, Qaboos, set off like a train, putting the fun back into fundamentalism and modernizing the place: a bit of music, something called "TV", a university and an end to slavery.

Given its arid setting Muscat is surprisingly green, its streets lined with bougainvillaea and grassy verges. It rains in Oman like nowhere else on the peninsula, and due to the green Dhofar hills to the south, shrouded in mist around monsoon time, it is often called the Switzerland of the sands.

Muscat is not and does not strive to be as wild as its up-state neighbour, Dubai. Sure, the modern city lives off oil and tourism, and wealthy Omanis swan around in Armanis, drive their 4WDs over the dunes and go surfing and sand-skiing at weekends. But there is less grandiloquence in its architecture and the city feels more genuine.

On the edge of this cauldron of a desert – both real and figurative – Muscat, lush, pristine and as subtle as its perfume, is an oasis of calm.

FEW CITIES HAVE DEVOTED themselves to promoting the restorative powers of retail and leisure therapy with such gusto as Dubai. Just in case anyone had missed the point, the city even hosts a Shoppers' Festival every winter. The "shop till you drop" mentality which the city purveys is deliberate, a hard-headed business decision to build up an alternative stream of revenue for the emirate once the oil reserves run out – in 10, 15, maybe 20 years. Dubai has always been a merchant port; a century ago it was trading in precious metals, pearls and spices to supplement the income from fishing. The ruling Al Maktoum family have simply taken all that to an extravagant new dimension.

To draw in the visitors, Dubai is hardly lacking in other natural resources. At the eastern end of The Gulf, on its southern shore, the city sits next to warm turquoise waters; its beaches are safe, clean and sandy. Add to that mix the lure of high-class golf and tennis tournaments, a horse race that is synonymous with wealth (the Dubai World Cup), fishing charters, sandboarding, waterskiing and 4x4 desert excursions, and the tourist-friendly appeal of the city becomes self-evident. And of all its futuristic hotels, the 1,000-feet (305-m) sci-fi sail of the Burj Al-Arab, soaring up on its own

islet, is a startling vision of opulence and post-modernism – it brands itself the world's first seven-star hotel.

The Maktoums have even more ambitious plans for the future, already becoming a reality in the form of three gigantic man-made islands, each in the shape of a palm tree, and a cluster of over 200 more creating a jigsaw map of the world. These environmentally contentious developments will be home to luxury villas, hotels and golf courses, and - the PR hyperbole claims - visible from outer space.

If then, the city is so geared to pulling in visitors, particularly from Europe, who are pampered by largely Asian staff before being dispatched to air-conditioned malls to spend their *dirhams*, what is there of the original Dubai? The modern resort area (Deira) lies north of the Khor Dubai creek. South of the waterway – across bridges, under the Al Shindagha tunnel, or by *abra* water taxi – lies the older quarter, Bur Dubai, where some sense persists of the mosques, souks, *dhows* and the gold, frankincense and myrrh of yesteryear. Although Dubai may have chosen to style itself like Las Vegas or Hong Kong, it is still a Middle Eastern city; sometimes the clash is startling, not least in the city's ice-rink where the sight of traditionally-clad skaters in mid-lutz can be quite bemusing.

"Thirty years ago
Dubai was a tiny
fishing port.
Now it flaunts
skyscraper hotels
which would be
run out
of Nevada
for being
over the top."

Julie Burchill

> DUBAI, UAE > LONGITUDE: 55°17' E > LATITUDE: 25°14' N > ALTITUDE: 0 feet/0 metres > POPULATION: 862,400 > TWINNED WITH: Casablanca, Detroit, Shanghai

309

TEHRAN IRAN

51°23' E

IN THE AMORPHOUS GEOGRAPHICAL term that is "the Middle East" Iran is often mistakenly lumped together with the Arab world. And yet the Iranians are not Arabs. Modern Iranians are descendants of the ancient kingdom of Persia, with all the feline connotations of carpets and plush luxury which that implies, and they speak not Arabic but Farsi (from which our word "Persian" is derived). The country has only been called Iran since 1934, supposedly after the Persian word "Aryan" meaning "of noble origin".

Essentially a sprawl of thoughtless functional blocks, Tehran may not have the architectural splendour of Persia's former capital, Isfahan, or of Qom, the holy city that is arguably still the country's spiritual centre and administrative grey eminence. Nor is Tehran's setting as pretty as blossoming Shiraz, the original home of the famous grape, since the city lies low and flat, cloaked in an almost permanent yellow custard of smog. But Tehran is most importantly Iran's largest city and commercial hub, with a young and dynamic population, catalyst and barometer of an Islamic state in the throes of exciting modernization.

While the image of Persia past in the form of emperors such as Darius and Xerxes might be known through the history books, the modern image most likely to be emblazoned on Western minds is the piercing countenance of the Ayatollah Khomeini who led the Islamic Revolution on his triumphant return from exile at the overthrow of the last decadent Pahlavi Shah in 1979. Like a forerunner of the Taliban he denounced all things Western and was famous for issuing the *fatwa* that had Salman Rushdie stacking shelves in disguise at the supermarket.

A talisman to the Muslim world, the Ayatollah died in 1989, with ten million mourners attending his funeral. Since then Iran under Khatami has been moderating Khomeini's absolutism, and this hospitable country is irresistibly opening up. This is most noticeable in its capital, flush with oil revenues from the Caspian fields. A people that once worshipped the Zoroastrian deity of Ahura Mazda now worships a different kind of Mazda (no doubt named after the God) that clogs up the streets, pollutes Tehran's air and makes the city unsafe to navigate on foot. Though the *hejab* dress code is still adhered to and the tent-like *chador* shawls still abound in the old generations, emerald-eyed young Tehrani girls are flirtatious and conspicuous by their make-up. The well-heeled go skiing up on the nearby towering Alborz range at weekends – segregated pistes of course.

Ancient Persian grandeur and exoticism is here only visible in the odd glimpse of turquoise tiling, carpets and the saffron, caviar and pistachios, ingredients of one of the world's most ancient cuisines. But a slogan on a Tehran bus still hints at an innate Farsi wisdom: "In the sea of love there are no beaches. In the desert of my heart you are her only poppy." *Also sprach Zarathustra!*

"Neither Eastern nor Western, but with a character of its own, colourless but clear, like water – and I do not mean the Tehran drinking water."

Freya Stark

> TEHRAN, IRAN > LONGITUDE: 51°23' E > LATITUDE: 35°39' N > ALTITUDE: 3,800 feet/1,158 metres > POPULATION: 7,722,900
> NATIVES: Angylina, Abbas Kiarostami, Mohsen Makhmalbaf, Azar Nafisi, Harold Nicolson, Mohammed Reza Pahlavi
> RESIDENTS: Shirin Ebadi

OCCUPYING THE GENTLY south-facing slopes of the promontory which juts out from the eastern edge of the Caucasian isthmus into the Caspian Sea, for most Baku is an obscure Asiatic city with a strange yet powerful-sounding name. Almost as if it had to be so, the capital of the tiny state of Azerbaijan is a city with a past as murky and colourful as the rainbow-glints off the petroleum for which it is famous.

A boom town whose modern proportions are as recent as the turn of the 19th century when it supplied half the world's oil, Baku's medieval citadel is one of modern tourism best-kept secrets. Better known for its eerily beautiful Valhalla backdrop of miles of nodding oil jacks, flames, desert and Soviet blocks, at the core of Baku stands a charming sea-front fort surrounded by crenellated walls encircling a tight warren of streets. These in turn are home to rambling flat-roofed nests of houses-upon-houses made of pale, sun-baked clay bricks with overhanging wooden balconies. At the heart of this ancient core stand the magnificent palace of the city's once Shrivanshah ruler, Ahistan I, and the eccentric column of the so-called Maiden's Tower.

Beyond these lie fine 19th-century stone mansions, built along boulevards by those who were lucky enough to become overnight oil barons by striking a black-gold gusher in their back garden, and which give Baku a strange Eurasian imperial feel. Downtown Baku holds other sights surprising in an Asian city, such as a Lisbonesque funicular (now sadly defunct), an old station built in an amazing hotchpotch of Disney, art nouveau, Persian and orthodox cupolas, and an underground railway with striking and ornate stations to rival those of Moscow. Along the sea-front boulevard of Neftchilar Avenue, Azeris can be found relaxing to tea and chess (this is the home of Gary Kasparov) wearing their characteristic black fezzes made of voluptuous *karakul* wool. One of the five biggest cities of the former USSR, central Baku is surprisingly graced with trees and parks, while the bazaars and *caravanserais* still hint at the city's importance before the invention of the car.

The origins of the city's name are shrouded in myth but one theory is that the name is a translation of the ancient Persian for "place of fire" or "city of God". Seeing flames springing from the ground at places where the oil-sodden earth had caught fire, it is possible Persian fire-worshippers founded a holy city here. (A more popular modern etymology is the Azeri Bad Kube, meaning "blustering wind", on account of the wind that gives Baku its nickname, "the Chicago of the Caspian".)

Oil has been both Baku's foundation and its undoing. A treasure so sought-after would quickly become fought over, and most of the 20th century saw the city plunged into bloodshed, and espionage. But now for once it seems to have hit a rich seam of peace, and Baku, home of saffron and world capital of caviar, is back.

"Oil is the life of Baku.

The earth is soaked with it and for miles round the waters of the Caspian Sea are coated with an oily film."

Fitzroy Maclean

"Faded grandeur and cracked façades, crumbling swags and cherubs, wooden gingerbread balconies, old apricot-coloured paint daubed with graffiti."

Wendell Steavenson, *Stories I Stole*

AT THE EDGE OF THE classical world, Georgia is a land of legends. Home of the Golden Fleece sought by Jason and his Argonauts, the Caucasus mountain range is also said to be where Noah's Ark landed. The original Garden of Eden is just down the road and Georgian folklore has it that while God was out making the world they were out drinking to his name, and so, flattered, God granted them his favourite mountains and the most beautiful land of all. The names of some of the kingdom's unruly secessionist states – Ajaria, Ingushetia, Ossetia, Abkhazia – seem oneiric and invented. And their landscape of tumbling mountains and fortified hilltop villages would not seem out of place in *Lord of the Rings*.

> TBILISI, GEORGIA > LOCAL NAME: T'bilisi > LONGITUDE: 44°48' E > LATITUDE: 41°42' N > ALTITUDE: 1,430 feet/436 metres > POPULATION: 1,240,200 > TWINNED WITH: Atlanta, Palermo
> NATIVES: Boris Akunin (Grigory Chkhartishvili), Nina Ananiashvili, Nana Djordjudze, Aram Khatchaturian, Georgiou Kinkladze, Nutya Kukhianidze, Berthold Lubetkin, Katie Melua, Tigran Petrosian
> RESIDENTS: Edouard Shevardnadze

There is something fantastical, comic and grotesque about the Georgians themselves. Strikingly handsome, wiry, dark and aggressive, they are a unique race with a unique language and zany alphabet. A bacchanalian race, they fuel and dine out on their eccentricity with knowing zeal. This is a wedge of land that has long harboured Russia's non-conformists, turning them into Cossacks, guerillas and rebels. As the writer Philip Marsden noted, it is "the place where the sea-like flatness of the steppe breaks against the Caucasus and all its scattering of non-Russian peoples".

It is not hard to see in Georgia the roots of the wild impulses that were to drive the country's most infamous son, Joseph Djugashvili, aka Stalin, the peasant's son from the hills who was studying in Tbilisi to be a priest when he got distracted.

The structure of the city itself is zany. Essentially a 19th-century construction (the AD 452 original was razed by the Persians) the old quarter is a rambling sequence of clustered, tottering and crazed wood-balconied houses which themselves are perched precariously like birds' nests in the side of a hill.

The Mktvari River bubbles through its basin, feeding the "hot springs" that give the city its name, while up on the cliff top of Mount Mtatsminda stands the fortress of Narikala Castle.

After a rare period of enforced silence under Moscow, this land of music, wine and blood feuds has seen some hot political water, in 1992-3 playing host to its own sulphurous civil war at the hands of the typically colourful dissident Gamsakhurdia. But the recent "Rose Revolution", which deposed former Gorbachev side-kick Edouard Shevardnadze, may have set the reluctant nation on a straighter course.

Tbilisi boasts civilized tree-lined lanes, a plethora of intricate mosques, synagogues and churches. Under Tsarist Russia the city had already become a place of exile, inadvertently populated by a liberal intelligentsia who brought with them the *langage du salon*. And this cosmopolitan and educated, almost jazz-age mood still prevails in modern Tbilisi, adding to its distinct leisured grace and southern charm that is unlike any other outpost of the former Soviet Union.

"Baghdad looked fascinating from the air. Minarets, mosques, date palms and camels, the Tigris, its banks lined with opulent oriental palaces…" Noel Coward

AFTER LANDING IN BAGHDAD on a trip to gee up Allied forces in 1943, Noel Coward went on to remark waspishly that Baghdad from the air "may be fascinating and fraught with Eastern glamour but close to is one of the least attractive places I have ever seen. It is stifling, dirty and without charm." Agatha Christie observed that it was "the name really that so fascinates one". Well, what a name: evocative of *One Thousand and One Arabian Nights*, of Ali Baba, Aladdin, Sinbad and Scheherazade...

For some twenty years few people who lived outside Iraq had a clear or coherent picture of what Baghdad actually looked like. There were the grainy nocturnal images of cruise missiles threading their way through the city's streets which CNN transmitted during the Gulf War, and the occasional sanitized interview conducted in one of Saddam Hussein's 60-odd palaces. But come the war of 2003, and suddenly 24-hour coverage from Baghdad provided a close-up, if militaristic, travel guide to the city.

Sadly, it merely proved that Coward's observations 60 years earlier remained generally true. After a decade or so of sanctions, followed by the onslaught of Operation Iraq Freedom and accompanying looters, Baghdad was permanently impaired. The middle classes who had hung on in the faded splendour of their Ottoman-influenced houses had been forced to sell everything they owned simply to survive. Sandstorms and dust – Baghdad, like most Arab cities,

rises out of surrounding desert – had also taken their toll. The infrastructure, bombed and plundered, was wilting.

And yet, and yet, battered Baghdad survives. The glory might have gone, but the River Tigris ("lion-coloured, like the Tiber or Arno" if you're Freya Stark, "sluggish brown" if you're not) continues to slide through the city where the Caliphs once ruled, and which was built by Abu Ja'far al'Mansur, Brasilia-style, in 4 years during the 760s. Overgrown, untended palm gardens line the river and barbecues of the *masghouf* fish are still consumed along its banks, accompanied by Rothmans and Johnny Walker Black.

Baghdad, once famed for its beauty, is now, according to Mario Vargas Llosa, "the ugliest city in the world". But those who have explored it recall that its plainness is offset by a sense of charm as offbeat as the sliced Easter-egg design of the Martyrs' memorial, alongside which "touristic" sites like the Kadhimiya or Shahid Mosques seem rather predictable fare. The city has begun to rediscover some kind of normality, with the re-opening of cinemas, bars, racecourses, bodybuilding gyms and beauty salons. The billboards that once extolled Saddam now advertise consumer goods. Yet the new vitality is dysfunctional, a return to life fractured and frustrated by insecurity and fear, as Baghdad attempts to embrace democracy and a new beginning in which it can welcome vistitors once more to 'the City of Peace'.

THE TRAVELLER WHO PASSES beneath the gateway of Bab Al-Yemen into the old city of San'a is about to take a voyage back through time. While outside the walls, and spreading out across the plain in which San'a sits, there is a new city of modern houses and petrol stations, through Bab Al-Yemen there exists a world that has remained essentially unchanged for hundreds of years. Not because the city is fossilized or abandoned – on the contrary, it is as full of life as ever – but because San'a, probably more than any other Arab city, is in touch, emotionally and spiritually, with its pre-Islamic past.

Its inhabitants value that past highly, as they do all things Yemeni. Restaurateurs will proudly announce that it is Yemeni meat that they are serving along with wheat bread, and a fenugreek-flavoured *hulbah* broth. Western clothes are rare, the garb of choice is traditional: coloured *sitarah* cloaks, coiled headscarves and curved *jambiyah* daggers, the women's all-embracing black *sharshaf*. Nobody is actually sure when San'a was founded. Some consider it the world's first city. One legend has it being founded by Shem, son of Noah, begetter of the Semites. However vague its origins, this city is seriously ancient, and feels as old, not as the hills, but as the ring of mountains that surrounds it.

San'a is also the treasurehouse of a unique urban architecture. The city's extraordinary tall houses, sometimes eight storeys high – skyscrapers for centuries before the term was invented – were built out of mud bricks on basalt foundations, and decorated with white stucco, alabaster and plaster friezes. Perched on the plain of San'a, "the rooftop of Arabia", at an altitude of 7,710 feet (2,350m), the houses are themselves surmounted by a *mafraj*, a penthouse or belvedere with views out across the rooftops. The *mafraj* is modelled on the one on top of the 2nd-century AD Palace of Ghumdan from Sana's past; nothing physical remains of the palace, but the concept of the belvedere perpetuates its memory.

Up in the *mafraj*, local men will disappear for hours to indulge in the ritual of chewing leafs from the qat tree, an action which – according to those who have experienced it – produces an effect which is not so much mind-altering as mind-extending, where the brain goes into slow-motion and time seems to stretch for ever. From their vantage point the qat-chewers can ponder the mountains, the city below, life and death and history.

Recent problems in Yemen – the attack on the USS Cole at Al'Adan, the old port of Aden, 200 miles (322km) south, or kidnappings and murders in the interior – have reduced the number of visitors to San'a. They are missing something quite special. With or without a mouthful of qat, it is a city that expands the mind.

"'There are three earthly paradises,' said the Prophet. 'Merv of Khurasan, Damascus of Syria, and San'a of Yemen. And San'a is the paradise of these paradises.'" Tim Mackintosh-Smith, *Yemen*

42°15' E

WHEN RASTAS IN KINGSTON talk about "roots" they're not referring to their hair; but not many of them may know that the place they're talking of is the city of Harar in the green hills of Ethiopia. For it was here that Ras Tafari, son of Ras Mekonin, Duke of Harar, was born and spent most of his childhood before becoming Haile Selassie, Emperor of Ethiopia.

The Rastafarian movement was the brainchild of a Jamaican, Leonard Howell, who, fresh from battles against the British with the Ashanti in West Africa, hailed Ethiopian King Menelik II's victory in 1896 over the Italians as a victory over white supremacy. Back in JA he put a spin on the *Book of Revelations*, hailing the advent of

fortifications – the crenellated wall that still today circles the old city with its five magnificent city gates and 24 watch-towers.

East of the Great Rift Valley, surrounded by soaring mountains, with a cool climate, views over the Danakil Desert to the north, lush hillsides to the east and fertile pastures to south, even today Harar is a spinner of myths and exotic tales, and a city whose treasures are still coveted by travellers. According to legend, the women of Harar are the most beautiful in Africa. The first European to enter the city was the explorer Richard Burton, who returned with evidence of wonderful silver craftsmanship in the form of necklaces, bracelets and chains that are still to be found in the

> ## "A place of riches and security which easily became a splendid legend, it retained something of the gracious fragrance of Fez or Meknès." Evelyn Waugh, *Waugh in Abyssinia*

Selassie and preaching the opium (or, in his case, clouds of ganja) of a new, anti-white and dread-locked religion, Rastafarianism.

Whatever the fashion, Christianity, Islam or Rastafarianism, the walled city of Harar was always a fiercely religious city. From the 16th to the 19th centuries it was, like Timbuktu, a closed and forbidden city at the centre of the Islamic expansion into Africa, masterminded by the great Islamic conqueror of the highlands, Ahmad ibn Ibrahim, aka Gragn, meaning "left-handed". With its 82 mosques Muslims still regard Harar as the fourth holiest city in the Islamic world after Mecca, Medina and Jerusalem. It was Gragn's nephew, Emil Nur, who built Harar's distinctive

city's markets. The coffee cultivated in the surrounding hills is some of the world's finest.

Leonard Howell apart, Harar has always seemed to attract colourful characters. In the 1880s, as if enacting the unchained longings of his poetry, the peripatetic French Romantic poet, Arthur Rimbaud (known locally as "Rambo" or "Rainbow") ended up here, setting himself up as a photographic agent and freelance gunrunner to the King. It may have something to do with the allure of a fairytale city built like a child's sandcastle, a warm adobe Camelot with a delirious, colourful warren of secretive alleyways squeezed into barely a third of a mile (a square kilometre), set high up in a cloud-cuckoo-land of hills.

> HARAR, ETHIOPIA > LOCAL NAME: Harer > LONGITUDE: 42°15' E > LATITUDE: 9°14' N > ALTITUDE: 6,000 feet/1,829 metres > POPULATION: 99,500
> NATIVES: Haile Selassie > RESIDENTS: Arthur Rimbaud

THE CITY OF MOMBASA was built on trade. As Kenya's access point to the rest of the world it first bartered gold, ivory and slaves for textiles in the 11th century, doing deals with traders arriving from Arabia and Persia; commerce has been the city's lifeblood ever since. Located on a coral island in a bay surrounded by mangroves and open to the Indian Ocean, Mombasa is anchored to the mainland by both causeway and bridge – at the end of the 1890s the construction of railway lines to Nairobi and Uganda anchored it even more firmly to the very heartland of Africa. It remains the largest port in Eastern Africa, a coastal outlet for landlocked countries like Uganda, Burundi and Rwanda. So there is a nip of salt in the air, and plenty of spices too. The city, like a sailor's face, is weathered and wrinkled from exposure to sun and brine.

As with any commercially successful harbour city, it was not long before the predators started circling and looking for a slice of the action. In Mombasa's case, the Portuguese were the most persistent offenders. Vasco da Gama sailed up to Mombasa in 1498 after rounding the Cape of Good Hope, but was repelled; the Portuguese returned seven years later and intermittently through the 1500s until they secured it, for a while, before being turfed out... by the Omanis. The uncompromising Fort Jesus, the Portuguese citadel, full of turrets and tunnels, is only a stroll from the present-day downtown area.

The old town, which slopes down to the harbour, is crowded and compressed, with a faded yet alluring 19th-century feel. The dominant note is that of Swahili culture: women in traditional black *bui-buis* or printed cotton *kangas*, the men wearing *kunzu* robes. Some houses retain their Swahili shutters and latticed balconies, but the original massive wooden entrances and door frames carved with flowers, animals or geometric designs survive only in the Fort Jesus museum or further up the coast at Lamu. And the legacy of centuries of trading with Arab *dhows* can be seen in the 16th-century Mondhry and Basheikh mosques, which stand alongside Sikh and Hindu temples.

On Moi Avenue, the main shopping street in central Mombasa, a set of crossed, carved tusks recalls a visit by the then Princess (but imminently to become Queen) Elizabeth in 1952, on her way to view the wildlife of the interior. Visitors to Mombasa now tend to come for the nearby beaches, and to enjoy a city that is softer and generally safer, more indolent perhaps, than Nairobi. The white coral-sand beaches, Tiwi, Shelly and Diani to the south, and the string beyond Nyali to the north, are shark-free, the only downside being that they are often thick with seaweed.

"At Mombasa we reach the true Africa of the Victorian illustrations."

Cyril Connolly

DAR ES SALAAM TANZANIA

39°16' E

MUCH OF THE TIME, visitors to Dar es Salaam, shooed along by their tour operators, can only grant the city a fleeting glance, en route to Tanzania's collection of exotic destinations: its game parks and reserves (most notably the Serengeti), the Great Rift Valley, Mount Kilimanjaro or the musky allure of Zanzibar 50 miles (80km) to the north of the city. Few are able to fully appreciate its unusual, possibly unique, mix of the African, Arab, Asian and German.

First and foremost, Dar es Salaam is a harbour. A sultan of Zanzibar, one Majid bin Said, saw the commercial potential of the site (that is, of the slave and ivory trade), and began the construction of his summer pleasure palace in 1865: Dar's history as a city, although its name sounds splendidly ancient, is relatively recent. The Sultan died only five years later in a fall in his brand-new palace, but the name he gave it, Bandur ul Salaam ("Palace of Peace") endures.

In any case, shortly afterwards, in the late 1880s, the German East Africa Company took control, making Dar es Salaam the capital of their colony of Deutsch Ostafrika. They imported a rectilinear grid of streets along the waterfront (it is far too tempting to call such a pattern Teutonic) and the necessary elements to create a chunk of Germany in Africa: a hospital, the Kaiserhof Hotel, a Lutheran church for zealous missionaries and St Joseph's Cathedral, as well as a railway, the Mittelland Bahn, running inland from the harbour to Lake Tanganyika, a project which was completed a tad too late, in 1914. Following the First World War, the British acquired Tanganyika – a name beloved of schoolboy philatelists – until the country gained independence in 1963. So Tanzanians have had a mere four decades to oversee their city, which remains the heart of the country (even though the capital was relocated to Dodoma in 1974). It is a blend of all its influences, which gives the city its strength, and should perhaps detain the transient tourists a little longer.

From the waterfront, the harbour unrolls, and traditional Arab *dhows* with triangular *lateen* sails still ply their trade, nowadays overtaken by the hydrofoils buzzing off to Zanzibar. In the city, not only is the Arab influence still strong, but in the west around Indira Gandhi Street, a little India, where Hindu, Muslim and Sikhs tolerantly coexist, adds yet another cosmopolitan layer. The wooden balconies of the German colonial buildings now grace government offices. For a sense of Africa, the Kariakoo market and the ubiquitous communal *daladala* minibuses could only hail from that continent, and – although Dar es Salaam is a Muslim city, and bars are infrequent except out in Dar's swollen suburbs – the music of the city, a joyous guitar and brass-driven dance band form, articulates the laid-back fun of this busy port. And, refreshingly, Dar has also turned out to be one of the world's most self sufficient cities, a model of sustainable urban agriculture, where nearly 70% of households actively produce their own fruit and veg.

> DAR ES SALAAM, TANZANIA > LONGITUDE: 39°16' E > LATITUDE: 6°48' S
> ALTITUDE: 47 feet/14 metres > POPULATION: 2,489,800
> RESIDENTS: Roald Dahl, Robert Koch

"Dar es Salaam lies like a **dormant bush-baby** curled round a blue bay fringed with **coconuts and flamboyants.**"

Elspeth Huxley

"As the sun burns off the morning mist, the skyline of Jeddah is clearer. There's no minaret, dome or crescent moon in sight. It is the formidable face of a boom economy." Michael Palin

FOR SOME 1,400 YEARS, ever since Caliph Othman bin Affan declared it so, the Red Sea port of Jeddah has been the entranceway to Medina and Mecca, the portal – by sea and now by air – for hundreds of thousands of pilgrims en route for the final stage of the *hadj* that every Muslim aims to complete within his lifetime. The Caliph's decision was the major turning-point in the city's history, giving it an all-encompassing *raison d'être*, but this "Bride of the Sea", on the western shore of Saudi Arabia, is more than just some desert terminal.

Although Jeddah, like Dubai, has spent much energy over the last couple of decades constructing a skyline of new buildings that would fit right in as part of Paris's La Défense or London's Docklands, the Al-Balad quarter, old Jeddah, offers a completely different cityscape. Here are fine examples of Jeddah's trademark merchant houses: thin, tall, limestone buildings of three, four or five storeys providing plenty of shade for the streets they line. Their façades are covered by huge rectangular, darkwood balconies on which carved screens enclose the window spaces, there to catch any breeze that might ease the heat and humidity, but also to preserve the modesty of the women of the house. The walls of these houses are flecked with coral and shells, evidence that the stone was quarried from the reefs down near the seashore. One of the finest examples, the Nassif House, constructed for the then governor of Jeddah in 1881, and now a cultural centre and museum, contains a total of 106 rooms and was once known as "the Tree House", since it was the only residence in Jeddah that could boast a tree, a venerable neem that still lives on.

Although Jeddah tentatively welcomes Western tourists, this is still an intensely devout city that observes its religion's rules. Restaurants and shops close for prayer times; fast food outlets are for "bachelors only", with a separate hatch to serve women. More dramatically, the car park of a mosque is where punishments meted out by the courts may include the severing of a hand or a head. Post 9/11 there are other issues at play, not least that Jeddah is the corporate HQ of the wealthy Bin Laden family's construction business.

Yet Jeddah possesses an unexpected dash of whimsy. Along the corniche, a string of lights which once illuminated the sea front at Blackpool now brighten the way. And some 400 sculptures, including works by Jean Miró and Henry Moore, are scattered throughout the city, most curiously on a series of roundabouts which are topped off with bicycles, planes and huge replicas of mathematical dividers, protractors and set squares.

LIKE DELHI IN INDIA or St Louis in Senegal, the Eritrean capital of Asmara bears the imprint of its former European colonizers. But the redolence that lingers in Asmara is not that of tiffin or Gauloises, but the aroma of good Italian coffee. Here the espressos and cappuccinos are as lovingly prepared as in any streetside bar in Rome or Naples, and of a late afternoon the local Eritrean gentlemen saunter down Liberation Avenue for their *passeggiata* sporting elegant borsalinos and black suits. In the Catholic cathedral, Benito Mussolini is listed among the donors. Outside, 1950s Fiats and Vespas buzz hither and thither.

The Italian influence in this far-flung highland city arrived in the 1890s, when Governor Ferdinando Martini appointed the small village of Asmara to be the capital of Italy's new African colony. The community itself dated back seven centuries, to a settlement in which four warring clans had been brought together in peace by their womenfolk, and was consequently given the name Arbaete Asmara, or "the women united the four".

To the south side of the city's main thoroughfare, Liberation Avenue, the architecture relates the story of Italy's occupation, and also of Mussolini's desire to create a new Roman Empire in Africa. The Rationalist design of the Cinema Impero or the Ministry of Education are straight out of Il Duce's Fascist manual. The Governor's Palace and the 1930s villas are pure Lake Como. The 1938 Fiat Tagliero building is a glass art deco classic that would be right at home in Miami. To the north of the city, though, there is a spicier feel, where the markets and mosques remind you that this is, in fact, Muslim Africa.

Asmara has been under threat for a long time. Following the Second World War the United Nations placed Eritrea in an uneasy federal union with Ethiopia; in 1962 the Ethiopians annexed Eritrea, leading to decades of bitter conflict. But, amazingly, the fluctuating war devastated the countryside and not the city. Asmara's isolation helped: the link to Massawa 40 miles (64km) away down on the Red Sea used to be best traversed via *téléphérique*. The city was able to exist in its own bubble, legendarily both safe and clean, although it could not completely fend off the ravages of time on its buildings and infrastructure.

Now, during a tentative cease-fire, the front line of the Ethiopian army is still often only half a day's drive away. The possibility of further invasion remains. Whether this city of palms, hibiscus and bougainvillaea, of time in stasis – "Africa's Pompeii" as it has been dubbed – will survive is debatable. But to date it has proved remarkably durable. Long may the cappuccino machines steam and the Vespas buzz.

> "It takes coffee seriously, people try to dress well and have their shoes cleaned outside the old opera house. One might think the place was in Southern Italy."
>
> Thomas Keneally

ADDIS ABABA ETHIOPIA

IN CONTRAST TO THE COUNTRY'S antique name, Abyssinia, Ethiopia's capital is a relatively new affair. The city was founded in 1887 by King Menelik II, a dynamic visionary of a king, who rose above the warring fiefdoms that were tearing the Horn of Africa apart and sought to reunify them in the face of covetous colonial nations scrambling for their piece of the dark continent. He was to the Ethiopians what Ataturk was to the Turkic tribes, the founder of a new city and a revived and strengthened national identity with a modernized society. His new city was christened "new flower" by his wife, Empress Taytu.

Set high in the foothills of the Setoto Mountains, Addis, as the city is known for short, stands 7,875 feet (2,400m) above sea level, making it, after La Paz and Quito, the third highest capital in the world. At his wife's desire Menelik built the city around the hot springs at Filwoha, which although now shrunk to a muddy pool, still form the city's hub.

From here the city spreads out in modern, low-rise, unspectacular 20th-century style. The main thoroughfare, surprisingly called Churchill Avenue, is testament to the Allied expulsion of Mussolini's Fascist soldiers who invaded the city in 1936 and for five years laid claim to the country. Surprisingly, there are more English references in the city, perhaps none more so than the solid octagonal form of St George's Cathedral, dedicated coincidentally to England's patron saint but built in commemoration of Menelik's repulsion of the first Italian colonialist advances at the Battle of Adwa in 1896.

The Italians stayed long enough to name the two main meeting forums for the Addis populace: Mercato, possibly the largest market in Africa and a labyrinth of stalls, shops and warehouses selling an infinite variety of the useful and useless; and, the other side of Churchill Avenue, Piazza, a more upmarket yet still teeming version, lined with jewellers, silversmiths and craft shops.

The revered Emperor Haile Selassie took Ethiopia through to 1974 when he was deposed following famines and pent-up public disgust at the riches of the nobility and the church (Haile Selassie was said to parade around with a lion on a leash when receiving distinguished visitors). A brief flirtation with Marxism followed under the ensuing Dergue regime, since when war with neighbouring Eritrea and the famine that spawned Live Aid and revived Bob Geldof's career have been the images of Addis and Ethiopia broadcast to a generation around the world.

But Addis is up and running again, as is best illustrated by Ethiopia's new national hero leaving renamed streets in the wake of his Adi Dasser trainers, the new emperor of long-distance running, Addis native Haile Gabrselassie.

330 > ADDIS ABABA, ETHIOPIA > LOCAL NAME: Adis Abeba > LONGITUDE: 38°45' E
> LATITUDE: 9°01' N > ALTITUDE: 7,875 feet/2,400 metres > POPULATION: 2,638,500
> NATIVES: Meseret Defar, Haile Gabrselassie, Liya Kebede, Wilfred Thesiger

"I'd expected somewhere very hot and dusty rather like towns in New Mexico. But it was **very open and cool,** and fresh with the **scent of eucalyptus.**"

Bob Geldof

AS SOME CITIES HAVE THEIR sights and others their sounds, so Moscow has its unique smell. A musty, slightly sweet compote of black bread, vodka, unrefined petrol and soap, it permeates every nook and cranny of the city. With the power to evoke vivid images, to find it strangely not unpleasant is to be captured by the spell of Russia.

The façades of St Petersburg may once have presented its aristocratic sophisticated face but Moscow is the real and – founded in the 12th century – original home of the eccentric and drunken Russian soul, epitomized by former Mayor Boris Yeltsin. Here, amid the bleak grey boulevards that led one writer to call Moscow "LA without sun and grass", and where, in Byron's eyes, "like black ghouls on the soundless snow Muscovites went their way", are incongruous displays of glitter and hedonism. The cathedral of St Basil on Red Square, built in celebration of Ivan the Terrible's victory over the Mongols to free Moscow from the Golden Horde, is a boiling pot of bulging domes and churches that Lewis Carroll saw as "bunches of variegated cactus". Along with the city's other occasional churches and palaces it seems distorted, exaggeratedly religious, almost tasteless, capricious, and without a standard of beauty, built seemingly by imagination and not from plans. This Russian salad of styles, a mix of Oriental irregularity and bizarre beauty, led many 19th-century travellers to call Moscow an inland Constantinople.

A whole century would subsequently come to identify Moscow with just the opposite, a symbol of suppressed individuality and metaphor of the Cold War, its *matrioshka* of ring roads lined by rows of uniform *krushchoby* slum apartment blocks. But even then the odd aesthetic extravagance could not be resisted. Stalin's metro was a needlessly opulent underground palace of chandeliers and socialist art galleries, his Seven Sisters towers flawed follies, and Soviet women became famed for excessive application of cheap eye-shadow.

And in the post-*glasnost* world the newly rich Moscovites, people in the right place at the right time ennobled by privatized oil and mineral rights, are no less gaudy. High on conspicuous consumption, discretion is a swear-word and understatement unheard of. Jaded by years of conformity these new tsars of the capitalist age minx down fashionable Kusnetsky Most in search of Prada over Pravda, their entourages climbing out of *shestsotki* Merc sedans. At weekends they retire on their Harleys to the gently rolling land of the suburbs, to Gorki, Nikolina Gora, Barvikha, and Zhukovka – not gulags but the Moscow equivalent of the Hamptons, where they have equally flashy *dachas* with turrets, towers and monuments to their own vanity.

From mafia and corruption to accepted respectability, that age-old route of kings, Moscow is in the throes of the necessary rise of a professional ruling class whose organized crime will one day beget stability and a middle class. Only then will a much-needed equilibrium, and maybe with it some taste, prevail.

"Moscow: those syllables can start a tumult in the Russian heart."

Alexander Pushkin, *Eugene Onegin*

> MOSCOW, RUSSIA > LOCAL NAME: Moskva > LONGITUDE: 37°38' E > LATITUDE: 55°45' N > ALTITUDE: 512 feet/156 metres > POPULATION: 8,299,000 > TWINNED WITH: Bangkok, Chicago, Dusseldorf, Valencia, Warsaw > NATIVES: Elena Dementieva, Fyodor Dostoevsky, Vasily Kandinsky, Evgeny Kissin, Anna Kournikova, Prince Peter Kropotkin, Boris Pasternak, Serge Poliakoff, Alla Pugacheva, Alexander Pushkin, Marat Safin, Alexander Scriabin, Stanislavsky, Andrei Tarkovsky, Tatu (Yulia Valkova & Lena Katina) > RESIDENTS: Guy Burgess, George Blake, Donald Maclean, Kim Philby

"In *Out Of Africa* Nairobi is portrayed as a sunny little country town, so I am disappointed to find that at some point they took away that pretty scene and replaced it with Omaha." Bill Bryson

NAIROBI KENYA

COMPARED TO THE CITY OF Karen Blixen's day, the skyline of Nairobi may now look more like a mid-Western downtown, but the wildlife that inhabits its environs is still distinctly African. Giraffes, lions and zebras gaze nonchalantly at the skyscrapers from the savannah of the National Park just beyond Nairobi's outskirts, the only reserve of its kind located so close to a major conurbation.

The animals were there long before Nairobi. There is no long, rich history to recount. In the late 1890s, British engineers, constructing a railway from Mombasa to Uganda, simply set up camp near a swampy watering hole (its name, Ewaso Nairobi, is the Masai for "stream of cold water"), while they took a breather and mulled over how to tackle the highland slopes coming up ahead of them. For a decade or so there was nothing much but a handful of tents, a supply store and shunting yard. Yet by 1905, shortly after the first permanent buildings had been erected, the nascent city had become the capital of the colony of Kenya, and big game hunters were arriving to update their trophy walls.

The city has not stopped growing since, and is already the largest city between Johannesburg and Cairo, although in other continents its population of two million people would scarcely merit a mention. This upward spurt over only a century or so has given Nairobi a relentless growth curve reflected in the crescendo of noise that it generates each morning after the comparative quiet of the night (other, that is, than in the CBD nightclubs or the legendary Buffalo Bill's bar, a magnet for the louche and maverick of Nairobi).

Compared to Mombasa down on the coast, Nairobi has a reputation for being hard, fast – and dangerous. Although the city contains the African HQs of a number of major UN agencies like the World Bank, and has its fair share of smart office blocks and suburban mansions for the seriously wealthy, it is surrounded by extensive slum areas and has also become known for a dangerous level of mugging. The locals coined a word for it, "Nairobbery". To add to this impression of lawlessness, the city was seriously unsettled by the terrorist bombing of the US Embassy on Moi Avenue in 1998. As a result many businesses and restaurants have relocated to Westlands, north of the centre.

There is plenty of energy, both positive and negative, a constant flux of the legal and illegal, particularly down along River Road, and a certain amount of chaos. It is said that the only punctual things in Nairobi are the short, sharp showers, which frequently douse the pavements of an afternoon, and provide an opportunity to spot a galloping herd of busy umbrella vendors.

> NAIROBI, KENYA > LONGITUDE: 36°48' E > LATITUDE: 1°17' S > ALTITUDE: 5,450 feet/1,661 metres > POPULATION: 2,043,300 > TWINNED WITH: Denver > NATIVES: Richard Dawkins, Govindas Desani, Richard Leakey > RESIDENTS: Iman

STILL KNOWN BY ITS LATIN NAME, Damascus is one of the great, mythical sites, dating back some 7,000 years and almost "half as old as time". From the Phoenicians, via the Greek and Romans to the Arabs, Mongols and Ottomans, Damascus possibly the longest continually inhabited city in the world.

Situated in an oasis east of Mount Lebanon on an otherwise uninhabitable plain, the setting is biblical, conjuring up images of the proportionate success of seeds sewn on barren and fertile land. And in her youth, as a centre of learning and civilization, Damascus embodied the classical sense of everything a city should be. The ancient Syrians invented the numbering system used everywhere in the world (except, ironically, here and throughout Arabia); in Roman times Damascus became renowned for its prized woven fabric known as damask; and Syrian poets were responsible for penning some of the most famous lines in Arabian literature, notably a tome called *Alf Layla wa Layla* which translates as the best-selling *One Thousand and One Arabian Nights*.

As its Arab name, "Ash Sham", suggests, the modern city is a bit of a shambles. Modern Syria of which Damascus is capital was born from the break-up of the Ottoman Empire after the First World War. Until independence in 1946 it enjoyed a restless relationship with its new owners, the French, who in 1936, following serial insurrections, decided, rather uncharacteristically, to bomb Damascus. Divided by the Barada River the old city to the south, encircled by the original Roman walls has essentially survived, if in a state of somewhat charming and gracious decay with dilapidated wooden Ottoman mansions hung precariously over the river.

Through the great Arab gates of Bab as-Salaama ("Gate of Safety") and Bab Touma in the old city are to be found many architectural treasures of the Arab world. The Great Omayyad Mosque, designed

> DAMASCUS, SYRIA > LOCAL NAME: Ash Sham > LONGITUDE: 36°20' E > LATITUDE: 33°30' N
> ALTITUDE: 2,296 feet/700 metres > POPULATION: 1,803,700
> NATIVES: Bashar al-Assad

"And as he journeyed he came near the city of Damascus and suddenly there shined around him a great light that came from Heaven."

The Bible, Acts 9

to be the greatest ever is resplendent with its golden mosaics. Outside its walls is the red-domed mausoleum where lies the great Arab knight, Saladin (that famous warrior but little-known Kurd!). Alongside the 19th-century souk still stands an arrangement of Corinthian columns from the original Roman temple of Jupiter. In the east of the old city, off "the street that is called Strait" is the ancient Christian quarter and St Paul's chapel on the spot where the disciples lowered the saint out of the window so he could flee the Jews. Modern-day travellers on this road will have their eyes opened to Damascus's charms.

Hospitality is everywhere in the world but here a national pastime. This tight maze of cobbled streets is packed with tea-houses patronized by wise old men with white beards smoking their *narguileh* water-pipes in beatific contemplation. From every shop door ring polite invitations to pass the time, drink tea and chew the falafel, always punctuated with the country's seeming motto, *tafaddel* ("you are welcome"). Only occasionally are these the cunning solicitations of Assad's *mukhabarat* secret police.

BEIRUT LEBANON

VENUS WAS THOUGHT TO LIVE in the hill-caves of Lebanon. Once one of the most dangerous places on earth her capital is again the *femme fatale* of the Middle East, its visitors no longer hostage to fanatical terrorists but instead to a seductress's charms.

Although several decades of internecine civil war might indicate otherwise, Beirut was historically a byword for the peaceful cohabitation of a cocktail of diverse faiths. "Beryte" to the Phoenicians, the ancient city was always an important trading port coveted by successive invading powers, crusaders, Arabs and Ottomans. Under the Romans, Berythus had become an important school of law. As a potential trampling ground Beirut's solution for survival was to become a centre for reason and culture in the form of publishing and education.

The other trick she developed was to become a seductive haven for banking and gambling, a Switzerland of the Middle East, unusually Western in her pursuit of material success and in the licentious pursuit of pleasure that goes with it. To desert Arabs, West-facing, Western-spirited Beirut was "a sore thumb that stuck out in the wrong direction".

Lebanon was born of the break-up of the Ottoman Empire and was made a French protectorate. Amid the minarets and fine Ottoman mansions were added villas in honey-coloured French neoclassicism. A corniche and a Parisian Etoile were built. "Beyrouth" became an exotic mix of Eastern mystery and the language of love.

While Beirut's diversity was the reason for her effervescence, following independence and the creation of Israel after the Second World War she was also a tinder-box waiting to explode. Beirut was taken hostage by fleeing Palestinians and became a minefield of political allegiances, a cause appropriated by states beyond Lebanon's borders, split across the infamous "green line" between East and West, Christian and Muslim, but with all factions firing Katyushas seemingly at everyone in sight. Peace returned in the early 1990s, and although the checkpoints of the peace-keeping Syrian army are still very much in evidence, the once-ominous black flags of the Hizbollah faction are now the symbol of a legitimate political party.

Much of the city still lies in red rubble and to its south are the reminders of the refugee camps, Sabra and Shatila. But the Parisian Lebanese *émigrés* have returned. The Solidere redevelopment of the historic centre is almost artificially polished while the developers regularly unearth ancient ruins before demure locals who sup a *mezze* of the Middle East's best cuisine, chuck back *arrak,* suck *hookah* pipes and shoot backgammon at the cafés on Rue Monot and Rue al-Maarad.

People-watching is a favourite pastime of this vain but beautiful race, never more so than by day in the bikinied-Venusland of the Riviera cafés and by night in some of the Mediterranean's steamiest nightclubs in the loft-world suburbs of Jounieh, La Quarantaine and Achrafiye.

Her body abused and contested by so many creeds, Beirut's true deity is the pagan goddess of beauty.

> BEIRUT, LEBANON > LONGITUDE: 35°30' E > LATITUDE: 33°52' N > ALTITUDE: 16 feet/5 metres > POPULATION: 1,878,200
> NATIVES: Fairouz, Mustafa Farroukh, Mona Hatoum, Nicholas ("Mr Swatch") Hayek, Keanu Reeves, Nada Saleh, Pascal Tarabay, Gabriel Yared

"Nubile,
bikini-wrapped
oil-girls, with
figures like
greyhounds and
waists as pliant as
a bundle of
banknotes,
inhaled and
exhaled their
exquisite physical
presences up and
down the sun-
spotted terraces."

Laurie Lee, *Arrack and Astarte*

"My heart has never failed to lift at the sight
of those milk-white walls,
those spires and towers,
those steep red-tiled roofs,
the incomparable golden dome
that still dominates the city." John Simpson

35°13' E

THERE IS A MOMENT WHEN THE GLORY and the tragedy that is Jerusalem becomes completely and unforgettably comprehensible. Standing on the top of the noble sanctuary of Haram Esh-Sharif, the Temple Mount which rises above the old walled city, a tight cluster of historic sites reveal themselves, of huge significance to three of the world's great religions.

Islam: the Mount, and Jerusalem itself, is dominated by the 7th-century Dome of the Rock, its copper roof now resplendently gleaming with gold leaf; this is the place from where, according to the Koran, the Prophet Muhammad made his Miraj, the ascent to Heaven, to be in the presence of God.

Judaism: tucked just below the Mount, the Western Wall is a remnant of the great Second Temple, destroyed by the Romans in AD 70. Under the Ottomans, Jews began to come here to lament the loss of their Temple (hence its more famous name, the Wailing Wall); ever since, it has been a sacred destination.

And Christianity: to the west of the Mount is the Church of the Holy Sepulchre, the tomb of Jesus Christ. His final walk, the Via Dolorosa, where stations of the cross mark the places where he stumbled under the weight of the crucifix, wends through the Muslim quarter. Across to the east the groves of the Garden of Gethsemane are where Christ was betrayed by Judas.

The whole area reverberates with intense emotional impact. It should, or could, be a cause of multi-faith celebration. Instead it is the rift fault that has created unhappiness, bitterness and death. When news reports break of another suicide bombing, the unpretentious beauty of Jerusalem on a sunny spring morning is jarring. And the meaning of the city's name – Ursalim, "city of peace" – seems poignantly inappropriate.

For three millennia, Jerusalem has been fought over. Like dogs scrapping over a bone, Egyptians, Syrians, Greeks, Romans, Crusaders, Saladins, Mongols, Turks and the British have wrested control of the city, only to relinquish it to another. And, for now, Jerusalem remains part of Israel. The young nation's recent painful past is recalled by Yad Vashem, west of the city centre: a memorial, museum and tribute to the dead of the Holocaust as well as those, like Oskar Schindler, who plucked some lives from the deluge for which there was no hope.

Beneath the bell-tower of the art deco YMCA and the pink façade of the 1930s King David Hotel, modern Jerusalem reflects the returning diaspora. Ethiopian and Russian voices overlap; teenagers relax in the alleyways of Nakhalat Shiva while their friends patrol in battle fatigues and with semi-automatics; the 19th-century Eastern European clothes of the Ultra-Orthodox in Mea Shearim offset the Versace on Ben Yehuda Street. Alongside them the Palestinians are still stateless, and Jerusalem's Armenians almost extinct. Jerusalem has never truly known peace; may it one day do so.

> JERUSALEM, ISRAEL/WEST BANK > LOCAL NAME: Yerushayalim/El Quds > LONGITUDE: 35°13' E > LATITUDE: 31°47' N > ALTITUDE: 2,500 feet/762 metres > POPULATION: 670,000
> TWINNED WITH: Cairo, New York, Seattle > NATIVES: Yasser Arafat, Farid & Rami Chehade, David Grossman, Yasmin Levy, Dorrit Moussaieff, Amos Oz, Natalie Portman, Yitzhak Rabin,
Edward Said, Avraham B. Yehoshua > RESIDENTS: Samuel Agnon, Teddy Kollek, Boris Schatz, Abraham Ticho

341

TEL AVIV ISRAEL

THE JOURNEY BETWEEN Tel Aviv and Jerusalem is an hour or so's drive, most companionably undertaken in a *sherut* or shared taxi. However, the two cities are radically different. Compared to the inland, history-imbued, religiously divided capital, weighted down with all the baggage and the memories of the past, Tel Aviv, yet to celebrate its first centenary, is a carefree, hormonal teenager, beach-loving, secular and sexy – and now Israel's most populous city.

In 1909, with the formation of the Republic of Israel still four decades away, a group of peace-loving Jews moved out of the ancient, crowded and mainly Arab port of Jaffa to establish a community for themselves, and acquired 12 acres of land for that purpose. To coin the name of this new community, the founders turned to the Hebrew translation of *Altneuland*, a novel by the Zionist Theodor Herzl – Tel meaning "ancient", Aviv "springtime", the clash of old and new that Tel Aviv would come to symbolize.

A few of its first generations are still alive, genteel and European in attitude, but they are now outnumbered by Tel Aviv's distinctly Israeli youngsters, who like the energy, the night-life – a nightclub will open anywhere, even in the back of a petrol station – and above all the

beaches, eight miles (13km) of white sand along the Mediterranean. The shoreline is lined with hotels; the Dan has a 1960s vibe, the Hilton could be in Florida. But not all the culture here is of the beach variety. The city is home to the National Opera (in a Ron Arad opera house) and the Israel Philharmonic, though perversely, given the emphasis on youth here, it is Jerusalem rather than Tel Aviv where Israel's underground music scene is most active.

The earliest architecture in the centre, dating from the first decades of the 20th century, includes fine examples of 1930s modernism created by architects who had relocated from Europe and so were directly influenced by the work of Le Corbusier and the Bauhaus. Though many are in desperate need of restoration, they announce Tel Aviv's modernity. Old Jaffa, which the founders left behind, is now a southern suburb with restaurants, art galleries and artists studios on its stone-flagged streets.

Life is not all milk and honey, though. Along the shoreline the buildings are tall since land is expensive, squeezing a lot of people into very little space, and with no tram or metro system, gridlock – Bangkok-style, sometimes – is a regular event. Nor has Tel Aviv, the commercial and financial hub of Israel, been immune from bomb attacks. But in general it is breezy, upbeat, even brash, a personality typified by the local transsexual singer Dana International, who, to the horror of the ultra-Orthodox, triumphantly carried off the 1998 Eurovision Song Contest.

"More Sunset than Gaza Strip. More West Coast than West Bank."

Janine di Giovanni

> TEL AVIV, ISRAEL > LONGITUDE: 34°46' E > LATITUDE: 32°04' N > ALTITUDE: 0 feet/0 metres > POPULATION: 365,300 > TWINNED WITH: Milan, Warsaw > NATIVES: Dana International, Uri Geller, Ofra Haza, Tzipi Livni, Binyamin Netanyahu, Itzhak Perlman, Yaakov Shabtai, Topol, Pinchas Zukerman > RESIDENTS: Nathan Alterman, Ben Gurion, Esther Raab

"Turks, Greeks and Armenians dwell intermingled, bitter enemies at heart, and **united solely by their love for the land of their birth.**"

Archduke Louis Salvador
of Austria, 1874

EXACTLY 100 YEARS after Archduke Louis recognized the strength of feeling that existed between the different ethnic groups in Nicosia, the intermingling he described was brusquely un-mingled. Following a Greek-backed coup, and the Turkish invasion of 1974, a ceasefire was called, and Cyprus divided in two by the so-called "Green Line".

The northern third of the island became an enclave for Turkish Cypriots (though many chose exile in London or Australia) and the blue berets of the United Nations arrived to patrol the buffer zone created between their sector and the Greek south. As in Berlin, a wall – complete with barbed wire, landmines, sandbags and pillboxes – was constructed, creating unexpected dead ends and slicing through the heart and the psyche of the old city. The Berlin wall fell, and Beirut and Belfast reconciled internal divisions, but Nicosia, despite the best efforts of potential peacemakers, remained the last divided capital city in the world.

Then, in April 2003, travel restrictions were relaxed, and for the first time in 30 years the two communities could cross the barrier. In the first three weeks alone, half the population took the opportunity to visit "the other side". Turkish Cypriots tasted McDonalds for the first time, while Greek Cypriots headed north to view former homes long abandoned (and, some said, to dig up stashes of buried treasures). They could also take advantage of cheaper prices, whether offered by mechanics or prostitutes. And previously menacing blockades overlooking no man's land became places of music, drinking and frivolity, despite the presence of armed, but now very casual, soldiers.

If full unification is achieved it will re-bind an attractive and historic Mediterranean city of warm, honey-coloured buildings. In the more modernized Greek area, Lefkosía, the Saint Sophia Cathedral, was modelled on Paris's Notre-Dame; in the Archbishop's Palace, which looks Venetian but was built in the 1950s and '60s, the heart of the Greek nationalist hero Archbishop Makarios (the "Castro of the Mediterranean") is preserved for posterity. The Turkish quarter, Lefkosa, where the much admired Ottoman minaret of the Arabahmet mosque keeps watch, has remained more traditional, and quieter. Indeed, some Turkish Cypriots fear reunification will mean an influx of reckless developers and that the pleasure of lunch on the unspoilt harbourfront of Kyrenia may be forever marred.

Both sectors are contained with the old city walls, a star-shaped enclosure of mighty ramparts built in the 16th century by the Venetians, who occupied the city to control their trade routes. Beyond the fortifications, modern Nicosia spills outwards, the suburbs spreading past a racecourse whose location rivals that of Goodwood or Cheltenham to the hills where the eucalyptus, orange and lemon trees will still be growing whenever the Green Line is finally erased.

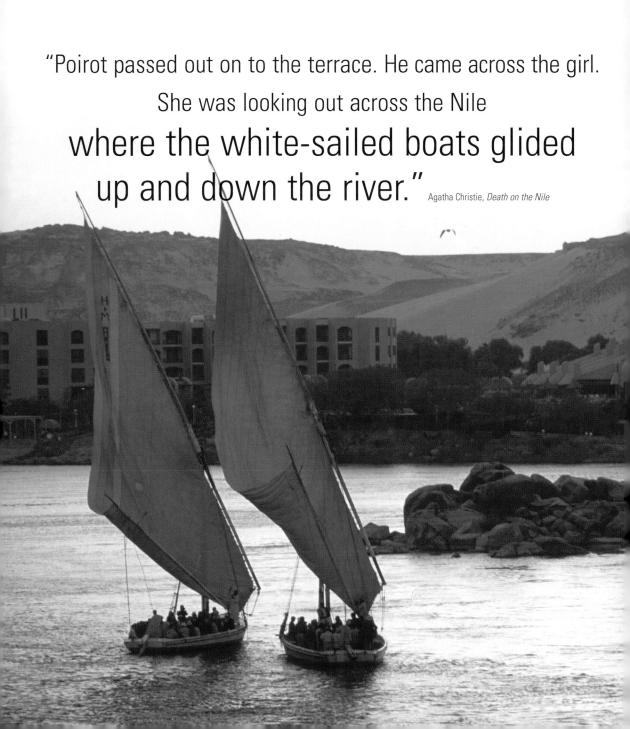

"Poirot passed out on to the terrace. He came across the girl. She was looking out across the Nile where the white-sailed boats glided up and down the river." Agatha Christie, *Death on the Nile*

32°56' E

THE TERRACE WHERE HERCULE POIROT strolled is still there.
The Old Cataract Hotel in Aswan, built by Thomas Cook in 1899,
sits on an outcrop above the River Nile, a cocoon of tea and biscuits,
gin and tonics at sundown, with a Moorish vaulted dining-room that
catered to Winston Churchill, Howard Carter and Tsar Nicholas II.
Little, on the surface, has changed. Below the hotel the *feluccas*,
manned by tall, *djellaba*-clad crewmen, ferry visitors from Aswan's
corniche out to the islands in the river – only now they come with
beatboxes which pump funky Nubian music out across the waters.

Aswan has long been the frontier town between Egypt and Nubia
to the south, and – as the farthest anyone could navigate up the Nile
– once known as the end of the civilized world. Here was the river's
first unnavigable cataract, hence the hotel's name. For many, this
is the Nile at its most stunning. The city, on the East bank, faces
golden desert sands that run down (past the mausoleum of the Aga
Khan, who loved to winter in Aswan) to the emerald-coloured river
where red granite rock is tempered by fringed palm-trees.

It was granite that made Aswan's name: the red stone of Pompey's
Pillar in Alexandria came from the quarries nearby. Stern quality control
means it is still possible to admire from close up a remarkable, but
flawed, obelisk that was abandoned mid-hew, testament to the
engineering prowess of the ancient Egyptians: 1,000 tonnes or more
of stone that would have been excised, manhandled and delivered
to the other end of the country. Aswan's original name, Sian, came,
apparently, from the word for red granite. The later, Coptic name,
Souan, means "trade", and the city's souk stalls are heady with the
aromas and colours of saffron, paprika, indigo and leather.

Nature, rather than craftsmen, fashioned Aswan's two main
islands. Kitchener Island was presented to the British general for
leading Egyptian forces in the Sudan. Shady oleanders, sycamores
and date palms, ripe for romantic trysts, reflect his passion for
botany (and rumour has it, dusky young men). On Elephantine
Island, named after its pachyderm contours, the Nilometer, a
calibrated series of steps, measured the critical rise and fall of the
thin strip of river that determined whether the riverine dwellers
would experience fertility or drought.

Upstream, egrets, parakeet and Horus-like falcons swoop. Higher
again, the Aswan dams hold back the waters of the Nile. To protect
irreplaceable ruins due to be flooded, the temples of Philae and
Kalabasha were painstakingly moved and reconstructed, as were
the immense statues of Abu Simbel, further south, way into the
Nubian Desert. A long drive through the dark of early morning to
catch the figures illuminated in the sunrise is more than worth
the 3.30am alarm call.

> ASWAN, EGYPT > LONGITUDE: 32°56' E > LATITUDE: 24°02' N > ALTITUDE: 367 feet/112 metres >
POPULATION: 220,000 > NATIVES: Abass Mahmoud El Akaad, Mahmoud Fadl
> RESIDENTS: Aga Khan III

347

KAMPALA UGANDA

UGANDA LIES WHERE THE West African rainforest meets the eastern savannah, a tropical, green, wet and fertile land of mountains and plains, home to abundant wildlife and, famously, the mountain gorilla. But if its scenery conforms to the image of the African jungle beamed through Western television sets in the adventures of Tarzan, the history of Uganda and, by default, Kampala, its capital, is no less of a jungle.

Until Europe's 19th-century discovery of the "dark continent", Bantu Buganda (the Swahili drops the "b") was the most influential and largest kingdom of the Bacwezi kings. The name Kampala is the elision of an expression "Kosozi Mapala" meaning "Hill of the Antelope" – a reference to the domestic impala grazing at the royal court. In 1890 the Treaty of Berlin called a halt to the scramble for Africa and decreed that Uganda fall under British control. Of all the tribes native to Uganda the Victorians, deciding to rule from afar, found the Bagandans most suitable for civil service and positions of office. Naturally, the Bagandans lauded it over the other tribes and in time declared the dynasty of Kakaba kings, in the process inciting a jealousy that was set to ignite in postwar independence. The 1950s saw the rise of a human gorilla, one of Africa's and the world's most infamous and insane tyrants in the form of Idi Amin, at whose hands Kampala's Hindu and Asian population were expelled and minority tribes perished in obscene acts of torture and human decimation.

Subsequent decades saw tyrants and false dawns come and go as Kampala was looted and peppered in a cross-fire of "gorilla" warfare. In 1996 comparative peace and stability was brought to Kampala's streets with the iron Afro-Marxist grip of President Museveni. He has guided Uganda out of the red mist of civil war and restored Kampala beyond expectation.

Once the showcase city of Eastern Africa parts of Kampala are gleaming once again. The city sits on just one of its seven hills, Nakasero, overlooking distant Lake Victoria. It is a green city whose upper suburbs are a garden of airy boulevards flanked by embassies and the luxury residences of those who have plotted their way to the top. While down below out of sight is the mess of scavengers and the not-so-cunning – among them Kampala's population of marabou storks, like giant seagulls – a topsy-turvy clamour of blaring *lingala* hip hop and street markets selling an A-Z of odds and ends, of poverty and disease – *ukimwi* (AIDS) has found a capital here, too.

But at least Kampala is safe again, one of few African cities to have drinkable tap water. The city is still suffering from a considerable hangover – similar to the effect of a night drinking the local *pombe* banana beer – but, be it rose-tinted spectacles or beer goggles, Kampala is on the way back to being what Churchill once called "the Pearl of Africa".

> "Like Rome and Lisbon, Kampala is built on seven hills. 'How refreshing,' one Briton said, **'to see a view in Africa that has an end.'"** John Gunther

> KAMPALA, UGANDA > LONGITUDE: 32°34' E > LATITUDE: 0°20' N > ALTITUDE: 4,298 feet/1,310 metres
> POPULATION: 1,150,000 > RESIDENTS: Idi Amin

"South Africans used the word **continental** in just the same way as the English do, meaning **Latin, warm, spicy, relaxed and exotic.**"

Richard West, *The White Tribes of Africa*

32°34' E

ON A CONTINENT DOMINATED by bland eyesores for cities, Mozambique's capital is a refreshing burst of character, atmosphere and faded elegance. Whereas many African cities seem to have been built yesterday, there is here a tangible sense of history and culture.

This is down to the Portuguese. In 1502 the trader-explorer Lourenço Marques discovered the natural harbour at the mouth of the Rio Maputo. Like most explorers of the era he couldn't resist naming the place after himself, and only when Mozambique won independence in 1974 was the city renamed after the river.

The city didn't take off immediately: within a few decades it had been abandoned, only to be resuscitated in 1721 by the Dutch East India Company, who built a trading factory and fort before leaving within a few years. It was not until 1886 that the city's golden age arrived, coinciding with the discovery of gold in neighbouring South Africa's Witwatersrand. The state of Transvaal and Portugal decided to build a railway between Pretoria and Lourenço Marques, and at the turn of the 19th century, as a major port handling one third of South Africa's gold and other imports and exports, Maputo took its current shape. In 1890 the modern state of Mozambique, previously a collection of warring *mazungo* chieftains, was born.

The capital of Mozambique was moved here from the tiny northern island outpost of Ilha de Moçambique and the Portuguese

splashed out on recreating a little piece of imperial Portugal in their East African colony. Downtown Maputo feels a little like Lisbon, the buildings in both cities sharing in the same delicious decay – the same faded pastel-coloured façades of colonial villas built in the Portuguese Gothic Maunelini style. The jacaranda and palm-lined *avenidas* are flanked with street cafés and seafood restaurants alive with the nasal twang of an exotic Afro-Portuguese dialect and the latino rhythms of a music so absent in the other southern states of Africa. Maputo feels European, Mediterranean. And yet there are surprises. The backstreets of the old town, which lend themselves so delightfully to getting lost, harbour creole-style 19th-century

houses of wood, iron filigree and covered balconies that could be New Orleans and seem imported from the Caribbean.

The 20th century was not so kind. The rule from Lisbon of Antonio Salazar's dictatorship held Maputo back as it did Lisbon, his Marxism still evident in Maputo's Avenidas Mao Tse Tung, Lenin and Ho Chi Minh. The Frelimo liberation movement has ruled since independence in 1974, but the South African policy of destabilization at the hands of the Renamo guerillas has ensured that the country has been known to a whole generation only through war reports. The civil war is at last over, and although the countryside is still a minefield, Maputo can be enjoyed as a surprisingly sensual African metropolis.

> MAPUTO, MOZAMBIQUE > LONGITUDE: 32°34' E > LATITUDE: 25°56' S > ALTITUDE: 194 feet/59 metres
> POPULATION: 1,114,000 > NATIVES: Al Bowlly, José Craveirinha, Eusebio, Mariza
> RESIDENTS: Mia Couto, Graça Machel, Hennig Mankell

351

KHARTOUM SUDAN

KHARTOUM WAS ONCE THOUGHT to be laid out like the Union Jack. Nothing remains of Kitchener's patriotic urban planning and the city is instead a village capital of low-scale, low-rise houses and shacks that stretch for miles into the sandy distance. But although its British urban topography may have been eroded and confused, Khartoum's history echoes with the story of one of those typically eccentric Victorian gentlemen campaigners, General Charles Gordon, subject of the Charlton Heston Hollywood epic, *Khartoum*.

Gordon had been the governor of Khartoum between 1874 and 1880. In 1882 he was sent back to ensure the safe exit and passage of the city's population of Europeans in the face of Mohammed Ahmed al-Mahdi, a self-proclaimed Messiah, who had started a holy war to free the Upper Nile from colonial power. No sooner had Gordon arrived than the city came under attack. He telegraphed London for back-up but was ignored, and so with a small garrison of soldiers he attempted to hold out. Through an eccentric Victorian combination of cheek, stoicism and wit he did so for a full 320 days despite the city haemorrhaging turncoats and being outnumbered by several thousand. Even in the closing days of the siege he was still sending telegrams saying "Khartoum all right; could hold out for years." A few days later he was killed.

Khartoum sits at the confluence of the White and Blue Niles. At their meeting point the two tributaries, known as the Mogran, form a huge oxbow curve shaped like the "elephant's trunk" that gives the city its name. One of the more unusual destinations in a bird watcher's holiday brochure, the florid Nile islands in the middle of this momentous swathe of water are temporary home to a rich population of migratory birds.

Capital of the Sudan, Khartoum is in fact composed of three indistinct cities, Khartoum itself on the left bank of the Blue Nile, Khartoum North on the opposite bank and then, round the bend, the city of Omdurman, whence came Gordon's fate and where lies the tomb of his conqueror, al-Mahdi.

Today one can barely imagine the colonial city. Apart from the chic quartier of al-Riyad where Osama bin Laden is said to have had his villa until expelled from Sudan in 1996, there is little semblance of urbanism. The industrial core of the city was bombed by the US following bin Laden's embassy bombings in Dar es Salaam and Nairobi, and with an ever expanding population fleeing the civil war with the Christian Africans in the south, the most these new arrivals can be bothered to put up are mud and straw huts providing just enough shelter and some sense of privacy.

Save for the colourful saris of the Sudanese women, Khartoum is a sand-kicked, brown city under an unchanging blue sky that makes you forget such things as clouds exist; a slow-motion, almost sedated city, the world's largest waiting-room.

"I see a crumbling metropolis that seems to be fluttering its dusty eyelids after a long slumber beneath the sands." Paul Salopek

> KHARTOUM, SUDAN > LOCAL NAME: El Khartûm > LONGITUDE: 32°32' E > LATITUDE: 15°32' N > ALTITUDE: 1,247 feet/380 metres > POPULATION: 1,244,500
> TWINNED WITH: Cairo, Istanbul, Wuhan (China) > NATIVES: Basil Dearden > RESIDENTS: Charles Gordon, Horatio Herbert Kitchener

JAN MORRIS described Cairo as "one of the half-dozen supercapitals – capitals that are bigger than themselves or their countries". For Egyptians, country and capital city are one and the same – Misr ("Egypt City").

Although the banks of the Nile were the birthplace of the Pharaohs, the walled city of Al-Qahira ("the Conqueror") was a comparatively young creation, dating from the 10th century of the crusader-bashing Fatimid leader, Salah al-Din. The Pharaohs had held their capital at Memphis across the river to the south and a millennial interlude of colourful kingdoms preceded the Islamic conquest. You cannot help but sense this detachment in the culture-less opportunism of today's tourist touts and ubiquitous hawkers of alabaster Nefertiti figurines. It is as if the proxy gifts of another civilization have fallen – lucratively – into their laps.

The Coptic Christians (true descendants of the ancient Egyptians and still 10 per cent of the population) had founded the fortress of Babylon-in-Egypt, whose remnants can still be found by their Mar Girgis monastery. The first Arabians to arrive were Persians, under Amr, who founded the city of Fustat, now a mere shantytown for the *zebaleen* (rubbish-gatherers). Following Greek rule, Iraqi *khalifs* razed and rebuilt successive fortresses and it was to this agglomeration that Saladin gave shape, erecting mosques and *madrassas*, and the city walls and gates which form the perimeter of Islamic Cairo. Herein lies the great Khan el-Khalili souk, a labyrinth of alleys with *mashrabiyah* wood-latticed balconies, full of the cries of spice, perfume and cotton traders, and misty with wafts of *tofa* (apple-scented tobacco) from the *ahwa* (coffeehouses), where Cairene men bang down dominos and suck squint-eyed from bubbling *sheesha* pipes. Boy-waiters dance through the human traffic with precarious trays of *shai* (tea) and *karkadeh*

"Such monuments are an integral part of even the most contemporary of lives. Their resonance has carried down the ages, and can speak to us today with a relevance they never abdicated." Naguib Mahfouz

hibiscus infusions, while street-merchants dish out guava juices and the ubiquitous diet of bean *fuuls*, *falafeels* and *sheema* bread.

Cairo remained feudal until the 19th-century reformer Mohammed Ali updated the city. His memory as Egypt's great modernizer is celebrated by the majestic mausoleum-citadel on the southern hills. The 19th century also brought European influence. Khedive Ismail commissioned the art deco and neoclassical Etoile of streets around Midan Ataba – an attractive blend of arabesque and colonial styles. Thereafter Cairo sprawled, its streetmap splintering like a dried-out waterhole, to accommodate one of the densest populations in the world, with supposedly just 13 square centimetres of green per inhabitant. The fumes of black and white taxis – Ladas and Peugeot 504s from the Soviet Nasser years – further clog Cairo's lungs. Limousines queue behind laden oxen and donkey-carts. The city is at bursting point, its limits seemingly defined by the Pyramids which, disappointingly, are lapped at by the expanding Giza suburb. They stand, sphinx-like for their enigmatic symmetry and ancient simplicity, challenging modern Cairo to resolve the riddle of her 21st century.

> CAIRO, EGYPT > LOCAL NAME: Misr > LONGITUDE: 31°15' E > LATITUDE: 30°01' N > ALTITUDE: 72 feet/22 metres > POPULATION: 10, 772,000 > TWINNED WITH: Abu Dhabi (UAE), Amman (Jordan), Astana (Kazakstan), Baghdad, Barcelona, Beijing, Damascus, Frankfurt, Houston, Istanbul, Jerusalem, Khartoum, Minsk (Belarus) New York, Ottawa, Paris, Rabat (Morocco), San'a, Seoul, Stuttgart (Germany), Tokyo, Tripoli, Xian (China) > NATIVES: Boutros Boutros-Ghali, Raffi Cavoukian, Dalida, Thomas Dolby, Atom Egoyan, Farouk I, Julian Fellowes, C.S. Forrester, Penelope Lively, Naguib Mahfouz, Karim Rashid, Claudia Roden, Sylvain Sylvain (Ronald Mizrahi), Alan Whicker, Sheik Ahmed Yamani > RESIDENTS: Lord Cromer, Nawa El Saadawi, Ibn Khaldoun, Umm Kalthum, Auguste Mariette

ODESSA UKRAINE

THE ODESSA STEPS SEQUENCE in Eisenstein's *Battleship Potemkin* is seared into cinema's consciousness. The moment when a baby's pram, the mother mown down by Tsarist gunfire in the 1905 uprising, bounces untended down the flight of steps, is a seminal piece of film which Brian de Palma later paid homage to in *The Untouchables*. Although Eisenstein was slightly economical with the *cinema vérité* (the flight ends not at the edge of the Black Sea, but a roadway full of trucks), the majesty of the 192 steps remains intact, best viewed looking up the steep tree-covered bluff towards a statue of the Duc de Richelieu, great-nephew of the more famous Cardinal.

The Duc, fleeing the French Revolution, proved useful to Russia's Catherine the Great, who had issued a decree in 1794 to turn Odessa into a military base to control the local Cossacks and Tartars. Richelieu was a formidable adminstrator, and under his direction Odessa grew not just into a fortified port but into a cosmopolitan resort full of *émigrés*, the playground of Russia's elite, a Black Sea Biarritz.

The city planners built an airy, alfresco city of broad boulevards (or "Bulvars"), crescents, courtyards, squares and onion-domed churches. On this coastal edge of the barren steppe they refoliated the land. Odessa is full of chestnuts, acacias and, above all, the plane-trees which line the boulevards. The local beaches of white sand are gently sloping and child-friendly. And the women of Odessa are noted for their chic beauty: "Ukraine girls really knock me out", sang the Beatles, so it must be true.

The buildings of Odessa have retained their elegant air – pastel ochres, yellows and blues, a rococo cathedral – and, in keeping with Odessa's reputation as a city of the arts (Babel, Pushkin, Tolstoy and Kandinsky all lived here), a sumptuous Opera and Ballet House. It was designed by the architects of the Vienna equivalent, although it is now sinking into the catacombs which were created by the quarrying of the local shell-limestone, and which hid partisan fighters during German occupation in the Second World War.

Following the disintegration of the USSR, there have been good and bad moments for Odessa. A hefty segment of the Russian mafia relocated here, but restored many crumbling buildings as they moved into property speculation. The beaches are emptier now that Russians prefer to summer in St Tropez. But the caviar, smoked herring and local vodka is still as tasty, the city's vistas always impressive, and the locals have never lost their sense of humour. They even have a public holiday on 1 April: the Humourina Festival, when they crack Ukrainian jokes (lack of space prevents their inclusion) and wear red noses, which, unusually for this neck of the woods, are not the result of too much vodka.

"The scene on the Odessa steps fuses events where the impulses of the common people, assembled to rejoice in the vernal air, were mercilessly crushed by the boots of Reason." Sergei Eisenstein

> ODESSA, UKRAINE > LOCAL NAME: Odesa > LONGITUDE: 30°39' E > LATITUDE: 46°28' N > ALTITUDE: 115 feet/35 metres > POPULATION: 1,027,000
> TWINNED WITH: Baltimore, Liverpool, Marseilles, Valencia, Vancouver > NATIVES: Anna Akhmatova, Isaac Babel, George Garnow, Emil Gilels, David Oistrakh, Irina Ratushinskaya, F.A. Rubo
> RESIDENTS: Oksana Baiul, Chaim Nachman Bialik, Armand-Emmanuel Duplessis (Duc de Richelieu), Vasily Kandinsky, Yuri Olesha, Alexander Pushkin, Leo Tolstoy, Leon Trotsky

KIEV UKRAINE

MOSCOW AND ST PETE'S MAY STEAL the tourist limelight but Kiev is the Jerusalem of Russia. And contrary to popular expectation it has the architecture and heritage to match.

It all started here. When settlers from Scandinavia arrived in the Ukraine, a vast buffer between Europe and Asia whose name means "borderland", the native Slavs called these settlers the "Rus" (from which the word Russian is derived). But in time under their leader, Svyatoslav, they became the region's rulers. In the 11th century, Svyatoslav's son Volodymyr fell in love with a royal from Constantinople, and in order to ask for her hand embraced and imported Christianity. There followed a golden period of cultural activity during which the very roots of the Russian Orthodox Church, its language, art and architecture were founded. The Rus empire subsequently disintegrated, begetting a splinter empire in the north-west that was eventually to become Russia and to dominate the region. But Russia is descended from the Ukraine.

The Ukrainians made the seat of their empire in Kiev, on the site of the one of the original 5th-century Slav leaders, Ki, where today the gilded Asiatic heritage of their vision survives in the form of the inexhaustible Santa Sophia Cathedral complex, a facsimile of the one in Istanbul, and the Caves Monastery in the Pechersh district, home to mummified monks and definitely not for the claustrophobic.

A truly resilient Scythian city, Kiev was raped by the Mongols and then passed from pillar to post, between Turks, Poles and finally Russians, increasingly becoming a pool for refugees and misfits. These people became the Cossacks, from the Turkic word "kazak" meaning a combination of outlaw, adventurer and free spirit, a murky people so innate to the wild landscape of the Ukrainian steppe.

Kiev's distinct heritage survives remarkably intact. WWII threatened to raze it; instead the Nazis decided to shunt the city's Jewish population into the ravine at Babyn Yar in the north of the city, now a housing estate. Under the Soviets the Ukraine was the USSR's ill-managed laboratory, backfiring in 1986 when Reactor 4 at the Chernobyl plant north of the city exploded during testing. The recent so-called Orange Revolution, although apparently rotting, may yet give the city new zest.

The city sits on an amphitheatre of wooded hills above the Dnipro River, full of picturesque islands, bridges and bays. The Podil historic merchants' quarter is a dazzling bohemian district alive with traditional *kobza* and *bandura* lute and guitar music, and with bars and nightclubs as glittering as the city's onion domes. Dynamo Kiev is one of Europe's leading football teams, and the *pysanky* painted eggs are the deserved prize of the city's few visitors. And of course the city is home of the famous *kotleta po-Kyivsky*, better known to the world as Chicken Kiev. But the mother of all Russian cities deserves more than a place in the frozen food section of a supermarket.

"Overlooking
the river, Kieff
reminded me
of Quebec and
if Quebec
has the finer
site, the
picturesqueness
of Kieff
architecture is
more than
sufficient
compensation."

R.H. Bruce-Lockhart,
Memoirs of a British Agent

> KIEV, UKRAINE > LOCAL NAME: Kyiv > LONGITUDE: 30°34' E > LATITUDE: 50°26' N > ALTITUDE: 548 feet/167 metres > POPULATION: 2,595,300 > TWINNED WITH: Bratislava, Edinburgh, Florence, Kyoto, Munich, Toronto, Toulouse, Warsaw, Wuhan (China) > NATIVES: Oleg Antonov, Vadim Brodsky, Mikhail Bulgakov, Vladimir Horowitz, Serge Lifar, Golda Meir, Vaslav Nijinsky, Igor Sikorsky > RESIDENTS: Anna Akhmatova, Taras Shevchenko

359

"Who is to say that all this is not some person's dream, and there is not a single actual person here, not a single real action? That somebody may suddenly wake up who is dreaming all this, and it will all suddenly disappear."

Fyodor Dostoevsky, *Crime and Punishment*

30°18' E

ST PETERSBURG was the dream of Peter the Great, and 300 years after its foundation the city still retains the same unreal phantasmagoric quality, as if it were the figment of the imagination that has haunted so many of its souls.

Many of them lie in its foundations. In 1703 Peter took back these mosquito-infested mudflats on the Gulf of Finland from the vanquished Swedes. At his feet lay an empire but it lacked a suitable capital. Peter was embarrassed by Moscow's Byzantine and outmoded mindset and appearance. He wanted a showcase that could stand alongside the great European capitals, so he ordered a madcap project to raise a brand-new city, as if from the sea.

Built at unreal speed and at great cost of life, St Petersburg suddenly appeared, a composite city incorporating the latest in English, French and Italian architectural vogues: a London Embankment and Admiralty, French neoclassical boulevards exotically called *prospekts* and twiddly Italian baroque façades.

Blue, green, grey, with touches of gold here and there, the city is all about façades. The European face of a country that stretches to the Pacific Ocean, St Petersburg is commonly thought to have no connection with the rest of Russia. Yet it is only superficially European. In this land of the silent north under whose calm and snowy skin courses hot Eastern blood, St Petersburg is a typically mad and grandiloquent gesture.

And so began the story of the Romanov dynasty, a rose-tinted starry epoch of Tsarist style when the court of Catherine the Great received the great thinkers of the time such as Diderot and Voltaire and amassed in her Winter Palace a vast art collection for private enjoyment in her own hermitage, now one of the world's great museums – an era of unparalleled splendour, artistic endeavour and excess, epitomized by the yearly Fabergé egg.

But splendour became a metaphor for how out of touch the Tsars were, and the 1905 warning shot across their bows went unheeded. In 1917 Lenin made his famous secret train journey back

from Finland, the old certainties were swept away and in the new world order the city became Leningrad. During the Second World War the city endured 900 days under siege from Hitler, and when the epicentre of Communism was transferred to Moscow, St Petersburg's beauty was left to blanch.

Since 1990 it has taken St Petersburg a long time to regain its metropolitan prowess, but in many ways it has not changed. Looking at its cold blue river-front across the broad expanse of the Neva, it is still a place of ethereal beauty. A new fur-lined aristocracy, albeit of the gun, eat blinis with caviar in the art nouveau cafés down Nevsky Prospekt. And in the Dostoevskian interior of its brooding backstreets the city still seems powerfully and engagingly malevolent: Peter's heroic dream begat Raskolnikov's heroic crime.

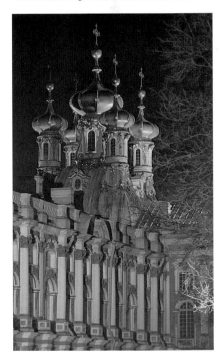

> ST PETERSBURG, RUSSIA > LOCAL NAME: Sankt-Peterburg > LONGITUDE: 30°18' E > LATITUDE: 59°56' N > ALTITUDE: 13 feet/4 metres > POPULATION: 4,774,200 > TWINNED WITH: Bangkok, Barcelona, Gdánsk, Helsinki, Los Angeles, Manchester, Osaka, Takamatsu (Japan), Warsaw > NATIVES: Oksana Akinshina, George Balanchine, Alexander Borodin, Artur Chilingarov, Nicolas de Staël, Peter Carl Fabergé, Oxana Fedorova, Michel Fokine, Al Jolson, Natalia Makarova, Vladimir Nabokov, Anna Pavlova, Vladimir Putin, Alexander Rodchenko, Dmitry Shostakovich, Boris Spassky, Leon Theremin, Anastasia Volochkova > RESIDENTS: Fyodor Dostoevsky, John Field, Nikolai Gogol, Mikhail Lermontov, Dmitri Mendeleyev, Alexander Pushkin, Igor Stravinsky, Ivan Turgenev

ALEXANDRIA EGYPT

THE ALEXANDRIA IMMORTALIZED by Lawrence Durrell, Cavafy and E.M. Forster has dissipated. Some traces linger, a few spoors drifting on the sea breezes which aerate Alexandria and which have long persuaded Cairo's inhabitants to flee their congested, dusty, hot capital for the hotels and villas that lie along its sweeping corniche – as refreshing a prospect as the chilled beers that awaited Sylvia Sims and co. in *Ice Cold In Alex*. From the sea front, the face of the city is turned north to Europe, giving it a flavour as much Mediterranean as Middle Eastern, and one that is very different from the rest of Egypt.

Way back in the 3rd century BC, the city was constructed on the orders of, and dedicated to, a 25-year-old Alexander the Great. Alexandria always aimed high. The Pharos Lighthouse, built by one of Alexander's successors, Ptolemy II, was one of the seven wonders of the ancient world, the tallest building of its time, reputed to be able to capture and cast the sun's rays 30 miles (48km) offshore. Ptolemy also established the world's most extraordinary library: the Bibliotheca Alexandria, hundreds of thousands of linen and vellum-wrapped scrolls representing a repository of the civilized world's knowledge as it stood at the time. By 200 BC Alexandria was the richest and largest city in the world.

From this high point destruction ensued. Julius Caesar unsportingly torched the library; "history", it was said, "lost its memory". During an earthquake the lighthouse tumbled into the sea. Cleopatra (whose Needles in London and New York hail from here) met her serpentine end. And when, under Arab control, Cairo took over as Egypt's capital, the city began to wither. By the time Napoleon arrived in 1798, he found a small fishing village with a mere 5,000 inhabitants.

The revival of Alexandria's fortunes came through the construction of the Mahmudiyya Canal in the 1820s linking the city to the Nile, and half a century later with the Suez Canal; Alex became fashionable once again, hence the influx of immigrants from Europe and the Levant who later populated Durrell's novels, occupying the Turkish quarter of Gumrok, late 19th-century Greek and *belle époque* Italian villas, and congregating in coffee houses like the Petit Trianon and Pastoudis, both still extant.

Now the city's ancient past is resurgent. Beneath the waters of the bay, archaeologists have located what they believe to be the remains of the Pharos near Fort Qaitbey. In the autumn of 2002 the New Library of Alexandria opened, a bold attempt to revive the great Bibliotheca, in an elliptical granite Norwegian design. Though the shelves were far from full at the opening ceremony, the library is a symbol, a new beacon, of Alexandria's determination to turn its past into the future, and to gainsay that school of nostalgists who would hold that the best of Alex is long gone.

> "The ponderous azure dream of Alexandria burning like some old reptile in the bronze Pharaonic light of the great lake."
>
> Lawrence Durrell

> ALEXANDRIA, EGYPT > LOCAL NAME: El Iskandariya > LONGITUDE: 29°56' E > LATITUDE: 31°13' N > ALTITUDE: 6 feet/2 metres > POPULATION: 3,341,000
> TWINNED WITH: Baltimore, Cleveland > NATIVES: Constantine Cavafy, Stewart Copeland, Sayyid Darwish, Rudolf Hess, Filippo Tommaso Marinetti, Gamal Abdel Nasser, Demis Roussos, Omar Sharif, Giuseppe Ungaretti > RESIDENTS: Cleopatra, Lawrence Durrell, Marthe El-Kayem, Euclid, E.M. Forster, Ptolemy

"It seems to me
that while other cities are mortal,
this one will endure
as long as there are men on earth."

Petrus Gyllus

28°58' E

NO OTHER CITY in the world can claim to straddle two continents. With one foot firmly planted on European soil, Istanbul vaults eastwards across the channel of the Bosporus to Asia. In both Istanbul's previous lives, as Byzantium and then Constantinople, the city's name and fame has been the stuff of legend: its history has been torrid, and its intrigues suitably Byzantine.

The European side of the city contains Istanbul's most celebrated gems, not least the vast, awe-inspiring space beneath the unsupported, golden-tiled dome of Aya Sofya. Built by the Emperor Justinian in AD 537 as the finest church in all of Christendom, it was converted into a mosque under the Ottomans, and, in Kemal Ataturk's modernized, secularized Turkey, is now a museum. On the low hills above the freshwater of the Golden Horn, its rocket-like minarets are matched by those of the Süleymaniye and Blue mosques, creating the city's signature skyline. Just along from Aya Sofya, the Topkapi Palace encapsulates the exotic, opulent Ottoman splendour which entranced the imagination of artists like Ingres. Here the sultan kept his harem, and amongst the courtyards, screens and shutters, an erotic frisson still lingers.

Across on the Asian side of the Bosporus lies Üsküdar – once known as Scutari – where a youthful Florence Nightingale tended the wounded of the Crimean War; sadly, a quest to find her lamp, rumoured to be still on display, is fruitless. Northwards, up the busy Bosporus towards the Black Sea, ferry boats pass the rococo Dolmabahce Palace and wonderful late 19th-century timber villas – the yalis owned by Istanbul's wealthy – clinging to the sides of the steep high banks.

Istanbul, and especially its cluster of buildings above the Golden Horn, has been sending out a siren call to tourists for

centuries. Alphonse de Lamartine gushed that "God, Man, Nature and Art have conspired to create the most marvellous view that the human eye can contemplate on earth." A tad over the top perhaps, but he had a point. Later visitors, arriving after their cosseted journey from Paris on the Orient Express, could enjoy the vista from the grand Pera Palas Hotel, built specifically to cater for them by Georges Nagelmackers of Wagons-Lits.

Sean Connery's James Bond arrived to film *From Russia With Love* in 1962, conducting romance beneath the minarets and espionage in the catacombs, but in the following decades the city lost some of its glamorous sparkle. However, 40 years later, Istanbul is back with a vengeance, its special mix of souks (the Kapali Carsi truly the grandest of bazaars), *hammam* steam baths, domes and minarets bubbling away like the hookahs which are once more in vogue after dinner in the restaurants of the buzzing quarter of Beyoglu.

> ISTANBUL, TURKEY > LONGITUDE: 28°58' E > LATITUDE: 41°07' N > ALTITUDE: 90 feet/27 metres > POPULATION: 9,413,000
> TWINNED WITH: Cairo, Florence, Houston, Jeddah, Khartoum, St Petersburg, Skopje (Macedonia), Stockholm, Warsaw
> NATIVES: Kutlug Ataman, Emre Belozoglu, Roza Eskanazi, Terfik Fikret, Elia Kazan, Rifat Ozbek, Orhan Pamuk
> RESIDENTS: Gheorghe Hagi, Nazim Hikmet, Pierre Loti, Florence Nightingale

365

JOHANNESBURG SOUTH AFRICA

SOME SAY THE BEST PLACE to be in Johannesburg is the airport because you're likely to want to leave quite quickly and while you're there it's also the safest. Mythically dangerous and lacking the physical beauty and sophisticated veneer of its Europeanized Cape cousin, Jo'burg is nevertheless the heart of the real South Africa, a brash and physical city rushing with adrenalin.

At the end of 19th century it was the Boers who were rushing to this valley in the Transvaal (Jo'burgers are known as "*vaalies*") on their Great Trek north from the Cape. They came in search of the rich seams of gold that had been discovered in the surrounding plains – the city's name is attributed to Johannes Meyer, the first mining commissioner. Its natural reserve of the precious yellow metal has always been Jo'burg's equity and the backbone of its wealth. It sits in a valley surrounded by square-sided hills, the mounds of mine deposits accumulated over a century of gold-digging.

Jo'burg is the commercial centre of Africa, accounting for around a quarter of the whole continent's gross national product. The wealth comes not only from minerals but a highly-tuned service industry, which has fuelled many Jo-burgers to new heights of wealth, or into space as was the case of Mark Shuttleworth, the first man to pay for a holiday in orbit. With its glistering banks and malls, Sandton district is the richest square-mile in Africa. Two hours drive east is where tycoon Sol Kersner founded his African Vegas, Sun City, complete with the stunning pleasuredome of the Lost City luxury hotel and gambling complex.

You could make a rand or two from security systems as well. Muggings and carjackings have long been the subject of whiteman dinner-party horror-stories ever since the *chiaroscuro* of wealth and poverty replaced the black and white segregation of apartheid. Unlike, say, India where the poverty is mixed in with daily life, Jo'burg is still surrounded by satellite black townships, most famously in the south-west – "Soweto". The once Sohoesque downtown district of Hillbrow is a virtual no-go zone, and even in the northern middle-class white suburbs – in pretty, 19th-century Parktown (the original Boer settlement), Rosebank and Houghton – tension is high. At its roots Jo'burg is a masculine, hard nugget of a city built on the black and white religious Boer-farmer psyche.

But "just now" (as Jo'burgers would say) with the Midas touch of Mandela, the "City of Gold" is moving on, trying to present a softer image as "Joey". There is a rising and expanding black middle class driving around in Beamers. No longer burdened by the mantle of oppressor, the whites can relax and have fun. There is a buzzing multiracial arts scene and Jo'burgers are never more united than when supporting the Bafana Bafana national soccer team, watching Allan Donald charge in at the Wanderers or as when the Springboks lifted the 1995 Rugby World Cup at Ellis Park, together with the new black President wrapped in the flag (colloquially known as "the Y-fronts") that represents all the colours of this rainbow nation.

"An extended brickfield is the first impression; a prosperous powder-factory is the last." John Buchan

366 > JOHANNESBURG, SOUTH AFRICA > LONGITUDE: 27°59' E > LATITUDE: 26°09' S > ALTITUDE: 5,750 feet/1,753 metres > POPULATION: 2,599,000 > TWINNED WITH: New York City
> NATIVES: Peter Abrahams, Pearl Argyle, Andre Coetzee, F.W. De Klerk, Ernie Els, Retief Goosen, Christopher Hope, Sid James, Miriam Makeba, Manfred Mann, Dave Matthews, Rifat Ozbek, Gary Player, Basil Rathbone, Andrew Strauss, Janet Suzman > RESIDENTS: John Buchan, Nadine Gordimer, Nelson Mandela, Mongane Wally Serote

BUCHAREST ROMANIA

LINGUISTICALLY CLOSER to Italian and French – both of which are commonly spoken in its capital – Romania is a Latin island surrounded by Slavs. Its history dates back to the Dacians, who inherited their language from the conquering Romans. Today the only remnant of this Roman people is in the Dacia cars whose ersatz Renault 12 chassis became the country's enforced automobile imprint under dictator, Nicolae Ceauçescu.

While Prague was going through its Velvet Revolution and other capitals were settling peaceful divorces with Moscow, Bucharest was the scene of the bloodiest of all the 1989 regime changes, conducted with Latin passion and impetuosity. From a treacherous and shifting four-way battle between the people, Ceauçescu, the miners from Timisoara who normally supported him and the Securitate (the Romanian KGB), between the summer of 1989 and January 1990 the city descended into a continuous series of riots and reprisals until all were united in one voice against Ceauçescu. He and his wife were summarily executed in what came to be remembered as one of the most amazing pieces of footage of those tumultuous months.

Retrospectively, many think Ceauçescu was hastily removed so that he would be unable to testify against those corrupt Communists who replaced him – and who benefited from his death but benefited little a country that has progressed, other than by virtue of Hagi on the football pitch, slower than almost any other former Eastern bloc nation. Ceauçescu's tomb is invariably decked in fresh flowers.

Ceauçescu left behind him a legacy of pseudo-architectural grandeur and unfinished buildings. Most infamous of these is the behemoth of the so-called House of the People, one of the largest buildings on the planet, but redundant, closed and architecturally unsound despite six years of the work of 700 different architects, none of whom were allowed to see the overall plans. It remains a ludicrous piece of brutalist-Byzantine-cum-baroque-Romanesque fantasy, as absurd as the theatre of Bucharest's famous avant-garde playwright Eugène Ionesco. Equally successful, the project to divert water through a city that has no natural river yielded the sewer-like trickle that is the Dimbovita canal.

Ceauçescu had a Parisian vision for this city, of tree-lined boulevards, pompous fountains and Versailles-esque lakes, but it is arguably the parts of the old city he did not bulldoze that retain the most French flavour, where you can still hear *doina*, the Romanian *fado*. And around the market stalls of Lipscani ring the Asiatic cries of the bazaar.

Founded by a shepherd named Bucur on the Wallachian plains between the Carpathian Mountains and the Danube, Bucharest is a city in limbo between Latin, gypsy and Orthodox mystic, a blend that lends it a bucolic, yet wild and impetuous streak quite unique in this corner of the world.

"Carr: Bucharest.
Tzara: Oh, yes. Yes.
The Paris of the
Balkans.
Carr: Silly place to
put it, really..."

Tom Stoppard, *Travesties*

> BUCHAREST, ROMANIA > LOCAL NAME: Bucuresti > LONGITUDE: 26°06' E > LATITUDE: 44°26' N > ALTITUDE: 240 feet/73 metres > POPULATION: 2,027,500
> TWINNED WITH: Atlanta > NATIVES: Alina Cojocaru, Mircea Eliade, Dinu Lipatti, Ilie Nastase, Edward G. Robinson > RESIDENTS: Angela Gheorghiu, Eugène Ionesco

"There's a river near Vilnius, where my grandfather taught me to fish."

Sean Connery as Captain Marko Ranius, *The Hunt for Red October*

25°16′ E

IN VILNIUS CITY CENTRE, there is a stone bust in memory of the late great Frank Zappa, perhaps not the most obvious recipient of a municipal monument, but nonetheless his sculpture is a clue to the slightly offbeat and elusive charm of the capital of Lithuania, the largest of the Baltic countries. It has been said that the personality of Vilnius is particularly hard to define, being neither Eastern European nor Scandinavian, Russian nor German – and "not even Lithuanian".

Vilnius was part of the Russian Empire for 120 years, before the Germans occupied it during the First World War. There followed a phase when it bounced like a pinball between Lithuanian rule, the Bolsheviks, Poles, and the Soviet Union. Eventually the League of Nations delivered it back to Lithuania, only for the USSR (with the Nazis in between) to regain control.

In common with Riga and Tallinn, the other principal Baltic cities, Vilnius has its distinctive old quarter, complete with cobblestones, spires and red roofs. Where it differs is in its location: the other two cities are on or close to the Baltic Sea. Vilnius is deep inland, in the south-east of Lithuania – and the atmosphere is one of a countryside city, close by hills and forests and far from the salty air of the Baltic. According to calculations by the National Geographic Institute of France, the centre of Europe lies a few miles north of Vilnius (the actual spot is marked by a sculpture park) – this is serious Central Europe.

Although Vilnius has made major efforts to modernize its infrastructure under the leaderships of two dynamic mayors, Arturas Auokas and Rolandas Paksas – the latter upgraded to the post of

president of Lithuania in a somewhat shock election result in 2003 – the city's civic and religious buildings combine an eclectic and occasionally dilapidated collection of styles.

There are a high number of churches (religion is an important element in Lithuanian life), one seemingly on every corner of the city. The finest is the much loved and extremely graceful St Anne's, one of the few remaining Gothic buildings in the country. The city's cathedral is an unexpected 18th-century structure of classical columns and pediments, the centre of Vilnius's spiritual life, but also a favourite place to meet for a date, with its high tower and unmissable clock.

Although general consensus has it that Vilnius is an earthier city than Riga and Tallinn, more Polish, more emotional and less sophisticated, it is proud of its culture, with numerous orchestras and choirs, and a Jewish artistic tradition now being rediscovered (the city's Jewish community was all but eradicated during the Second World War).

But Vilnius has no need to play down its earthiness – it is part of its character. As Jonathan Frenzen wrote of his character Chip Lambert in *The Corrections*, "All in all, he found Vilnius a lovely world of braised beef and cabbage and potato pancakes, of beer and vodka and tobacco."

> VILNIUS, LITHUANIA > LONGITUDE: 25°16' E > LATITUDE: 54°40' N > ALTITUDE: 699 feet/213 metres > POPULATION: 542,300 > TWINNED WITH: Ålborg (Denmark), Chicago, Madison WI, T'aipei
> NATIVES: Bernhard Berenson, Alexander Berkman, Marija Gimbutas, Jascha Heifetz, Witold Kawalec, Onute Narbutaite, Andrew Schally > RESIDENTS: Kerry Shawn Keys, Muza Rubackyté

HELSINKI FINLAND

HELSINKI HAS A SPECIAL kind of light.
Across these northern latitudes it glides in
horizontally, refracting through the glass
casing of Steven Holl's new Kiasma art
museum – which has impacted on the city
like the Guggenheim in Bilbao – or the
curves of one of Alvar Aalto's vases, as
luminous as the 20-hour days of Finland's
all too short summers.

Far-flung, in European terms (and
consquently a haven for dissidents
and émigrés – Lenin once holed up in
the city), Helsinki spent its formative
years wedged between the competing
ambitions of Russia and Sweden, a pawn
in their power struggles; only since
Finland's independence in 1917 has it
been able to develop unhindered. The
Swedes founded the city in 1550, under
the name Helsingfors, as a counter to the
Hanseatic League's Talinn; it existed as
little more than a Swedish outpost until
Tsarist Russia annexed Finland in 1809
and appointed Helsinki its capital (over
Turku). The city's wide boulevards and the
onion domes of the Uspenski Cathedral
convey a sense of the mini-St Petersburg
the Russians constructed.

The city is compact, still the smallest
venue ever for an Olympic Games, which
it hosted in 1952, and good for walking,
biking or roller-blading around. The
surrounding countryside of birch woods,
lakes and islands lies close by. There is
little urban sprawl or skyline, and the main
sights – the greeny-blue domes of the
Lutheran cathedral, the Finlandia concert
hall, and the Kauppatori market full of
mushrooms, berries and herring – all cluster
round the harbour area. The flip side is that
for some of the city's teenagers, growing
up with their eyes on a different horizon,
Helsinki is too small and too provincial:
"Hell-stinky", some of them call it.

> "Every building, every work of architecture, is a symbol which has the aspiration to show that we want to build a paradise on earth for ordinary mortals."

Alvar Aalto

But for such a diminutive place, its influence on global culture has been far-reaching. In the 1950s Helsinki style evolved a strong personality. Alvar Aalto designed both the city's Finlandia concert hall and the Easy Chair 400 which graces the living-rooms of style-aware homes. The bold, bright patterns of Marimekko, produced by founder Armi Ratia and textile designer Maija Isola, were brought to instant world attention when Jackie Kennedy purchased some of their fabrics. And Tove Jansson's hippomorphic *Moomintroll* books have been translated umpteen times.

Not everything, of course, is so light and bright. Come winter, when the nights seem to go on forever, the city's saunas are welcoming, un-PC furs warming, the Internet cafés humming (in the land of Nokia, communication technology is its lifeblood) and a bottle of strong spirits always handy. Jean Sibelius, the creator of Finlandia – the music, not the vodka – spent many a night in the Kämp and König restaurants hitting the bottle during his own dark days. Nowadays, however, Helsinki's preferred alternative to hard liquor is a cup of Kahvi, the coffee which has become a local obsession to an extent even Seattle never reached.

TALLINN ESTONIA

TALLINN HAS BEEN DESCRIBED as the "most beautiful German city in the world", a reference to its collection of pewter-tinted steeples, turrets and towers which hint of Bavaria and the steep-roofed houses that seem to have been transported directly from Alpine slopes. It is said that the old city, Toompea, represents less than one per cent of Tallinn's area, but possesses all of its charm. The overall effect of its dense, medieval skyline is almost picture postcard-perfect, a quaint vision of a fanciful fairy-tale township, although Tallinn's history is drawn from the Grimm Brothers end of the canon.

By a fluke, Toompea survived intact (apart from one bombing raid in the Second World War) throughout a whole series of invasions and occupations, by the Danes, Swedes, the Tsars, Nazis and Soviets. The Danes bequeathed the city's name: in Estonian *taani* means Danish, *linn* means town.

Tallinn has now celebrated, like its Baltic neighbours, the first decade of its independence; Estonia was the first of the states to break away from the USSR, during the failed Moscow coup of August 1991. There are, naturally enough, reminders of the city's former Russian connections: most prominent is the Nevski Cathedral, a slice of pure St Petersburg; Kadriorg Palace and its parks were commissioned by Tsar Peter the Great, who made a dozen visits to Tallinn, such was the importance to him of its ice-free port. Soviet rule has left its own relics, from a massive but melancholy memorial celebrating the "Fighters for Soviet Power", to the suburb of Lasnamäe, which is such a quintessential late-1970s piece of monolithic Soviet planning that one can almost imagine it becoming designer-chic. Period pieces from other eras include the 1930s houses in the suburb of Nõmme, constructed during a brief phase of independence that Estonia managed to squeeze in between the two World Wars, and the summer villas of the seaside area of Pirita.

Tallinn now advertises itself as "medieval and wired", not a reference to illicit black-market substances, but its Internet habit – cybernet cafés have proliferated. The city had always kept its finger on the pulse; during the Soviet years residents pointed their TV aerials towards Finnish television signals to make sure that they were plugged into what was going on, just as fashion followers will now make the trek across to Baltic to Stockholm to replenish their wardrobes. Tallinn is getting into its own stride, looking for opportunities to display its entrepreneurial flair and flex its once atrophied capitalist muscles. Meanwhile, its music scene is locating its own voice: the unlikely combination of Dave Benton and Tanel Padar became local heroes overnight by winning the oft-derided Eurovision Song Contest of 2001, starting a mini-run of Baltic success (Latvia carried off the 2002 title).

"These ancient stones are a part of ourselves,

flesh of our flesh.

Hold your breath and listen,

for these stones speak of our distant childhood." Lennart Meri

"I'm interested in the happy-go-lucky attitude shown by young Latvian women. For young people in Latvia, the Riga lifestyle has seemed very much a Western one." Ralf Vulis, *Crazy Sexy Girls – Latvian Girls In Riga*

> RIGA, LATVIA > LONGITUDE: 24°07' E > LATITUDE: 56°56' N > ALTITUDE: 7 feet/2 metres > POPULATION: 764,300 > TWINNED WITH: Ålborg (Denmark), Cairns (Australia), Dallas, Florence, Santiago (Chile), T'aipei > NATIVES: Mikhail Baryshnikov, Isaiah Berlin, Sergei Eisenstein, Mariss Jansons, Marija Naumova, Wilhelm Ostwald, Raimonds Pauls, Andrejs Pumpurs, Mother Maria Skobtsova, Mikhail Tal > RESIDENTS: Janis Rozentals, Ralf Vulis

24°07' E

OF THE THREE BALTIC CAPITALS – Riga, Tallinn and Vilnius – which emerged in the immediate aftermath of the collapse of the Soviet Union like a sleepyhead stirring after a troubled night, the common consensus is that Riga, the capital of Latvia, has emerged brightest and with the bushiest tail. The city does not possess the picture-perfect cityscape of Tallinn or the eclecticism of Vilnius, but it was always dynamic; and just as it was once believed that whoever had control of Riga would rule the Baltic, so Riga has taken firm control of its own destiny since independence in 1991.

Like both the other cities, Riga has its old core, girded by stone walls for protection, a network of sinuous narrow, cobbled streets, tucked between the city's canal and the Daugava River that heads ten miles north to the Baltic. A few buildings remain from the city's medieval prime, when Riga was the centre of the Hanseatic League. Commercial trading gave it strong links to the rest of Europe – Napoleon, who had a fondness for these kind of comparisons, once called Riga "a suburb of London", although he never managed to capture the city. Others did, and Riga endured a series of external rules, from the Teutons and the Swedes to the Nazis and Communist Russia.

There are plenty of Stalinist remnants in the guise of indistinguishable housing blocks, but Riga retained a level of sophistication throughout that era. The city's outstanding architectural feature is the presence of a substantial number of buildings constructed in the Jugendstil, the Germanic twist on art nouveau. The finest examples of this somewhat baroque decorative style, full of devices from nature – birds, animals, shells – are on Alberta iela, some designed by Mikhail Eisenstein, the father of Sergei, the director of Battleship Potemkin; Sergei unsportingly pooh-poohed his father's work, dismissing him as a "maker of cakes". After

decades of neglect during which these houses gently and genteelly crumbled, a programme of restoration is in hand to preserve their quirky delights.

Despite the 90 years from 1621 when Riga was under Swedish sway (it was Sweden's second capital, and the flag of Latvia still sports the blue and yellow), the more predominant flavour is Russian, as it once was the most Soviet of the three Baltic capitals; approximately half the population are of Russian origin, the language is still spoken widely, and the cuisine is heavy on cabbage and beetroot.

After celebrating 800 years of existence – and ten of independence – in 2001, Latvia went on to win the following year's Eurovision Song Contest, guaranteeing a new international focus on the city; however, it is the centuries-old *dainas*, laconic folksongs, a kind of Latvian *haiku*, that guarantees a link between the rejuvenated, forward-looking city and its subjugated past.

23°43' E

IF THE GREEK GODS looked down from Mount Olympus they would not recognize the city of the ancient people who invented them – always assuming they could see it through the smog. For centuries it seemed that Athena, Goddess of Wisdom herself, had spurned her urban namesake.

Ancient Athens was a tiny place and the modern city was not made capital until 1834. Until then, and arguably still now, Greeks looked towards just one city, "to THE city" or "*stin poli*", now Istanbul, formerly Constantinople. Spared by the Spartans and Alexander the Great, under 400 years of Ottoman rule Athens had shrunk to a village. It was only a bit of 19th-century nation-building under Bavarian import, King Otho I that restored the chance of greatness to Athens. He spotted the brand potential of the city's 5th century BC golden age – the legacy of Pericles, the dramas of Aeschylus and the political and philosophical heritage of Plato, Aristotle and Socrates, commissioning the sophisticated neoclassical city that survives in the Plaka district and the steep Montmartre-like streets of Kolonaki.

Modern Athens' problems began with the influx of Greeks from Anatolia fleeing Ataturk's modern Turkish state, among them the other Aristotle – Onassis. The city swelled, but without planning, becoming a famously haphazard sprawl of sclerotic arteries, asphyxiated by the asthma of traffic pollution. Then, having hosted the inaugural event in 1896, the Olympic flame came home and Athens was awarded the 2004 Games. The city

began its own race against time and became a building site. The only "Prime Movers" were JCB diggers, the Gods of Reconstruction bestowing a ringroad, new airport and Calatrava-designed stadium. The city's underground was "Fosterized" by gleaming state-of-the-art stations and barely an ancient stone was left unturned as façades were lifted and a new Museum of the Acropolis built, the better to care for Athens' ancient treasures, such as the marbles the Greeks lost to Lord Elgin.

Along with its architecture, Athens' social life was reborn. Visitors who used to stay just long enough to see the Parthenon and grab some *dolma* in Plaka on their way to Mykonos are now detained by Hellenic hip-hop and the lively nightlife of up-and-coming neighbourhoods Psiri, Pagrati and Thissio. The city is once again worthy of the Greek national character, generous, exuberant and passion-packed.

It was a marathon not a sprint - or neither as it turned out for Paula Radcliffe and the disgraced Kosta Kenteris and Katerina Thanou. But after two millennia Athens carried the Olympic baton successfully and at least finished the race. The national team having just brought home the football European Championship the city certainly went higher and further, if not exactly faster, to do justice to the five precious rings. Zeus and his entourage, especially the ancient Goddess of Victory (and latterly Goddess of Quality Footwear) can look on with renewed belief in their city and smile at the free publicity from the collective feats of so many Nike trainers.

"Let there be light! said Liberty, And like sunrise from the sea, Athens arose!"

from *Hellas* by Percy Bysshe Shelley

> ATHENS, GREECE > LOCAL NAME: Athina > LONGITUDE: 23°43' E > LATITUDE: 37°59' N > ALTITUDE: 230 feet/70 metres > POPULATION: 3,192,600 > TWINNED WITH: Chicago, Los Angeles
> NATIVES: Alcibiades, Theodoros Angelopoulos, Aristophanes, Demothenes, Arianna Stassinopoulus Huffington, Yannis Kokkos, Melina Mercouri, Stavros Niarchos, Pericles, Solon, Katerina Thanou
Socrates, Sophocles, Xenophon > RESIDENTS: Aristotle, Costa-Gavras, Aristotle Onassis, Plato

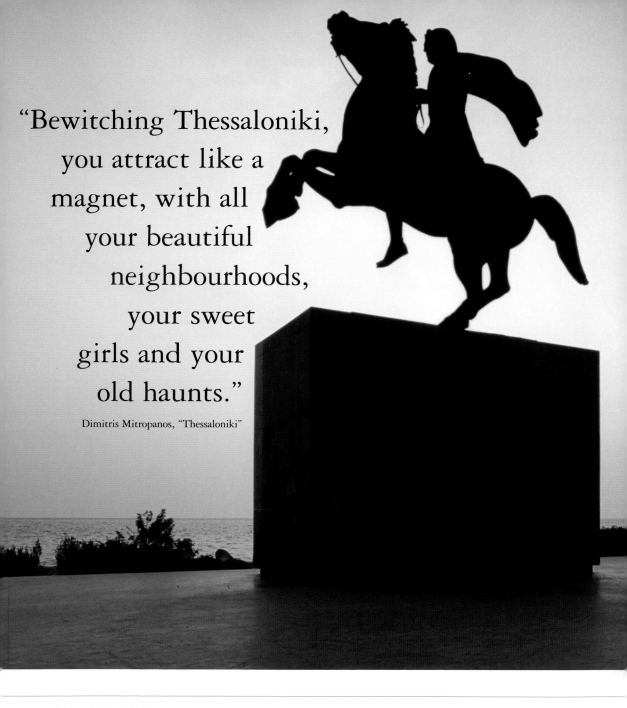

"Bewitching Thessaloniki,
you attract like a
magnet, with all
your beautiful
neighbourhoods,
your sweet
girls and your
old haunts."

Dimitris Mitropanos, "Thessaloniki"

> THESSALONIKI, GREECE > LONGITUDE: 22°57' E > LATITUDE: 40°38' N > ALTITUDE: 7 feet/2 metres > POPULATION: 1,083,000 > TWINNED WITH: Cologne, Leipzig, Melbourne, San Francisco
> NATIVES: Mustafa Kemal Atatürk > RESIDENTS: Eusthathius, Leo the Mathematician

THESSALONIKI GREECE

WHEN THE DECISION was made by the IOC that the Olympics would finally return to Greece in 2004, it meant that world focus would necessarily fall on Athens in the south of the country. Little thought was spared for Thessaloniki, Greece's second city, up in the north-east – for many its coolest, but never as well-known as the capital.

There is a marked difference to Athens. Thessaloniki, or Salonica as it was long known outside Greece, is Eastern in orientation by virtue of its location. Within the Byzantine Empire it ranked only behind Constantinople – now Istanbul – in importance, and the city was under Turkish control for the best part of five centuries, from 1430 to 1912. Thessaloniki had been founded in 315 BC by Cassander, king of Macedonia, and named after his wife, a sister of Alexander the Great; Alexander's father, Philip of Macedonia, was buried here. The Byzantine, Ottoman and Balkan strands are still deeply woven into the soul of the place. Athenians, especially the capital's football fans, disparagingly dub Thessaloniki "Bulgaria".

The city's churches, especially the imposing Agios Dimitrios, are full of Byzantine mosaics and frescoes. Ottoman remnants include the Bey Hamam bathhouse and the Bezestémi textile market; in the upper town, Kemal Atatürk, the father of modern Turkey, was born in a typical Ottoman house of overhanging balconies and gables. Other communities also left their mark, including an influx of Anatolian refugees in the 1920s, although the Jewish quarter was brutally depleted from 55,000 to 2,000 during the Second World War.

Surrounded by an amphitheatre of low hills off a horseshoe bay on the Aegean's Thermaikos Gulf, modern Thessaloniki is a large city with plenty of student life buzzing around the arcaded square, Platia Aristotelous, down on the waterfront; the people of Thessaloniki have a reputation for a level of friendliness more associated with village life.

The city suffered a devastating fire in 1917, and sections were rebuilt under the direction of the Frenchman Ernest Hébrard; there is a breezy 1920s openness and modernity to its avenues and squares, and the streets he constructed parallel to the sea (the waterfront is known locally as Paral'a). There are other winds too: from the north comes the Bardaris, a cold and harsh wind that blows in from Bulgaria, such a characteristic part of life in Thessaloniki that songs have been written about it. The city has a strong musical tradition, including the subversive, spontaneous lyrics of *rembetika*, and anything from industrial to reggae can be heard in Ladadika, the old oil and olive trading quarter, now the centre of the city's night-life.

The people of Thessaloniki know how to appreciate the good things they have, especially their food, from spicy Anatolian dishes to cream pies, called *bougatza*, served with cinnamon. And at the end of the day they will still take the time to pause and watch the sunset.

WARSAW POLAND

WARSAW SAW WAR LIKE NO OTHER European city. A walk through
the Stare Miasto (the old town) reveals a city of cobbled streets,
north-European mustard- and pale pink-coloured buildings adorned
with Gothic and baroque decorations, wood-beamed interiors, arched
vaults, the odd sgraffitied façade, and, at Zankowy Square, the
remains of a medieval castle. It is all a fake.

Pictures depicting Warsaw at the end of the Second World War
show a flat expanse of rubble stretching from the foreground to the
horizon with just the lonely spire of a church in the distance – a prong
of hope in this religious city, disrupting the level skyline. An incredible
85 per cent of Warsaw was literally flattened by Nazi and Soviet
bombardments, and half of the city's then population perished with
it, 350,000 of them Jews deported to the death camps from the
city's famous Jewish ghetto in the Mirow-Muranow district. It is said
that blood will run from a handful of Warsaw soil if you squeeze it.

It is testament to the pride of its citizens – and a surprisingly surge
of aesthetic responsibility on the part of Soviet Warsaw's governors –
that in 1945 the old city centre was entirely and lovingly rebuilt, stone
for stone. Today the city's harrowing history is poignantly set out in the
small but powerful Museum of Warsaw in the old central square. It
seems Warsaw's destruction is now a marketing opportunity – black
and white images of the flattened city are on sale everywhere.

War-saw: there is an inherent sadness to those two syllables,
enforced by a language whose combination of consonants looks at
times like an electrocution warning. To several generations the word
Warsaw symbolized the sadness on the other side of the Iron Curtain,
the city associated with the Communist anti-NATO military pact.
And yet the origins of the city's name are so much merrier. Wars, a
fisherman, and Sawa, his girlfriend, were a Polish Romeo and Juliet.
Legend has it that a mermaid appeared to them and commanded
them to found a city here on the banks of the Vistula River.

Warsaw has been the capital of Poland since 1596 (moved here from
Kraków) and its 18th-century cultural heyday saw the construction of
many churches and palaces such as the summer palace-on-the-water
of the last king of Poland in Lazienki Park. In the 19th century Poland
became part of the Russian Empire, then Soviet in the dust of 1945,
with all the architectural beauty that that implies – although Stalin's
Palace of Culture, similar to the Seven Sisters in Moscow and lone
monu-statement on Warsaw's modern skyline, has a Soviet-chic appeal.

Home of Chopin, Warsaw still carries the mantle of Polish arts and
culture, its blinis and duck dishes part of the only East European
cuisine to emerge internationally. It is no longer the sad city behind
the curtain. It is alive, educated and youthful, a student city fuelled by
a native brew. For do the Poles drink wodka? Is the Pope Catholic?!

> WARSAW, POLAND > LOCAL NAME: Warszawa > LONGITUDE: 21°01' E > LATITUDE: 52°15' N > ALTITUDE: 312 feet/95 metres > POPULATION: 2,269,000 > TWINNED WITH: Berlin, Chicago,
Den Haag (Netherlands), Düsseldorf, Hamamatsu (Japan), Harbin (China), Istanbul, Kiev, Moscow, Rio de Janeiro, St Etienne (France), St Petersburg, Seoul, T'aipei, Tel Aviv, Toronto, Vilnius
> NATIVES: Zbigniew Brzezinski, Marie Curie, Sam Goldwyn, Agnieszwa Holland, Krzysztof Kieslowski, Osip Mandelstam, Pawel Pawlikowski, Joseph Poniatowski, Marie Rambert, Krzysztof Zanussi
> RESIDENTS: Frédéric Chopin, Jan Paderewski, Wladyslaw Szpilman, Andrzej Wajda

"The Warsaw of the late '90s reminded me of my grandad's old travelling bag with a false bottom: **there was much more to it than met the eye."** Vitaly Vitaliev, *Borders Up!*

> BELGRADE, SERBIA > LOCAL NAME: Beograd > LONGITUDE: 20°29′ E > LATITUDE: 44°48′ N > ALTITUDE: 433 feet/132 metres > POPULATION: 1,576,100 > TWINNED WITH: Beijing
> NATIVES: Marina Abramovic, Alex Bogdanovic, Dejan Savic, Vukan Stojanovic > RESIDENTS: Dragan Stojkovic

AS THE SERBS HAVE BEEN continually cast as the villains of the complex ethnic jigsaw that is the Balkan peninsula, so Belgrade has found itself a continual flashpoint and has suffered as a result. Historians calculate that the city has been destroyed and rebuilt a total of 40 times in its 2,300-year history.

Capital of Serbia since 1403, the city sits at the confluence of the Sava and Danube rivers – the strategic citadel fort of Kalemagdan still stands proud, if not intact, overlooking the junction – just to the west of the old Stamboul Road linking Turkey to Central Europe. The Serbs became serfs to Turkish rule in the 16th century; it is from there, as a buffer between the Ottoman and Christian worlds, that all Belgrade's woes stem.

But the citizens of Belgrade are so used to it that they have their bunker routine down to a T and it seems that long experience of war has done little to beat them down. A walk through the battered streets of Stari Grad (what's left of the old town), Terazije (Belgrade's modern heart) and the pedestrian boulevard of Kneza Mihaila reveals a chic and sophisticated café society specializing in that saggy-eyed, wearily omniscient, dissident look of swarthy, bristled intellectuals and regulars conversing through clouds of pungent Soviet tobacco exhaled from filterless cigarettes permanently glued to their lower lips.

Yet this apparent inner calm is combined with an irrepressible, mad effervescence, the exterior manifestation of a mindset that betrays a people

"Everything is crazy and beautiful no matter what."

Emir Kusturica

From the ashes of the Second World War emerged a federation of the south ("Yugo-") Slav states held together by the iron grip of Marshal Tito, and ruled from Belgrade. However, after his death in 1980 (Tito's grave is in Belgrade), there was always the suspicion that as the dominant force in government his Serb successors dreamed of a Greater Serbia; and so the Balkan peninsula splintered across its old faultlines. Belgrade is now picking itself up from its 41st sacking, this time at the hands of United Nations bombs intent on ousting Slobodan Milosevic, the "Butcher of Belgrade" who spent his last years lambasting the judges at The Hague, having led his nation on a collision course with the U.N. over Kosovo.

who would appear to love as easily as they kill. Nowhere is this conveyed more strikingly than in the music of the *blehmuzika* brass bands – a crazy mélange of snake-charming *zurla* (oboe), oom-pah tubas, melancholy accordion and screaming trumpets, all combined into a jazzy Balkan ska groove that accelerates from calm exposition into a frenzied ritualistic trance in the midst of which you feel anything could happen.

It lends a bizarre fairy-tale atmosphere to the former capital of a mythical short-lived country – Yugoslavia, 1929-1999, R.I.P. Meanwhile, the latest Belgrade, whose name means "white city", may have found the white flag of a more lasting truce.

KRAKÓW IS POLAND'S ROYAL CITY, the kingdom of Poland's capital for 500 years between the 11th and 16th centuries. Unlike Poland's other, less fortunate major cities such as Warsaw and Gdansk, Kraków was miraculously saved from destruction in the Second World War – surrounded by the Soviet Army in 1945 the Nazis evacuated the place – and thus all its undisputed beauties have the advantage of being original. As such, many Poles would call Kraków the mother of their nation's historical soul.

The jewel at the heart of Kraków is its royal cathedral, with its golden-domed Renaissance chapel, and castle, Wawel, where a dynasty of Polish kings held their coronations and sat enthroned. Under their reign they made Kraków one of the great arts centres of Europe, inviting craftsmen to gild their Catholic churches in luxuriant gold leaf. Even at the turn

of the last century Kraków was home to skilled craftsmen who decorated the city's church windows with fine art nouveau stained-glass designs and depictions. The city's Czartoryski Museum houses an unsuspected collection of fine art, including works by Rembrandt and Leonardo that rarely travel as part of international exhibitions.

At the heart of the city is the main market square, Rynek Glowny, with its arched central covered market whose darkened, shadowy central aisles are at once atmospheric and ablaze with gold leaf and the sparkling opulence of an Asiatic bazaar. A picturesque and natural setting for cafés, bars and people-watching, this and the lively Florianska Street are the magnetic centre of Kraków. Across the square stands St Mary's Church, whose Transylvanian pointed spire forms a lone and eerie silhouette against the night sky.

To the south of the city, outside Planty – the green ring around the old city that follows the line of its medieval moat – lies the district of Kazimierz, so founded and named after King Casimir the Great in 14th century, and until the 1820s an independent town. This is the heart of the former Jewish Ghetto, housing all the Jews that were expelled from the city in the 15th century. At number 4 on Lipowa Street in Podgorze district, where the Jews were relocated under Nazi occupation, is the site of Oskar Schindler's factory, rendered famous by the film *Schindler's List*. Schindler was plotting to save the Jews from deportation to the nearby former camp of Plaszow while further west, a mere 37 miles (60km) from the heart of a rejuvenated, newly carefree, cultural and affluent pretty city, lies a town called Oswiecim – better known to the world by its German name, Auschwitz.

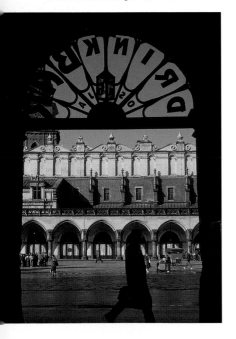

"The city, like the nation, is a sort of outpost. That balance of the mind we call philosophy is here balanced on the edge of an abyss." G.K. Chesterton

> KRAKÓW, POLAND > LONGITUDE: 19°56' E > LATITUDE: 50°03' N > ALTITUDE: 810 feet/247 metres > POPULATION: 870,000 > TWINNED WITH: Rochester NY
> NATIVES: Stefan Banach, Eva Hoffman, Jan Matejko, Helena Modjeska, Stanislaw Wyspianski > RESIDENTS: Copernicus, John Paul II, Roman Polanski, Zbigniew Preisner

19°56′ E

"Budapest is the loveliest city on the Danube.
It has a crafty way of being its own stage-set, like Vienna,
but also has a robust substance and a vitality
unknown to its Austrian rival." Claudio Magris, *Danube*

STRADDLING THE BANKS OF THE middle Danube, Budapest is a violent tale of two distinct cities. Linked by a necklace of spectacular bridges, on the west bank lies Buda dominated by the verdant, craggy Vorhagy Castle hill. On the flatter eastern bank stands the city of Pest, fronted by the Westminster look-alike parliament buildings. Buda reflects Budapest's Hungarian heritage, while Pest recalls the imperial times when the city was the Eastern-looking seat of the twin-capital Austro-Hungarian Empire. This alliance brought its downfall in 1914 but ultimately saved Budapest from the Communist yoke in the summer of 1989 as Austria opened the borders to her old friends and so drew back the Iron Curtain.

Buda had been established in the 5th century and named after Attila the Hun's brother. The Magyars under Arpad arrived in 896, a date considered the founding of the Hungarian nation, bringing with them a strange island of a language, related to Finnish and considered a linguistic "*steppe*" so monotone is its delivery. Pest (a Slavic word), meanwhile, had been settled by Germans, who called their home "Ofen" ("Oven", on account of the city's prevalence of lime kilns). A period of development was halted by the Mongols' characteristic bull-in-a-china-shop arrival. Then in 1526 the Magyar kingdom was defeated by the Turks, and Budapest became the most western outpost of the Ottoman Empire, a legacy of which are the popular baths at the foot of the Gellert Hill spa.

After the 1848 Revolution, the Kaiser of the dual monarchy (nicknamed "K & K") sought to reimpose Austrian authority with new imperial architecture. The citadel on Buda was fortified with Habsburg canons, and Pest granted the Grand Boulevard, a Heroes' Square and regal tree-lined thoroughfares in the Parisian mould. The two cities were first linked in 1873 by the sturdy elegance of the Chain Bridge.

The churches, bastions, squares and fortifications of Buda seem old but were in fact rebuilt following the devastating Nazi siege of 1944. This was the start of Budapest's darkest decades, when, in Hungarian parlance, the city found itself "under a frog's arse down a coalmine". Matyas Rakosi was installed by the Communist Party, continuing the Nazi persecutions and becoming Hungary's "Little Stalin". Then, in 1956, Soviet tanks rolled in to quell the revolution that had been sparked by the liberal policies of Rakosi's successor, Imre Nagy.

Budapest always retained a form of more open, "goulash socialism" that endeared it to the West, and was the liveliest, brashest city in the Eastern bloc – Habsburg encouragement of prostitution translating in the modern world into a seedy reputation that drew the label "the Bangkok of Europe". With such colourful exuberance, a Liszt of great musicians and the imperial heritage of its architecture and famed Hussar horsemen, Budapest exudes an air of *fin de siècle* sophistication. Unlike precious Prague or downtrodden Bratislava, Budapest is the full-blooded capital of Central Europe.

> BUDAPEST, HUNGARY > LONGITUDE: 19°04' E > LATITUDE: 47°30' N > ALTITUDE: 377 feet/115 metres > POPULATION: 1,821,071 > TWINNED WITH: Fort Worth TX, Hangzhou (China), Kosice (Slovakia), New York, Osaka, Taejon (South Korea) > NATIVES: Robert Capa, Michael Curtiz, André Deutsch, Krisztina Egerszegi, Eva and Zsa Zsa Gabor, Andy Grove, Theodor Herzl, Harry Houdini, André Kertész, Arthur Koestler, Ernö László, Stefan Lorant, Ferenc Molnar, Eugene Ormándy, Judit Polgár, Ferenc Puskas, Tommy Ramone, Miklós Rósza, Erno Rubik, Andras Schiff, Márta Sevestyén, Georg Solti, George Soros, Ilona Staller (la Cicciolina), Edward Teller > RESIDENTS: Béla Bartók, Tibor Fischer, Franz Liszt, Raoul Wallenberg

389

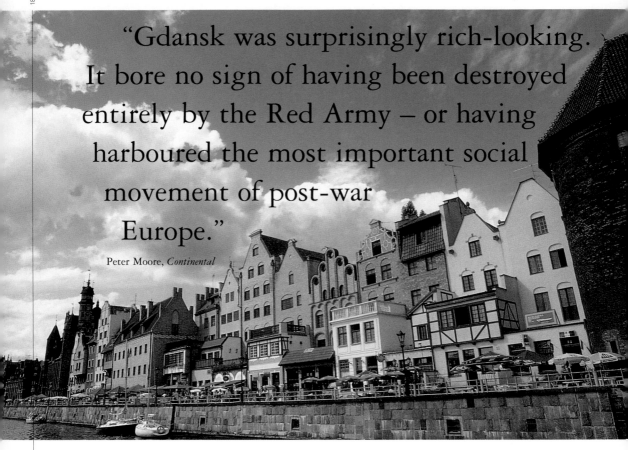

"Gdansk was surprisingly rich-looking. It bore no sign of having been destroyed entirely by the Red Army – or having harboured the most important social movement of post-war Europe."

Peter Moore, *Continental*

NAPOLEON IS SUPPOSED TO have said that Gdansk was "the key to everything". Just over a century later Hitler was clearly of the same opinion – as it was here at Westerplatte, the city's harbour entrance onto the Baltic Sea, that he decided to invade Poland and spark off the Second World War. The battleship *Schleswig-Holstein* started shelling the city at 4.45am on 1 September 1939.

Like Warsaw, the old city of Gdansk was lovingly restored brick-by-brick after the war, so that it resembles very accurately its former glory. A visit to the city is to go back in time to the 14th century, when Gdansk was at the beginning of its heyday. At that time, under the control of the Teutonic Knights, the city was called Danzig and its

architecture had then, as today, a flavour that is more Flanders than Kraków – yellowy, pinky, tall, narrow, multi-floored townhouses with tapering roofs in staircase crenellations. The lively ul Mariacka is banked by picturesque 17th-century burgher houses, while the Town Hall is a fine example of Teutonic Gothic architecture. In 1361 the city became rich, as part of the elite Hanseatic League of cities that joined in an alliance of trade, predominantly in textiles. The Poles arrived in 1454 and the monarchy changed the name to Gdansk but allowed the city to maintain its independence as a city-state.

Neither German nor Polish, this architectural and ethnic ambiguity is Gdansk's charm, making it uniquely cultured and cosmopolitan,

> GDANSK, POLAND > LONGITUDE: 18°39′ E > LATITUDE: 54°21′ N > ALTITUDE: 30 feet/9 metres > POPULATION: 462,500 > TWINNED WITH: Cleveland, St Petersburg, Sefton (UK)
> NATIVES: Jan Dantiscus, Johannes Hevelius, Günter Grass, Gabriel Fahrenheit, Arthur Schopenhauer > RESIDENTS: Lech Walesa

as befits a city that harboured Arthur Schopenhauer and Gabriel Fahrenheit among its famous sons. But Gdansk has also borne the tensions of standing on a historic faultline. For centuries the sandy and lake-filled Baltic coast province of Pomerania was a battleground between Poland's neighbours. This is the now-vanished kingdom of Prussia, which briefly prevailed over the city in the 18th century: it is little surprise that when temperatures rose Gdansk ended up in the front line.

Modern Gdansk is in fact a three-city conurbation. Beyond the gates of the old city, through which Polish royalty used to pass on their way to the seaside, are the sub-cities of Sopot, where Napoleon had baths and whose beaches are a regular Danziger weekend attraction, and Gdynia, a modern Soviet-style industrial suburb. Gdansk is a major shipbuilding centre, and its shipyards on the northern outskirts were the birthplace of Lech Walesa's Solidarnosc movement in August 1980, perhaps the first reformist engine in the former Eastern bloc, which begat Glasnost and the fall of the Berlin Wall. In these workers' suburbs stands a monument of confession unique in Communist times – the Solidarity monument to the fallen shipyard workers was erected to commemorate victims of the regime even while the regime itself was still in place.

"People who live here know what kind of weather to expect by glancing at Table Mountain. It is the world's largest barometer."

H.V Morton, *A Traveller in South Africa*

> CAPE TOWN, SOUTH AFRICA > LONGITUDE: 18°28′ E > LATITUDE: 33°57′ S > ALTITUDE: 39 feet/12 metres > POPULATION: 3,092,000 > NATIVES: Paul Adams, Billy Butlin, J.M. Coetzee, Marlene Dumas, Brenda Fassie, Abdullah Ibrahim, Alex La Guma, Antony Sher, Pieter-Dirk Uys, Solly Zuckerman > RESIDENTS: Christian Barnard, Breyten Breytenbach, Nuruddin Farah, Nelson Mandela, Cecil Rhodes

ANY CITY BUILT AT THE END of Africa had a chance of being spectacular. Cape Town does not disappoint. The fractious meeting of the cool Atlantic with the warm Indian Ocean is still further south at Agulhas. But set on the prong of the Cape Peninsula with the decapitated flat red loaf of Table Mountain at centre stage, for sheer physical beauty Cape Town must rank alongside Rio and Sydney.

"Kaapstad" is S.A.'s oldest settlement, founded in 1652 by the Dutchman, Jan van Riebeck. It is also the country's most cosmopolitan city. In fact, were it not for the indigenous Hottentot-settler half-caste Cape Coloureds, some would argue it has nothing to do with the rest of South Africa; more a chunk of Europe bolted to the bottom of the continent, such is its popularity among European expats and gastronomes. For its climate, Baywatch-style bars and beach-life it feels like California dancing to an African beat.

But Cape Town is not a postcard city, all khaki-clad neo-colonialism, whale-watching, and sun-downers on Camp's Bay. While the tourists sip Cape beer down on the revitalized Victoria and Alfred waterfront, industrious Cape Towners contribute to the boom, bringing substance to their city's obvious charms. The international film circus has been attracted by the spectacular locations, bringing in its wake an entourage of advertising talent, fashion models and the trendy clubs and restaurants they need to hang out in – "no biltong and rooibos, darling,

I'll have the impala and a glass of Stellenbosch red". An artistic centre since Herbert Baker planted his Hellenistic architecture here, modern painters and sculptors now find inspiration in the unique Cape light. With its Cape Dutch facades - pastel-shaded à la Cubana - the rickety hillside district of Bo Kaap, until the 1960s a black ghetto, is now the city's affirmed boho neighbourhood, pink strip and prime real-estate.

Cape Town is strangely disorientating. Table Mountain's flat face points north. Behind lies the Peninsula reached on the temperate Indian side via the Victorian marine base of Jamestown with its land-based colony of penguins; and returned from on the windswept Atlantic side by the stunning Chapman's Peak Drive beneath the mountain's Twelve Apostles so often shrouded in the "Table Cloth".

From his residence at Grootte Schuur Cecil Rhodes cooked up the Cape-to-Cairo dream of painting the whole of Africa pink. 100 years later this was supplanted by the dream of freedom. While down on Bloubergstrand Cape Town's surf-dudes harness the wind in power kites, from their city a wind of change has swept the country. From the Nelson hotel, guests now look out over a multi-ethnic Newlands cricket ground, the multi-coloured Kirstenbosch botanical gardens across to Robben Island, Cape Town's Alcatraz, former leper colony and after 27 years no longer the custodian of Nelson Mandela. This is Raleigh's "fairest cape of all" and the Cape of Good Hope indeed.

SARAJEVO BOSNIA-HERZEGOVINA

18°25' E

THE SUBURBS OF SARAJEVO are still recuperating from the siege by Serbian forces which the city endured between 1992 and 1995. Battered, shrapnel-perforated tower blocks stand as relics of the pounding they received from the big guns dug into the surrounding hillsides; rusting trams disintegrate in disused sidings.

However, the old centre, Bascarsija, relatively untouched by the siege, remains distinctively Muslim with a multitude of mosques, cafés and rows of wooden-fronted workshops giving the city its aromatic Ottoman feel. Sarajevo was originally a Turkish creation, founded in the 1460s by Isa-Bey Isakovic and endowed by Gazi Husruv-bey; the mosque that bears the latter's name is one of the city's finest. But the heart of the city is not just a well-preserved souk. Designer bars and boutiques have sprouted up alongside the more traditional ateliers and bathhouses to create a glamorous, funky and confident centre.

The Bosnians are noted for being an attractive race, and in the early evening young Sarajevans, the girls mini-skirted, bare-midriffed and all blinged-up, strut their own version of the Roman *passeggiata* up and down the pedestrian streets. Late at night the main drag, Fedarhija, becomes a spectacular outdoor catwalk. It is as though the inhabitants of Sarajevo have communally agreed on complete denial as the best way to deal with the trauma of their recent past. They look blank if asked for directions to the tunnel museum, the permanent reminder of the three-mile-long, two-yard-wide (5km x 1.8m) shaft excavated by the besieged citizens to gain access to precious, life-giving supplies from the outside via an arduous, dangerous journey.

Journeys in Sarajevo have often carried a heavy price, as the Austrian Archduke Franz Ferdinand found to his cost one sunny day in June 1914. Dispatched to Sarajevo to smooth things over in a dispute between local Bosnian Muslims and seething Serbian nationalists, the Archduke and his consort were assassinated by Gavrilo Princip, releasing the uncoiling of events that led to the First World War.

Eighty years later, in another round of Balkan turf wars, Serbian nationalists were once again lying in wait. Sarajevo lies in a natural amphitheatre, a sitting duck for Serbian artillery and the sharpshooters ready to pick off anyone foolhardy enough to venture outside along what became known as "Sniper Alley" during the 1400 days of siege. The most familiar images of Sarajevo became those of scurrying pedestrians, bullet-spattered streets and gutted buildings. only a decade before Sarajevo had been optimistically presenting itself as an ethnically harmonious city hosting the 1984 Winter Olympics.

The people of the city are naturally wary and tough. They have lived under threat for so long, and tensions are never far away – the buffer line with Republika Srpska (the region annexed by the Bosnian Serbs) is just outside the city. Yet each month that passes the springs unwind a little more. Legend has it that if you drink from the fountain in the main Bascarsija square, a little of the city will stay with you forever. The spirit of Sarajevo is famously indestructible.

"Forget the past.
Live the future.
Viva Sarajevo!"

Bono, Kosevo Olympic Stadium, Sarajevo, 1997

> SARAJEVO, BOSNIA-HERZEGOVINA > LONGITUDE: 18°25' E > LATITUDE: 43°51' N > ALTITUDE: 1,804 feet/550 metres > POPULATION: 434,000
> TWINNED WITH: Dayton OH > NATIVES: Aleksandar Hemon, Emir Kusturica, Vedran Smailovic, Jadranka Stojakovic

395

"In Dubrovnik life still has something of the value it must have had in Venice when she was young."

Rebecca West, *Black Lamb and Grey Falcon*

WITH ITS TALL, THICK RAMPARTS, towers, turrets and buttresses Dubrovnik looks exactly like a child's idea of a fortress – a fairy-tale Camelot-style castle. If you were to take your bucket and spade to the beach, this is exactly what you would build. The original old town occupies just a small area of headland beneath the steep slopes of the Dinaric mountain range, which at its peak divides Croatia from Bosnia in a spectacular spine of arid grey massif. Built on a mound climbing steeply up the hillside, it is a perfect example of the earliest principles of human fortification.

Through the drawbridge of the Western Gate is Stradun, the main street that bisects the town. Here, warm honey-coloured limestone greets the eye in a delightful blend of delicately carved Romanesque columns, medieval arches, starker Moorish façades and Arabian windows. Old Dubrovnik is an entirely pedestrian zone and inhabitants and visitors alike swan carefreely and decadently up and down its streets whose slabs of paving stone have been worn by 500 years of footsteps into a smooth soft sheen, like that of marble. In contrast, the balconies, fountains and bell-towers remind one of a miniature Florence and the Piazza San Marco in Venice. With the unmistakable Slavonic red-tiled roofs, Dubrovnik betrays the influence of its many occupants and besiegers down the centuries. The more casual observer will simply delight in its secretive alleys

and passageways, its steep and twisting steps where cats steal, liquid, between the shadows.

You can forget your bucket and spade though, since Dubrovnik offers little in the way of beaches for sandcastles or sunbathing. The Dalmatian coast is formed from hard limestone rock called "karst", which time has worn into knobbly spikes like stalagmites, impossible to walk on without appropriate footwear. Stoic local bathers repair to the satellite of Lokrum, one of the thousand islands on a coastline with more islands than a salad-dressing, where nudity on specially-crafted smooth platforms is encouraged.

From 1991-92, Dubrovnik's historic centre suffered considerable damage during a two-year siege at the hands of the Yugoslav Army, and a plaque and detailed map is at pains to point the finger of blame. Now a UNESCO World Heritage site, Dubrovnik is an agent of postwar propaganda in a country where ethnic tensions still run high. It is hard to think it possible to engender a similar partiality should the same fate one day befall the city of Milton Keynes (or for that matter modern Dubrovnik, which has sprawled unimaginatively and unattractively north up the Lapad peninsula).

Unfailingly welcoming, Dubrovnik is a city resonant with history. With its tales of people, fairy-tale architecture, mountains, lakes and islands, it is the perfect place for a gallant prince to bring his princess.

STOCKHOLM SWEDEN

IT IS FITTING THAT Ingmar Bergman should have been so unemotional about Stockholm. His comment suits the mood of the city, a mix of pragmatic maritime nous and relaxed attitudes. In the past decade, its stock among British- and American-style gurus has rocketed sky-high, but you get the impression that they have got considerably more animated about Stockholm than its inhabitants.

This is a small-town city, intimate and manageable, but with the necessary accoutrements of a major capital – an opera-house, a Grand Hotel and a massive royal palace (the present family is descended from one of Napoleon's marshals, Jean-Baptiste Bernadotte, who managed to get himself adopted by the childless Charles XIII and ascended the Swedish throne in 1818).

Stockholm still offers a welcome to contemporary visitors (though not all have such dynastic ambitions) as warm as the ochre and russet colours of the houses of Gamla Stan, which contains the city's old town, and is one of the 14 islands that make up the city. Further out into the Baltic another 24,000 islands of varying sizes make up the scattered Skärgard archipelago. Consequently, water is a primary element of the city – the long-standing equation being that Stockholm is one third water, one third light and one third space – and never very far away from any part of the city.

Steamers that have been serving the same routes for decades putter up and down along the waterways, past tree-clad islands which provide a glimpse of a boathouse, a villa or a flagpole: the blue and yellow of the Swedish national flag seems to be everywhere. In the heart of the city, three-masters set sail past Viking longboats (restaurants for the tourists) and slide elegantly behind the sloping grounds of the annual jazz festival. On Djurgården a museum protects the recovered and beautifully restored remains of the Vasa, the gigantic and impressive, but top-heavy, royal warship, which was launched in 1628, flags and streamers flying, and almost immediately sank to the bottom of the bay.

These celebrations of Stockholm's past are offset by its trendier-than-thou present, which has blown away the old – and unfair – image of Sweden as a deeply dull world of Björn Borgs and Volvos. Visitors can now frequent the groovy underground stations or boutique hotels like Benny Andersson's Hotel Rival in the once blue-collar, now bohemian Södermalm district; locals sport the fashion designs of Filippa K and Gul & Blå. There has also been an explosion in high-class cuisine – decent portions but exquisite tastes, although a platter of meatballs with lingonberry sauce on the side still hits the spot.

In the summer of 1973, during a six-day siege at the Kreditbanken, the bond formed between hostages and captors (the hostages later refused to testify against them) led to the coining of the term "Stockholm Syndrome". A few days in the Swedish capital can have a similarly captivating appeal.

"It is not a city at all. It is simply a rather large village, set in the middle of some forests and some lakes.

You wonder what it thinks it is doing there, looking so important."

Ingmar Bergman

> STOCKHOLM, SWEDEN > LONGITUDE: 18°04' E > LATITUDE: 59°20' N > ALTITUDE: 144 feet/44 metres > POPULATION: 743,700 (metro: 1,803,300) > TWINNED WITH: Chicago, Istanbul > NATIVES: Benny Andersson, Gunnar Asplund, Carl Michael Bellman, Ingrid Bergman, Franz Berwald, Neneh Cherry, Britt Ekland, Thomas Enqvist, Greta Garbo, Artur Hazelius, Jenny Lind, Anna Lindh, Dolph Lundgren, Hennig Mankell, Alfred Nobel, Claes Oldenburg, Olof Palme, Staffan Scheja, Hjalmar Söderberg, Annika Sörenstam, Art Spiegelman, August Strindberg, Emanuel Swedenborg, Marie Taglioni, Raoul Wallenberg > RESIDENTS: Astrid Lindgren

399

17°06′ E

"Perhaps it had something to do with the three names of the city: the juxtaposition of tongues made me feel I had crossed more than a political frontier.

A different cast had streamed on stage and the whole plot had changed."

Patrick Leigh-Fermor, *A Time of Gifts*

QUESTION: "WHAT DO THE Czechs and Hungarians have in common?" Answer: "The Slovaks." For a thousand years up to 1918 modern Slovakia was known as Upper Hungary – still a four-letter word to Slovaks. When the Hungarians were ousted the Czechs became the new landlords (save for a six-year hiatus during World War II). This shared and fought-over piece of land was only recognized as an independent country in 1993.

While the Ottomans controlled Buda, Bratislava, as Poszony, was from the 16th to the 19th century capital of Hungary. Its cathedral was the site of coronation of the Magyar kings, the Hrad, its huge, gaunt castle, the seat of Hungarian royalty. Following the defeat of the Turks, imperial splendour bled out of the city and floated back downstream to Budapest, leaving Bratislava adrift, throneless and roleless until made capital of Slovakia in 1969.

Pozsony in Hungarian, Pressburg in German, and now Bratislava (by popular myth a post-independence concoction of *slava*, meaning

> BRATISLAVA, SLOVAKIA > LONGITUDE: 17°06′ E > LATITUDE: 48°09′ N > ALTITUDE: 440 feet/134 metres > POPULATION: 616,900 > TWINNED WITH: Cleveland, Kiev, Vienna
> NATIVES: Ernö Dohnányi, Johann Nepomuk Hummel, Rudolf von Laban, Lucia Popp > RESIDENTS: Béla Bartók, Daniela Hantuchova

"glory" and *brat* evoking "brotherhood") was the trilingual city of the 20th century, the very epicentre of the concept of Mitteleuropa. Bratislava bears traces of all three peoples in its many strata – the power of the German culture, the adventurous chivalry of the Hungarians and the subdued, patient humility of the Slovaks. "*Ostlich von Wien fängt der Orient an*" ("East of Vienna the Orient begins") was the famous phrase of that post-Napoleonic Austrian statesman, Metternich. In modern terms the Asiatic undertones of Slavic tongues and echoes of an eastern musical idiom begin approximately an hour's drive east of the Austrian capital. The Viennese have long regarded Bratislava as a suburban citybreak. They come in search of the white wines that have been cultivated since the Romans founded Posonium and cultivated grapes on the slopes of the Carpathians, which begin just beyond the Iron Gate of Romania.

Post the Velvet Divorce, while Prague steals all the limelight Bratislavans are mellow and sarcastic about their city's comparative lack of history. And they are happy in the knowledge that, although full of neo-baroque theatres and art nouveau palaces, Bratislava is not known as a city for tourism, but rather for living - so much so that it has marketed itself to the low-cost stag weekend crew as Partyslava. Especially in the Stare Mesto old town around the Hlavane Namestie old main square, in the "four streets" of the *korzo* night-time Bratislava has become a whacky, straight-up party-town, fuelled by shots of powerful borovicka juniper brandy. By day the city still retains an air of intellectualism and localism in its cultured cafes. Bratislava is a greyer, more industrial city, outwardly less beautiful, but a city whose charms are more subtle and genuine for having to be discovered and matured at a slower pace. This is where Hans Christian Andersen fell in love; and the fairy-tale beauty of the local girls is said by one publisher to make the city very hard for people who are engaged.

FOLLOWING THE BALKAN upheavals of the 1990s, the tourists who once used to stream into Split are returning. The physical charms of the city and its nearby Adriatic beaches (among the most beautiful in Europe) are undiminished. A warm offshore current delivers mild, dry summers. Located round a harbour on the leeside of a peninsula, Split has made sure that the less palatable elements – at least for visitors – of the industrial area and military base are tucked out of sight on its far side. Along the waterfront, palm trees shade the walk. Offshore lie the lush islands of Brac, Hvar and Vis. To the west, at the end of the peninsula, the hills of Marjan Park offer a wooded retreat.

The Roman Emperor Diocletian, born in nearby Solin, made the sensible decision, following his abdication in AD 305, to spend the remainder of his days here, indulging in a relaxing mix of meditative musing and a little light gardening. The palace he had constructed is still very much the dominant, and imposing, feature of the city, built out of the same white stone from Brac that was used for the White House in Washington DC. Diocletian also imported a sphinx or two from Egypt, one of which guards the entrance to the site of his mausoleum, now the cathedral of St Domnius, the doors of which are decorated with impressive 13th-century carvings depicting the life of Christ. The palace was always something of a fortified town in its own right, and nowadays, behind its gates, there is still a living community, complete with shops, a café and a nightclub.

In an inversion of this penetration of contemporary life into what could have become the mothballed museum of the palace, elements of Roman masonry have been recycled throughout Split, cropping up in the medieval buildings along streets that, like those of Venice (unsurprisingly, given the Venetians' three centuries in control of the city), will suddenly open up unexpectedly into a small square. Rather larger public spaces were required to contain the celebrations when local boy Goran Ivanisevic played his wild card to perfection at Wimbledon 2001 and was welcomed home by 150,000 overexcited inhabitants.

As the main port for the Dalmatian coast, there is plenty of hustle along the harbour as the passenger ferries head off to the islands, while other boats deliver cargoes of fish, and bring back bushels of the rosemary, heather and lavender which grows freely on sunny Hvar. Along with those scents, less innocent merchandise has been arriving – illicit alcohol and drugs – and there are concerns about the underworld's influence in Split. But a more positive change has been the opening up of the unspoilt island of Vis, unspoilt because for years it was a military reserve, which is now ready to receive a new and more peaceful generation of visitors.

"During my match there wasn't a single car out on the streets of Split. Everyone was watching. Now I am a hero once again." Goran Ivanisevic

> SPLIT, CROATIA > LONGITUDE: 16°27' E . LATITUDE: 43°31' N > ALTITUDE: 203 feet/62 metres > POPULATION: 188,700 > TWINNED WITH: Los Angeles, Ostrava (Czech Republic)
> NATIVES: Mario Ancic, Goran Ivanisevic, Bruno Sundov, Franz von Suppé > RESIDENTS: Diocletian, Ivan Mestrovic

403

VIENNA AUSTRIA

OF THE MANY things Vienna is famous for – opera and waltzes, schnitzels, coffee, a song by Ultravox – perhaps the most unusual is its sewers. Even the most casual film fan will know the sewer-chase scene in *The Third Man*, Carol Reed's film about corruption and opportunism in interwar divided Vienna. They probably do sewer tours...

For seven centuries before its capitulation sparked the First World War Vienna had been capital of the Austro-Hungarian Empire and seat of the Habsburg dynasty who left their indelible imprint of pompous imperial architecture on the city. Central Vienna is contained within the Franz Josef Ring, a circular, grand boulevard of, in Graham Greene's words "heavy buildings and prancing statuary", commissioned by the eponymous emperor. Within this are chunks of heavyweight baroque and rococo such as the Rathaus (the town hall), St Stephen's Cathedral and the famous Opera House, witness of many Mozart premières, solid and rigid, but with details as twiddly as a Viennetta ice-cream. Amid these are fine examples of the Jugendstil and modern post-Habsburg Secessionist architecture of Otto Wagner and Alfred Loos. Meanwhile, the sewers are not the only spectacle underground. Many of Vienna's subway stations are as ornate as anything in Moscow, especially the Kaiser's own personal stop, Kaiser Pavilion in the Hietzing district.

Vienna's cultural heritage is not just musical (Mozart, Beethoven, Schubert and Brahms are just a few of the great composers buried here). After all, every dynasty has to have an art collection. West of the central ring among a clutch of Biedermeier buildings is one of the largest museum complexes in the world, while the refurbished Albertina Museum within the Hofburg royal palace is once again open. To the north-east across the Danube canal – which is far from

blue – lies the famous Prater district (from the Italian *prato* meaning "lawn") the former royal hunting ground and site of the Ferris wheel from where Harry Lime delivered his famous speech about the Swiss and cuckoo clocks. Nowadays it is basically a Vienna Eye, from which you can look down on the famous Lipizzaner stallions of the Habsburg's Spanish riding-school.

Out on a limb at the eastern edge of its eastern kingdom ("Oesterreich"), Vienna has receded into the European Hintergrund. However, it is still the city of writers, artists and musicians, of ideas and illusions that it was when Hitler the young painter studied and planned his Anschluss here and Freud conjured up his theories on dreams. They and others gathered in the ornate, arm-chaired *Kaffeehäuser* around Kaertnerstrasse that still survive unchanged in this Starbucks world, sipping creamy coffees (it was the Turks who had introduced the bean in the 17th century) and gluttonous *Sachertorte* sponge cakes.

The coffee might be sensuous, but, like its architecture, halfway between rigid and playful, and its waltzes, halfway between formal and gay abandon, the Viennese ego seems charged with suppressed sexual energy.

> "I never knew the old Vienna before the war with its Strauss music, its glamour and easy charm – Constantinople suited me better."
>
> Graham Greene, *The Third Man*

404 > VIENNA, AUSTRIA > LOCAL NAME: Wien > LONGITUDE: 16°23' E > LATITUDE: 48°12' N > ALTITUDE: 561 feet/171 metres > POPULATION: 2,072,000 > NATIVES: Marie Antoinette, Alban Berg, Karl Czerny, Carl Djerassi, Gustav Klimt, Hedy Lamarr, Niki Lauda, Brian Laudrup, Lotte Lenya, Frederick Loewe, Otto Preminger, Lucie Rie, Egon Schiele, Romy Schneider, Arnold Schoenberg, Franz Schubert, Max Steiner, Johann Strauss elder and younger, Josef von Sternberg, Erich von Stroheim, Anton von Webern, George Weidenfeld, Billy Wilder, Ludwig Wittgenstein, Joe Zawinul > RESIDENTS: Ludwig van Beethoven, Johannes Brahms, Anton Bruckner, Sigmund Freud, Joseph Haydn, Adolf Hitler, Gustav Mahler, Wolfgang Amadeus Mozart

ZAGREB CROATIA

OF ALL THE URBAN JEWELS to emerge from the break-up of the Eastern bloc, perhaps Zagreb is the least touted. Prague, Kraków or St Petersburg attract far more admirers, while visitors to Croatia tend to ignore its capital in favour of the picturesque cities of the Dalmatian coast.

They miss an atmospheric city of Gothic steepled churches, baroque stately mansions and manicured parks; of funiculars and twisting tramways that are equally playful as, say, Lisbon; of secretive arches and passageways that are every bit as Kafkaesque as the Czech capital; and of pleasantly symmetrical sequences of steps that with their lanterns are reminiscent of Montmartre. Parisian cylindrical posterboxes advertising a flourishing intellectual and artistic life dot the main thoroughfares and on the Italian-style piazzas the cafés are appropriately full of aloof poseurs – for Croats have an Italian sense of *figura*. Between 1918 and 1943 Croatia was Italian, and even in that short time, like cappuccinos on the Ethiopians, it must have rubbed off on them.

From atop the steep forested Medvenica uplands Zagreb commands a panoramic view over the landscape of a history as checkered as the angry red chessboard of its bold flag.

"I was surprised how European Zagreb looked.

Here was a stately park, stately buildings and ageing bronze statues of generals riding horses that wouldn't have looked out of place in London, Vienna or Paris."

Peter Moore, *The Wrong Way Home*

Zagreb stands on the cusp of its Venetian and Austro-Hungarian roots. In the Second World War Croatia was briefly a puppet of the Nazi regime (with the German name, Agram), its Ustasa police guilty of some of the war's worst extermination programmes (until overthrown by Tito, himself a Croat). West to the Adriatic stretches the plain which bore some of the worst fighting of the Yugoslavian split. But since peace returned to the region Croatia has stood tall on the international stage, with the only basketball side able to give Team USA a game, and a national football squad to be reckoned with.

Zagreb rolls royally from the Sava River. In the lower town, theatres, museums and galleries inhabit the neoclassical Franco-Balkan villas of the 19th-century commercial centre. Separated by the affluent main Ilica Street with its elegant cafés and stylish boutiques, is the medieval city, its topography still reflective of the old divisions between merchants and the church. Zagreb grew up as twin towns, based around two main squares: the town of Kaptol around St Stephen's Square, historically the dominion of the local Catholic church, and Gradec, based around St Mark's Church for traders. In the modern Zagreb the two are united into an energetic market square cut into the steep incline of the city's hill beneath the twin steeples of the Gothic cathedral. By day this teems with colourful stalls, while by night the staircase of throbbing surrounding bars becomes a little tricky to navigate after a few too many Ozujsko beers or shots of Croatia's lethal plum brandy, *slivovica*.

BRAZZAVILLE CONGO

DURING THE SECOND WORLD WAR, while his country lay beneath the combined heels of the Nazis and the collaborative Vichy administration, Charles de Gaulle turned to France's overseas colonies to create a new power base. What was then known as French Equatorial Africa became a prompt recruit, and de Gaulle chose the city of Brazzaville as the symbolic capital, with Radio Brazzaville as its unfettered voice. Following Congo's independence in 1960, Brazzaville became the country's capital; it was in the city, 16 years earlier, that a grateful de Gaulle had announced the principle of self-determination for all France's former African colonies.

For those not fully intimate with the physical geography and borders of Central Africa – probably the majority of us – a subsequent 1997 change of name by neighbouring Zaire to a new life as the Democratic Republic of the Congo was bound to create confusion. That one country is now called Congo-Brazzaville and the other Congo-Kinshasa may not have entirely helped clarify matters. Brazzaville's Congo is the smaller of the two, although its relatively short coastline, between Gabon and Angola, is nonetheless longer than its alter ego's maritime toe-hold.

Brazzaville lies opposite Kinshasa on the other side of a broad pool on the River Congo. The two cities have always been rivals, ever since Brazzaville was founded in 1880 by the explorer and colonizer Pierre Savorgnan

de Brazza (he also gave his name to the de Brazza monkey) as a Gallic counterpoint to the Belgian Léopoldville, as Kinshasa was then known. A consistently high level of humidity creates a semi-permanent murk over Brazzaville, through which Kinshasa can occasionally be made out on the other side of the wide river. Output from both cities' radio and TV stations, and the arrival of refugees from the latter-day heart of darkness that has been former Zaire, further deepens the intermingling. Of the two, Brazzaville is generally deemed to be more mellow, friendlier and – at least, when there is no civil war – safer. Above all it is lushly green; the fingers of the surrounding jungle seeming to penetrate the city itself.

Like much of West Africa, Brazzaville's recent past has seen periods of turbulent political upheaval. A damaging civil war in the late 1990s gutted many of its houses and left the soccer stadium a magnificent ruin, but a tentative and tenuous cease-fire led to a "peace train" reopening the railway line out to Pointe-Noire on the coast, and the city's splendid Basilique St Anne happily survived intact. In the pockets of peace, Brazzaville's lively quarter of Poto Poto can return to being vibrant, the Plateau commercial area is able to concentrate on business as usual, and the nightclubs of Moungali resound to home-grown Congolese rumba-like *soukous* music.

> BRAZZAVILLE, CONGO > LONGITUDE: 15°11' E > LATITUDE: 4°17' S > ALTITUDE: 984 feet/300 metres > POPULATION: 1,133,800
> RESIDENTS: Jean-Baptiste Tati-Loutard

"Palms shot up like geysers of emerald green into drifting layers of cottony mist; winding tar roads were flanked by shoulders of cream-coloured sand; old-fashioned colonial houses sat placidly behind whitewashed walls."

Jeffrey Tayler, *Facing The Congo*

THE COUNTRY WHOSE CAPITAL sounds as if you are trying to speak underwater is a calm and unassuming party in the ethnic *bortsch* that is the Balkan peninsula. Clean, ordered and industrious Slovenia has more in common with Germany than with the other republics of the former Yugoslavia; a green country over half-clad in forests, bathed by lakes with island castles, it would seem to be the address of the Grimm brothers' imagination.

Complete with hilltop castle, the city of Ljubljana itself also seems plucked from a storybook; a Lilliputian toytown of stately but undersized mansions and squares, capital of some small, fancy or forgotten realm.

The realm in question was the old Roman province of Illyria, and a town has existed here on the banks of the Ljubljanica River since the Roman settlement of Emona. These Latin roots were briefly revived under Napoleon but now only subsist in the *rizota* (risotto) that

comes from having Italians for neighbours. Napoleon bequeathed his educational, legal and public administration values, but otherwise Ljubljana was always firmly a Habsburg city – known until the First World War as Laibach – brought up in the Viennese way, from a healthy café culture to a strait-laced attitude to life, at least among the German-speaking aristocracy. It was the Habsburgs who commissioned the pretty, rather Alpine pale-coloured mansions, villas and churches that are the city's signature, sometimes earning it the soubriquet "White Ljubljana". One of the city's favourite sons, the architect Joze Plecnik, is otherwise responsible for most of Ljubljana's stately public buildings and spaces, including the gracious river embankment and the addition of two delicate bridges either side of the Habsburg original that form the postcard and favourite tryst site of the Triple Bridge.

> LJUBLJANA, SLOVENIA > LONGITUDE: 14°30' E > LATITUDE: 46°03' N > ALTITUDE: 978 feet/298 metres > POPULATION: 321,200 > TWINNED WITH: Chemnitz (Germany), Cleveland, Tirana (Albania)
> NATIVES: Matija Jama, Joze Plecnik > RESIDENTS: France Preseren

14°30' E

> ## "Ljubljana is a city where people are at home when you telephone in the middle of the day. At home, available, and willing to talk."
>
> Zoe Brân, *After Yugoslavia*

Having also been settled by Slavs from Poland, Ljubljana had looked east as well, and in 1929 Slovenia became part of the Union of Yugoslav Republics, in fact its most productive and most affluent member. But when in 1991 the autonomy of Yugoslavia's constituent states became increasingly threatened by Belgrade, Slovenia's inevitable sense of difference resurfaced and the republic was the first to break away, suffering only a brief salvo with war before silently and bloodlessly creeping out of the union.

Since then happy little Ljubljana has been minding its own business, a sort of Geneva without the guilt. Inhabited by a demure yet glamorous polyglot population, the city enjoys a cultural life disproportionate to its tiny population, full of theatres and a calendar charged with arts festivals. The young still unchain themselves to the legacy of the punk music that put them on the map in the late 1970s in the form of Pankrti and Kuzle, or chill out over a locally brewed Union beer on Cupova Street and among the atmospheric cobblestone streets of Mestni and Stari under the castle hill, where the girls are mythically tall and beautiful, as befits a city whose name means "beloved".

IT IS PRECISELY BECAUSE Prague's beauty was spared by the Second World War and then accidentally preserved during five subsequent decades of unmindful Communism that one feels the tension caused by its abrupt and total Westernization.

"Kafkaesque" and "bohemian" are two words already bled of meaning by indiscriminate use, never more so than here in their birthplace: the Czech capital lies in the province of Bohemia, named after its original settling tribe, the Celtic Boii. While by day the famous Karluv Most (Charles Bridge) creaks under the weight of visitors, pseudo-court jesters, ersatz Jewish violinists and strains of "Eine Kleine Touristmusik" (Mozart penned *Don Giovanni* here) it is hard to think of anything less Bohemian, unconventional and artistic, or to imagine the city shrouded in any macabre paranoiac anxiety.

But Prague will always have dominion over the twilight and nocturnal hours. Across the River Vltava the long façade of the Hradcany Castle on the hill, with its many windows for eyes, cannot help but hover unsettlingly, an inescapable presence like an all-knowing, all-seeing conscience; while in the Mala Strana beneath it a game of shadows is played out between the recesses of secretive arches and narrow sequence of steps and hidden passages bathed in the billowing coppery light of street lanterns. Prague is a spiritual place that inspires belief in invisible forces, in magic. It is the city of the *golem*, the clay automaton that runs amok, the creation of the Jewish ghetto at Josefov, Europe's richest and most rooted, inspired by the spirit of the alchemist. Among its thousand golden spires and in its night-time imprint of anxiety, estrangement and totalitarian extremity, the imprint of K's fiction on Prague's reality, however clichéd, is undeniable.

It was the Holy Roman Emperor, Charles IV (he of the bridge) who presided over Prague's first golden age, when the Gothic look of Stare Mesto (old town) was formed, most famously in the magnetic heart of Staromestske Namesti main square with its story-book clock tower, complete with astronomical clock, and the striking twin steeples of Tyn Church. The second, baroque, golden age came under Habsburg rule, when in 1784 the disparate quarters of the city were first brought together into one city. This included the art nouveau and deco treasures of the Nove Mesto such as the façades along Vaclavske Namesti, Wenceslas Square – scene of the peaceful demonstrations that begat Prague's Velvet Divorce from Moscow but also the 1968 invasion of Soviet tanks to quash the liberalization of Dubcek's Prague Spring. But the freedoms rioting in the restaurants and department stores of this Central European Champs-Elysées do little justice to the sadness that went before and the suffering that fought for them.

Land of Staropramen and the original Pilsner, Prague has led the newfound Western rhapsody for Eastern Europe, but now finds itself ravished for the first time, by an irrepressible post-modern invader – flooded with tourists, and more recently, water.

"This little mother has claws."

Franz Kafka

> PRAGUE, CZECH REPUBLIC > LOCAL NAME: Praha > LONGITUDE: 14°26′ E > LATITUDE: 50°04′ N > ALTITUDE: 951 feet/290 metres > POPULATION: 1,213,800 > TWINNED WITH: Chicago, Kyoto, Phoenix AZ
> NATIVES: Madeleine Albright, Patrick Berger, Peter Brandl, Max Brod, Vera Caslavska, Jaroslav Drobny, Jaroslav Hasek, Vaclav Havel, Franz Kafka, Ivan Klima, Jan Kodes, Herbert Lom, Hana Mandlikova, Martina Navratilova, Rainer Maria Rilke, Miroslav Vitous, Bertha von Suttner, Jaroslav Vejvoda > RESIDENTS: Antonin Dvorák, Milos Forman, Johann Kepler, Milan Kundera, Alphonse Mucha, Bedrich Smetana, Josef Sudek

NAPLES ITALY

WHEN THE ITALIAN GOVERNMENT introduced the compulsory seat-belt law in the 1980s, in Naples they printed white T-shirts with a thick black diagonal stripe to make it look to the police as if you were strapped in while driving and so avoid being fined. If you're being given a parking fine by a Naples traffic warden, chances are he's an impostor. Or you may be convinced to buy a stereo at a knock-down price in one of Naples's Arabian-style street *kasbahs* but the box you take home will be full of wood.

Neapolitans are the natural persuaders of Italy yet their con tricks are performed with such artistry and theatricality as to be forgivable, and with the sureness that has made them successful immigrants across the globe. All the creativity of a nation that once discovered and illuminated the world is resident here in the Neapolitan genes. Imagine what it could achieve were it channelled differently!

Most people come to Naples for its setting, one of the world's great locations in the perilous lee of the slumbering volcano, Vesuvius, atop a glistening azure bay sprinkled with the pristine and exclusive islands of Capri, Ischia and Procida. But most give a wide berth to the city's hawkers and a reputation for crime and seediness that goes back to Spanish and Bourbon rule, when the city was the sex capital of the continent (if people saw Naples and died, it was usually due to syphilis). Visitors hasten instead to the Sorrentine peninsula, romantic images and natural beauty denying an opportunity to enter the unique southern Italian mindset.

Naples is the capital of the dark and lawless *mezzogiorno*, the open-handed, lazy and ignorant South so derided by the hard-working North. It is a lawless city with its own rules, where millions of northern euros are syphoned into fictitious pension accounts; of extreme riches and desperate poverty and illiteracy; an extraordinary mix of extreme Catholicism and almost pre-forgiven sin where bright neon madonnas stare out from the alcoves of churches while ageing mothers, dressed in black, sell contraband cigarettes on street corners sitting on market crates; and with a strange twisted dialect incomprehensible to most Italians. And yet it is the birthplace of so much of what Italians and foreigners hold dear about the country – the original fast food, pizza (traditionally thin and oily), and humble street café cuisine that is better than any northern restaurant; of extra thick coffee, limoncello and the *canzone napolitana* Italian lyric tradition hijacked in classic Neapolitan style by those "Italians", Frank Sinatra and Andrea Bocelli.

The Romans, the Spanish, the Bourbons and a myriad of postwar governments have all sought to bring this unruly city to heel. But in a refreshing fable of civil obstinacy, diffident Naples continues to resist all impositions. Until Vesuvius turns it into a latter-day Pompeii, like the medieval families of the local Camorra mafia, this city will carry on and look after its own.

> NAPLES, CAMPANIA, ITALY > LOCAL NAME: Napoli > LONGITUDE: 14°15′ E > LATITUDE: 40°51′ N > ALTITUDE: 33 feet/10 metres > POPULATION: 993,000 > TWINNED WITH: Kagoshima (Japan)
> NATIVES: Gian Lorenzo Bernini, Enrico Caruso, Antonio Clemente (Totò), Victor Emmanuuel, Carlo Gesualdo, Luca Giordano, Valeria Golino, Ruggiero Leoncavallo, Francesco Rossi, Domenico Scarlatti, Massimo Troisi, Ben Vautier, Giambattista Vico > RESIDENTS: Vittorio di Sica, Diego Maradona

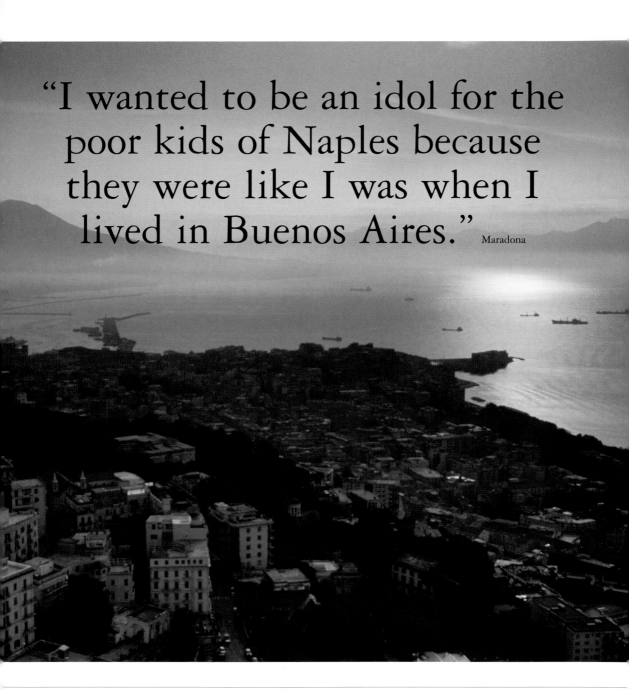

"I wanted to be an idol for the poor kids of Naples because they were like I was when I lived in Buenos Aires." Maradona

FEW COUNTRIES CAN HAVE AN outpost so alien to the national whole as Trieste is to the rest of Italy. Rarely can a place have been so defined by the geographical hand that history has dealt it.

Straddling the faultline between the Latin and Slavic worlds, Trieste occupies the end of a steep and thin sliver of land jutting into the Slovenia headland of Istria, a protusion that on the black and white of a map makes a mockery of apparently arbitrary national borders. Yet it is precisely the designs on its sovereignty which have plagued Trieste's history that make it so startling and intriguing.

Although the Romans had a settlement here named Tergeste, the city's history is murky and illusory until the influx of Austrian capital in the 19th century when the Habsburgs chose Trieste as the southern port of their empire. It was here that they imported the coffee that would become the luxury of the intelligentsia in the Viennese Kaffeehäuser. Trieste is still today the leading coffee port of the Mediterranean, and a place where coffee consumption is taken very seriously indeed. Modern Trieste was built on Habsburg money, which accounts for the tight, ordered layout of its centre, for the yellow colourations of the neoclassical and baroque lines around the central Borgo Teresiano (so named after the Habsburg Empress, Maria Teresa), more reminiscent of northern cities, and for its unmistakable Central European air.

> "In the **immobility and silence**, city, sea and hills became one entity, formed and coloured by some bizarre artist, divided, sliced by lines marked by the yellow dots of streetlamps." Italo Svevo, *Senilità*

Political temperatures had always run high even under the Austrians when the local Friuli people formed the *irredentismo* movement to try to gain independence from the Austrians. But with the end of the Austro-Hungarian supremacy, after a First World War that had seen some of its fiercest trench warfare on the limestone plateau above the city, Trieste was effectively up for grabs. The city passed briefly into Yugoslavian hands but was reclaimed by the Italians - under a nationalist movement spearheaded by the eccentric romantic poet Gabriele d'Annunzio. Trieste has been a hotbed of Italian nationalism ever since. In the Second World War the old rice-hulling plant of Risiera San Sabba was the site of one of Italy's two concentration camps, and these days its fiercely localist Friulano population (many roadsigns are bilingual, in Italian and Friulano) are sympathizers of the northern separatist Lega Nord movement. Incredibly, the border dispute with neighbouring Yugoslavia only fizzled out in 1975, leaving old fears to resurface briefly following Slovenian independence in 1991.

The Adriatic setting is idyllic but the city beautifully remote and indifferent. With a shrunken trade role its quays have been left to run down, its buildings scruffy and crumbling. Like its architecture, a synthesis of Venetian and Habsburg and Slav, Trieste is a schizophrenic place, slightly spooky, cultish, on the margins of Italy – and of reality.

> TRIESTE, FRIULI, ITALY > LONGITUDE: 13°46' E > LATITUDE: 45°39' N > ALTITUDE: 7 feet/2 metres > POPULATION: 215,600 > NATIVES: Leo Castelli, Paul Henreid, Rachel Luzzato Morpurgo, Salvatore Pincherle, Umberto Saba, Santorius Sanctorius, Italo Svevo > RESIDENTS: James Joyce, Pier Paolo Pasolini, Pasquale Revoltella   417

"Dresden gave me great pleasure, and my desire to think about art was revived. There are unbelievable treasures of all kinds in this beautiful place."

Johann Wolfgang von Goethe

THE BAROQUE GLORIES OF DRESDEN were once almost lost to the world. During February 1945, the RAF and USAF launched five raids against the city as part of Operation Thunderclap to support the advancing Red Army. This was far from the Allies' finest hour, as they poured (partly in revenge for the bombing of Coventry) a firestorm of incendiary bombs onto "the Florence on the Elbe", the pride of Saxony.

Photographs of the city's gaunt ruins – burnt, blackened, buckled and bent – cast considerable doubt on the military purpose of the tactics, especially as Dresden possessed little in the way of heavy industry. Allied leaders carefully disavowed any responsibility, leaving Air Marshal Sir Arthur "Bomber" Harris to face the flak alone.

Since those torrid days, the city fathers of Dresden – both under Communist rule as part of East Germany, and since reunification – have undertaken a monumental programme of new

> DRESDEN, SACHSEN, GERMANY > LONGITUDE: 13°45′ E > LATITUDE: 51°03′ N > ALTITUDE: 400 feet/122 metres > POPULATION: 463,600 > TWINNED WITH: Chicago, Columbus OH, Coventry, Florence, Ostrava (Czech Republic) > NATIVES: Hans von Bülow, Erich Kästner, Paula Modersohn-Becker, A R Penck, Gerhard Richter > RESIDENTS: Heinrich von Kleist, AR Penck, Robert and Clara Schumann, Johann Schiller, Heinrich Schütz, Ludwig Tieck, Richard Wagner, Carl Maria von Weber

architecture (notably a see-through VW factory) but more importantly, of renovation - its highlight the symbolic resurrection of the Frauenkirche after decades of ruin, the church's cross crafted by the son of one of the RAF's Lancaster pilots. There were rich jewels to restore. During the reign of Augustus the Strong, elector of Saxony, and also king of Poland, Dresden had blossomed during the early 18th century. The culmination of Augustus's vision – and it is generally conceded that Dresden is his city, his legacy – was the Zwinger, one of the highlights of the recent reconstruction work (and undisputedly the oldest Zwinger in town). Originally conceived as a pleasant orangery set within a fortress complex, it evolved under architect Matthaus Pöppelman into a palace replete with German baroque stylings – "boisterous, but never crude", said Pevsner. Its Alte Meister gallery contains gems from the Italian Renaissance (Giorgione, Raphael) and the Dutch and Flemish masters (Vermeer and Van Eyck respectively).

Dresden, however, has had plenty of homegrown artistic talent. For here, amongst the cupolas and spires of its baroque palaces and churches, German Romanticism was nurtured, at salons where Schiller and the Schlegel Brothers sought sympathetic company, and through the music of Weber and Schumann. At the Opera House, built by Gottfried Semper, architect of London's V&A Museum, Richard Wagner arrived in 1841 and within four years had premiered *Rienzi*, *The Flying Dutchman* and *Tannhäuser*. When that first Opera House burnt down, Semper created a second masterpiece, which hosted the debuts of a raft of Richard Strauss operas.

From the Brühlsche terrace, known as "the Balcony of Europe", above the city, the extent of Dresden's renaissance is evident, proof of an inbuilt durability, despite the best efforts of bombs or the record floods of 2002, that Jerome K. Jerome appreciated. Dresden did not have "the gaiety of Paris or Vienna, which quickly palls", he remarked. "Its charms are more solidly German and more lasting."

13°23' E

"The nervous, endlessly quivering Berlin air works upon people like alcohol, morphine, cocaine, exciting, inspiring, relaxing deadly: the air of a world city ."

Conrad Alberti, *The Old and the Young*

ON 9TH NOVEMBER 1989 the first breach was made of the Berlin Wall. Ten years later, if you stuck together all the pieces of souvenir wall that had been hawked by "*Ostalgie*" opportunists you'd probably end up with a wall twice as high. After all, there has been enough substitute rubble to exploit since Marlene Dietrich's "*ewig junge Stadt*" ("eternally youthful city") was turned into the biggest building site in Western Europe – a playground for the world's leading architects, part of a massive post-reunification rejuvenation programme.

Four nations used to share it. JFK famously said he was "*ein Berliner*". Now everyone wants a piece of it.

Berlin was always a hotbed of experimentalism. If for some its name is a haunting epitome of the Cold War Checkpoint Charlie stand-off, for others Berlin has the soft-focus silver tint of its most famous rose, Marlene Dietrich – the icon the modern city still wants to believe in, of the city's golden age, when it was the alternative pole of the Parisian avant-garde. Continuing the licentious liberalism of Friedrichstrasse in the inter-war cabaret years, since July 1989, and as if anticipating the Soviet collapse and reunification, Berlin has been the home of the yearly techno shagfest that is Love Parade – one million people making the future in the appropriately-named Tiergarten (literally "animal garden" and formerly the royal hunting grounds) either side of the Unter den Linden central boulevard leading up to the sought-after dancefloor of the Brandenburger Tor. In the words of Bob Fosse's camp MC, "liife iz bioodivul, ze girls are bioodivul, even ze orkestra is bioodivul". This is Berlin at its pierced, peaked black leather cap, Polizei-chic best.

The avant-garde years were also the period of Bauhaus, Walter Gropius's functional aesthetic marrying art with design.

This architectural heritage, coupled with an urgent post-GDR need to reinvent itself, has been the impetus that has caused the rush for real estate and the *einstuerzende Neubau* (the speedy erection of new buildings) that characterizes the Bundesrepublik's born-again capital: from Foster's impressive Reichstag dome and the KaDeWe (Kaufhaus des Westens) monument to triumphant Western materialism, to the thoughtful zig-zag zinc of the Jewish Museum by favoured memorial architect of the moment, Daniel Libeskind.

There are some, however, especially those who are not particularly into cranes, glass and aluminium, who don't see what the fuss is about. Even as the Western-weighted imbalance fades and the centre of life shifts from the Ku'damm to the old Jewish ghetto of Mitte (literally "middle") and the acknowledged buzz of Friedrichshain, Berlin remains an unusual metropolis, quiet, spread-out and utterly rural in parts. But, beneath the deceptively soft and lambent light that reflects off Berlin's surrounding lakes, has always thrived a culture of ephemeral underground clubs, and a chaotic, carnal yet northern energy quite unlike any other place in Germany if not the whole of Europe.

> BERLIN, GERMANY > LONGITUDE: 13°23' E > LATITUDE: 52°31' N > ALTITUDE: 161 feet/49 metres > POPULATION: 3,395,738 (metro: 4,500,000) > TWINNED WITH: Beijing, Jakarta, Los Angeles, Tashkent
> NATIVES: Ursula Andress, Frank Auerbach, Hans Jurgen Eysenck, Dietrich Fischer-Dieskau, Marlene Dietrich, Frederick the Great, Lucien Freud, Bill Graham, Walter Gropius, George Grosz, Nina Hagen, Gerard Hoffnung, Nastassja Kinski, Max Liebermann, Ernst Lubitsch, Herbert Marcuse, Me'shell Ndegéocello, Helmut Newton, Mike Nichols, André Previn, Leni Riefenstahl, Andrew Sachs, Elke Sommer, Kaiser Wilhelm II
> RESIDENTS: Willy Brandt, Bertolt Brecht, Albert Einstein, Rainer Werner Fassbinder, the brothers Grimm, Rudolf Hess, Christopher Isherwood, Vladimir Nabokov, Kurt Weill

"The Southern people
are a drama themselves;
they are experts because they live
life on a stage."

Domenico Dolce, co-founder of Dolce & Gabbana

PALERMO HAS HAD MANY HEYDAYS. Sicily's location plumb in the middle of the Mediterranean, the football to Italy's boot, made it a highly desirable prize for a succession of invaders and colonizers, some of whom, though not all, brought much glory to Palermo. Frederick II, the 13th-century polyglot, polymath king of Sicily and Holy Roman Emperor (who rejoiced in the nickname "the Wonder of the World") constructed cultural and architectural masterpieces. Previously, under the Normans, Palermo was the wealthiest city in Europe, with only London, also then in Norman hands, in contention for the title.

The Moors, even earlier, had built pleasure palaces and planted luscious orchards of citrus trees and mulberries which thrived in the local lava-rich soil, and the city's splendour was said to rival that of Baghdad. But as in the Iraqi capital, time – and the intervention of American and British bombs – took its toll on Palermo. The legacy of its past is magnificent, but for decades was decrepit; gradually restoration has begun, but there is much, possibly too much, to do.

Palermo's great buildings are scattered around the city like undiscovered art treasures in a junkyard. In the Cappella Palatino, the royal chapel within the Palazzo dei Normani (Arab-built, despite its name), the geometric mosaics of red, green and gold are some of the finest examples of their kind anywhere in the world. The exterior of the 12th-century cathedral is disfigured by an unsympathetic dome added 600 years later, but inside there are sumptuous works of art. Trees grow in the nave of Lo Spasimo, the ruined church and monastery now converted into a cultural centre. The Teatro Massimo, the largest opera-house in Europe, is undergoing renovation. Crumbling 18th-century *palazzi* hopefully await their turn.

The architectural rebuilding has been parallelled by a gradual cleaning up of *mafioso* activity, the dark side of Palermo. The shadow of the Cosa Nostra (and the *omerta* tradition of obedient reticence) still hangs over the city, but the official crackdown that followed the murders of anti-mafia magistrates in the 1990s has significantly weakened its influence. What were once no-go areas are now can-go areas; even the dilapidated areas of La Vuccina and La Kalsa, the old Arab quarter, are dusting themselves down and picking themselves up.

Life in Palermo is certainly *vivace*. The decibel level is high, and the pollutants ubiquitous, the water is frequently rationed and there are regular street protests (although as one observer notes, these are "invariably over by lunch"). Insular by nature, the citizens of Palermo can be guardedly silent, a throwback to the Mafia years, but behind the sombre façade they have an innate

Latin warmth and an enticing sense of beauty. One of the city's lesser known relics is their local Sicilian dialect – clipped and baroque, it draws on the influence of all their colonizers, both the enlightened and the corrupt – which Dante declared was one of the most beautiful languages he had ever heard.

TRIPOLI LIBYA

13°08' E

UNTIL RECENTLY, LIBYA was an unlikely destination for a holiday in the sun. Before other countries and individuals took its place, Libya and its absolute leader Colonel Muammar Gaddafi were Western catch-alls for Islamic fundamentalist terrorism, its capital off limits due to undesirable associations that invited Clinton's missiles in 1986. It retaliated with the bombing of PanAm flight 103, over Lockerbie.

Now that Gaddafi is positively courting the West, and the country opening itself up to a fad of desert-chic holidays (a week away from commuting, riding a camel with the Tuareg nomads) and revealing long-obscured archaeological treasures from the city's Roman and early Arab conquest origins.

Oea was the name of the settlement the Romans established here in the province of Tripolitania, to provide grain, oil slaves and exotic African goods to their empire. Following the Roman decline, the Vandals swept through northern Africa with a Mongol's respect for its architectural heritage. Following a brief period of Byzantine resuscitation it was not until the Arab invasion of the 7th century that the city's fortunes began to look up. The Arabs rechristened the city Tarabulus, converted it to Islam and in almost nine centuries of rule built the city that survives today. Tripoli is dominated by the vast red castle, Assai al-Hamra, a labyrinth of courtyards and houses-added-to-houses which sits on the city's northern promontory, whence it used to overlook sea but now sits stranded above a motorway and several miles of reclaimed land. The city's medina, the focus of all life in Arabic cities, is exceptionally peaceful for the lack of consumerism under Gaddafi, its souq one of the most authentic and hassle-free of the Arab world.

Three hundred years of Ottoman rule followed, until in 1911 Italy made its bid for a piece of the African continent and set about a vicious period of extermination and enforced exile of Tripoli's indigenous population. Figuratively and architecturally, in the *hammams* and traditional *khan inns* and flurries of frilly neoclassical architecture, the Turkic and Italian colonial periods left a distinctive mark on the city.

Other suitors had included the Spaniards and the Knights of Malta but after the Second World War Libya gained independence under King Idris. Then, in the 1960s an air of pan-Arabism was sweeping across the region, whose coat-tails were caught by then Captain Gaddafi, who deposed the king in a coup. Since 1969 he has run his country according to his little Green Book (the Arabic equivalent of *Das Kapital* or *Mein Kampf*, depending on your point of view) – a doctrine that declares Libya as a Jamahirya (a state of the masses) and prescribes a more equal distribution of the country's oil wealth but which is fundamentally a military dictatorship.

Caked for years in the sand of neglect, Tripoli and its beaches have lost some of the allure that once attracted the cryptic title "White Bride of the Mediterranean". But the brochure-designers already have this under control.

"There was something unmistakably forlorn and beautiful about this city, a wistfulness and largely unspoken resentment. There was nostalgia and regret in the peeling paint of the colonial Turkish and Italian mansions." Justin Marozzi, *South From Barbary*

> TRIPOLI, LIBYA > LONGITUDE: 13°08' E > LATITUDE: 32°52' N > ALTITUDE: 23 feet/7 metres > POPULATION: 1,279,500 > TWINNED WITH: Cairo, Tashkent
> NATIVES: Claudio Gentile, Hazem el Masri > RESIDENTS: Muammar Gaddafi

SALZBURG AUSTRIA

SALZBURG OWES ITS NAME and rich baroque splendour to the salt transported down the Salzach River which flows past its old city walls. But the city's saline origins could easily be forgotten amid the saccharine industry that has grown up in the 20th century – in fact ever since the Victorians deigned to start including the city as a destination on the Grand Tour (or Grand Sneer) – on the back of the city's most famous son. Wolfgang Amadeus Mozart is to Salzburg what Shakespeare is to Stratford. And like the Cotswold village, Salzburg accepts to be totally dominated by the composer, raking in the royalties from visits to his Geburtshaus (birthplace) on the ornate thoroughfare of Getriedegasse, or to the Domkirche, where he was christened, endless concerts and piped crucifixions of his Koerchel to the half-baked local delicacy, Mozartkugel cakes. Birthplace of kitsch, Salzburg (or Schmaltzburg) is Mozart's Graceland (although unlike Memphis there are as yet no Amadeus look-alikes).

The sound of music dominates Salzburg. The city is not just a one-hit wonderland, it has a symphony of world-famous orchestras and chamber music groups, all of which blow their trumpets during the music festival that dominates the city through the months of July and August. And if it's not Cherubino and Figaro it is the strains of Julie Andrews in the eponymous modern-day operetta (and Christmas movie favourite) by Rodgers and Hammerstein, of which the chirpy Amadeus would have been proud. The bars and restaurants are alive with "Edelweiss" while "My Favourite Things" pursues the visitor around the city like a mariachi band in Mexico.

The city occupies a beautiful Alpine location, surrounded by the dramatic scenery of the Salzkammergut hinterland of lakes, glaciers and mountains. Before Maria von Trapp fled across over these hills they were the muse of Salzburg's less celebrated residents, Gustavs Mahler and Klimt.

At the centre of the old city rises the rock on top of whose sheer sides sits the imperious fortress of Hohensalzburg, menacing and impregnable as the Schloss in *Where Eagles Dare*. A funicular now carries tourists up to superb views over the gushing river and picturesque Altstadt (the old town) focused around Mirabellplatz and Dreifaltigkeitsgasse whose delicate elegance, cobbled streets and timbered baroque houses evoke, as if deliberately, the nostalgic innocence of those well-known lyrics.

Not all Salzburgers are violinists, composers or conductors (least of all some of the city's buskers) but those who are not play second fiddle to the city's heritage and its greatest benefactor. Given the telephone "hold" music and enormous record industry Mozart bequeathed to the world, it is as halting as his piano concerto in D minor (the saddest of all keys) to remember that the child prodigy died a pauper and after being afforded the cheapest of funerals was buried in an unmarked grave in Vienna.

> SALZBURG, AUSTRIA > LONGITUDE: 13°03' E > LATITUDE: 47°48' N > ALTITUDE: 1,394 feet/425 metres > POPULATION: 145,500
> TWINNED WITH: Atlanta > NATIVES: Christian Doppler, Angelika Kirchschlager, Wolfgang Amadeus Mozart, Herbert von Karajan
> RESIDENTS: Anke Huber, Gustav Klimt, Gustav Mahler, George and Maria von Trapp

"Cream coloured ponies and crisp apple strudels, Doorbells and sleighbells and schnitzel with noodles."

Oscar Hammerstein, *The Sound of Music*

COPENHAGEN DENMARK

"Other cities put up statues of generals
and potentates. In Copenhagen they
give you a mermaid.
I think that's swell." Bill Bryson

> COPENHAGEN, DENMARK > LOCAL NAME: København > LONGITUDE: 12°34' E > LATITUDE: 55°40' N > ALTITUDE: 16 feet/5 metres > POPULATION: 1,096,100 (metro: 1,785,000) > TWINNED WITH: Osaka
> NATIVES: Niels Bohr, Victor Borge, August Bournonville, Helena Christensen, Carl Dreyer, Johannes Ewald, Peter Høeg, Arne Jacobsen, Sören Kierkegaard, Per Kirkeby, Peter Martins, Peter Schaufuss,
Sandi Toksvig, Lars von Trier, Jørn Utzon, Thomas Vinterberg > RESIDENTS: Hans Christian Andersen, Georg Jensen, Carl Nielsen

COPENHAGEN DISTILS, within its relatively small confines, a number of apparently contradictory personalities: weather-beaten mariner, toytown soldier and, most recently, elegant designer. All coexist in Denmark's modest capital.

Sometimes Copenhagen feels like a saltier version of Amsterdam, but though it offers canal cruises past a thicket of spires and a canopy of bronzed rooftops, the city's port life is far more prominent: towering cruise ships line up an anchor's throw from Nyhavn, the groovy quayside area, where antique ships' figureheads are on sale. Herring – in many guises – is available, although many locals eat it only at Christmas.

The more sentimental side of Copenhagen emerges nightly at the Tivoli Gardens, the brainchild of a 19th-century Danish socialite inspired by the former pleasure gardens of London and Paris. After dark, hundreds of muted lights create a luminous fairyland, while children in miniature soldiers' uniforms perform a changing of the guard. Well, this is the country of Lego and Hans Christian Andersen, after all: the statue portraying Andersen's Little Mermaid – one of the world's great city icons – is a petite, wistful and, for many, disappointingly insignificant statue a few yards offshore in the harbour waters. Over the years, her body has been variously decapitated, dismembered and filleted, for ransoms or pranks.

This twee vision of "Wonderful, Wonderful Copenhagen" would probably send the city's designerati into paroxysms of agony, unless they viewed it as a piece of post-modern irony. Silversmith Georg Jensen and the multifaceted Arne Jacobsen, who oversaw the design of the SAS Hotel from façade to coffee cups, blazed the trail for a phalanx of designers (including Hans J. Wegner and Finn Juhl) renowned for blending cool functionalism and beauty.

Copenhagen has a long legacy in the arts. The Carlsberg brewing family collected widely – their Ny Carlsberg Glypotek is full of Etruscan statuary and Roman art. South of the city the contemporary Arken art gallery slices its way across the marshes; to the north the sea view from the Louisiana Museum is as seductive as its modern art. Peter (*Miss Smilla's Feeling For Snow*) Hoeg and Lars (*The Idiots*) von Trier both challenge existing rules, the same attitude that, in the 1950s and '60s, drew US jazz musicians, notably gravel-voiced saxophonist Dexter Gordon, to the city's Montmartre Club.

Following the July 2000 opening of a sweeping bridge-tunnel link between Copenhagen and Malmö in Sweden, a combined metropolis called Øresund, the biggest city in the Baltic and Northern Europe, has been created. But one suspects that Copenhagen's own distinctive neighbourhoods – elegant Kongens Nytorv, vibrant Vesterbro, the alternative (though somewhat scruffy) free city of Christiania – will survive, and that it will continue to offer a menu of moods as extensive as the *smørrebrød* options on offer at Ida Davidsen's world-famous restaurant.

"Rome is a careless city in which you stumble upon its landmarks by accident as if **its citizens are impatient of so much culture standing in the way of a cappuccino or a parking place.**"

Anthony Mingella

> ROME, LAZIO, ITALY > LOCAL NAME: Roma > LONGITUDE: 12°30′ E > LATITUDE: 41°54′ N > ALTITUDE: 331 feet/101 metres > POPULATION: 2,688,000 > TWINNED WITH: Tokyo
> NATIVES: Gustave Apollinaire, Asia Argento, Dario Argento, Lucrezia Borgia, Paolo di Canio, Juan Carlos I, Julius Caesar, Bonnie Prince Charlie, Enrico Fermi, Giancarlo Fisichella, Massimiliano Fuksas, Sergio Leone, Sophia Loren, Anna Magnani, Maria Montessori, Alberto Moravia, Ennio Morricone, Alessandro Nesta, Anita Pallenberg, Isabella Rossellini, Roberto Rossellini, Elsa Schiaparelli, Alberto Sordo, John William Waterhouse, Lina Wertmuller > RESIDENTS: Caligula, Federico Fellini, Natalia Ginzburg, Horace, John Keats, Marcello Mastroianni, Nero, Ovid, Pier Paolo Pasolini, Percy Byshe Shelley

ORSON WELLES FAMOUSLY SAID Italy was full of actors, almost all of them good, and that the only bad ones were in films. The streets of Rome are Italy's greatest theatre, an urban stage of eloquent, deep brown eyes, animated gestures accompanied by constant exclamation, full of the relentless buzz of Vespas, frenetic espresso-drinking and an apparent fear that the world might stop turning should the Romans fall silent.

In a country of strong local identities, Milan may be Italy's economic capital, Turin its industrial heartland and Florence its cultural mecca, but each of these cities is in its way provincial. Only Rome has the insouciant metropolitan swagger and arrogance of a city that is sure of its global resonance, and like London's cockney and New York's patter, Rome has a lax-jawed arrogant "*romanaccio*" dialect to match.

In this land obsessed by *figura*, Rome wins out. Milan may have beauty in its clothes and Venice in its architectural excess, but Roman beauty is the most Doric and natural of all. Classic Roman beauty seduced the English Romantic poets, who ascribed Roman boys a patronizing innocence, and entrapped the homosexual poet-film director Pierpaolo Pasolini, who was murdered by a rent boy on the beach at Ostia. This is the seedy side of Rome, still redolent in the louche streets of the former medieval trading quarter of Trastevere. In Rome, capital of the Catholic world, piety and licence are open but uneasy bedfellows. Beyond the Vatican, country within a city, goodness cohabits with sleaze. This is the home of *La Dolce Vita*, all hair-gel and sunglasses, although the Via Veneto looks better in black and white. Here even the traffic wardens are beautiful. Romans believe that beauty will save the world.

It will have to save their city. Luigi Barzani wrote that "the Italian way of life can only be deemed a success by the temporary visitor". Rome has long not been the paradigm of civilization that the ancient city once represented. Modern "*Roma Ladrona*", (the big thief) is the land of political larceny at the centre of the 1992 Tangentopoli (bribe-gate) scandal when all fingers, let alone roads, pointed at the city's lupine government. Rome is the start of the Italian South and does nothing to hide its meridional sense of *mañana*.

Rome's arrogance derives from the grapes and chaises-longues decadence of its ancient imperial past. We all know the legend of the wolf, and the city is littered with antiquity and global landmarks – the Forum which was the basis for so many cities, the Colosseum and Baths of Caracalla, Anita Ekberg's Trevi Fountain, Campo dei Fiori, the Spanish Steps, Bernini's fountain and his prescient baroque colonnade in St Peter's Square, an arena seemingly designed to host two million disciples and showcase on television the passing of the first Pope of the media age.

Amid the scattered antiquity and jumbled topography of its seven hills, the eternal city is also one of the world's greenest, watered by the Tiber, its avenues and parks shrouded under a canopy of signature dark-green pini ombrello pine trees that, together with its rose-red walls, cast the magic purple and gold aura that engulfs the city at dusk.

IT WAS ONE OF Dorothy Parker's Algonquin sparring partners, the humorist Robert Benchley, who on arriving in Venice wired back to New York the plaintive message "Streets flooded. Please advise." Behind his *bon mot* lies a genuine truism. Because the thing that is most striking on arriving in Venice for the first time – most elegantly done via a sleek motor boat to the Cipriani or Gritti Palace – is that the streets are indeed full of water.

Other cities, like Amsterdam and Copenhagen, have canals, but here they are everywhere, of every shape, size and mood. France's Venise Verte or London's Little Venice are tame simulacra. Nothing can compare with the original's profusion of waterways, the arteries and veins of Venetian existence. *Vaporetti*, *traghetti*, gondolas, barges, skiffs and water transport of every description criss-cross the water – carrying not just tourists but piles of coal, food supplies, or patients heading to hospital. This is a living community, not a Disney fantasy, nor a Canaletto canvas.

Venice is a great place to get lost. There is no handy grid system for easy orientation, but a sinuous layout with signs that occasionally and vaguely point towards the Rialto or the Piazza San Marco. So there is nothing easier than fleeing the madding, maddening summer crowds: exploring, out of season, the far-flung – and often exquisitely malodorous – *fondamente* shrouded in the fog of *Don't Look Now*; joining the locals (all of whom know each other – the population without tourists is tiny) for a Sunday afternoon in one of the much-coveted Lido beach huts; savouring a plump *tramezzino* sandwich and a glass of *prosecco* in a quiet square; or stumbling across a Vivaldi concert in an out of the way church.

Apart from Venice itself, the lagoon is home to another 40 islands. Many are completely deserted, others are used for sports facilities, quarantine hospitals and market gardens. But the most visited are those islands that form a kind of Greater Venice – the perky fishing village of Burano with its brightly painted houses, the glassworks of Murano and the quietly dignified Torcello. Tucked close by Venice is the cemetery island of San Michele, where Serge Diaghilev, Igor Stravinsky and Ezra Pound reside in perpetuity.

Back in Venice, the classic sites – Piazza San Marco, the Doge's Palace and the Ponte di Rialto – throb, but are still inspiring. Fabulously rich in both art (from the Accademia to Peggy Guggenheim's modern art collection) and magnificent churches, Venice is an architectural marvel, a city no one would now have the courage or stupidity to build, although the threat of its sinking appears to have been over-hyped. Above all, Venice provides a remarkably direct link to a history of seafaring empires, exotic hedonism and sinister intrigue, which often seems both palpable and contemporary.

"Venice is like eating an entire box of chocolate liqueurs in one go."

Truman Capote

> VENICE, VENETO, ITALY > LOCAL NAME: Venezia > LONGITUDE: 12°20' E > LATITUDE: 45°26' N > ALTITUDE: 3 feet/1 metre > POPULATION: 308,717 > TWINNED WITH: Sarajevo, Suzhou (China), Talinn
> NATIVES: Tomaso Albinoni, Giovanni Bellini, Canaletto, Giacomo Casanova, Luigi Enrico Ferro, Carlo Goldoni, Marco Polo, Giovanni Battista Tiepolo, Jacopo Tintoretto, Antonio Vivaldi, Ermano Wolf-Ferrari
> RESIDENTS: Peggy Guggenheim, Donna Leon, Maria Taglioni, Titian, Veronese

GOTHENBURG SWEDEN

SWEDEN'S SECOND CITY owes its character, at least in part, to two other European countries. Established in 1621 by the Swedish monarch Gustav Adolphus, "the Lion of the North", on the mouth of the Gota River, the city was laid out and built by Dutch designers. Their influence on Gothenburg is still visible, in the tall houses lining Linngaten, and the canals cruised by flat-bottomed boats known as *padden* (toads), although many of the original waterways have long gone. Later on, a 19th-century vogue for things Britannic led to the city acquiring the nickname "Little London", and Scots and English benefactors donated money for the construction of a hospital, library and university.

The city shows a considerate concern for the comfort of its citizens, laying pipes underground to heat the surface of the Kungsportsavenyn – known simply as the Avenyn, or avenue. This is the Champs-Elysées of Gothenburg, half a mile (1km) long and 40 yards (36m) wide, where Swedish boulevardiers can relax at one of the pavement cafés and watch the world saunter past. With superb beaches within easy reach, plenty of greenery and some healthy ocean air, it makes perfect sense that one opinion poll revealed that nearly six out of ten Swedes would like to live in the city.

From the harbour outwards trams trundle through Gothenburg's neighbourhoods:

"Here I will build my city."

King Gustavus Adolphus

That Gothenburg drew some of its personality traits from outside Sweden is consistent with its role as a trading port – the Swedish East India Company operated out of the city – and its geographical position, turned towards the rest of Europe, whereas Stockholm stares out across the Baltic. The harbour rarely, unlike other Swedish ports, freezes during the winter, and although there is skating on the city's lakes and its many parklands look delightful under a coating of snow, Gothenburg has a reputation for offering a warmer welcome than Stockholm (which is welcoming enough). Its charms have attracted major corporations; Volvo and Saab have their headquarters here, as does Hasselblad, the Rolls-Royce of cameras.

from studenty Vasastaden to the once rundown working-class district of Haga, now a revitalised bohemian quarter of low wooden houses and cobbled alleyways, and further on out to vibrant Linnstaden, named after Carl von Linné, creator of the Linnean nomenclature we use for the whole of natural history.

But perhaps it is back down the tram line, in the harbour area, that Gothenburg's true soul lies. Appropriately a statue of Poseidon, God of the Seas, stands in the middle of the Gotaplatsen, and the port is full of maritime museums and restored or replica ships. The restaurants serve salt fish, and even the new opera-house, reflected in the waters, seems to be a collection of prows, sterns and gunwales.

> GOTHENBURG, SWEDEN > LOCAL NAME: Göteborg > LONGITUDE: 11°58' E > LATITUDE: 57°43' N > ALTITUDE: 32 feet/10 metres
> POPULATION: 462,500 (metro: 730,000) > TWINNED WITH: Chicago, Shanghai > NATIVES: Karin Boye, Jose González, Fredrik Jacobson, Victor Hasselblad, Ingemar Johansson, Johan Eric Rydqvist, Björn Ulvaeus RESIDENTS: Bedrich Smetana

IN MANY WAYS Munich showcases all the traditional German stereotypes. This is the land of Bayerische Motoren-Werke ("Beamers") and the Oktoberfest of oom-pah bands, pretzels, big-bosomed *frauleins* and beer-swilling moustachioed Bavarians slapping *lederhosen*-clad thighs.

Yet the Bavarians set themselves apart from the rest of Germany, just as other Germans set the queer Bayerisch folk apart. If Milan is the most southern state of Germany, Munich is the most northern state of Italy. The two nations and cultures meet here amid the Alpine foothills, fairy-tale castles, lakes and trees in a cultured mix of strong local dialect and cosmopolitanism.

Parts of Munich have a sunny, laid-back atmosphere that is more Mediterranean than Milan, an outdoor life of aromatic cafés and wine connoisseurs. And yet the architecture and fashions are definably Teutonic: the fifteenth century cobblestone Altstadt (old town) is a huddle of yellowy façades, Tudoresque timber, broad low arches and circular attic windows. The Baroque onion domes of the city's old churches are reminiscent of the steeples seen in Romantic portraits of a bygone rural Germany, while the Rathaus (town hall) in Marienplatz is pure robust Germanic neo-Gothic, as is the Residenz in Max-Joseph Platz of the Wittelbach family, rulers of Munich from 1385 until 1918. To the north of the city the Englischer Garten is a stage for that favourite German pastime, nude sunbathing. Meanwhile, students from one of Germany's most illustrious universities pedal around earnestly on Brechtian black bicycles, cloth-capped and with leather satchel swung around the waist. On a lazy afternoon or in the Gothic night dotted by the warm glow of Bierkellers (beer halls) Munich can seem transposed from a Grimm fairy tale. Small wonder that it should inspire such nationalism in the country's most famous Pied-Piper who held early meetings of his National Socialist Party in the Hoffbrauhaus beer hall on Platzl.

But Munich also has a sleek and modern other side that has had it branded "the city of laptops and Lederhosen." It has long been a publishing and media centre, home to black-clad, roll-neck dot com start-up types who flash their cash in the boutiques of Maximilienstrasse. In counterpoint the vibrant now-gentrified district of Schwabing close to the university is the domain of scruffy eternal students lost in more abstract thoughts.

Munich has always had a powerful sporting tradition, steeped in Germanic resilience and competitiveness. Bayern Munich, one of the city's two teams, has always been a dominant force in European football, while many Münchner avail themselves of their city's surrounding natural beauty, turning their bodies into temples on the naturalist work-out circuits of the Bavarian hinterland or on the snows of Garmisch-Partenkirchen underneath the Zugspitze.

"I felt bad when I thought of that Babylon of races... I belong to that town more than to any spot in the world, inseparably bound up with my own development." Adolf Hitler

> MUNICH, BAVARIA, GERMANY > LOCAL NAME: München > LONGITUDE: 11°35' E > LATITUDE: 48°08' N > ALTITUDE: 1,700 feet/518 metres > POPULATION: 2,306,000 > TWINNED WITH: Bordeaux, Cincinnati OH, Edinburgh, Kiev, Sapporo (Japan) > NATIVES: Markus Baabel, Andreas Baader, Franz Beckenbauer, Theobald Boehm, Eva Braun, Hanne Darboven, Alfred Einstein, Lion Feuchtwanger, Michael Haneke, Werner Herzog, Heinrich Himmler, Franz Marc, Rudolph Moshammer, Carl Orff, Walter Sickert, Richard Strauss > RESIDENTS: Adolf Hitler, Paul Klee, Thomas Mann, Lola Montez

437

BOLOGNA ITALY

11°22' E

WITH PROCESSIONS OF CLASSICAL columns that march harmoniously along its medieval avenues and thieving shadows cast by the half-moons of its winding narrow alleys, Bologna inspires a furtive combination of illicit intimacy and poetic wandering. An ivory tower, calm and serene, Bologna hides the secrets of lovers in her shady alcoves.

Above and between the porticoes, Bologna is a rose-red city of bombastic churches and vainglorious palaces, lasting testaments to the architectural flattery bestowed down many turbulent centuries by the papal and civic forces that vied for control of the city. For although all roads might lead to Rome, in Italy, they almost certainly pass through Bologna. Sitting on a fertile plain at the centre of a thin and mountainous country, Bologna has always been a strategic city and a vital trading junction. To render immortal their ephemeral reigns, the city's patriarchs commissioned lavish chapels, frescoes, tombs and staircases to their vanity, patronizing some of the finest artists of the time and creating, with the help of the brothers Caracci, one of the most influential schools in the history of Italian art.

But invaders also sought to contain the Bolognese propensity for free thinking that has led it to be the Pope's *bête noire* and emancipated gay capital of Italy. From the foundation of Europe's oldest university at its heart, Bologna has always been the Italian residence of pioneering thought and revolution, earning it the soubriquet "*Bologna la dotta*" (the learned). Here in the Middle Ages were laid down the basic principles of European law, and hundreds of years later, around the same time as a Bolognese physicist Guglielmo Marconi was discovering radio, Bologna became the birthplace and home of the Italian political Left. Already dubbed "*la rossa*" (the red) for its famed red buildings, Bologna's second nickname gained a figurative meaning, which attracted the neo-Fascist bombing of its station in 1980.

Bologna is a city for walking and talking, if only to digest one of its famous meals. Bologna is to food what fashion is to Milan (any Italian who says otherwise is talking a load of the city's *mortadella* sausage, aka "boloney") fabled for such fine things in life such as *tortellini* and *tagliatelle al pomodoro* (bastardized by students worldwide into "spag bol"). The Bolognese live in a land of plenty, totally devoted to epicurean pleasures, and their affluence and famed papal corpulence – Bologna's third nickname is "*la grassa*", "the fat" – rather take the edge off the social conscience and belie the image of the starving student. If there are any partisans left, they are probably of the *prosecco* variety. Perhaps this was always the city's alluring and ultimately workable paradox. It is twinned with industrial Coventry in the UK. Personally I'd rather be sent to Bologna.

> BOLOGNA, EMILIA-ROMAGNA, ITALY > LONGITUDE: 11°22' E > LATITUDE: 44°29' N > ALTITUDE: 178 feet/54 metres > POPULATION: 380,500 > TWINNED WITH: Coventy (UK), Kharkiv (Ukraine), La Plata (Argentina), Leipzig (Germany), Nizhny Novgorod (Russia), Portland OR, St Louis, San Carlos (Nicaragua), Thessaloniki, Toulouse, Valencia, Zagreb > NATIVES: Giorgio Bassani, Stefano Benni, Agostino, Annibale and Lodovico Caracci, Pierluigi Collina, Lodovico Ferrari, Lavinia Fontana, Pope Gregory XIII, Guglielmo Marconi, Giorgio Morandi, Pier Paolo Pasolini, Ottorino Respighi, Christian Vieri, Alessandro Zanardi RESIDENTS: Umberto Eco, Vasco Rossi

"Bologna is the Italy that works."

Charles Richard, *The New Italians*

TWICE A YEAR, the Piazza del Campo becomes more than ever the absolute epicentre of Sienese life and history. After months of preparation, parades, trial races, flag-throwing and ceremonial blessings, horses representing ten of the city's districts erupt in a 80-second burst of equestrian madness and pandemonium round the piazza's sand-covered surface, less Derby Day than stock-car derby: this is the race known as the Palio.

The 17 city wards, the *contrade*, each with its own quaint symbol – the Hedgehog, the Porcupine or the Giraffe – and

history of the Palio, first run in 1283, is riddled with tales of low tricks, nobbled jockeys and lucrative backhanders.
The Jockey Club would have an apoplectic fit.

That the Palio is run with as much passion as ever is a clue to Siena's deep connection to the past. Built on three hills, the city is still close to the natural landscape it emerged from. The stunning scallop-shaped Piazza del Campo (into the suntrap of which the visitor suddenly bursts from the approaching shaded passageways) follows the contours of the original meadow that lies beneath it.

"Più di chiunque altro, Siena ti apre il cuore."
"More than anywhere else, Siena opens up its heart to you."
Inscription on the Porta di Camollia

strident colours, were demarcated in the Middle Ages. Marriages used to be arranged strictly within each *contrada*; love affairs outside them carried the potential of a *Romeo and Juliet* tragedy. Some *contrade* have historically been allied, others bitter rivals. Only ten of the wards can run horses to win the Palio, the victor's banner – known locally as *il cencio* or "the rag", a typically offhand Sienese dismissal of something so excruciatingly important. The

Anyone who makes the vertiginous climb to the rather rickety platform at the top of the Torre del Mangia, which rises high above the Piazza, can gaze out across the red roofs of the city to the olive groves and orchards that nestle up to its edge.

The sense is very much one of travelling back in time. The overall shape of the city and the warm brown colour (burnt sienna) of its stonework has changed remarkably little since the 14th century. The striped Romanesque-Gothic Duomo, decorated in a style that Henry James described as "goldsmithery in stone", and that epitome of civic pride, the Palazzo Pubblico, are free of distraction by modern neighbours. When they wanted to create a centre for contemporary art, the city fathers did not summon Frank Gehry or Rem Koolhaas, but converted the 15th-century Palazzo delle Papesse.

Once Florence's main rival, Siena has taken a more leisurely path than its more frenetic Tuscan cousin. But that does not mean the Sienese are not proud; they are, fiercely so. And given that some outsiders consider them the most beautiful citizens of Italy, that pride can spill over to a haughtiness that rather belies the inscription at the Porta di Camollia; Dante declared they were "vainer even than the French." They do not need the outside world, their whole world is their city.

> SIENA, TOSCANA, ITALY > LONGITUDE: 11°20′ E > LATITUDE: 43°19′ N > ALTITUDE: 1,056 feet/322 metres > POPULATION: 55,600
> TWINNED WITH: Buffalo NY > NATIVES: Tino di Camaino, Duccio, Guido da Siena, St Bernadine, St Catherine

FLORENCE ITALY

THE TERRACE AT FIESOLE is a short Vespa ride up into the hills outside Florence. Looking back towards the russet roofs of the city below, the Duomo rises like a beacon, especially when the mist is lying low over the River Arno. It is an appropriate symbol for Florence. The great dome of the cathedral, conceived and constructed by Filippo Brunelleschi between 1420 and 1461, is a physical manifestation of the vaulting ambition and confidence that the capital of Tuscany enjoyed under the Medicis.

Their wealth, derived from banking, was the most alluring of the patronage on offer to artists in the 1400s: Botticelli, Cellini, da Vinci, Michelangelo and Raphael represent only a partial roll-call of those who flourished as a result. The Medicis would supply the Vatican with two popes (Leo X and Clement VII) and were intensely political animals – this is the city of Machiavelli – but they did love their art, especially Lorenzo "the Magnificent", and for that we can only thank them. For art lovers, Florence is a happy, but exhausting, hunting ground.

At the Uffizi Gallery, a deep breath is required before heading in to gaze at Titian's *Venus of Urbino* and Botticelli's *Birth of Venus*, or the portraiture of Bronzino and Piero della Francesca. A quick schlepp across town, at the Accademia, the statue of *David*

by Michelangelo – or as one visitor was heard to remark, "the statue that David did of himself" – tends to overshadow the rest of the collection. And that's before the footsore aesthete delves into the Bargello, where more Michelangelo sculptures stand alongside Giambologna's bronze *Mercury*. Florence's churches are as rich in art as any of the museums and galleries. Santa Maria Novella contains extraordinary frescoes by Masaccio, Ghirlandaio and Uccello; at Santa Croce works by Giotto and Donatello are scattered among the tombs of Galileo, Michelangelo and Machiavelli.

Their artistic heritage has, unsurprisingly, made Florentines proud, if not downright arrogant, although much of their aggression is down to the fact they can't walk along the web of medieval lanes in the centre of Dante's city without being steamrollered by phalanxes of tour groups heading for the Ponte Vecchio. They are more likely to congregate away from the centre, in the wine cellars around Santa Croce, near the university in San Gallo, or south of the river in Oltrarno.

For its residents, Florence is the last bastion of civilization before what they see as the philistine wilderness of the South, the *meridionale*. This is definitely not the Mediterranean: here, the local cooking is inspired by the forest, a sylvan cuisine

of wild boar, porcini, truffles and beans. Florentines are as intense about food as they are about cars, football – either their soccer team, the purple-clad Fiorentina, or their own medieval no-rules, Rollerball-style equivalent, *calcio storico* – and elegant clothes, on which they spent an unseemly proportion of their annual budget. In a graceful, harmonious city, where the view over the Arno at sunset can bring tears to even the most jaded traveller's eyes, the people are as elegant as their surroundings.

> FLORENCE, TOSCANA, ITALY > LOCAL NAME: Firenze > LONGITUDE: 11°16' E > LATITUDE: 43°46' N > ALTITUDE: 125 feet/38 metres
> POPULATION: 461,000 > TWINNED WITH: Asmara, Edinburgh, Istanbul, Kiev, Kyoto, Nanjing, Philadelphia, Sydney > NATIVES: Dante Alighieri,
Sandro Botticelli, Agnolo Bronzino, Filippo Brunelleschi, Benvenuto Cellini, Maria Luigi Cherubini, Clement VII, Donatello, Lorenzo Ghiberti, Oriana Fallaci,
Leo X, Fra Filippo Lippi, Jean-Baptiste Lully, Niccolò Machiavelli, Cosimo Medici, Lorenzo Medici, Florence Nightingale, Richard Rogers, John Singer Sargent,
Paolo Uccello, Amerigo Vespucci, Franco Zeffirelli > RESIDENTS: Gabriel Battistuta, Giovanni Boccaccio, Galileo Galilei, Cosimo Medici, Michelangelo, Raphael

"Everything about Florence seems to be coloured with a mild violet, like diluted wine."

Henry James

10°46' E

MUNCH'S IMAGE OF A LONE FIGURE against a turbulent sunset, mouth wide open and with hands clamped to bulging temples is one of the world's most recognized paintings. But the Oslo of today would be unrecognizable to the artist in whom it inspired such anguish.

The Scream – now returned after its theft in 1994 – may conveniently symbolize the alienation and isolation of modern life, but Munch was reacting to an overcrowded 19th-century Oslo plagued by a Dickensian squalor of open sewers and tuberculosis. Rumour has it he had also been on a drinking binge just before his apocalyptic vision. Nowadays Oslo is a nanny-state model of cleanliness, affluence and efficiency, as clean as the sound of Keith Jarrett's piano at one of his locally-recorded ECM sessions. People who are easily bored and like their cities as fast-moving and eternally stimulating as London or New York might find themselves, after a visit to his magnificent museum, sympathizing with Munch.

The truth is the Norwegians are naturally naturists, not city-builders: lovers of nature and nudity who, in the words of the Monty Python "Parrot" sketch are "pining for the fjords". Oslo is surrounded by forests, lakes and hills that are a constant irresistible draw to its citizens. In the long summer days the city virtually empties and shuts down; walking and intellectualizing in the nude take precedence. In the long dark winter come cosy evenings of carefree rural drinking, skiing (this is the home of the balletic Telemark turn) and typically of this part of the world, ski-jumping – the Holmenkollen ski-jump, built for 1952 Olympics, is one of the more bizarre features of Oslo's skyline. The Oslo fjord itself is full of islands where businessmen retire at weekends or hold meetings after which a signed contract might be celebrated with a quick skinny-dip.

Until Norwegian independence Oslo was a small provincial city called Kristiania on the fringes of the Scandinavian empire and dominated by Stockholm. Although the latter may be the domain of cutting-edge, polo-necked interior design, Oslo, still the smallest of Scandinavia's capitals, is now arguably the livelier city. Underneath the tree-lined, village-y "oh-

"Suddenly the sky became blood red. I stopped, leaned against the railing, dead tired. And saw the flaming clouds as blood over the blue-black fjord and city. I stood there trembling with angst. And I sensed a loud, unending scream pierce nature."

Edvard Munch

so-slow" exterior of Vigeland Park. And despite its rather Calvinist views on the sale and over-pricing of alcohol, it has a robust fun-loving Viking mentality of strapping Thors and tall blonde Hildegaards. Along the Karl Johan's Gate, Oslo's most famous thoroughfare, named after the 18th-century king and formerly home to the artistic community where Munch, Ibsen, Grieg and friends would have hung out, are humming bars and nightclubs (albeit serving low-alcohol beer). Reminders of the Norwegians' supreme sailing credentials lie close at hand in a clutch of museums housing the Kon-Tiki, the Fram, Nansen's polar ship, and examples of the Viking vessels that ruled and terrorized the seas and, some say, discovered America. It is odd to think this race of red-bearded warriors inclined to suffer a touch of the red mist have turned over the centuries into a softly-spoken nation synonymous with Scandinavian peace-brokering. Within the democratic functionality of the city's red-bricked Radhus (town hall), every year the Nobel Peace Prize is awarded.

> OSLO, NORWAY > LONGITUDE: 10°46' E > LATITUDE: 59°55' N > ALTITUDE: 164 feet/50 metres > POPULATION: 758,900 > TWINNED WITH: Madison WI > NATIVES: Gro Harlem Brundtland, Lars Saabye Christensen, Mariella Frostrup, Jostein Gaarder, Sonja Henie, Terje Rypdal, Greta Waitz > RESIDENTS: Edvard Grieg, Henrik Ibsen, Edvard Munch

TUNIS TUNISIA

TUNIS, LIKE ALGIERS, is a city of whiteness set against the azure blue of the Mediterranean. But, unlike the capital of neighbouring Algeria, it has not, recently, been wracked by internal violence, and has preserved both its infrastructure and its charm, as seductive as the perfumes on sale in the el-Attarine souk, or the scent of jasmine and oleander that on a summer evening drifts through the lanes of the seaside suburb of Sidi Bou Saïd.

With a comparatively laid-back attitude to its colonial past, Tunis has been described as "a dusty Paris with palm-trees", although the overall impression is that the city is neither predominantly Arab, African nor European. The French left behind traces of art nouveau and deco, the Parc du Belvédère, built for their wives and children to escape the relentless summer heat, and broad avenues that run courteously up to the medina, the old Arab town.

There, in the el-Zitouna Mosque, hundreds of columns were imaginatively recycled from the ruins of an early civilization, Dido's Carthage. Once Rome's most powerful North African rival, the empire she created was crushed after the Carthaginian general Hannibal's initially successful invasion of Italy in the 2nd century BC had faltered. Carthage, vindictively destroyed by the Romans – who sowed salt to prevent anything growing – has become a salubrious and very desirable bougainvillaea- and geranium-filled suburb to the north of Tunis. A short distance to the west, the Bardo Museum is a world-renowned collection of Roman and Punic mosaics, statuary and antiquities.

The mesmerizing alleyways of Tunis's flat-roofed old town gravitate towards the *casbah*, where each of the specialist souks is identified by an extremely French blue enamel sign stating the profession which is selling its wares, from the engravers of the Goldsmiths' souk to the distinctive red felt *chechia* (the tarboosh or fez) manufacturers based in the Echaouachia souk - although there is the usual quantity of 21st-century tat.

The bourgeoisie and the aristocrats have long moved away from the old quarters towards their modern apartment blocks and villas – or their mansions alongside the golf course in Carthage – and especially to the northern coastal suburbs of La Goulette and La Marsa, or Sidi Bou Saïd, where the doors and shutters of the houses are painted the blue of Aegean villages, a destination for chic Tunis teenagers heading out on the TGM train to congregate in the cliffside cafés.

Tunis itself often has the feel of an empty city, a quiet, almost eerie atmosphere (despite incessant traffic jams), either out of apathy, regret for the greatness of its past or pure nonchalance. Likewise its flat topography gives no sense of the sea so close hand; consequently, it is a city that seems to exist a little distractedly, and distanced from the realities of the modern world – which may be no bad thing.

446 > TUNIS, TUNISIA > LONGITUDE: 10°16' E > LATITUDE: 36°46' N > ALTITUDE: 10 feet/3 metres > POPULATION: 699,700 (metro: 1,660,300) > NATIVES: Anouar Brahem, Alain Boublil, Claudia Cardinale, Gerald Incandela, Ibn Khaldun, Albert Memmi, Selima Sfar, Georges Wolinski > RESIDENTS: Baron Rodolphe d'Erlanger, Paul Morand, John Howard Payne

"I fell in love with Tunis when I saw it from the window of the Salle du Divan in the Bey's palace. Your gaze soars over terraces and old tiled roofs, and peers through plaster grilles."

Paul Morand

> AARHUS, DENMARK > LOCAL NAME: Århus > LONGITUDE: 10°12' E > LATITUDE: 56°09' N
> POPULATION: 274,500 > NATIVES: Olaus Roemer

THE CITY OF AARHUS HAS rather proudly adopted Peter Ustinov's one-liner as a wryly self-deprecating marketing slogan. Denmark's second city does not aspire, at least not overtly, to the ultra-cool pose of the capital Copenhagen, but has gently pursued an unpretentious lifestyle on the east coast of Jutland, that finger of land perched on top of Germany which beckons towards Sweden and Norway.

The city in many ways sums up the history and the discreet charm of Denmark. Its central maze of small streets, around the Gothic Domkirke Cathedral, is medieval, dating from a time when Denmark was one of the dominant European powers; under its 14th-century king, Valdemar IV, the Danes held sway over Greenland, Iceland, Sweden and Norway. Just outside the city, at Den Gamle By (the old town), a kind of Danish Epcot, several dozen half-timbered houses from the 17th and 18th centuries have been reconstructed to create a living village, complete with bakery and bookstores.

But this celebration of Denmark's past does not mean that Aarhus is some twee olde-worlde theme park. The best of modern design and architecture is also on display. One of the two architects of the Radhus, Aarhus's City Hall, was Arne Jacobsen, father of Danish design and creator of many of its classic icons, including the curvaceous wooden Sevener chair. The Hall, built during the Second World War (when the Nazis, ignoring Denmark's neutrality, had invaded and occupied the country), is topped off by a scaffold-clad campanile which resembles nothing less than a fire-station training tower. "We think scaffolding looks nice," the architect later remarked. He had wanted the tower to stand in a separate garden, but the city council insisted it should be attached to the Hall. "Not the most exquisite architectural solution," Jacobsen observed. The modernist style police, though approving of his work, would have a severe attack of the heebie-jeebies if they saw Aarhus's statue of a pig relieving itself, which definitely errs on the side of kitsch.

As part of its microcosm of things Danish, Aarhus also offers honest food – sausages from street vendors, or pork and parsley and salted herrings at one of the restaurants on Åboulevarden, the promenade running alongside the River Århus – and the great

outdoors. Nothing is very far from anywhere else in Denmark, and the sea is no distance at all from the centre of Aarhus. The youthful city (where one in ten of the population is a student) lies close to rolling beech woods and white sandy beaches, of which Moesgaard Strand is the most popular. This is where the Danish royals choose to summer, at Marselisborg Slot, and non-royals to cycle, hike or take a refreshing dip in the wooden swimming baths by the harbour waters.

"The world's smallest big city."

Peter Ustinov

"Auf der Reeperbahn Nachts um halb eins

Ob du ein Maedel hast, oder auch keins." Hans Albers

WHEREAS FRANKFURT is rightly the home of the Frankfurter sausage, Hamburg cannot be blamed for Whoppers or the Royale with Cheese. But you are just as unlikely to see the city's real speciality, *aalsuppe* (eel soup) on the menu at your local McDonald's.

Germany's second city lies 50 miles inland but is in fact the country's most important container port: and shipping is the historic basis of Hamburg's wealth. Vast cargo vessels from the world over come up the broad estuary of the River Elbe, right to the heart of the city. As one of Europe's great merchant cities and member of the Hanseatic alliance, Hamburg is still today a city of noble shipping families, of born and bred Hamburgers with a long history of sea-beaten inner strength.

This is a handsome city whose skyline set against a bleak North Sea sky is instantly recognizable for the coppery tops of the churches and buildings of the Hafengegend (harbour district). Water surrounds and flows through the city from two river-lakes, the Binnenalster and Aussenalster, around which is a network of canals spanned by more bridges than Venice. Up river are the Strandhauser (beach houses) of the Elbstrand, a beach of the city's hottest bars almost in the midst of clanking industry.

Between the wars the classic image of Hamburg was the seedy strip of the Reeperbahn in Sankt Pauli, Hamburg's answer to Berlin's cabaret, immortalized by the blond charm of Albers. Then the Reeperbahn was Europe's most colourful and notorious red-light district, more famous even than Amsterdam. As always, the red lights seem to attract and signify life in all its colourful variety. Now somewhat sanitized and less seedy, Sankt Pauli is still red but also boho, a muse for a new breed of artists in search of the flesh of life. But cheap Hamburg always had its antithesis in the fine upstanding image of its merchant lineage,

and this is still epitomized by the leafy affluence of Blankenese district, just a short river taxi ride upstream.

In the midst of the Altstadt is Hamburg's enormous fish market, an institution and an overpowering slippery mêlée of silvery scales from the North Sea that has had Hamburgers nicknamed "Fischkopp" (fish-heads) by their compatriots. On the menu is the aforementioned speciality – "waiter, there's an eel in my soup!" – definitely an acquired taste. Appropriately for a city sharing its name with the original meat sandwich, Hamburg also has a vibrant gay scene, a fact which contributes in no small portion to the city's nocturnal vibrancy and cultural life. Industry comes with culture, and Hamburg's Kunsthalle Friedrich art gallery is particularly well hung.

One of the world's great port-cities Hamburg has the architecture and outward-looking tradition that make it well-suited to the contemporary vogues of loft-living, raves and home-offices for post-industrial art- and lifestyle-chic; a make-up that puts it now at the forefront of the German urban expression.

> HAMBURG, GERMANY > LONGITUDE: 9°59' E > LATITUDE: 53°34' N > ALTITUDE: 23 feet/7 metres > POPULATION: 1,715,400 (metro: 4,014,800) > TWINNED WITH: Chicago, Osaka, Shanghai > NATIVES: Hans Albers, Fatih Akin, Heinrich Barth, Wolf Biermann, Johannes Brahms, Bill Brandt, Ralph Dahrendorf, Bert Kaempfert, Karl Lagerfeld, Felix Mendelssohn, Angela Merkel, Sandra Nettelbeck, John Neumeier, H.A. and Margaret Rey, Helmut Schmidt, Axel Springer > RESIDENTS: C.P.E. Bach, Hanne Darboven, Cornelia Funke, George Philipp Telemann, Michael Stich, Monika Treut

MILAN ITALY

THE WORDS "CAPITAL" AND "FASHION" usually appear in most first sentences about Milan. But that is like reducing Cannes to its yearly film festival. It is true that when you emerge into the foggy haze of Linate airport to be greeted by the huge neon insignia of Emporio Armani there is little doubt what image the city wishes to project of itself. This may be brand-ville, but fashion is just the exterior.

The title of fashion capital was only recently annexed from Florence, and the shows that parade periodically into the city during the year are no more relevant to the average Milanese than the film festival is to the people of Cannes. An exaggerated sensitivity to style is innate to all Italians, and the retail empires of its fashion aristocracy, modern-day equivalents of the Viscontis and Sforzas who embellished its past with castles and *palazzi*, are by now more global than local.

For most Milanese fashion is a rigidly conformist "V-neck and brogues" elegance modelled on the English country gentleman. At heart, Milan has always been a conservative city, sometimes termed the most southern state of Germany, in line with its self-stated role as the *capitale morale* centre of a hard-working Italy. Behind it all Milan is rare in Italy for its outward gaze; and the Milanesi are obsessed with being seen as international and cosmopolitan.

Milan is Italy's financial centre, address of Italy's stock market, and capital of the rich and most educated region, Lombardy, which drives the Italian economy. Under Silvio Berlusconi, who runs his media empire from Milan, some might even argue it is the country's administrative capital. And given this domestic platform Milan has always reached out, like Berlusconi's government, to be considered *al livello internazionale* – up with the global Jones's. The business and social language in Milan is the most Americanized in the country, and the taxis that greeted you at the station were once a deliberate New York yellow.

Milan often disappoints visitors expecting a Tuscan version of the Italian experience. Badly bombed in the last war and littered with ill-judged and speedy rebuilding projects, it represents a firmer aesthetic challenge. But visitors willing to explore the backstage of its catwalk high streets and undoubted artistic treasures (the most famous dinner party ever to be painted resides here, after all!) will be rewarded with a glimpse of a city, arguably alone in the country for not resting on its laurels: its unfortunate looks do not allow it to.

There was once no greater gulf than that between Milan's image and the reality. But the city is shrugging off its dour image to be "romanized" by a love of the aperitif, brunch and late lounges. Youth and innovation, supported by the city's traditional affluence, have given it one of the most vibrant present tenses in Italy.

"Milan is a **very prudish city,** though people try to make it seem modern and provocative. The Milanese bourgeoisie makes its influence felt even on the younger generation. If they let their hair down, they do it in London or Paris, not at home." Giorgio Armani

> MILAN, LOMBARDIA, ITALY > LOCAL NAME: Milano > LONGITUDE: 9°11' E > LATITUDE: 45°28' N > ALTITUDE: 400 feet/122 metres
> POPULATION: 1,700,000 > TWINNED WITH: Chicago, Daegu (Korea), Osaka, Tel Aviv > NATIVES: Claudio Abbado, Pietro Antigoni,
Giuseppe Arcimboldo, Silvio Berlusconi, Dino Buzzatti, Robert Calvi, Paola Capriola, Caravaggio, Joe Colombo, Bettino Craxi,
Elio Fiorucci, Stefano Gabbana, Giulia Grisi, Paolo Maldini, Alessandro Manzoni, Mario Merz, Gio Ponti, Luchino Visconti
> RESIDENTS: Giorgio Armani, Umberto Eco, Ettore Sottsass, Giuseppe Verdi, Gianni Versace, Leonardo da Vinci

GENERATIONS OF BREADLINE students owe their survival to the Genoese, whose culinary invention gave the world that "when there's nothing else in the fridge" paste of basil, parmesan, pine nuts and olive oil, better known as pesto sauce. But mass-produced supermarket jars do not stand up to the original. A plate of *gnocchi al pesto*, a Ligurian speciality, is one of the treats of a visit to Genoa.

Although it has passed from obscurity to "the new sauce" to fridge staple, pesto was first confectioned to ward off scurvy, a disease to which sailors on long voyages used to be particularly prone. You can bet Genoa's most famous son, Christopher Columbus, had a jar or two on board when he set off across the ocean blue.

The Genoese were well placed to know the maladies of the sea. For centuries, together with the Venetians, the Genoese held supreme power in the Mediterranean. As the principal sponsors of exploration and expansion, the Genoese aristocracy acted as an early World Bank. It was when Columbus felt he had to go to Spain for funding for his project to discover the West Indies (still today the Genoese are known for being tight) that marked Genoa's decline. Venice's more singular beauty has obscured interest in Genoa and its past maritime glory, but of the two

only Genoa still fulfils its historic role as an important trading port, and the restored waterfront of warehouse-museums is beginning to do justice to Genoa's important and noble history.

A true port of oil, rust and brine, refreshingly unselfconscious Genoa has a deliciously seedy side and shows an edge to modern Italian life often obscured by the country's art treasures. Set against the undulating steep verdant slopes of the maritime alps on whose slopes, like the circles in Dante's Hell, lies the enormous Staglieno cemetery, Genoa is a city of neoclassical architecture, laid out on steep, criss-crossing porticoed streets of faded, salt-eaten townhouses with frescoed façades, marble aristocratic residences and in the old medieval centre, tight and playful *caruggi* (alleyways). Among these are classical *palazzi* such as the Palazzo San Giorgio where Marco Polo, while incarcerated, set down in writing his travels to far off lands. In 1904 Filippo Marinetti, father of Futurism had called Genoa "the most futuristic city in Italy". Today set against these classical lines is the modernity of the waterfront Expo area redesigned by the Genoese architect, Renzo Piano, including Europe's largest acquarium and Piano's own "il Bigo" panoramic crane.

Genoa has always been a point of departure, through which, from Buenos Aires to New York and Australasia, has passed a large portion of the world's diaspora. In summer it is invaded by hoards of Italian families boarding ferries to Sardinia, Corsica and Elba. An urban

hub on the Italian Riviera, Genoa is rarely considered a destination in itself (famous jewels such as Portofino, the Cinque Terre and San Remo lie just kilometres away). In the 19th century a group of English sailors went ashore with a football here and founded Italy's oldest football club. Meanwhile, the city gave its name to the famous twilled-cotton cloth the world now knows as jeans.

> "In that bay on your coastline where you can see the sun rise and gently set, the harbour seems not a piece of terra firma but rather a celestial demure." Petrarch

FRANKFURT GERMANY

THE VISITOR ARRIVING at Frankfurt's international airport is greeted by a phalanx of sleek purring Mercedes taxicabs, the standard car of Germany's financial capital, whereupon he or she is whisked in noiseless comfort down the Autobahn and into a gleaming city of abstract, glass towers where the sun does not shine, it merely reflects dazzlingly off the architecture. This is "Bankfurt" – a hi-tech, almost computerized city unashamedly designed around the pursuit of money.

Straddling the banks of the River Main, Frankfurt is also Germany's most American city. Its Tetris skyline leads some to call it "Mainhattan". The taxi-driver may well speak English better than most New Yorkers and if not, will pepper his language with Anglicisms, whether pointing out "*die* Nightclubs" with "*schöne* Ladies" or referring to his "Lifestyle" or "Handy" (mobile phone).

But Frankfurt was not always a futuristic city. Flattened in the Second World War it is the epitome of the German "*Wirtschaftswunder*" (economic miracle); of the hard work and efficiency that have become Germanic bywords, and a desire to put the past behind and build to the future. The "*es muss etwas geschehen*" ("do something!") work ethic is writ large in the form of a chilling, gargantuan golem statue metronomically swinging its anvil outside the tradefair zone. It seems *Arbeit* (work) still "*macht frei*".

The post-war rebuilding process was powered by Germany's *Gastarbeiter*, (guest-workers), principally Turks invited to deploy their manpower and skills. Between businessmen and the extended families of that generation over a quarter of Frankfurt's population are of foreign origin.

Lurking not far beneath Frankfurt's futurism are stout German traditions such as a thick regional dialect, a taste for *Apfelwein* (cider), steak wedges cooked on a stone slab, and the famous sausages that have found their way onto hotdog stands worldwide. The cobbled streets of Sachsenhausen on Frankfurt's Rive Gauche are lined with convivial *Kneipe* full of merry and burly Frankfurters tucking into some serious elbow-grease out of large heavy beer glasses. The picturesque facsimile of Romerberg Square, with its reconstructed timber housing, gives an idea of what the city would have been like when Goethe was born here.

Goethe's *Faust* was the original Romantic fable of a pact made with the devil Mephistopheles in return for an experience to transcend the hollowness of rational knowledge. Modern Frankfurt has made a pact with Mammon in return for a free-wheeling materialistic lifestyle which expresses itself equally in the plush luxury of the city's buildings but also in the seedy underbelly of business-oriented peep-shows and dishevelled parasites that lurk in its windy lees and shadowy alcoves.

Publishers at their beloved, world-famous Book Fair (just one of a cycle of mammoth trade fairs) often will not see more than their hotel, an apparently deserted city and the airport hangars of the city-within-a-city that is the *Messegelände* (Fair Zone). But those that do venture out are rewarded with the experience of a little-suspected parallel universe, of a monied underground youth culture, living it up in innovative bars and clubs – a welcome dose of life and reality among the monuments to illusory stocks and shares that dominate above the surface.

456 > FRANKFURT, HESSEN, GERMANY > LOCAL NAME: Frankfurt am Main > LONGITUDE: 8°41' E > LATITUDE: 50°07' N > ALTITUDE: 338 feet/103 metres
> POPULATION: 650,800 (metro: 3,700,000) > NATIVES: Heinrich Anton de Bary, Ilse Bing, Adam Elsheimer, Marie de Flavigny (aka Daniel Stern), Anne Frank, Johann Wolfgang von Goethe, Michael Gross, Heinrich Hoffman, Willi Messerschmitt, Mayer Amschel Rothschild, Uwe Schmidt (aka Señor Coconut), Regula Venske > RESIDENTS: William Forsythe

"That silver and gold
hole through which
flows from German
lands everything that
flows, grows, or is
coined and beaten."

Martin Luther

ZURICH IS THE HOME OF the fabled Swiss Bank Account, that byword for measureless untouchable wealth, rendered shadily glamorous by decades of espionage and gangster films and their stories of eight-digit numbers left in airport lockers.

Geneva and Zurich are the two international metropolitan faces of the Confederation Helvetica, but while the former, French and Romansch capital, is the gentile residence of retirees and diplomacy, its German counterpart, as befits the sharp zig-zag of its name, is the land of snappy suits and Alpine quartz, stop-watch precision.

Like Geneva, Zurich is also a lakeside city. The thin, placid mirror of the Zurchersee extends east of the city, offering up calm reflections of a bucolic, lego-like countryside of neat red-roofed villages and church spires – and beyond them, the Alps, weekend playground of bankers: some of the finest skiing in Europe is only a short drive away, in nearby Flims, Zermatt or that original resort of the jet set (and now the Easy Jet set), St Moritz.

Bonds, drafts and funds have long provided Zurich with its lifeblood and smooth assured lifestyle, but they have also ensured the city's injection of youth, and all the zest, regeneration and constant reinvention that brings. The right bank of the River Limmat is a cosmopolitan hub of cutting-edge designer bars, and the city's former warehouse district, ZuriWest, is undergoing the obligatory summary loft conversion, by night the scene of an experimental DJ rave scene revelling in little-suspected Swiss drum 'n' bass and techno-trance. Such swilling wealth attracts parasites, and Zurich has long been cursed with a seedy underbelly and prolific drug scene that littered its public parks and belied the smooth clockwork exterior. But in a gesture of classic Swiss revisionism Zurich's authorities have now largely swept this under the carpet.

Yet beneath the ephemeral fads of global youth fizzles a stoutly distinct local culture. Zurich's "*Back und Brau*" bakery-cum-brewery restaurants are still thriving: the local speciality of raclette and cheese fondu is not just a tourist attraction but a staple of Switzerland's rural mountain roots, and Sprungli still serves the best Swiss chocolate confections in the city. And while the language of investments and interest rates may be an Anglicized patois, even speakers of *Hoch Deutsch* (high German) may find themselves floundering in the local dialect of Schweizer Deutsch. To balance its materialist image Zurich also boasts culture of international import, such as Chagall's stained-glass windows in the Gothic Fraumunster Church (a rare flourish in the austere climate of Zurich's underlying Protestantism) and the Kunsthaus, whose collection of Picassos, Rodins and Impressionists is priceless in comparison with any gilded vault.

Zurich feels as if it ought to be a capital in a country whose multi-facets resist such classification. So, instead, it lingers in between, not quite central to European affairs but a safe deposit box for when the markets have closed. Smooth, confident and accountable only to itself, and the very definition of swish.

"So there was mystery in Zurich; there was more than cuckoo clocks. There was irony. There was rebellion. There was the cafe Voltaire and the birth of Dada, right in the middle of the bloodiest war ever fought." Carlos Fuentes

> ZURICH, SWITZERLAND > LOCAL NAME: Zürich > LONGITUDE: 8°32' E > LATITUDE: 47°23' N > ALTITUDE: 1,339 feet/408 metres > POPULATION: 363,000 > TWINNED WITH: Kunming (China)
> NATIVES: Alain de Botton, Fischli and Weiss, Robert Frank, Max Frisch, Johann Füssli, Bruno Ganz, Johann Pestalozzi, Hermann Rorschach
> RESIDENTS: Jean Arp, Albert Einstein, Carl Jung, Patricia Kass, Thomas Mann, Tina Turner

459

STRASBOURG FRANCE

THE AVENUE GÉNÉRAL-DE-GAULLE in Strasbourg has, over the years, variously been named after Napoleon, the Kaiser, the French Republic and Adolf Hitler, an indicator of the pendulum effect of the French and German influences which have long vied for domination over the city. The French held sway from 1681 until the 1870s, when the Prussians took control until the end of the First World War; in the Second World War it was re-Germanized under the Nazis. Strasbourg is now part of France, and has been for nearly 60 years, but Germany is only a matter of miles east across the Rhine. Here in Alsace, the renowned dish of *choucroute garnie* is, by any other criterion, sauerkraut, sausage and bacon.

The twin forces at play have not, however, created a curate's egg (nor even an *oeuf de vicaire* or a *Hilfspfarrersei*), but something particularly Alsatian, a race who are something of a law unto themselves. There is enough space between the city and the French capital to give Strasbourg plenty of elbow room: the city contains France's only other National Theatre, and the Alsatian dialect, Elsässisch, is still an actively living language.

The city occupies a central position within Europe, roughly equidistant between Paris and Salzburg, or Malmö and Barcelona – in fact it was the Franks who first dubbed it Strasbourg, the city of roads.

So it was perfectly natural that after the Second World War there was support for a proposal, by the British politician Ernest Bevin, that the Council of Europe be based here; in time the European Parliament and Court of Human Rights followed suit.

Strasbourg offers the Eurocrats much to appreciate. The pink Vosges sandstone mass of the Romanesque-cum-Gothic cathedral is surmounted by a 15th-century spire and a double cross of Lorraine which made it the tallest building in Christendom until the 19th century (from the top of the spire the Black Forest is visible). Marie Antoinette was in fact received there on her way from Vienna to marry the future Louis XV1. Nearby the opulent palace of the Rohan family, who provided the city with a clutch of bishops and cardinals, is now home to three museums, while the south-western corner of the city's main island, the *Grande Ile*, is the extremely photogenic Petite France, full of willow trees, covered bridges and half-timbered houses, where tanners, fishermen and millers once worked.

Throughout each December the island is home to a Christmas market, the *Christkindlesmärik*, where warming *Glühwein* is the tipple of the season; among the cobbled streets of Petite France, the twin cultures of Strasbourg continue to co-exist.

"Sire, Strasbourg is yours."
The Marquis de Louvois to Louis XIV, 1681

> STRASBOURG, BAS-RHIN, FRANCE > LONGITUDE: 7°44' E > LATITUDE: 48°35' N > ALTITUDE: 141 feet/43 metres > POPULATION: 258,800 (metro: 451,200) > TWINNED WITH: Boston, Kyoto,
Leicester (UK), Miami Beach FL > NATIVES: Jean Arp, Gustave Doré, Sébastien Erard, Jean-Baptiste Kléber, Marcel Marceau, Jacques Martin, Charles Munch, Marie Tussaud, Arséne Wenger
> RESIDENTS: John Calvin, Johannes Gutenberg, Albert Schweitzer

"The industrial capital of Italy,
famed for its architecture..."

The Italian Job

> TURIN, PIEMONTE, ITALY > LOCAL NAME: Torino > LONGITUDE: 7°41' E > LATITUDE: 45º04' N > ALTITUDE: 784 feet/239 metres > POPULATION: 963,000 > TWINNED WITH: Chambéry (France), Cologne, Córdoba (Argentina), Detroit, Gaza, Geneva, Glasgow, Haifa (Israel), Liège (Belgium), Lille, Lyon, Rotterdam, Shenyang (China), Volgograd (Russia) > NATIVES: Gianni Agnelli, Giacomo Balla, Alessandro Baricco, Alighiero Boetti, Camillo Cavour, Massimo d'Azeglio, Luciano Fabro, Battista Farina, Joseph Lagrange, Carlo Levi, Primo Levi, Rita Levi-Montalcini, Rita Pavone, Nina Ricci, Paolo Soleri, Victor Emmanuel II > RESIDENTS: Italo Calvino, Natalia Ginzburg, Mario Merz, Friedrich Nietzsche, Cesare Pavese

TURIN DESERVES A SPECIAL place in the hearts of film fans. It was here that in 1969 Charlie Croker, the swaggering cockney played by Michael Caine, was sent by Noel Coward along with Benny Hill and a bunch of public school rally drivers to steal 4 million dollars in gold from the Italian government, "to help with Britain's balance of payments".

The capital of Piemonte sits in the foothills of the Italian Alps, that made it host city for the 2006 Winter Olympics, under the teeth of Mont Blanc and the Matterhorn. The film opens with Beckermann sweeping romantically through breathtaking Alpine scenery in his Lamborghini to the accompaniment of Matt Monro singing "On Days like These".

Unlike the concentric chaos of most Italian towns, Turin's centre is laid out in a Parisian grid of regal and imperial boulevards dating from the city's time as Italy's capital under the Dukes of Savoy. When the convoy escorting the gold bullion arrives it turns left by the grandiose Porta Nuova station, up the utopian marble of Mussolini's Via Roma, the city's arcaded central column, and through the baroque Piazza San Carlo, whose shaded arches are home to the Turin's most decadent bars and cafés. Turin's symmetry turns out to be its downfall, as Caine, cunningly disguised as an English fan, is able to make his way through a network of courtyards and inter-connecting arches straight into the ornate marble foyer of the Museum of Egypt, the largest Egyptian museum after Cairo.

At the delta of Via Roma is Piazza Castello,

nowadays a much calmer place since revision of Turin's traffic circulation gave priority to the city's beautiful rickety, orange trams. A fountain now provides for calmer contemplation of the square's splendours – the centrepiece Palazzo Madama, the ornate balconies and window-trimmings of the burgeoning opera-house, and the faded rosy grandeur of the Palazzo Reale, reminiscent of Versailles and once the seat of the Italian royal family.

The scene is set for one of cinema's most famous car chases, first sacrilegiously down the museum's baroque staircases, in and out of arcades, eluding blundering *carabinieri* on motorcycles and disrupting the leisurely *passeggiate* of the locals, up onto the Fiat factory's rooftop testing track, skirting the edge of the romantic Parco Valentino, and arriving at the edge of the majestic River Po. The three minis then cross the weir to the riverside *murazzi*, Turin's former cargo bays and boathouses, and now the centre of a night-life that has made the city a real pole of alternative music from reggae and jazz to disaffected rap.

With not a thought for the famous Shroud (or is it?) or the delectable Gianduja chocolate, in his haste, Michael Caine was not the most curious of tourists. He missed the understated treasures of an underrated city only to find himself minutes later with the fortunes of the British treasury and the fate of his ill-starred gang hanging very much in the balance in a bus off the edge of an Alp.

MONTE CARLO MONACO

WHAT AN EXTRAORDINARY PLACE Monte Carlo is: an exquisite Fabergé egg of a city on permanent display between the Alps and the Mediterranean, the private fiefdom of the Grimaldi family for some seven centuries. In their backyard this tiny city half the size of Central Park (Monaco is the name of the principality) hosts a motley crew of high rollers, tax exiles and, at the Grand Prix every May, the circusfolk of Formula One, some working flat out in the heat and dust, others simply lounging in high-octane luxury, raising a glass of champagne their only hardship. The allure of the Côte d'Azur and the power of the automobile came together all too tragically in the 1982 car accident that took the life of Princess Grace, middle America's very own fairy princess, the bride of Prince Rainier III, and cast a pall over the whole city. Rainier's forefathers had first wrested it from the control of the Genoese in the 14th century, and after much protracted tussling, the Grimaldis eventually gained Monaco's complete independence from France: to ensure the name was not in danger of dying out, any man who married a Grimaldi woman promptly adopted their surname.

At one low point in the family fortunes (they'd already sold off the towns Menton and Roquebrune to France), the then prince, Charles III, hit on the wheeze of installing a casino at Monte Carlo, inspired by the one at Baden-Baden. Opened in 1863, it became a massive money-spinner for Monte Carlo which became a byword for idle raffishness ("a sunny place for shady people" was Somerset

Maugham's much quoted aphorism) and only regained an aura of glamour courtesy of Rainier and Grace. Such were the revenues that taxation was expendable, and to this day Monte Carlo remains a tax haven. Amongst the beneficiaries – who tend to live in the anonymous 1980s apartment blocks of Fontvieille – are a high proportion of Formula One drivers. The Grand Prix, first staged in 1929, is the last of the street races on the F1 calendar. As World Champion Phil Hill once said, "If you suggested running a race here for the first time, you would be considered to be mad and out of touch with reality." The two-mile (3.2 km), 80-second route touches almost all of the key parts of Monaco, zipping across the everyday road markings, up steep climbs, round the tight bends of La Rascasse or Ste-Devote, the cars flashing past the frontages of Gucci and Chanel, yards from packed restaurant terraces and hotel balconies. They pass the royal palace (with its toytown cannons and pith-helmeted sentries) and pile through the Casino square before dropping down to the arcaded curve of the waterfront tunnel and onto the tamarisk-lined promenade.

It may be that, as some social observers bemoan, there has been a decline in Monte Carlo's cachet – too many nouveaux riches, too few manners – but, regardless, most cities would only too happily accept this level of tarnish. Following Rainier's death in 2005, the city's well-heeled inhabitants were left to wonder just how long the benefits of his lengthy rule would last.

> MONTE CARLO, MONACO > LOCAL NAME: Monte-Carlo > LONGITUDE: 7°25' E > LATITUDE: 43°44' N > ALTITUDE: 23 feet/7 metres > POPULATION: 15,400
> NATIVES: Fanny Ardant, Léo Ferré, Caroline and Stephanie of Monaco > RESIDENTS: Björn Borg, Anthony Burgess, Shirley Conran, David Coulthard, Alain Ducasse
Daniela Hantuchova, Grace Kelly (Princess Grace), Ringo Starr

"The harbour is always full of boats
and beautiful people,
but you can't let it distract you.
When you see the ladies, topless
and drinking champagne,
you have to keep focused." David Coulthard

"The days succeed one another here
with a beauty I would
describe as brazen."

Friedrich Nietzsche

> NICE, ALPES-MARITIMES, FRANCE > LONGITUDE: 7°17' E > LATITUDE: 43°42' N > ALTITUDE: 32 feet/10 metres > POPULATION: 343,100 (metro: 888,784) > TWINNED WITH: Edinburgh, Houston, Miami
> NATIVES: Arman (Armand Fernandez), Albert Calmette, Henry Cavendish, Nicole Farhi, Giuseppe Garibaldi, Yves Klein, Jacques Médecin, Simone Veil > RESIDENTS: Alphonse Karr, Maurice Maeterlinck, Henri Matisse, Friedrich Nietzsche

IF BRIGHTON IS a worn-out window-girl, Nice has matured from one of the beautiful girls who still decorate its combed private beaches in summer to a mature, sophisticated *femme d'un certain âge*; slightly past her prime, but without the need for make-up – an experienced *grande dame* of a city, the Catherine Deneuve of the French Riviera. Nice is the French alternative to Britain's fish 'n chips.

It took a while to catch on with the English – they would not come, it is rumoured, until they had the Promenade des Anglais named after them – but in time Nice became the colony and continental bathing place of choice among the jet set, jazzmen and "itsy-bitsy teenie-weenie yellow polka dot bikini" brigade of the roaring '20s.

Nice had been joined to France only in 1860, and the first train steamed through the Alpes Maritimes and into the station in 1864, aboard it the trend-setting Romanov, Tsar Nicholas and King Leopold II of Belgium. Nice still has the largest Russian Orthodox church outside the motherland, on Rue Paradis, and it can be no coincidence that the Romanov love for Nice led to so many paintings by Henri Matisse ending up in the Hermitage. Today Russia's nouveaux riches contribute significantly to Nice's expat contingent. But they are just part of a *salade niçoise* of international Louis Vuitton dandies with delusions of aristocracy who swan day-long past the sky-blue iron chairs on the promenade, men hands behind back and ladies with spoilt yapping poodles at their heeled feet. Always a con-strip of pickpockets and *artistes ambulants*, nowadays they also have to circumnavigate the roller-bladers and skate-boarders (some of Europe's best) who treat their catwalk as a competition arena. More Club Med than Gentlemen's Club, even the palm-trees were imported from Africa.

But like Brighton there is inevitably more to France's fifth city than its deckchairs. Skyscrapers and office blocks are the substance behind the baroque façades of the sea front and Negresco Hotel. Both are undeniably cities of the flesh, and in summer there is little Niçoise that goes unbronzed. The busy, open main square of place Massena indicates a working city that is more than a resort, while on rue de Suède the café and bars are alive with a vitality that outlives *les vacances*. Beneath the château on top of the hill of *vieux* Nice is a steep maze of medieval streets, wall to wall with fish restaurants and bars serving local *socca* (egg pancakes). Such picturesque old mazes are typical of the Riviera, but in Nice the air is more metropolitan.

"*Plus ça change, plus c'est la même chose*," said Alphonse Karr, a famous resident of the city. Summers will come and go, but Nice will always be the entry point for the Côte d'Azur, a beautiful ageing actress superior to the newcomers that adorn la Croisette every May at nearby Cannes, who knows all the secrets of femininity and has palms already at her feet.

COLOGNE GERMANY

IF THERE IS A SYMBOL THAT encapsulates the romantic German soul it is the Rhine, river of legend and lore, hiding place of the Ring at the core of both Wagner's opera cycle and Tolkein's trilogy and, on a rock just south of Cologne home of the Lorelei, the original femme fatale and siren who attracted sailors to her beauty only to dash them on the rocks.

The Rhine has been Germany's lifeblood for centuries, and the barges that still ply the greeny-blue swell past Cologne, so laden as to seem submerged, are reminiscent of trade in a romantic pre-motorcar age.

Water was always central to Cologne, from the time the Romans founded the original settlement here on the Rhine's banks and bequeathed it 12 still-standing romanesque churches, to the original perfumed toilet water (originally thought to be an aphrodisiac) that has been splashed on generations of hopeful smooth-shaven cheeks in search of a nightclub Lorelei. Still today the classic view of Cologne is of its skyline first perceived from the river, the brick and half-timbered architecture of the *Fachwerkhaeuser* prefacing the neat romanesque symmetry of the Altstadt, with, towering above it, the spiked spires of Cologne's mighty gothic cathedral, which critics chastize as being a tourist-trap out of synch with the city's Roman origins, and which is so big that the locals joke it has never not been covered in scaffolding, undergoing repairs ever since it was finished.

The Kölner are an irreverent lot, known throughout Germany for a spontaneous talkativeness and relaxed air that is positively southern Italian. Appropriately, Cologne is Germany's carnival city, whose proceedings begin with German precision at 11am on 11/11 every year on the Alter Markt marketplace in the old centre and reach their peak in February in the Sudstadt southern district of the city. Their city is the capital of German comedy (if there is such a thing), Edinburgh-style theatre and art, and the streets of the up-and-coming Belgisches Viertel district are littered with trendy galleries. None is more famous, though, than the central Ludwig modern art museum wallpapered with Picassos.

True to its carnival soul Cologne knows how to have a good time, and its Italianate manner and climate of artistic experimentation have made it coincidentally the gay capital of Germany. Beer here is a connoisseur's art form, with many of the bars having their own special brew (with 24 breweries in the city, beer is the real eau de Cologne), each a brand of the light, highly-fermented and aromatically bitter *Kölesch*, always consumed with the obligatory *Reibekuchen* (grated roast potatoes), and *Sauerbraten* (marinated beef with raisins). In the best and most raucous establishments this is traditionally served by barmen known as *Kobes*, famed for their sparring and upfront demeanour who carry around great wooden crates of the local tall thin beer glasses and notch up dashes for each beer on your table like days on a pleasurable prison wall.

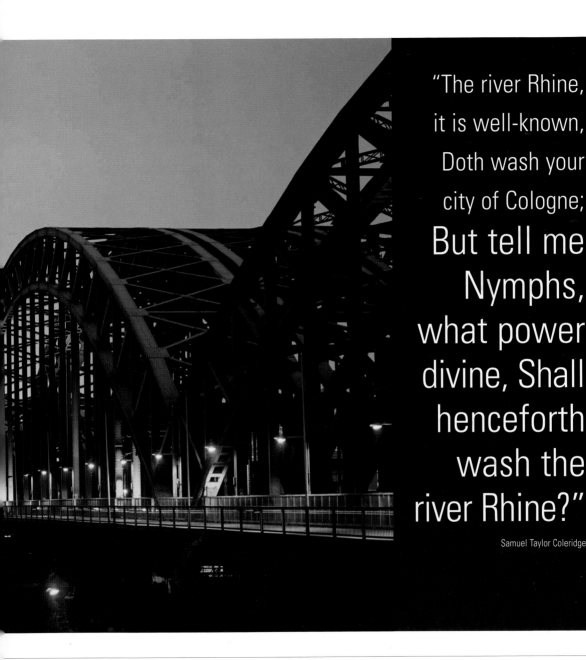

"The river Rhine,
it is well-known,
Doth wash your
city of Cologne;
But tell me
Nymphs,
what power
divine, Shall
henceforth
wash the
river Rhine?"

Samuel Taylor Coleridge

> COLOGNE, NORDRHEIN-WESTFALIA, GERMANY > LOCAL NAME: Köln > LONGITUDE: 6°57' E > LATITUDE: 50°56' N > ALTITUDE: 141 feet/43 metres > POPULATION: 960,000 (metro: 3,067,000)
> TWINNED WITH: Bethlehem (West Bank), Cork, Indianapolis IN, Kyoto, Lille, Liverpool > NATIVES: Agrippina the Younger, Konrad Adenauer, Dirk Bikkenbergs, Heinrich Böll, Max Bruch, Hans Haacke, Nico, Jacques Offenbach, Ruth Prawer Jhabvala, Benedikt Taschen > RESIDENTS: John Duns Scotus, Max Ernst, Stefan Lochner, Gerhard Richter

469

"On the bank
of that lovely
stream, where
Folly grows
upon the green
mountains,
is harvested in
the autumn,
put in a cellar,
poured into
vessels, and
sent to foreign
countries."

Heinrich Heine

6°47' E

DÜSSELDORF IS A CITY WITH two very distinct personalities. It is the sober business capital of Nordrhein-Westfalia, Germany's most heavily industrialized and populous state, but it is also a serious party town where the number of drinking establishments along the Altstadt has earned it the nickname of "the world's longest bar". This combination of hard work and harder play proved rather appealing to the media and advertising agencies of Germany, who relocated *en masse* to the Medienhafen dockland area, and whose creative gurus are able to air-kiss each other when they bump into each other on the Königsallee. The "Kö" is an elegant, chestnut and plane tree-lined avenue which is one of the country's most upscale shopping streets. For good or ill, status and conspicuous wealth are sought-after commodities in Düsseldorf.

Accordingly, the architecture of the city is forward-looking. It received its fair share of bombs in the Second World War, but whereas Dresden has spent vast efforts renovating its baroque buildings to their former glory, Düsseldorf took the opportunity to move ahead. A combination of steel, glass and aluminium presents a vision of a bright, shining (and prosperous) future as gleaming as a smile from local girl Claudia Schiffer. This is the fashion hub of Germany, although when Napoleon called it "*mon petit Paris*", he was referring less to any *haute couture* comparisons than to the city's elegant confidence.

Though modern in outlook, Düsseldorf does appreciate its past. The twisted spire of the St Lambertus Basilica and the circular Schlossturm are both medieval relics. The Kaufhof department store is an art nouveau treat, and one of Germany's first skyscrapers, the Wilhelm-Marx-Haus of 1924, is a precursor of its contemporary cousins.

Beer is big in Germany, and in Düsseldorf the speciality is Altbier, a dark and slightly sweet, malty brew, best grabbed at a stand-up table under a heater in winter, or supped at any one of the 300 or so pubs, bars and beerhalls on the cobbled Altstadt – perhaps accompanied by a platter of *Sauerbraten, Blutwurst* (black pudding) and onions, or even *Martinsgans* (goose) served with red cabbage, apple and chestnuts.

But although the cuisine is hearty, solid fare, and the city's old nickname "*Schreibtisch des Ruhr*" ("clerks' desk of the Ruhr") is a reference to a preponderance of accountants and paper-pushers, a love of art is not overlooked, especially as Düsseldorf is slightly touchy about the cultural prominence of Cologne, only 25 miles (40km) south. At the Kunstsammlung, the centrepiece is a collection of works by Paul Klee, a professor at the Art Academy until he was denounced as degenerate by the Nazis, and the city is extremely proud to be the birthplace of the 19th-century poet Heinrich Heine.

> DÜSSELDORF, NORDRHEIN-WESTFALIA, GERMANY > LONGITUDE: 6°47' E > LATITUDE: 51°13' N > ALTITUDE: 125 feet/38 metres > POPULATION: 563,000 (metro: 2,978,696) > TWINNED WITH: Haifa (Israel), Moscow, Osaka, Reading (UK), Warsaw > NATIVES: Peter von Cornelius, Heinrich Heine, Heike Makatsch, Reinhard Mucha, Claudia Schiffer, Jan Wellem, Wim Wenders > RESIDENTS: Joseph Beuys, Andreas Gursky, Paul Klee, Friedrich von Schadow, Robert Schumann, Xenia Seeberg, Thomas Struth

CONVENTIONALLY, GENEVA IS viewed as a paradigm of neutrality, diplomacy and consensus. Admirable traits but also attributes that attract derision and have not granted the city the kind of colourful history and consequent personality that make it a destination. When assessing the benefits of war and corruption on a country's culture, Orson Welles's character in the classic film *The Third Man* famously attributed the emergence of Italy's Michelangelo and Leonardo to the Borgias' bloodbath, while claiming that Switzerland's centuries of democracy and peace had produced only the cuckoo clock.

No doubt that Geneva-born *penseur* par excellence Jean-Jacques Rousseau would have thought very differently, as would Henry Dunant, the winner of the first ever Nobel Peace Prize in 1901 and founder of the Red Cross. It seems somehow appropriate that the country whose flag is a white cross on a red background – paradoxically known to most through that misnomer and favourite military accessory, the Swiss Army penknife, should be here in Geneva the home of the organization whose flag is its mirror and complement.

The Geneva Convention set out new standards for human rights, and the city is the European headquarters of the United Nations (or "Untied Nations", depending on your point of view), whose diplomats account both for a third of the city's population and for the city's generally sedate and sobre air.

Split by the Rhône River Geneva occupies a chocolate-box setting on the south-western tip of Lake Geneva. Joining the city is the Pont du Mont Blanc, on one side the diplomatic quarter of hotels, residences and the famous row of international flags outside the Palais des Nations; on the other the clean, even twee, cobbled streets of the *vieille ville*, the old town and the lively embankment of bars and restaurants along Quai General Guisan. To the east, through the intermittent plume of the 390 foot (119m) Jet d'Eau fountain and across the mirror of water woven by the wakes of yachts, wind-surfers and motorboats, rise the peaks of the Alps, among them the white shoulder of Mont Blanc itself, which for many are Geneva's principal attraction and for which the city is a springboard. Verbier, Megève, Chamonix – many of Europe's oldest and most famous ski resorts, virtual suburbs of the city, are within an hour's drive, and many of Geneva residents have second homes in the mountains, a favourite year-round retreat at weekends.

Geneva itself seems something of a retreat. Predominantly inhabited by a now-mature postwar generation, a rarefied air of old-world courtesies remains and Geneva still symbolizes a Switzerland that is a haven of affluent calm where, as if nowhere else, life's little luxuries can be found and truly enjoyed in peace.

"His 'Let's go to Palermo' was an unambiguous erotic message and her 'I prefer Geneva' could only have one meaning: his mistress no longer desired him."

Milan Kundera, *The Unbearable Lightness of Being*

> GENEVA, SWITZERLAND > LOCAL NAME: Genève > LONGITUDE: 6°9' E > LATITUDE: 46°13' N > ALTITUDE: 1,224 feet/373 metres > POPULATION: 180,000 > TWINNED WITH: Geneva AL
> NATIVES: Charles Bonnet, Henry Dunant, Jean-Etienne Liotard, Jean-Jacques Rousseau, Ferdinand de Saussure > RESIDENTS: Isabelle Adjani, Ernesto Bertarelli, Jorge Luis Borges, Albert Cohen, Jean-Claude Killy, Nastassja Kinski, Amélie Mauresmo, Carlos Moya, François Voltaire

LUXEMBOURG LUXEMBOURG

WHEN THE EMPEROR CHARLEMAGNE died he divided his kingdom between his three sons. The Frankish west, the Teutonic east and the kingdom in the middle each had a slice of Europe. But in the absence of the emperor's unifying grip the heirs descended into internecine feuding as two of the brothers sought to get their hands on the middle kingdom. An ethnic and linguistic faultline can be traced from Flanders through to the Alto Aldige in north-east Italy, and there is a school of thought that sees the whole history of Europe in the battle between these two big brothers. No city more than Luxembourg bears the scars of this conflict, and therefore the imprint of Europe.

Struck by its defensive capabilities it was Count Siegefroid of Ardennes who in the 10th century built his castle here on the rocky promontory known as the Bock, overlooking the gorges of the Petrusse and Alzette river valleys. To better defend his fortress Siegefroid built a labyrinth of *casemates,* subterranean passages hewn into the rock, and for its unassailability Luxembourg became known as the Gibraltar of the North. But the city's defences became the envy of warring European states, who sought to establish a stronghold there. Successively attacked by the Burgundians, French, Spaniards, Austrians and Prussians, Luxembourg was besieged and destroyed as many as 20 times in the space of 400 years.

The turning point came in 1830, when following the Belgian secession Luxembourg claimed independence from the United Kingdom of the Netherlands and turned its back on arms and defence. In a declaration of their future neutrality in European affairs, the citizens of Luxembourg torched their coveted fortress, so that today only a few ruined ramparts remain.

Throughout the industrial age Luxembourg lived off its iron-ore deposits, until, as these were waning, the Grand Duchy reinvented itself as an alternative Switzerland with favourable banking and taxation laws to woo the international rich. Ever since, Luxembourg has been one of Europe's most affluent states, a city that put the deluxe into the Benelux economic union. Luxembourg is an archetype and multilingual model of today's European union, with open borders and an identity drawn from its neighbouring giants, France and Germany (although Luxembourgish is still the language of the street).

Even without its fortress Luxembourg inspires a sense of medieval fortification that the modern eye finds romantic. Winding down from the Bock, the Chemin de la Corniche has been called Europe's most beautiful balcony, beneath which lies the cobblestone lower town of Grund, the Grand Ducal Palace and the meeting of two rivers. Luxembourg is a tiny place where the Duke can be seen shopping of a Saturday afternoon and, apocryphally, the government ministers' numbers are in the phonebook. But it is a proud and unique island in the geopolitical landscape of Europe, representing a foothold in a time when the continent was a patchwork of similar city-states.

"On a clear day, from the terrace, you can't see Luxembourg at all. This is because a tree is in the way." Alan Coren

> LUXEMBOURG, LUXEMBOURG > LONGITUDE: 6°08' E > LATITUDE: 49°36' N > ALTITUDE: 115 feet/340 metres > POPULATION: 80,700
> NATIVES: Robert Schuman, Edward Steichen

IN SOME CITIES, LIKE ALGIERS, each street corner offers a view of the sea; in others, like Kuala Lumpur or Toronto, it is a towering man-made structure that catches the eye. Grenoble, on the other hand, is dominated at every turn by the limestone massifs which surround it, the very mountains that brought the Winter Olympics here in 1968 – *ah oui*, the year Jean-Claude Killy cleaned up in the Alpine skiing events. Grenoble is effectively the capital city of the Alps; Austria's Innsbruck is its only rival for the title.

As the bubble-podded *téléphérique*, slanting up to the promontory-top Fort de la Bastille, rises over the red roofs of the city, forested slopes – snowbound in winter, meadow-clad in summer – come into view. Below, the loop of the Isère has the milky-green colour of all authentic mountain rivers, and when the visibility is good, Mont Blanc can be made out to the north east. Grenoble is a base for rock climbing, kayaking, trekking, mountain-biking – and skiing, of course: Chamrousse, the old Olympic village, is only 20 miles (32km) away up in the Belledonne range.

But it's not all hearty outdoor living – the crystal-clear Alpine air of the mountains (the city itself lies in a bowl that captures some rather nasty pollution) is as good for the brain as it is for the body. Of the "I'm a writer, not a hiker" fraternity, Stendhal is the city's most famed product. Grenoble has a reputation for enlightened urban thinking (especially under mayor Hubert Dubedout, whose 20-year reign began in 1966) and is now one of Europe's leading centres of hi-tech and scientific research.

A significant student population brings a youthful energy to the cafés and bars around the places St André, aux Herbes or Grenette – this is a city of squares – in the medieval quarter, which was built when Grenoble was the main city of the Dauphiné region, its Fort protecting this valley passage through the Massif de la Chartreuse. Up in those mountains, the viscous yellow and green Chartreuse liqueurs are produced by Carthusian monks to a recipe so sacrosanct that at any one time only three of the monks are allowed to know the recipe, and each of those is only allowed to know one part of the formula.

Now served by the TGV (three hours north to Paris or south to Marseilles), Grenoble's quality of life has attracted a new breed of residents, well-off but also eco-conscious, "*les bobos*" as the French call them. This is a city of discreet charms and a proud past; its stout resistance during the Second World War, when Italian forces occupied and the maquisards secreted themselves up in the Vercors massif, earned Grenoble the Croix de la Libération. Accordingly the city takes its civic duties seriously: Grenoblesse oblige.

476 > GRENOBLE, ISÈRE, FRANCE > LONGITUDE: 5°44' E > LATITUDE: 45°11' N > ALTITUDE: 702 feet/214 metres > POPULATION: 150,500 (metro: 419,300) > TWINNED WITH: Phoenix AZ, Ouagadougou, Oxford
> NATIVES: Jean Dréjac, St Rose Philippine Duchesne, Miss Kittin, Stendhal, Jacques de Vaucanson > RESIDENTS: Isabelle Bihr, Jean-François Champollion

"The poplars standing up in bright blue air, the silver turmoil of the broad Isère, and sheer pale cliffs that wait through Earth's long moon."

James Elroy Flecker, *From Grenoble*

MARSEILLES FRANCE

PROUD MARSEILLES IS in many ways the most North African of French cities: during the colonial era its quays and wharves were the gateway to Algiers, Tunis and Tangiers. But it is equally Provençal, from its olive oil soaps to its *terrains de boules* and plane trees, and the city's setting on a coastline pitted with the inaccessible rocky creeks called *calanques* could only be the South of France.

The capital of the Midi is rougher and tougher than the Côte d'Azur resorts or its scholarly neighbour Aix-en-Provence. Right in its centre, the rectangular old Port is chock-full of yachts and fishing boats, its sides clustered with hotels, restaurants and bars offering refreshing pastis. Behind the port are steep hills, on top of which Notre Dame de la Garde gleamingly surveys the bustle below. Off to the east the corniche sweeps past a shimmering sea in which the Château d'If – the prison island setting for *The Count Of Monte Cristo* – sits squat and implacable. The Cité Radieuse, Le Corbusier's imaginative 1940s housing project, offers views both of hills and a sea which Van Gogh described

(and which local boy Eric Cantona would probably have loved to have described) as having the ever-changing colour of mackerel.

Since the TGV opened up to Marseilles in 2001, whisking passengers down from Paris in just over three hours, the city has become very *à la mode* for out of towners seeking a 19th-century townhouse apartment with a sea view and sun. Earlier residents were the Ligurians and Phocaeans – hence the nickname for residents of "*phocéens*" – and then the usual Mediterranean crew of Romans and Greeks. The activities of the more unscrupulous incomers helped earn Marseilles a reputation as being (like all port cities) louche and dodgy, an image further fostered by *The French Connection*. It is a reputation the city is keen to shrug off and one hard to square with its friendly vibe, although Marseilles is capable, if required, of turning in on itself like an armadillo to reject all boarders as well as the mistral wind that scoots down the Rhône Valley.

Modern Marseilles retains a split between its poor and rich quarters (traditionally demarcated by the main avenue

La Canebière), but there is much change afoot, not least the regeneration of the docklands under the Euroméditerranée project. Marcel Pagnol's Marseilles trilogy of melodramatic plays evoking life in the city before the Second World War now seems rather dated – this is the hip-hop capital of France (a movement spearheaded by IAM), with a thriving culture of movie-making (led by Luc Besson) and thriller-writing.

One thing will never change: the mighty *bouillabaisse*, the traditional Marseilles dish for which the translation "fish stew" barely implies the richness of its nuances. Connoisseurs have their own favourite variations, but the constant is *rascasse*, the scorpion fish, plus the fresh catch of day and seasoning that includes fennel, saffron, thyme and bay-leaf. At serious *bouillabaisse* restaurants, a strictly codified preparation ends with the ritual bestowing of all-encompassing napkins. Starters and desserts are a luxury; one serving of the dish fills the stomach in the same way that Marseilles sates every one of the senses.

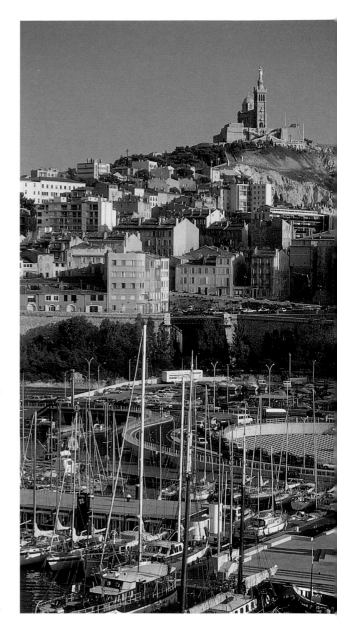

"The one great city in France that does not advertise the grandeur of the past, or oppress you with the weight of its monuments."

Bruce Chatwin

> MARSEILLES, BOUCHES-DU-RHÔNE, FRANCE > LOCAL NAME: Marseille > LONGITUDE: 5°23' E > LATITUDE: 43°18' N > ALTITUDE: 39 feet/12 metres > POPULATION: 800,500 (metro: 1,231,000)
> TWINNED WITH: Haifa (Israel), Hamburg, Kobe (Japan), Odessa, Portsmouth (UK) > NATIVES: Antonin Artaud, César Baldaccini, Maurice Béjart, Eric Cantona, Honoré Daumier, Fernandel, Sebastien Grosjean, Louis Jourdan, Marius Petipa, Joseph Pujol (Le Pétomane), Jean-Pierre Rampal, Edmond Rostand, Zinédine Zidane
> RESIDENTS: Yves Montand, Marcel Pagnol, Raymond Petit, Chris Waddle

479

AMSTERDAM OFFERS AN intriguing mix of the overt and the covert, the upfront and the clandestine. The city has achieved its justified renown for what it has been happy to expose, be it a Rembrandt painting or the prostitutes sitting in the "shop windows" of the red-light district. But on further acquaintance, the city offers less visible attractions, nuggets of beauty or history that merit exploration.

Thankfully, even Amsterdam's clichés are still rewarding. The canals are genteel and harmonious; the four concentric rings of the Grachtengordel form watery boulevards lined with soft trees, through which the light is definitively dappled. The tall, red-brick, round-gabled townhouses (from the top of which jut pulleys for drawing up supplies), humpbacked bridges and cobbled paths physically define the shape of the old city's heart and recall its 17th-century Golden Age.

There is art and culture aplenty, enough for a lifetime of viewing: Rembrandts and Vermeers are highlights of the massive Rijksmuseum (the only truly monumental building in this intimate city), Van Gogh merits a museum all to himself, and more recent stars, Mondrian in particular, are showcased at the Stedelijk. The Concertgebouw orchestra and the Dutch National Ballet are world-class. And then there is the counter culture, the earthier city of Jacques Brel's "Port Of Amsterdam": the whores – cheery, though oddly unerotic in their matter-of-factness – and the haziness of the marijuana coffee houses ("they, like, sell dope right over the counter, man, and you don't even get busted") and the magic mushroom stores. And yes, there are tulips from Amsterdam, although they are actually cultivated in the bulb fields between Haarlem and Leiden.

So Amsterdam delivers the preconceptions, but those who only take the standard boat cruise miss the secret corners revealed by wandering round the backwaters or through

the Jordaan district – a quirky museum or an exquisite antique shop in the basement of a canal house. In one group of town houses the top floors were converted into an ornate but secret Catholic chapel in 1663 and hosted services during the years when stern Calvinism was rampant. Two centuries later, in the attic of 263 Prinsengracht, Anne Frank and her family hid from the occupying Nazi forces; the simple museum is powerfully moving. Away from the centre the old docklands and port are where Amsterdammers have relocated; to the west lie boatyards, houseboats and warehouses converted into artists' studios, to the east architects are creating museums and desirable flats on Java- and Borneo-eiland, named after former colonies, whence came the spicy Indonesian food which is Amsterdam's signature cuisine.

Amsterdam shows both sides of its character at the end of April when, on the Queen's Birthday, the centre is cordoned off and the city erupts in the national colour, orange (the royal family is the House of Orange), for two nights of mayhem, orange wigs, orange T-shirts and orange beer. The day after, an early morning walk reveals that all the detritus of excess has been miraculously and Calvinistically cleared, and, as the bells toll, the serenity of the city feels as timeless as one of the Rijksmuseum's Vermeers.

480
> AMSTERDAM, NETHERLANDS > LONGITUDE: 4°54' E > LATITUDE: 52°23' N > ALTITUDE: 3 feet/1 metre > POPULATION: 731,200 (metro: 1,730,000) > TWINNED WITH: Halifax (Canada), Toronto
> NATIVES: Jan Akkerman, Karel Appel, Dennis Bergkamp, Johann Cruyff, César Domela, Ruud Gullit, Bernard Haitink, Patrick Kluivert, Rudi Krol, Baruch Spinoza, Hendrik Verwoerd
> RESIDENTS: Anne Frank, Geert Mak, Rembrandt

"The myth of Amsterdam
is a myth of the spirit,
where that of other European cities is,
especially, one of monumentality."

Geert Mak, *Amsterdam*

"Lyons is the larder of France."

Paul Bocuse, chef

> LYONS, RHÔNE, FRANCE > LOCAL NAME: Lyon > LONGITUDE: 4°52′ E > LATITUDE: 45°45′ N > ALTITUDE: 568 feet/173 metres > POPULATION: 445,000 (metro: 1,260,000)
> TWINNED WITH: Ouagadougou, St Louis > NATIVES: André Marie Ampère, Paul Bocuse, Claudius, Charles Antoine Coysevox, Gérard Desargues, Youri Djorkaeff, Hector Guimard, Maurice Jarre, Karen Lancaume, Jules Joseph Perrot, Marc Riboud, Antoine de Saint-Exupéry, Jean-Baptiste Say, Bertrand Tavernier, Sandrine Testud, Charles Marie Widor, Zenaida Yanowsky > RESIDENTS: Klaus Barbie, Auguste and Louis Lumière

SURROUNDED BY FERTILE plains at the confluence of the rivers Saone and Rhône, Lyons is the stomach and tastebuds, the Bologna of France. The daily market on the Quai Saint Antoine and Quai des Célestins is one of France's most abundant, favoured by the country's biggest chefs. On display here, according to the season, are the lush fruits of the Rhône Valley, richly-flavoured vegetables from the l'Ain plain, famed Bresse chickens, fish from the Alpine lakes and succulent Charolais meats, fresh forest mushrooms, oysters, heavenly breads and Savoie honey. Lyons is a veritable *mange-tout* city.

But it is not just the flavours, and rarely is there a *soupçon* of gastronomic snobbery. For the Lyonnais enjoy the rituals of the table in *bouchons* (literally "corks") – traditional and affordable wood-beamed eateries so named as patrons are crammed into elbow-to-elbow intimacy that ensures a convivial atmosphere. Waistlines too may pop and circumferences expand at the mountainous plates of rich food, from the starter of *quenelle* (pike mousse) via an *andouillette* (Lyons's answer to Scottish haggis) to the chocolate cake, all sloshed down with a litre of Côtes du Rhône-Villages. For all its size, style and modernity the gateway city to the French Alps retains a strong regional flavour.

Lyons is not just food glorious food. Asterix fans will know that Lugdunum was the capital of Roman Gaul, and two beautifully preserved Roman theatres still evoke the city's classical origins. Across the *presqu'île* ("almost island") that sits in between the two rivers, the cobblestone streets and medieval mansions with Florentine staircases of the St Georges *quartier* is the largest and best-preserved example of Renaissance architecture in France. Hidden between these narrow streets is Lyons' network of *traboules*, covered passages that were originally built to protect the material of the silk-weavers against the outside elements: medieval Lyons was founded on its silk industry. Nowadays the *traboules* seem built to be the secret passages

they became when during the Second World War France's second city was the centre of the French Resistance against Nazi occupation and the *traboules* were used to smuggle messages, arms and people under the nose of the infamous butcher of Lyons, Klaus Barbie.

Its secretive streets, recent dark past and the mocking mask of the city's favourite son, the clown-marionette Guignol, lend Lyons a macabre air. The city is said to be joined in a black magic triangle with Prague and Turin. Its quayside lined with *bouquinistes* may be as romantic as Paris, yet Lyons shares with its Italian and Czech partners in occult a brooding hillside and mysterious atmosphere incarnated by the neo-Gothic skeleton of the Fourvière Basilica that stands high up on the Croix Rousse hill, its reflection shimmering ghost-like in the river. During a digestive post-prandial stroll it is as if the very sin of gluttony is watching over you like guilt.

ROTTERDAM

"IN ROTTERDAM WE MAKE the money and in Amsterdam they spend it." So goes a local saying in Holland's second city. Hard-working, practical and pragmatic, Rotterdam epitomizes those quintessential Dutch traits which stem from two sources: from lowland winds that batter it from the east, and the sea that would threaten from the west were it not for the industry and ingenuity of the burghers who designed and built the network of canals that today make Rotterdam one of the world's major cargo ports. Windmills and maritime skill have made a source of riches out of Rotterdam's two natural enemies.

Rotterdam was the headquarters of the *Verenigde Oostindische Compagnie* (the Dutch East India Company), which for two centuries, until its capitulation to the British at the turn of the 19th century, ruled the seas and monopolized the worldwide trade in spices such as nutmeg and cinnamon, which were the stocks and shares of their day. The warehouses down in the old port area of Delfshaven are still emblazoned with the names of the far-off islands whence these exotic riches came: Sumatra, Java, Borneo. From its stern offices on the Bommpjes embankment of the Rhine, the VOC also governed the trade in coffee, imported from its trading post, called Mocha, on the Red Sea Yemeni coast. Delfshaven still exudes the austere Presbyterianism of the founding fathers, and there is a still an aroma of coffee and cigar smoke in the Hotel New York, from where the pilgrims once left for the New World.

Rotterdam is still one of the world's most important shipping centres, a hub of globalization handling four million containers a year and storing mountains of goods and produce from the world over in its hangar-like warehouses.

"Rotterdam is remarkably clean: the Dutch even wash the outside brickwork of their houses." Mary Shelley

But the face of Rotterdam has completely changed. Flattened to the level of the Netherlands landscape by German bombs in the Second World War, Rotterdam chose to reinvent itself anew.

The city has now for many decades been a byword for architectural innovation and experimentalism, no better exemplified than by Rem Koolhaas, who designed the city's major space-age exhibition area, the Kunsthal in Westzeedijk. Floating on pillars in a pond at the end of Wytemaweg, the Netherlands Architecture Institute is a literal think-tank, an engine room of digital designs and new architectural - isms. Dotted around the city's barge-filled channels, wide boulevards and bicycle tracks are experimental buildings such as Het Potlood (the Pencil) and the lopsided Kijk Kubus cubist houses.

Yet Rotterdam has not forgotten its roots. The city's origins meet with its aluminium future in the harp-like Erasmus Bridge, spanning the Nieuwe Maas southern fork of the Rhine. It is named after the city's most famous son, Desiderius Erasmus (neé, more prosaically, Gerhard Gerhards) the father of Humanism that begat Holland's famed ideals of progressiveness, education and tolerance, which would make their way on the breeze and grow like a weed in the country's more profligate and decadent capital.

ANTWERP BELGIUM

ANTWERP HOPES THAT DIAMONDS are indeed forever. They have provided the city with a major source of wealth: approximately half the world's diamond trade is scrutinized under the eyeglasses of its brokers, a community made up largely of Hassidic Jews, whose fur hats and black coats have changed little since the 16th century.
In those days drapery was the city's major moneyspinner, and a contemporary generation of fashion designers, all alumni of the Academy of Fine Arts, notably the Antwerp Six led by Anne Demeulemeester and Dries van Noten, offer a textile cutting-edge as sharp as anything in the diamond district.

That Antwerp ever enjoyed such commercial success was down to serendipity. Bruges had the misfortune to find its own river silting up, and so Antwerp, on the free-flowing River Scheldt, was handed the chance to trade with the British (for cloth) and the Portuguese (for spices). The city was far from backward in taking up the opportunity; as a local saying puts it, "God gave the Scheldt to Antwerp and the Scheldt gave Antwerp everything." Under the Burgundian emperors Maximilian and Charles V, it became so prosperous it was known simply as "Metropolis", the paradigm of a city.

The wealth that flowed in allowed Antwerp's merchants to bestow patronage and largesse. Artists from across Europe, including Gossaert, Brueghel and Massys, gravitated to the city for a slice of their munificence. But it was a home-grown talent, Peter Paul Rubens, along with Van Dyck and Jordaans, who was the jewel in the crown. His altarpieces in Onze Lieve Vrouw, the largest Gothic cathedral in Belgium, represent one of the pinnacles of Antwerp's golden age. That era ended abruptly in 1576, when an angry Philip II unleashed the "Spanish Fury", driving out what he saw as the city's heretics. And when the Scheldt was cut off by the House of Orange's malicious damming of its mouth, Antwerp was backwatered until a rail link opened to Brussels in the 1840s. However, the people of Antwerp, known as *sinjoren*, have never forgotten their former greatness, and their reputation for amiability is tempered by pride, or what some other Belgians see as stuck-up self-importance.

Antwerp is once again an active port (its name is derived from *aan de werpen*, on the wharves) and the inner city well-preserved, including medieval guildhouses in the streets around Grote Markt, the main square, and grand mansions on the Parisian-style boulevards of Middleheim. There is not much hi-rise – although one of Europe's first skyscrapers, the KBC tower, was erected in the 1930s – and following the Second World War urban planners replaced bomb-damaged quarters not with ugly tower blocks, but with thoughtful townhouses in communal lanes. It is a sign of the gentility that underlies Antwerp's plump, possibly Rubensesque, penchant for the good things of life, especially good Burgundian cuisine, a nip of *genever*, or a glass of one of the hundreds of locally brewed beers for which Belgium has become renowned.

> "Antwerp is one of my favourite cities. I love the diamonds and the designer clothes. All those beautiful things make me melt." Venus Williams

> ANTWERP, BELGIUM > LOCAL NAME: Antwerpen/Anvers > LONGITUDE: 4°26' E > LATITUDE: 51°12' N > ALTITUDE: 45 feet/14 metres
> POPULATION: 446,500 > NATIVES: Ambrosius Bosschaert, Joos van Cleve, Hieronymus Cock, Frans Hals, Jan Leys, Dries van Noten,
Panamarenko, Clara Peeters, Frans Snyders, Anthony Van Dyck > RESIDENTS: Jan Breughel, Pieter Brueghel the Younger,
Ann Demeulemeester, Jan Gossaert, Quentin Massys, Christophe Plantin, Peter Paul Rubens, Luc Tuymans

BRUSSELS BELGIUM

FOR MOST EUROPEANS BRUSSELS is an abstraction, not a city, synonymous with the European ideal of which it is parliamentary HQ. Appreciation of the Belgian capital is often caught up in political prejudices. Depending on your point of view, it is either the brain and talisman of European political harmony and economic strength, or the cause of identical-size supermarket chickens, year-round tasteless tomatoes and the general eradication of national variety and rural customs deemed unhygienic.

On the surface Brussels does nothing to dispel the latter view. Under a typical grey tupperware sky the concrete streets the city sprouted after the Second World War can appear as faceless architectural metaphors of identity loss. The sky seems to fill the glass voids of skyscrapers and vice versa, forming surreal images from a Magritte painting. The soulless apparently deserted buildings of the European Parliament on Rue Belliard and the EU zone, which by day absorbs so many of Brussels's inhabitants are testaments to the boredom of utopia and make a good case for never arriving at the eternal happiness of the European dream.

But "Europe", the idea, is also Brussels's lifeblood. A constant passage of young cosmopolitan professionals on short-term placements and with expenses to burn – Baudelaire showed great prescience – ensures a dynamic, free-wheeling subculture all too ready to wine, dine and party when the day's paper-pushing is over and who make up the vibrant café culture of what, among the cranes of its suburbs, is the city's only real beauty spot, the magnificent medieval Grand Place.

European Brussels has not lost any of its own specialities and the city's justly famous restaurants are full of diet-free Bruxelloises and would-be Poirotesque gourmets gorging themselves on the glutinous local fare of *moules*, thick red Leffe ale, chocolate truffles and the *frites* (usually with mayo) that gave all Belgians their nickname in the eyes of the French.

Brussels may be the centre of Europe but it was once the centre of a vast empire, whose king, Leopold II, in claiming the heart of Congo's darkness for Belgium precipitated the "scramble for Africa". The story and fruits of this colonization are on show at the Royal Museum of Central Africa, a museum which in the contradictory blandness of Brussels's streets also reminds one that Belgium has a royal family. Away from the iconic Atomium icon erected for the 1958 World Fair and the minuscule, limp (and barely tourist-worthy) Mannekin Pis urinating cherub, among the louche barge tableaux of commissaire Maigret's underworld, a sturdier Flemish culture lurks underneath Brussels: the city has an unrivalled collection of Brueghels and in the Musée de la Bande-Dessinée a unique tribute to the art of Hergé, the Belgian creator of *Tintin* – the country's other detective – and other exponents of the cartoon strip.

Whether its "*Death on the Senne*" (Brussels's river) or "*Cigars of the Eurocrats*", Brussels and its citizens would be keen to dispel all caricatures of their city as a bland servant to the blue and gold stars of Jacques Delors' flag.

"In Brussels there is no life, only corruption." Charles Baudelaire

> BRUSSELS, BELGIUM > LOCAL NAME: Bruxelles/Brussel > LONGITUDE: 4°21' E > LATITUDE: 50°50' N > ALTITUDE: 190 feet/58 metres > POPULATION: 977,900 > TWINNED WITH: Atlanta, Reykjavik
> NATIVES: Chantal Akerman, Pierre Alechinsky, Thierry Boutsen, Jacques Brel, Marcel Broodthaers, Jan Brueghel, Liz Claiborne, Julio Cortázar, Hergé (aka Georges Remi), Audrey Hepburn, Jacky Ickx,
Claude Lévi-Strauss, Jean-Baptiste Madou, Toots Thielemans, Agnès Varda, Maxime Weygand, Marguerite Yourcenar > RESIDENTS: Pieter Brueghel, René Magritte, Jean Claude van Damme

"Ghetto-dwellers are the great fantasists.
There was an extraordinary vibrancy there,
an imaginative life." Ben Okri, *The Landscapes Within*

AS JO'BURG IS TO the south and Cairo to the north, so Lagos is the compass point of western Africa, the violent and tumultuous magnet of humanity and the core of the continent's most populous nation.

Like many African nations, Nigeria is an invention, a federation of 250 languages and peoples arising in 1914 from the trading exploits of the British Royal Niger Company that had won exclusive trading rights in the river delta as a result of shelling the place.

Lagos's origins date back to the Portuguese explorers who founded the first settlement here in the 15th century, calling it Lago de Curamo. The city sits in a bed of mangrove swamps and is composed of a number of islands and lagoons (lagos) adjoined to one and other by a series of zooming freeways.

The oldest part of the city is Lagos Island, nowadays the commercial hub of a metropolis that is the country's economic capital. Lagos Island is a graphic equalizer of skyscrapers, peaks and troughs, home to international firms and in NITEL House, Africa's tallest building. But deep in its heart around Campos Square and Campbell Street are a few examples, like the Palace of Oba (Nigeria's traditional kings), of a unique and colourful Brazilian-style architecture that is half-neoclassical, half-Portuguese-modernista founded by returning slaves from the New World. Ikoyi Island is the former posh colonial neighbourhood still with some traces of Victorian influence, while the third major island, named after Victoria herself, is the plush retreat of embassies away from the Lagos's motorway flyovers of traffic jams and street vendors and relentless small-time commerce. Beyond these three islands and the focal mainland port berths of Apapa and Tin Can Island, Lagos stretches in shacks and shanty towns to an ill-defined boundary out of sight and mind.

Many things have put Lagos on the map since Sami Abacha's despotic regime came to an end in 1999. For drug barons the city is pivotal in their transport arrangements for hard drugs. The Super Eagles led by the twinkle toes of J.J. Okocha and Nwankwo Kanu have become a footballing force to be reckoned with, a languid carefree mix of effortless skill and discipline-less self-destruction that is incorrigibly African. But most of all Lagos boasts an exuberant music culture and an internationally-renowned intellectual life and literary voice, best known through the work of Ben Okri. Highlife, Juju, Fuji, Afrobeat are all musical movements born in Lagos that have hit the international dance scene through the grooves of artists such as King Sunny Ade.

Lagos has a raw night-time energy unparalleled in Africa. Whether in the dens of the dark city or down on the beach at Tarkwa Bay,

Lagosians are *ariya* ("havin' a good time" in the local Yoruba tongue), jiving, drawing on a joint of the local *maria giovanna*, snacking on some *dodo* (friend plantains) or sipping a pint of Guinness and blackcurrant known as "Nigerian black".

> LAGOS, NIGERIA > LONGITUDE: 3°20' E > LATITUDE: 6°26' N > ALTITUDE: 10 feet/3 metres
> POPULATION: 8,349,700 > TWINNED WITH: Atlanta > NATIVES: Gil Eanes, Reebop Kwaku Baah, Buchi Emecheta, Ben Okri > RESIDENTS: Fela Kuti, Femi Kuti

BRUGES BELGIUM

THE SILTING UP OF THE River Zwin in the 1540s directly affected the history and development of two major Belgian cities. Boats and barges could no longer navigate their way upstream from the North Sea, and thence via a linking canal, to the quays of Bruges. A critical key selling point in the city's marketing prospectus was erased, and consequently the trade that had provided its days of plenty shifted west to Antwerp, which received a significant boost to its own commerce and prosperity.

As far as the rest of the world was concerned, it meant that Bruges remained pretty much as it had been during its medieval heyday. In subsequent centuries, the story was one of decline, and by the 19th century there was a distinct danger that the city's buildings would collapse into rack and ruin. However, in the nick of time *Bruges-la-Morte*, a novel by the Belgian symbolist poet Georges Rodenbach first published in 1892, alerted attention to its plight. Bruges (named after its many bridges) is now one of the most perfectly preserved (or reconstructed – not everything is original) medieval cities in Europe.

Along the meandering canals of Bruges's River Djiver, and behind discreet brick walls, stand the mansions that once housed wealthy merchants. Gabled houses line the main square, the Markt. Civic and religious buildings proclaim the prestige of Bruges: the St Jans hospital, the Gothic Town Hall and the Romanesque

Basilica of the Holy Blood, home to a vial which, it is claimed, contains two drops of blood washed from the body of Christ by Joseph of Arimathea. Above all of this finery, the 47-bell carillon of the octagonal Belfort (described by G.K. Chesterton as "like a giraffe") rings out as it has done for nearly 800 years. The Béguine convent, like its Amsterdam equivalent, is a corner of calm next to the swan-studded lake of Minnewater.

Bruges got fat from spices, furs and textiles, thanks to the Counts of Flanders, who granted the necessary freedom to foreign traders. The lure of wealth attracted a posse of artists, and the Burgundian dukes who ruled the city until the 1460s were notable patrons. Michelangelo created the white marble Madonna and Child in the Church of Our Lady. Jan Van Eyck, Hans Memling and Rogier Van der Weyden also benefited from Bruges's bounty; examples of their work are the backbone of the collection in the city's Groeninge Museum.

As if the beauty of Bruges was not heady enough, the local beers (before the First World War the city had over 30 individual breweries) accompanying waffles, or fries and mayonnaise, are perfectly capable of sending the senses spinning. And for chocaholics, a visit to Bruges is one of the great pilgrimages. For a city that was once on its knees, Bruges has found its niche as a tourist centre, and seems contented with that. Long live Bruges-la-Morte.

"The difference between Bruges and other cities is that in the latter you look about for the picturesque, while in Bruges, assailed on every side by the picturesque, you look curiously for the unpicturesque, and don't find it easily."

Arnold Bennett

> BRUGES, BELGIUM > LOCAL NAME: Brugge > LONGITUDE: 3°15' E > LATITUDE: 51°12' N > ALTITUDE: 78 feet/24 metres > POPULATION: 116,200
> NATIVES: Frank Brangwyn, Hugo Claus > RESIDENTS: Hans Memling

THE *PIEDS-NOIRS*, those French colonials who were born and raised in Algeria and, following independence, expelled from it, still talk long into the night with great nostalgia about the country and the city they had to leave behind. Why they miss Algiers (and why they fought so fiercely to stay there) is understandable – its setting is spectacular and its architecture like a sun-kissed Paris – but the city can only live in their memories, as the internal troubles that have plagued Algeria since the early 1990s, and the imposition of a *fatwah* on all foreigners, let alone the French, have rather actively discouraged visitors.

For the brave few who dare to do so, the most uplifting way to approach Algiers is by ship. Not only is it a reminder of the passenger boat services that once plied across the Mediterranean to and from Marseilles, but it reveals the city in all its theatrical glory, on the flank of a mountain emerging from the water. The first impression of Algiers is its whiteness (its French nickname is "*Algers la Blanche*"), a Persil-bright whiteness against the azure of the sky and the sea. Through the accumulation of balconied houses, stairways and corridor-like backstreets rise and fall with the natural contours, from the poor neighbourhoods around the port to the grand houses up on the hill.

The façades are increasingly dilapidated, as generations of layers of chalk and white paint flake away and Algiers' Europeanness flutters into dust. Beneath the Martyrs Monument, dedicated to the freedom fighters who won independence from France in 1962, the colonial city has been resettled by its Arab inhabitants. The medina, the old Arab quarter – even whiter than the old colonial areas – was a secretive place even before Algiers closed in on itself: grilles protecting the windows, an occasional glimpse of proud, exotic women in white robes slipping through its lanes, hidden Turkish palaces and Moorish houses. In the rest of the city, with little work available and under the constant threat of violence, the public spaces are occupied by vaguely menacing knots of young men, wary and world-weary.

The Algerian capital's history harks back to the Phoenician town of Icosium, founded in 1200 BC, according to legend, by a handful of Hercules' best friends. Later it became a pirate stronghold in the 16th century, their Barbary coast citadel, from where the corsairs could pick off any ships unwise enough to cruise past their turf. The Ottomans imposed some order, and created the city's *casbah*, as well as capturing and incarcerating Miguel de Cervantes. But such moments in Algiers' past have been eclipsed by present and immediate danger, the unrest caused by the fundamentalist GIA, the Armed Islamic Group, which has sent Algiers into a downward slide where violence and unpleasantness have gained the upper hand. For now the city's eyes will continue to remain watchful and unyielding; any glint of a ready welcome will have to wait.

> "What I love about Algiers are the things that everybody thrives on: a glimpse of the sea around every street corner, the heavy intensity of the sunlight and the beauty of the people."
>
> Albert Camus, *Summer in Algiers*

> ALGIERS, ALGERIA > LOCAL NAME: Al Jaza'ir/Alger > LONGITUDE: 3°04' E > LATITUDE: 36°46' N > ALTITUDE: 98 feet/30 metres > POPULATION: 2,562,400 > TWINNED WITH: Amman (Jordan)
> NATIVES: Edmond Charlot, Tony Gatlif, Roger Hanin, Eddie Marnay, Martial Solal > RESIDENTS: Albert Camus

LILLE FRANCE

SINCE 1994, when the Eurostar train service finally made real the great dream of travel through the Channel Tunnel, Lille has become one of the major transport hubs of Europe, the epicentre of a system from which TGVs can branch off to Brussels or London, or head south across the tentacles of the French rail network. However, few of the passengers who make the journey ever emerge from the platform complex of Lille-Europe to explore the city visible through its glass walls.

What they would discover is the capital of French Flanders, possessing the futuristic, Rem Koolhaas-designed Euralille complex, but also a magnificent old quarter. Every September, just before *la rentrée*, the Grand Place and the cobbled lanes and little squares of *vieux* Lille are taken over by La Grande Braderie, a massive antiques-cum-flea market which attracts dealers from all over France. They are following in the footsteps of the traders in textiles who provided Lille with its original mercantile success. This 17th-century wealth is reflected in the ornate baroque styling of the Vieille Bourse, the old mansard-roofed exchange, which reveals the city's fondness for all things Flemish.

Lille's blend of influences is best described as "*flamand à la française*": a plate of *moules-frites* or *potjevleesch* (a white meat terrine) is as likely to

be washed down by some local red wine as a glass of amber-coloured beer. The French flavour really only arrived in force in 1667, when Louis XIV captured Lille – the name comes from "*l'Isle*", referring the its position on an island in the River Deule – and removed it from the control of the Spanish Netherlands. He raised his own mini Arc de Triomphe in celebration, and commissioned Marshal Vauban to build the Citadel that still overlooks the city.

The dominant cotton and linen industries, and the nearby coalfields, brought attendant slums and grime, and the city used to have something of the feel of a Flemish Manchester. Most of that dirt has gone in the 21st-century, spruced-up version of Lille, although it is still proud of its working-class roots and its socialist tradition: François Mitterand's first prime minister, Pierre Mauroy, was the city's mayor. There is certainly a healthy dose of civic pride among Lille's residents – known as "*ch'tis*" – who have a reputation for youthful energy (there is a large student population) and great warmth. Whether for politics or food, they are capable of a passion as strong as the cheeses served at the tables of Lille: the famous orange-rinded Maroilles, produced since the 7th century, or the lesser known, but equally potent, Mont des Cats.

> LILLE, NORD, FRANCE > LONGITUDE: 3°04' E > LATITUDE: 50°38' N > ALTITUDE: 69 feet/21 metres > POPULATION: 219,600 (metro: 1,000,900) > TWINNED WITH: Buffalo NY, Cologne, Erfurt (Germany), Esch-sur-Alzette (Luxembourg), Kharkiv (Ukraine), Leeds (UK), Liège (Belgium), Nabulus (West Bank), Rotterdam, Safed (Israel), St Louis, Turin, Valladolid (Spain) > NATIVES: Renée Adorée, Antoinette Bourignon, Jean-Alexandre Dieudonné, Carolus-Duran, Bruno Dumont, Charles de Gaulle, Edouard Lalo, Philippe Noiret, Roger Salengro > RESIDENTS: Pierre Mauroy, Louis Pasteur

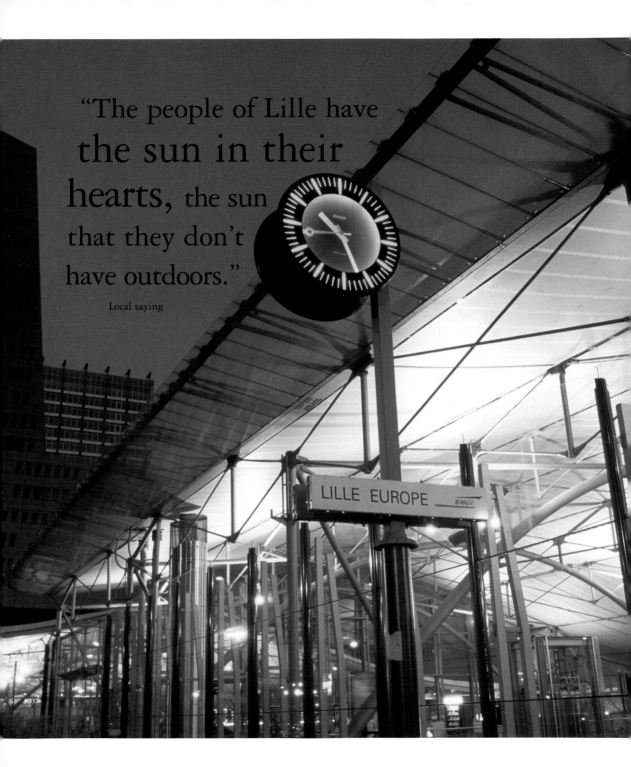

"The people of Lille have the sun in their hearts, the sun that they don't have outdoors."

Local saying

FRÉDÉRIC CHOPIN SPENT the winter of 1838-9 in Mallorca during the early days of his romance with Amandine Dupin, better known as George Sand; nowadays the music emanating from Palma is more likely to be the phat beat of this summer's Balearic dance classic rather than the exquisite preludes that Chopin completed during his stay; but, nonetheless, the sky and sea, as longer-term resident Joan Miró noted, are "at night and during the day, always blue".

Palma – not to be confused with Las Palmas, the capital of another major destination for package holidaymakers, Gran Canaria – was visited in its early life by an equally demanding and querulous queue

of invaders, drawn less by the promise of sun than by the value of the island's strategic position. This procession was brought to an end by Jaime I of Aragon, who captured Palma from its Arab rulers in 1229. "It seemed to me and to those who accompanied me," he later wrote, "the most beautiful city we had ever seen." Then, just like Hernando Cortés, who had said much the same about Mexico City, he promptly trashed the place.

Jaime set about converting the city's mosques into churches, and commissioned a massive cathedral, high on a rampart above Palma's harbour, to send out a robust and unmissable message to anyone

> PALMA, MALLORCA, SPAIN > LOCAL NAME: Palma de Mallorca > LONGITUDE: 2°40' E > LATITUDE: 39°35' N > ALTITUDE: 32 feet/10 metres > POPULATION: 323,138
> TWINNED WITH: Santa Barbara CA > NATIVES: Raymond Lully, Carlos Moya > RESIDENTS: Joán Miró

2°40' E

"The sky is turquoise, the sea blue, the mountains emerald. And the air? The air is as blue as the sky." Frédéric Chopin

sailing by of his aggressive Christian faith. Although work began in the 13th century, it was not finished until 1601: builders' excuses must have changed little over the years. The golden sandstone and flying buttresses of the cathedral, known as *La Seu*, "the Seat", dominate the city's skyline; at night, lit up, they do so even more. The Mallorcan nobility who flourished under Jaime constructed magnificent mansions, with massive wooden doors opening on to calm patios, in the old, upper, town, the Vila d'Amunt, where the Moorish influence remains visible in the old hot baths, the Banys Arabs, and the Palau de l'Almudaina, a blend of Islamic and Gothic.

Selected by *El Pais* newspaper as Spain's most desirable place to live, Palma is now a comfortable blend of the Iberian (tapas bars, hot chocolate, fluffy *ensaimada* pastries), the Catalan – it has a Rambla, mosaic *modernista* façades in the old red-light district of Sa Gerreria and fine Gaudi sculptures in the cathedral – and a distinctive, homegrown Mallorquian culture and language, the latter banned under Franco but now back with a vengeance. The nightlife in this capital city of the Balearic islands is also resurgent, a shade less frenetic than Mallorca's dance-till-you-drop clubbers' resorts, but vibrant enough along the Paseo Maritimo and in the former fisherman's *barrio* of Santa Catalina.

PARIS FRANCE

THE GREAT BEAUTY OF Paris is that it remains so fantastically and uncompromisingly Parisian. Shrugging its shoulders with a disdainful *moue* and an aloof "*bof!*", the city has accepted but essentially ignored the arrival of other cultures. When the first McDonald's opened, the names of the burgers had to be changed (remember John Travolta's "Royale with cheese" rap in *Pulp Fiction*); even the most global of brands has to toe the Parisian line.

Paris is enduringly homogenous. Baron Haussmann's 19th-century street plan – the imprint for so many subsequent city designs – held together by the arrow-straight Champs-Elysées, is essentially intact, despite the best efforts of revolutionaries, occupiers, liberators and the *évènements* of 1968. The tall three- and four-storey, mansard-topped apartment buildings are the city's architectural blotting-paper, able to absorb with equal ease the *ancien régime* Place des Vosges, the Pompidou Centre, or I.M. Pei's glass pyramid at the Louvre – while its best-known landmarks have been there for a least a century (the iconic Eiffel Tower and the whiter-than-white Sacré-Coeur), or nearly eight (Notre-Dame).

The city's centre (the *agglomération* beyond the *périphérique* is as infinite a sprawl as in most cities) is compact and wonderfully walkable. The surrealists set great store by walking as the best way to encounter "*l'impromptu*", and there is little better way to explore Paris than by taking a metro to one of the stations with such evocative and promising names – Jasmin, Glacière, Pyramides – and sauntering, without a map, through the spiral of *arrondissements* and *quartiers*. Through Montmartre or the Marais, St-Honoré or the Île St-Louis you can follow your nose, indeed all your vital organs: sniffing out a tiny bistro on the Rue St-Denis for a *croque-monsieur* or selecting foie gras at Fauchon, spotting a tiny atelier museum (the Zadkine, for example) tucked away down a passageway, or coming across the sculptures in the Jardin des Tuileries, away from the rush to view Rodin's *Thinker*, the *Mona Lisa* or Degas' *Ballet Dancer*.

Best of all, that walk should be *à deux*. It didn't really need Cole Porter to tell us that Paris is for lovers, or Robert Doisneau to capture that kiss on camera. Paris has been romancing for centuries, from Abelard and Héloïse to Jean-Paul Sartre and Simone de Beauvoir dining and debating at La Coupole, or, in a lustier vein, Serge Gainsbourg and Jane Birkin. Paris is a sexy city, and even better at night; as Terence Conran, that great Francophile, has noted, no city lights its monuments better than Paris.

There may be too many tourists these days – certainly Parisians tend to think so – and during the 1990s Paris may have lost a little ground to the new style centres of Stockholm, Seattle or Berlin, but it's merely a blip for this particular metropolis, which has been such an important cultural and intellectual powerhouse. Paris has many personalities – the atelier of Picasso, the gastronomic city of A.J. Liebling, the erotic playground of Henry Miller – and a rich multicultural mix to sustain it. Half the current population is not native to the city, proof positive that ultimately, in James Cameron's phrase, "Paris is an air and a scent and a state of mind."

"Paris was where the 20th century was.
Paris was the place to be."

Gertrude Stein

> PARIS, FRANCE > LONGITUDE: 2°21' E > LATITUDE: 48°52' N > ALTITUDE: 89 feet/27 metres > POPULATION: 964,400 (metro: 2,140,100) > TWINNED WITH: Cairo, Chicago, Kyoto, New York, San Francisco, Tokyo, Washington > NATIVES: Brigitte Bardot, Charles Baudelaire, Simone de Beauvoir, Sarah Bernhardt, Georges Bizet, Henri Cartier-Bresson, Manu Chao, Maurice Chevalier, Jacques Chirac, Edgar Degas, Catherine Deneuve, Serge Gainsbourg, Jean-Luc Godard, Stephane Grappelli, Johnny Hallyday, Françoise Hardy, Molière, Claude Monet, Anaïs Nin, Edith Piaf, Roman Polanski, Jean-Paul Sartre, Georges Seurat, François Truffaut, François Voltaire > RESIDENTS: Josephine Baker, Samuel Beckett, Constantin Brancusi, Brassai, Eugène Ionesco, James Joyce, Henry Miller, Man Ray, Gertrude Stein, Ossip Zadkine

THERE IS A HILL ABOVE Barcelona with the playful name "*Tibidabo*" on which sits a disused fairground. "*Omnia haec tibi dabo*" were the words the Devil used to try to seduce Jesus when he lured him up here – the Latin for "one day, son, all this will be yours". The Messiah must have been sorely tempted then and would be now, should he come again.

Beneath the Tibidabo the hill rolls away in a gentle curve down to a glistening azure Mediterranean, at its base, as if in a bubble, the capital of Catalonia, a singular and strange universe where the secretive and the gypsy sit alongside the glint and flash of the modern, where angular reality is interrupted by the curves and anti-logic of fantasy, and where a fierce regional identity conspires to be an international dialect. Arguably more progressive than the rest of the country, Barcelona is Spain's 21st century.

Architecture defines a city, but in Barcelona there is the sense that architecture is the mortal coil for a breathing being. There is some capricious soul that lives inside this architect's cage, distorting it in spasms like a benignly possessed spirit-child with a poltergeist's sense of chaos. Here and there the slide-rule precision of Cerda's 1910 Ensanche grid sliced through by the knife of Avenida Diagonal is insulted by the lawless petrified figments of Gaudi's imagination. In the unsettling wavy lines of la Pedrera on the sleek arrow-straight boulevard of Passeig Gracia it is as if light itself momentarily stops travelling in a straight line. Further north erupts the unfinished dream of Gaudi's Sagrada Familia, surreal before Dali and friends had thought of the word and at whose carcass, façades and spires writers have thrown vain similes ("dribbled candlesticks", "perforated cigarettes") for over a hundred years.

After decades of obscurity Freddie Mercury, local diva Montserrat Caballé and the 1992 Olympic flame, spectacularly ignited by an archer's burning arrow, illuminated Barcelona's assets to the world, joined the city to its sea and gave it a gleaming sea-front complex of marinas, bars and nightclub strips. There are those who lament the passing of a murky world that is losing its licentious grip on the alleys of the Barrio Gotic and Barrio Xino; of local inner fishing villages such as Barceloneta, Ribera and Raval, and the incessant expansion into the former industrial district of Poble Nou, now domain of lofts and warehouse parties; and that la Rambla has turned into a jesters' and hawkers' facsimile of the world's other great streets.

But the archaic cable-cars supported by Eiffelesque towers still connect the sides of the city's port, pointless like a fairground ride, Gaudi's Parc Guell will always be a Jabberwocky's playground, and in Picasso's cubist mindscapes even the straight lines are possessed. These and the city's latest addition, Jean Nouvel's multicoloured, translucent gherkin-shaped Torre Agbar are all symbols of Barcelona's innate spirit of invention and slightly wacky and much imitated take on things. Indeed, there are days when the whole of Barcelona, born under some strange once-off moon, seems like an avant-garde parody on the modern city theme.

> "The straight line is man's creation; the curved line, God's."
>
> Antoni Gaudi

> BARCELONA, CATALUNYA, SPAIN > LONGITUDE: 2°13' E > LATITUDE: 41°25' N > ALTITUDE: 20 feet/6 metres > POPULATION: 1,510,000 (metro: 4,654,000) > TWINNED WITH: Boston, Cologne, Kobe (Japan), Montevideo, Pusan (Korea), St Petersburg, São Paulo, Shanghai, Veracruz (Mexico) > NATIVES: Joan Brossa, Victoria de los Angeles, Ricardo Bofill, Montserrat Caballé, Julio González, Juan Marsé, Enric Miralles, Mañuel Vasquez Montalban, Frederic Mompou, August Puig, Jordi Savall, Antoni Tàpies, Carlos Ruiz Zafón. > RESIDENTS: Pablo Casals, Antonio Gaudi, Jean Genet, Pablo Picasso, Josep Pla

TOULOUSE IS A PRETTY CITY of many colours, "pink at dawn, red at noon, mauve at dusk", as a local saying puts it. The red bricks that predominate in the Renaissance buildings of the city centre give off the distinctive, blushing glow that has led to its "ville rose" nickname. In the 15th century the city benefited from a highly successful trade in the pastel, or woad plant, Isatis tinctoria, a clue to its importance – in an age before synthetic colours – to both textile dyers and artists, who appreciated and coveted its deep indigo blue pigment. The city's emblematic flower is the violet.

There is, indeed, something of a rainbow coalition feel about Toulouse, a spectrum of moods that comfortably balances the best of the old and the new, just as, politically, the council has traditionally been left-wing, but offset by a right-wing mayor. The city was an ancient capital under the Romans, for whom it was the centre of the Narbonne district, and the Visigoths. During four centuries in the early Middle Ages this was the site of the courts of the counts of Toulouse, where troubadours held forth in the poetry of the *Langue d'Oc*, the language of the Midi – a period cut short when the so-called Cathar heresy gave the rulers of France the excuse to bring the city into line in brutal fashion during the 13th century.

After the "pastel" years, when the merchants spent their wealth on the construction of lavish town houses – the Hôtel d'Assezat on the Rue de Metz gives a fine idea of their sumptuous lifestyle – Toulouse slumbered in a somewhat sequestered way until after the Second World War. The arrival of the aerospace industries (the city has been home to the Airbus, the Ariane rocket and the still supremely elegant, but now superannuated, Concorde) gave it a substantial lift, and a position in the vanguard of France's postwar technological revival.

Toulouse, the major city of south-west France, absorbed the festive spirit of Spain, across the Pyrenees, and the ethnic mix of its suburbs is reflected in the musical blend of rock, raggamuffin and *raï* performed by Zebda, who, along with singer-songwriter Claude Nougaro, have provided the city with its contemporary soundtrack.

Life in Toulouse is busy but relaxed, strolling along the banks of the Garonne, sorting through the flea market held near the landmark basilica of St-Sernin, or sitting down to savour the city's fabulous *cassoulet* stew. Differentiated from the rival Carcassone and Castelnaudry versions by the inclusion of *saucisse de Toulouse* and a *chapelure* breadcrumb covering, the city's *cassoulet* is as honest, self-confident and robust a dish as its people, a mentality typified by its Stade Toulouse "rugbymen", not least the legendary blond bombshell himself, Jean-Pierre Rives.

> "The St. Sernin church illuminates the night, a coral flower drenched by the sun. That's maybe why, despite your red and black, they call you the Ville Rose."
>
> Claude Nougaro, *Toulouse*

> TOULOUSE, HAUTE-GARONNE, FRANCE > LONGITUDE: 1°26' E > LATITUDE: 43°37' N > ALTITUDE: 479 feet/146 metres > POPULATION: 398,400 (metro: 800,000)
> TWINNED WITH: Atlanta, Bologna, Chongqing, Kiev > NATIVES: Jean-Marc Bustamante, Xavier Darasse, Edmund Dulac, Meredith Monk, Claude Nougaro, Jean-Pierre Rives, Zebda

TO THE INHABITANTS OF dark-blue Oxford, this little market town in the fens of East Anglia is "the other place", so symbiotic is the link of academic superiority between the two cities, to the exclusion of any other, so historic the rivalry between these two provincial cities known to millions of television viewers worldwide as annual adversaries in The Boat Race.

But whereas Oxford is a university in a city, Cambridge *is* the university. On a Saturday afternoon it is not uncommon to see students traipse through a crowded shopping mall wearing studs and their college colours muddied from an inter-collegiate game of rugby; or rowing VIIIs in college boatclub splashtops trundling through Trinity Street on knackered bicycles; or terrorists dressed up as undergraduates in ties sporting allegiance to one or other drinking club car-walking down King's Parade – all this without anyone batting an eyelid, as if it were normal behaviour. A bubble detached from reality and responsibility: this is the very definition of an ivory tower.

Cambridge is its colleges, themselves some of the richest foundations in the land. The central thoroughfare of King's Parade is dominated by King's College, its great court hidden behind William Wilkins's 19th-century screen above which rises, simple but perfect, King Henry VI's College Chapel, a city icon painted by Turner and Canaletto. The King's choristers are the angelic voice of England, the chapel's carol service one of the bastions of the traditional English Christmas.

Further down is Trinity College, alma mater to a litany of greats from Newton and Wittgenstein to Nabokov and Byron, who used to

506   > CAMBRIDGE, CAMBRIDGESHIRE, ENGLAND, UK > LONGITUDE: 0°07' E > LATITUDE: 52°12' N > ALTITUDE: 49 feet/15 metres > POPULATION: 108,900 > TWINNED WITH: Heidelberg (Germany), Szeged (Hungary) > NATIVES: Richard Attenborough, Syd Barrett, Dave Gilmour, Jack Hobbs, John Maynard Keynes, Olivia Newton-John, Tom Robinson, Ronald Searle, Eddy Shah, Judith Weir > RESIDENTS: Charles Babbage, Rupert Brooke, Stephen Hawking, A.E. Housman, F.R. Leavis, Rory McGrath, Isaac Newton, Bertrand Russell, Ludwig Wittgenstein

"The Backs of the colleges are like Dresden reborn in a garden, like an Ideal Château Exhibition on a toytown Loire."

Clive James, *May Week Was in June*

bath naked in the central fountain of the famous Great Court, a square mile made recognizable worldwide by the film *Chariots of Fire*. Trinity also mothered the infamous spies Philby, Blunt and Burgess, who in the 1930s discovered Communism in the college's cloistered courts, and the comic talent of *Beyond the Fringe*, which set the scene for decades of British satire.

Trinity was founded by Henry VIII, whose statue stands above the porter's lodge, the sceptre in his left hand long since replaced by a wooden chair leg. Pranks and dares have always been the prerogative of Cambridge undergraduates pitted against college porters in an outrage of lawless antics seemingly unanswerable to the civil code. The night-climbers of Cambridge, a university society dedicated to touring the city's rooftops without touching the ground,

have been replaced by gate-crashers using all their ingenuity to sneak or ambush their way into the university's famed May Week balls. The chain of drunken post-exam students stumbling from between garden parties on Suicide Sunday effectively holds the city to ransom.

But it is not all *Porterhouse Blue* and Byronic "din and drunkenness". Cambridge has a serious side as a powerhouse of scientific research. And there is a quiet aspect to the duck-egg blue city: an Impressionist tableau of punts and river-parties gliding silently past Wren's famous library on the immaculate florid lawns of the college Backs; of someone coming up to bowl on a college cricket ground; and of *déjeuners sur l'herbe* in Rupert Brooke's nearby Grantchester, where there is still honey left for tea.

Published by MJF Books
Fine Communications
322 Eighth Avenue
New York, NY 10001

The Book of Cities
LC Control Number 2007941361
ISBN-13: 978-1-56731-906-4
ISBN-10: 1-56731-906-8

Printed in China.

MJF Books and the MJF colophon are trademarks of Fine Creative Media, Inc.

WG   10   9   8   7   6   5   4   3   2   1